A Problem of Great Importance

THE BERKELEY SERIES IN BRITISH STUDIES

Mark Bevir and James Vernon, University of California, Berkeley, editors

1. *The Peculiarities of Liberal Modernity in Imperial Britain,* edited by Simon Gunn and James Vernon
2. *Dilemmas of Decline: British Intellectuals and World Politics, 1945–1975,* by Ian Hall
3. *The Savage Visit: New World People and Popular Imperial Culture in Britain, 1710–1795,* by Kate Fullagar
4. *The Afterlife of Empire,* by Jordanna Bailkin
5. *Smyrna's Ashes: Humanitarianism, Genocide, and the Birth of the Middle East,* by Michelle Tusan
6. *Pathological Bodies: Medicine and Political Culture,* by Corinna Wagner
7. *A Problem of Great Importance: Population, Race, and Power in the British Empire, 1918–1973,* by Karl Ittmann

A Problem of Great Importance

Population, Race, and Power in the British Empire, 1918–1973

KARL ITTMANN

Global, Area, and International Archive
University of California Press
BERKELEY   LOS ANGELES   LONDON

The Global, Area, and International Archive (GAIA) is an initiative of the Institute of International Studies, University of California, Berkeley, in partnership with the University of California Press, the California Digital Library, and international research programs across the University of California system.

University of California Press, one of the most distinguished university presses in the United States, enriches lives around the world by advancing scholarship in the humanities, social sciences, and natural sciences. Its activities are supported by the UC Press Foundation and by philanthropic contributions from individuals and institutions. For more information, visit www.ucpress.edu.

University of California Press
Berkeley and Los Angeles, California

University of California Press, Ltd.
London, England

© 2013 by The Regents of the University of California

Library of Congress Cataloging-in-Publication Data

A catalog record for this book is available from the Library of Congress

ISBN: 978-0-520-28954-3

22 21 20 19 18 17 16 15 14 13
10 9 8 7 6 5 4 3 2 1

For Lorri, Neave, and Caroline

Contents

Acknowledgments		ix
INTRODUCTION		1
1.	THE ORIGINS OF COLONIAL DEMOGRAPHY	15
2.	THE COLONIAL OFFICE AND THE POPULATION QUESTION, 1918–1939	48
3.	WAR, POPULATION, AND THE NEW COLONIAL STATE	83
4.	POPULATION AND THE POSTWAR EMPIRE	107
5.	POPULATION IN A POSTCOLONIAL WORLD	147
6.	BRITISH POPULATION POLICY IN THE POSTCOLONIAL ERA	177
	CONCLUSION: POPULATION AND THE LEGACIES OF EMPIRE	191
	Notes	201
	Index	289

Acknowledgments

This book has taken far longer to complete than I could have imagined when I began work on it more than a decade ago. Along the way I have incurred a number of debts to those who have helped me. The Limited Grant in Aid and Small Research Grant programs of the University of Houston provided financial support to undertake my research, as did the Center for Immigration Research at the University of Houston. The College of Liberal Arts and Social Sciences gave me a semester's leave in both 1998 and 2006 to allow me to write. My colleague Joe Pratt generously gave funds from his endowment to allow me a research leave as a junior faculty member, which gave me the opportunity to begin this project with an extended stay in London. During my time in London, Dudley Baines and Paul Johnson and other members of the Economic History Department at the London School of Economics befriended me and helped me access the unrivaled collection of population writings at the British Library of Political and Economic Science. Chris Langford helped me test my ideas and allowed me to view the Population Investigation Committee papers.

The staffs at the National Archives at Kew, the Wellcome Institute for the History of Medicine, the London School of Economics, Rhodes House, Oxford, the Women's Library, and Rice University Library greatly assisted my research. In particular, I thank Lesley Hall of the Wellcome Institute. A wonderful historian in her own right, she helped guide me through the rich collection of the Institute. I also thank the Galton Institute for permission to examine and quote from the papers of the Eugenics Society and the Family Planning Association for permission to quote from its papers at the Wellcome Institute.

My intellectual debts are many. The work of Alison Bashford, John

Caldwell, Matt Connelly, Frederick Cooper, Dennis Cordell, Joseph Hodge, Dennis Hodgson, Greg Maddox, John Sharpless, Richard Soloway, and Simon Szreter shaped my understanding of the history of demography and the British Empire. Richard Soloway encouraged me to pursue this project, offered assistance numerous times, and generously agreed to read the manuscript. His untimely death deprived us of one of the brightest minds in our profession. My current and former colleagues patiently waited for this project to come to fruition. In particular I thank Sarah Fishman, Joe Glatthaar, Jackie Hagan, Jim Jones, Marty Melosi, and Joe Pratt. My friends Greg Maddox and Dennis Cordell listened to my ideas and helped guide me through African history. Greg was kind enough to read the manuscript as well as papers, grants, and book proposals. Matt Connelly and Adam McKeown raised my awareness of the global context of my work. James Vernon and Mark Bevir helped me clarify the themes of this book and pushed me to link them to the broader intellectual history of Britain in the twentieth century.

My friends and family gave emotional and practical assistance over the many years I labored on this project. David Blackburn, Harvey Yunis, and Terry Lohrenz spent many Friday afternoons drinking beer and enduring yet another discussion of the book. My neighbors Stan O'Neal and Joellen Snow offered meals and sympathy when each was needed. My mother Leonore Ittmann, sister Pat Ittmann, brother Mike Ittmann, brother in-law Steve Kouris, sister-in-law Mary Murrey, and my nieces and nephew followed my progress and encouraged me. My wife's family—Joe and Nelda White, Nila Pollard, Troy and Amanda White—came later to the party but always acted interested in what must have seemed an esoteric topic and tolerated a historian in their midst. My daughters Neave and Caroline put up with my absences and long hours, and they continue to cheer and inspire me. Finally I owe the greatest debt to my wife Lorri White, who has endured five years of being a "book widow." She read and edited my manuscript soon after we met and gently pushed me over the finish line. Our marriage and life together made it possible to complete this project. Even more important, she has made my life immensely richer. For that I am forever grateful.

Introduction

In 1945, Robert Kuczynski, a leading figure in British demography, published an article in the *Eugenics Review* entitled "Demography: Science and Administration" in which he reviewed the history of British demography and lamented the weakness of the nation's population statistics. He ended with a call for a renewed emphasis on the training of demographers and officials in order to incorporate the science of demography into the operations of the state, arguing that "the increasing importance of the population problem will afford many opportunities of doing useful work in this country, and the great development schemes in the Colonies cannot be carried out effectively without the assistance of expert demographers."[1]

Kuczynski embodied the changing nature of the discipline he helped establish in Britain. Born and educated in Germany, he worked in the United States before coming to the London School of Economics in 1933, retiring as reader in demography in 1941. Beginning in the late 1930s he worked with the Colonial Office and was appointed as demographic advisor in 1944, a position he held until his death in 1947. A specialist in mathematical demography, he helped popularize the use of the net reproduction rate (NRR) as a measure of fertility and wrote widely about vital statistics in the United States and Europe. Yet from the mid-1930s onward, he became a specialist in non-European demography and capped his career with the multivolume work *A Demographic Survey of the British Empire*.[2] His belief in the scientific nature of his discipline and his conviction that in the future it would play a crucial role in the British state at home and in the empire was widely shared by other demographers, officials, and private activists.

To what extent then was Kuczynski's vision realized? This book suggests that population science played a significant role in British colonial policy in the twentieth century as the imperial state attempted to control colonial populations using new agricultural and public health policies, supporting private family planning initiatives, and by imposing limits over migration and settlement. Demography was one of several disciplines whose claims of scientific expertise offered officials new ways to understand colonial subjects as concerns mounted about the stability of imperial rule. The shift in demography in the early twentieth century toward quantitative methods raised the prospect of a science of population that could analyze and predict demographic trends. Colonial demography developed as a branch of the discipline in the interwar years as demographers attempted to apply these methods to the study of non-Western populations. Private activists and academics played a key role in creating the new field and worked closely with officials in designing polices to measure and shape imperial populations. Reflecting the ideological concerns of those who produced and consumed population data, race was invariably the critical variable to be measured in colonial demography. In the interwar years attention focused on the expansion of non-white populations and the steep fall in British and white settler birth rates, which appeared to threaten the racial and ethnic balance of power in the empire. To counter this threat, activists called for higher white birth rates and new measures to manage the size and distribution of indigenous colonial populations. The opportunity for them to influence the British government came in the late 1930s, as officials who were engaged in development planning turned to outside experts for help in improving demographic information gathering in the empire. These experts called for colonial governments to adopt European techniques of census taking and statistical analysis in order to improve population data, which created tensions between London-based staff and officials in the colonies.[3] As officials became more concerned about the potential threat posed by colonial population growth, they turned to these same experts for advice about how to counter its impact. Population experts pointed to the slow modernization of colonial societies, which led to rapid population growth as death rates dropped but birth rates remained high. This idea, formalized after 1945 in demographic transition theory, informed population control measures during the late colonial and postcolonial eras.

Kuczynski's vision began to falter in the 1950s when it was evident that the role of colonial demography in imperial governance had been compromised by overdetermined, poorly funded, and badly executed schemes. These failures highlighted the fragmentation of the colonial state as tensions developed between center and periphery as well as experts and officials over how best to govern the empire. That colonial demography was unable to secure the stability of the British imperial state was manifest with growing social unrest and ultimately movements for colonial independence. And yet colonial demography would continue to shape the postcolony. Many of the concepts used by British demographers and officials were incorporated into postcolonial family planning and economic development programs. These same officials and experts often found new careers with international agencies that hoped to use British expertise and networks to reach "Third World" populations.

Efforts to control colonial populations formed part of a larger expansion of the administrative and coercive powers of the imperial state. This expansion lies at the center of the new historiography of the late imperial state. Whereas previous imperial histories emphasized the quick progress of decolonization and the willingness of the British to cede power, more recent work has highlighted the imperial state's concerted efforts to retain and reshape the empire throughout the twentieth century. The political and economic problems of the empire in the interwar years led colonial officials to embrace more interventionist policies in the 1930s, a trend that accelerated during the Second World War.[4] The postwar era saw the continued expansion of state intervention into all areas of colonial life and the growth of such a formidable apparatus of military and police power that some have characterized it as the "second colonial occupation."[5] This consolidation and expansion of the imperial state enabled postwar British governments to maintain great power status and use colonial resources to bolster the British economy.[6] After the loss of India, officials and politicians determined that if decolonization had to be faced it should preserve British interests and control of the postcolonial political landscape.[7]

Yet the portrayal of the late imperial state as a Leviathan has led some historians to caution that its power has been overstated and that too little attention has been paid to the ways in which indigenous colonial societies exposed its ideological and material limits.[8] Moreover, even though experts played a key role in the extension of the late imperial state as part of the new imperial cadre abroad and as advisors to the Colonial Office, recent work has also highlighted the tensions and material constraints that compromised the assembly and deployment of expert knowledge.[9]

DEMOGRAPHY AND THE ORIGINS OF COLONIAL POPULATION SCIENCE

While colonial demography was mobilized by the aims and projects of the late imperial state, its development in the twentieth century reflected broader social and intellectual trends within Britain and the Western world. The emergence of quantitative demography in the early twentieth century followed the path taken by other social sciences like sociology, economics, and political science. Modeling themselves on the natural sciences, these human sciences embraced new methods of gathering and analyzing data that relied in part upon the new statistical techniques pioneered by Francis Galton, Karl Pearson, and R. A. Fisher. While the new techniques became central to all these disciplines, demography shared a particularly close relationship with the development of statistics. Galton, Pearson, and Fisher not only helped create standards for quantitative analysis, their concern with differential fertility, eugenics, and imperial population trends also defined the research agenda for population science.[10]

Galton's and Pearson's hopes for a biological science of eugenics failed to come to fruition in the interwar era. The emergence of a grand synthesis in biology between Mendelianism and Darwinian theory led to a growing divergence between the biological analysis of populations and the study of social determinants of human demographic behavior. In place of biometrics, demographers developed their own quantitative techniques. Building on the work of actuaries and medical statisticians, Louis Dublin and Alfred Lotka developed stable population theory, which allowed for more accurate measurements of growth rates and projections of future population size. In conjunction with techniques like component analysis and the net and gross reproduction rates (GRR) demographers in the interwar years acquired the tools needed for more accurate predictions about population characteristics and trends. For mainstream demographers, the new techniques laid the groundwork for a science of population and distanced the field from its association with eugenics.[11]

This positivist view of demography fits the prevailing orthodoxy within demography and other social sciences that portray them as objective and neutral sciences of social analysis.[12] While scholars have subjected the scientism of these disciplines to critical scrutiny, in recent years demography has been at the center of a debate about the nature of the modern state.[13] Using Foucault's concept of governmentality, historians and social theorists have traced how demography functioned as a technology of power, measuring, classifying, and ordering the population in order to govern in more effectively. Foucault suggested that it was because the security of populations became the energizing principle of the modern state that these became new techniques for governing that extended far beyond the state per se.[14]

This approach opened a variety of new perspectives on the history of population science, particularly the origins and functions of the national census. Studies of the invention of the modern census explored how enumeration required not only the expansion of knowledge but also its compression in order to present data in tabular form. The use of classificatory schemes of occupations and households required the suppression of diversity and difference in favor of patterns of similarity.[15] The work of Theodore Porter, Ian Hacking, and others explored how statistics more generally evolved from the description of social facts in simple quantitative terms to a sophisticated analysis of probability that sought to locate patterns of social behavior and provide causal explanations of those patterns. "The taming of chance" affected more than the presentation of social facts by states and experts; it also persuaded the general public of the existence of concrete social problems that could be studied and then corrected through state policies guided by statistical and quantitative analysis.[16] The recording and analyses of populations both created and measured social phenomena—whether disparities in health, differential fertility, or the status of ethnic and religious minorities—believed to be central to those who conducted the analysis.[17]

In theory, the colonial state possessed unlimited power to gather and use demographic information. Benedict Anderson and others see this ability to map the contours of colonial society as central to the growth of the colonial state.[18] These regimes used the knowledge they acquired to mobilize labor for economic projects and military service, often with unintended and disastrous consequences for indigenous societies.[19] Such unintended consequences point to the shortcomings of colonial demography. Although colonial states possessed the power to compel and coerce colonial populations, their ability to measure and map such populations remained woefully inadequate. Most accounts of African and Asian populations remained impressionistic, based on little more than travelers' reports and the ad hoc estimates of officials and others on the ground.[20] Demographic information remained fragmentary and unreliable throughout much of the non-European world well into the twentieth century.[21]

The new demographic techniques that offered more accurate tools of measurement and projection for European populations could not be used in the colonial environment. This situation reflected in part the limited investment in demographic and statistical infrastructure of the type created in Europe from the mid-nineteenth century onward. Lacking resources and trained personnel, colonial states produced little in the way of useable demographic information.[22] In many cases, they relied on indigenous informants to collect and compile information or simply asked indigenous leaders to produce their own estimates, which were then adopted as official ones.[23] The solution proposed by metropolitan experts to the problem of inadequate population data, the creation of European style census operations in the colonies, failed to resolve the issue. Efforts to impose European style censuses often provoked resistance from local colonial regimes who complained about the cost and asserted the superiority of their knowledge of indigenous society. Seen from the periphery, the plans of metropolitan officials appeared to be out of touch with colonial "reality."

However, the weaknesses of colonial demography reflected more than a lack of resources. It also revealed some of the inherent limitations of demographic instruments designed for use in Europe. The central document in these schemes, the enumeration form, represents an agreed upon set of significant facts that should be measured. Even then, census data collections are flawed, due to enumeration errors and the need to compress the diversity of individual-level data for ease of analysis and presentation. Such problems multiplied in the colonial setting as officials sought to record unfamiliar social and economic institutions. Even if they spoke local languages, officials remained outsiders, lacking the ability to read the social world they encountered and put it into terms useful for demographers. The ambiguities of recording social existence inevitably led to difficulties transcribing social facts into a neat package.[24] Nowhere was this difficulty more pronounced than in the efforts of the colonial state to map race and ethnicity. Colonial officials hoped that the census would provide a set of concrete demarcations within indigenous societies that would allow the state to better manage them. Yet in practice, such categories remained elusive.[25] The fluidity of race and ethnicity, as well as social constructs such as tribe and caste, resisted easy categorization, and it proved virtually impossible to police how individuals and groups identified themselves.[26] Indeed, as colonial subjects became more aware of the significance of such categories, they began to use the census and other social surveys as a way of establishing new identities or consolidating contested ones, often with an eye to gaining advantages vis-à-vis the state.[27]

Colonial demography also operated within a radically different political environment. In Europe and the Americas, where the census helped distribute political representation and state resources between and within regions, the demographic operations of the state enjoyed a reasonable level of legitimacy that engendered cooperation from its citizens.[28] In colonial societies, the gathering of demographic information often came to be associated with tax collection, forced labor, and military service. In such circumstances evasion and resistance exacerbated the difficulties of collecting information.[29] Despite its claims to superior knowledge, colonial demography as a field remained fragmented and ineffective. Only in the postcolonial era, as new forms of development aid internationalized population control, could the ambitions of demographers and officials for access to and knowledge about non-European populations begin to be fulfilled with the cooperation of newly independent states.[30]

POPULATION AND RACE IN THE BRITISH EMPIRE

While the history of British colonial demography resembled that of other of other empires, it was also shaped by a set of particular concerns and institutional arrangements that influenced the development of British population science since its origins in political arithmetic in the seventeenth century. William Petty, who coined the phrase in 1670, saw its value not simply in the production of numbers for the use of the state but also as a tool to reshape the population of the kingdom, most notably the Irish, who were to be assimilated to English norms.[31] In the eighteenth century political arithmetic delved into questions of national interest and power. Fear of larger continental rivals like France made the size and vigor of the British population crucial to national survival. Despite the ability of the English to draw upon the Scottish and Irish populations to bolster their military strength, Britain remained the smallest of the great powers. The need to maintain an overseas empire while waging war with larger European states made the size of colonial populations, the level of immigration, and rising death rates in London matters of public interest.[32] Opponents and supporters of the Whig regime used claims about the size and growth of the English and British population as part of a larger debate about the merits of parliamentary government and the efficacy of state policy, echoing similar debates on the continent.[33] Such debates reinforced the tendency to see British population trends not only as a domestic concern but an imperial one as well.[34] This linkage of the domestic and imperial would distinguish British population science into the twentieth century.

The absence of a national census in England meant that these debates relied on a variety of estimates and informed guesses from fragmentary records. This use of incomplete or even incorrect information characterized the work of Malthus. He derived his famous formula about the ratio of population to subsistence from a reading of accounts of population, most important in North America. The shakiness of his empirical claims failed to prevent the general acceptance of his theory.[35] The establishment of national censuses in Britain and the Western world and the development of an infrastructure for gathering and analyzing statistics of all kind would reduce this problem in the nineteenth century. However, in Britain the organization of the census remained flawed. The British government failed to create a permanent infrastructure for conducting a census and instead authorized each census as the date for enumeration approached. It also conducted separate censuses for Ireland, Scotland, and England and Wales.[36]

Despite the institutional problems of the census, the agency charged with conducting the English census, the General Register Office (GRO), established a reputation for innovation. Under the leadership of William Farr, the GRO pioneered the study of public health and its links to social conditions. It employed hundreds of clerks as well as actuaries and statisticians to carry out the arduous task of turning hundreds of thousands of hand-written records into tabular data. The need to compile and tabulate this information led to the adoption of new mechanical devices in order to speed up processing and increase accuracy.[37] Farr and the vital statistics movement relied heavily on the works of actuaries, who continued to develop their own life tables and other forms of demographic analysis throughout the nineteenth century.[38] In the 1880s, the GRO faced increasing competition from other government institutions for control over the analysis of social trends such as unemployment and mortality, even as its budgets remained static. Following the death of Farr in 1885, the GRO went into relative eclipse.[39]

The critical juncture for the development of modern demography in Britain came in the late nineteenth century. The development of new statistical and biometric tools by Galton and Pearson coincided with new concerns about the status of Britain's population. While both men are better known for their advocacy of eugenics in Britain, their understanding of Britain's perceived biological crisis drew on existing ideas about empire and population.[40] Galton, who traveled in Africa early in his career and served as president of the Anthropological Institute in the 1880s, saw the decline of "barbarous races" in temperate zones and the success of white settlements as proof the superiority of the white race.[41] Pearson for his part argued that the British maintained their supremacy by seizing territory from primitive peoples who gave up ground to more efficient races.[42] This belief in the demographic superiority of the British formed a staple of Victorian population discourse. Malthus contrasted the prudent reproductive behavior of the English with the recklessness of the Irish and saw the stagnation of Asian and Africa populations as evidence of their backwardness.[43] Mid-Victorian writers like Herbert Spencer, Alfred Gregg, and Walter Bagehot believed that competition between races for resources would lead to the expansion of the civilized races like the British at the expense of primitive peoples, a process elaborated on by Charles Darwin in *The Descent of Man*.[44] In the later nineteenth century writers like Charles Dilke and J. R. Seely linked the expansion of British power to its burgeoning and vigorous population, which swept aside "barbarous races."[45] In an age that increasingly saw race as a fundamental category, demography, like anthropology and craniology, helped map racial differences.[46]

Yet Galton and Pearson worried that Britain and other white nations were at risk from the falling fertility of "better stocks" at home and the problems of climate and racial intermixing abroad. Only a Britain where the best supplied future generations could continue the work of empire. The fear of degeneracy, widespread in the late Victorian and Edwardian eras, played a central role in the work of Galton and Pearson and inspired the creation of the eugenics movement.[47] The intense debate over the "condition of England" that raged in the decades before the First World War focused on social concerns defined by demographic analysis: the falling birth rate, class differences in fertility, and the poor health of the British population. For eugenicists, differential fertility represented a threat to the survival of Britain, and they called for measures to raise the fertility of the middle and upper classes and limit that of the poor and disabled.[48] Other reformers focused on the environmental causes of poverty and other social ills and suggested ameliorative measures like slum clearance, school meals, and maternal and infant clinics to raise the overall condition of the nation.[49] Forums like the Committee on National Deterioration, the Poor Law Reform Board, and the semi-official National Committee on the Birth Rate provided opportunities for activists to offer their opinions and attempt to persuade the public.[50]

Both sides used the tools of statistics and population analysis to strengthen their cases. Galton and Pearson's biometry labs sought to demonstrate the overriding significance of heredity for intelligence and social position.[51] Those who wished to demonstrate the significance of environmental influences played a key role in the first comprehensive attempt to use the census to as tool for social investigation. The 1911 Census, designed by T. H. C. Stevenson, employed an expanded census form to document changes in marital fertility.[52] It also saw the first widespread use of calculating machines to collate and analyze data and appeared to confirm the higher fertility of the working class and the sharp fall in family size among the middle class.[53]

In practice, many commentators blended environmental and hereditarian ideas in their discussions of British population.[54] H. J. Mackinder, a pioneer of geography, called on Britain to "increase your white manpower, both in number and efficiency," while C. V. Drysdale, the president of the Neo-Malthusian League, argued, "The security and prosperity of our Empire will be best served by having a maximum number of healthy, virile, efficient and patriotic inhabitants in every portion of it."[55] These calls to strengthen the British population coincided with a greater public concern about tensions among European powers, which many linked to population growth.[56] Support for efforts to achieve a larger and healthier population came from both sides of the ideological divide. Socialists, feminists, and supporters of New Liberalism proposed their own programs for social renewal, while on the right new organizations called for initiatives to bolster national strength and address the problems of poverty and social unrest.[57] This political environment formed the backdrop to the passage of a limited program of social reforms by the Liberals prior to 1914.[58]

The debate over Britain's population changed significantly after the First World War. The losses of the war combined with the continued fall in the birth rate raised fears about population decline. Using the new tools of demographic projection, Enid Charles and others painted a bleak future for Britain and its empire as the population aged and shrank.[59] Concerns about the birth rate coincided with increased attention to population growth outside of Europe, including a spate of work by popular writers focusing on race.[60] Signs of growth in Japan, the Dutch East Indies, and India, documented by a series of more reliable colonial and national censuses, appeared by the early 1930s. Demographers also noted evidence of population growth in the Caribbean and parts of Africa.[61] The prospect of a declining British population and growing colonial populations raised concerns about the survival of the British Empire. It also sparked a new wave of Malthusian anxieties that centered not on Europe, but on non-white populations in Asia, Africa, and the Caribbean.

The new demographic concerns highlighted the limits of demographic knowledge in interwar Britain. The principal tool of state demography, the census, remained underdeveloped in Britain. Demographers complained about the limited scope of the census and the relatively unsophisticated nature of census data presentation. The GRO was seen as unable to provide modern statistical analysis, and other organizations, like the Ministry of Health and the Governmental Actuaries Office, competed to gain control over the analysis and presentation of data.[62] Government agencies appeared uninterested in studying the question of depopulation, leading to calls for a Royal Commission to study British population trends and to suggest ways to reverse fertility decline.[63] The situation in the empire was even worse. Except in India, officials could only guess at the size and growth rates of colonial populations and efforts to create a uniform imperial census remained unrealized prior to the outbreak of the Second World War.[64]

Outside of government circles, demography remained a marginal field. The British government demonstrated little interest in funding social research in the interwar years, so it fell to private foundations to support such work. Like other British social sciences, demography struggled to find funding and a place in academic life.[65] It attracted little financial backing, and the only appointment in demography at a British university was a readership at the London School of Economics.[66] The discipline benefited from the expansion of state planning and intervention during the Second World War and the postwar era. The need to administer the welfare state led to the expansion of data collection by the British government and the employment of more experts to gather and analyze that data.[67] New opportunities appeared in the academic world as well as part of the larger expansion of social sciences in the postwar era.[68] Yet British demography lagged behind its American counterpart, which enjoyed far greater government and private support in the postwar era. While demographers like David Glass would establish international reputations, the impetus within the discipline increasingly lay in the work of Americans like Frank Notestein and Kingsley Davis, who enjoyed the support of universities, private foundations, and the U.S. government.[69]

The postwar empire saw a surge in interest in demography. Building on the work of wartime agencies like the Middle East Supply Center, the British tried to improve the demographic infrastructure of the empire and sponsor new research into colonial population problems. The formation of the Demographic Advisory Group in 1943 and the appointment of Robert Kuczynski as demographic advisor created an institutional base for demography in the Colonial Office under the aegis of the Colonial Social Science Research Council. Faced with the disarray of imperial statistical operations, demographers insisted that colonial governments adopt modern demographic procedures as a solution. Their belief in the power of science to help resolve colonial social disorder encountered the skepticism of local colonial officials and the difficulties of the colonial environment. Although colonial regimes resisted the suggestions of London-based experts, they lacked the resources to design and implement their own systematic censuses. The result was a piecemeal and incomplete expansion of statistical and census operations that left large parts of the empire untouched prior to decolonization.[70]

Despite the limitations of the demographic information available to them, officials proceeded with population control programs. Beginning in the interwar years, the Colonial Office experimented with allowing private birth control agencies to operate in colonial territories, imposed limits on imperial migration, and invested in new public health and agricultural programs. These efforts would become larger and more systematic in the postwar era. Officials expressed a greater sense of urgency about the threat posed by population growth to plans for imperial development, even in places previously believed to be underpopulated, such as Africa and the Pacific. Faced with increased resistance from colonial populations to agricultural reform and resettlement campaigns, the colonial state grew became more authoritarian. The use of such policies in counterinsurgency campaigns in Kenya and Malaya highlighted the potentially coercive nature of population control.[71]

The failure of these efforts became apparent as the pace of decolonization accelerated in the 1950s and 1960s. In even the waning days of empire, however, officials and activists still hoped to implement new population policies to slow the growth of colonial populations. For many of these officials and activists, the emergence of international population programs in the 1960s and 1970s offered the opportunity to continue their work, either with British aid agencies or the new international programs linked to the United Nations and U.S. bilateral aid. Ironically, even as these programs gathered steam, British activists and officials expressed alarm over the expansion of immigration from the former empire.[72] The emergence of a non-white minority within Britain posed new questions about the meaning of Britishness in a postcolonial world and raised fears about the consequences of global and domestic population trends for the future.

While several recent works place population programs and movements in a transnational frame, this book argues for the significance of the imperial in the development of population control.[73] For most of the twentieth century the empire remained central to how the British understood their world. Intellectuals, politicians, and ordinary citizens created their own visions of empire alongside the political and administrative realms that constituted the formal empire. These ideas about empire overlapped yet also contained different or even conflicting notions of the meaning and purposes of the British Empire. Individuals experienced a variety of ties to the empire in the form of investments, careers, bonds of friendship and family, and professional and social organizations. Imperial ideas and networks provided an avenue for private citizens, many of whom had limited direct contact with the colonies, to participate in the empire. These intellectual and human connections also gave the empire a global and transnational character. Almost until its dissolution, British officials and private citizens saw the empire as a global system, with its own linkages and networks that lay outside the control of other states or international organizations.[74]

The book traces the development of colonial demography and its role in the governance of the empire from 1918, when the British Empire stood at its greatest extent following the acquisition of new territories after World War I, to the effective end of the empire in the 1970s. However, this narrative does not cover the entire empire. It focuses on the efforts of officials in the Colonial Office in London as they attempted to formulate a coherent population policy for the dependent British Empire in Asia, Africa, the Caribbean, and the Pacific. This collection of territories possessed their own civil establishments, constitutional arrangements, and sources of revenues, which limited London's ability to exert control. India and the Dominions, the white settler territories of Australia, South Africa, Canada, and New Zealand, play a lesser role in this story. This is not to suggest that these regions did not matter, because both India and the Dominions featured in the larger debate about imperial population. However, both possessed their own governing structures. India had a government in Delhi and a secretary of state in London whose influence greatly exceeded that of the colonial secretary of state. In addition, although recent work on the Indian census and population makes clear the high level of interest in demographic issues in India, it also highlights the inability of the British government of India to create a population policy in the years before independence.[75] Many in Britain viewed the Dominions and its successor, the Commonwealth, as crucial to the maintenance of British global influence and hoped to bolster their populations and strengthen their ties to Britain. Sponsored immigration and the acceptance of the racially exclusive policies of the white settler governments involved a considerable degree of coordination between the British and the Dominions.[76] However, as independent states, these countries cooperated on their own terms and were not subject to control from London.

Chapter 1 examines the origins of the population movement and its role in the development of the field of colonial demography. Chapter 2 turns to the efforts of the colonial state to address population problems in the interwar years and the influence of the population movement upon colonial policy. Chapter 3 addresses the impact of the Second World War and its role in solidifying the influence of colonial demography and population activists within the British government. Chapter 4 focuses on the postwar empire and the attempt to forge a population control policy as part of a larger effort to sustain Britain and its empire in the face of colonial nationalism and the eclipse of Britain as a great power. Chapter 5 returns to the population movement in the postwar era as it dealt with the demise of the British Empire and the emergence of a global population movement dominated by the United States. Chapter 6 explores the creation of a postcolonial population policy in Britain and the continuing influence of British institutions and activists on the new international regime of population control.

The book concludes by examining the relationship between identity and population in postimperial Britain. The loss of empire, combined with an influx of Asian, Caribbean, and African migrants, raised questions about national identity. In this postcolonial world, demography still served to measure differences between groups as attention to birth rates and marriage patterns among the new arrivals fed fears about their impact upon Britain. The desire to limit the influence of "outsiders" on British society demonstrated the contradictions of Britain's efforts to construct a postimperial role and the continuing centrality of demographic ideas to how the British understood their place in the world.

1 The Origins of Colonial Demography

In 1920, a chance meeting in Julian Huxley's study at Oxford brought together Huxley, Alexander Carr-Saunders, and C.P. Blacker. Blacker, who was studying biology with Huxley, described the meeting many years later. He recalled asking Carr-Saunders, who already possessed a reputation as a population expert, how to define the concept of an optimum population.[1] This encounter marked the first meeting of the three most important population activists in twentieth-century Britain. Huxley, a biologist and popular writer on science, served as the first head of UNESCO (United Nations Educational, Scientific and Cultural Organization) and advocated UN support for family planning. Carr-Saunders was the preeminent British demographer of his generation and the head of the London School of Economics (LSE) from 1937 to 1956. Blacker, a physician, served as the secretary of the Eugenics Society and a senior official with the International Planned Parenthood Federation. These three men worked closely together over the next forty-five years in the birth control movement, as advisors to the British government and as leaders of the Eugenics Society. They would help define the agenda of the British population movement and played a central role in bringing the issue of non-white population growth to public attention. Collectively, they illustrate the many strands that went into the creation of modern demography and the British and global population movements. Each possessed scientific credentials, came from the upper reaches of British society and intellectual life, and all believed in the centrality of racial differences between humans.

This chapter examines the British population movement in the interwar era and how a coalition of demographers, eugenicists and birth controllers helped define the problem of colonial population. It begins with the evolving debate over population in Britain as the continued fall in the birth rate and evidence of growth among colonial populations lead to fears of a shift in the imperial and global balance of demographic power. As had been the case in the debate over British population prior to 1914, the fall in the birth rate and the growth of non-European populations would shape the development of demography as a discipline. Some of the earliest attempts to use new statistical methods and techniques of data gathering would be linked to efforts to explore these issues. Demographers increasingly turned away from descriptive statistics and biological models of population to more sophisticated quantitative measures and social explanations of demographic behavior. This new orientation facilitated the consolidation of demography as an academic discipline distinct from fields such as economics. Improved forecasting and analysis also increased the value of the field to the state, and both domestic and imperial ministries took interest in the new field. As concern mounted about population growth outside Europe, demographers turned their attention to the colonial world, applying the new methods to the study of these populations.

Among the most avid consumers of population science were eugenicists and birth controllers, whose interest in demography reflected their own intellectual and ideological concerns. Both groups believed that the new population trends offered additional reasons to pursue their agendas. For eugenicists, concern with colonial demography shifted the focus away from class differences in fertility toward racial differentials in growth rates as the greatest threat to biological fitness. For birth control advocates, evidence of accelerating growth justified the expansion of their efforts to meet the needs of women in Asia, Africa, and the Caribbean. While these organizations remained independent, many of their members belonged to more than one organization, creating an overlapping web of social and political affiliations. Despite their diversity, the groups involved in population issues often collaborated on projects, producing information for the broader public and lobbying government officials for assistance. This coexistence masked the dominance of eugenics within the movement. Due to its greater resources and the prominence of its members, the Eugenics Society would play a disproportionate role in the development of colonial demography.

The British population movement constituted one part of a larger international movement in the interwar years.[2] Before the First World War, eugenicists and neo-Malthusians held international conferences. In the early 1920s, conferences in London (1922) and New York (1925) reestablished links among population activists, particularly those from the United States and Great Britain. The World Population Conference in Geneva in 1927, organized by Margaret Sanger, proved to be a key moment in the international history of birth control and population studies. It produced a number of initiatives in its wake, including the founding of the International Union for the Scientific Investigation of Population Problems (IUSSP). In Britain, several organizations linked to this international movement appeared, including the British Population Society (BPS), the British arm of the IUSSP, organized in 1928.[3]

A number of British population activists participated in these international organizations. Many of them hoped that such bodies could help internationalize population issues. Julian Huxley was the best known of these internationalists, and his time at UNESCO would give him an opportunity to pursue his interest in creating "One World."[4] Harold Cox, the editor of the *Edinburgh Review* and a prominent economist who participated in the Geneva Conference, proposed a "League of Low Birth-Rate Nations" to limit the possibility of demographic competition in Europe and to ensure international peace.[5] The Cambridge economist Harold Wright and George Knibbs, the leading Australian demographer, echoed this call for international collaboration to solve population problems.[6] While such views reflected the growth of internationalism in the interwar years, supporters of the idea received little public support.[7] The one international organization capable of fulfilling their hopes, the League of Nations, steered clear of the controversial issues of population and birth control. The league and its constituent organizations like the International Labor Office confined themselves to statistical studies and conferences.[8]

The limits to internationalism went beyond the timidity of the League of Nations and its member states. British internationalists continued to argue that the British Empire played a unique role as a force for stability and progress and therefore must be maintained.[9] The continued belief in the importance of the empire can be seen in the activities of British population activists. They elaborated a vision centered on the need to protect the empire and Britain's role as a great power. Domestically they hoped to increase the size and quality of the population through environmental and hereditarian initiatives. Activists often used imperial rhetoric to justify such action, pointing to the need for a vital and growing population to defend the empire.[10] The movement also embraced more explicitly imperial measures, such as support for British overseas migration to dependent territories and the so-called White Dominions. In the face of expanding populations in Asia and elsewhere, activists called for the control of non-European populations through the promotion of birth control and increased supervision of imperial population movements.

The imperial and global thrust of their work led to expanded contacts with overseas activists. Birth controllers sought out feminists, health professionals, British expatriates, and colonial elites to construct an imperial network of clinics and organizations. Eugenicists increased their contact with eugenics organizations in the empire and Dominions, as well as Europe and the Americas. The growing coherence of the movement and its institutional growth allowed it to influence public opinion and attract the attention of government officials, particularly those in the Colonial Office.

POPULATION IN INTERWAR BRITAIN

The First World War cast a long shadow over British population debates. For those interested in demography, especially eugenicists, the war was a disaster; thousands of young and healthy men died, especially among the middle class and university educated. In addition to the loss of this "splendid manhood," the war threatened to exacerbate the problem of differential fertility. While many of the best young men died, often without having children, the next generation would be drawn from the ranks of the less fit, either the working class who received exemptions from combat or those who were incapable of military service. Despite the fears of eugenicists, public concern focused more on the fall of the birth rate, which accelerated during the war and continued to decline throughout the interwar period. The plunging birth rate shifted the focus away from class differentials in fertility toward the potential impact of lower fertility, even as differences in fertility by social class appeared to be diminishing.[11]

Anxiety about falling birth rates led to the great demographic controversy of the interwar years, the debate over the threat of depopulation. While some observers, like John Maynard Keynes, continued to argue that the Britain remained overpopulated, other prominent scholars argued that the current course of fertility and mortality would lead to a decline in population within the next twenty to thirty years.[12] From the mid-1930s onward, the prospect of an imminent decline in British population and its potential impact constituted the central theme in discussions of domestic and imperial population.[13] In 1934, Enid Charles's best-selling book *The Twilight of Parenthood* predicted that Britain's population would begin to decline as early as the 1940s.¹⁴ This estimate signaled the beginning a series of grim warnings about Britain's demographic future.¹⁵ Observers argued that the aging, shrinking population created by this trend would encounter a variety of problems in the future.¹⁶

As had been the case with the "condition of England" question prior to the First World War, the depopulation scare generated debate about the reasons for decline and how the state should respond. Conservatives cited their belief in the moral roots of fertility decline and blamed selfishness and feminism for smaller families.¹⁷ Charles, a socialist, blamed capitalism's impact upon the family and argued for far-reaching changes in what she termed the "ecology" of family life. She held out the Soviet Union as an example of the type of changes that would be necessary to reverse the decline.¹⁸ Others on the left, less enamored of the USSR, used depopulation as a justification for their own proposals. Richard Titmuss called for the expansion of social benefits to the working class, arguing that the difficulties of raising children in a free market society necessitated state support for families.¹⁹

Observers speculated about how a smaller population would affect Britain's role as a global power. Fears of decline in Britain coincided with the emergence of fascist regimes in Germany and Italy, which pursued pro-natalist policies and demanded more land to accommodate their expanding nations.²⁰ Similar anxieties emerged about the possibility that Soviet population growth could further unsettle the balance of power in the future.²¹ Concerns about changes in Europe were echoed in discussions of the empire. Observers worried about how the British would maintain their empire with a smaller population, a problem exacerbated by the accelerating decline in white birth rates in the Dominions.²²

As the depopulation panic gathered steam, demographers and popular writers called attention to the possible expansion of non-white peoples outside of Europe. Much of their concern focused on Asia and can be seen in part as a continuation of earlier invocations of the "yellow peril" in the nineteenth century.²³ A spate of popular books predicting an imminent clash between whites and other races were published in the 1920s on both sides of the Atlantic. American works such as Lothrop Stoddard's *The Rising Tide of Color*, Edward Reuter's *Population Problems*, and Edward Ross's *Standing Room Only* focused on the threat to white dominance posed by non-white populations at home and abroad and adopted an openly racist interpretation of demographic trends.²⁴ In England, books like J.W. Gregory's *The Menace of Colour*, Basil Matthew's *The Clash of Colour*, Lionel Money's *The Peril of the White*, and J. Swinburne's

Population and the Social Problem told a similar story for Britain and its empire.[25] These writers linked demographic changes outside of Europe to the improvements in security, medical care, and food production provided by European empires.[26] They predicted that this benevolence would come back to haunt Europe. In Gregory's words, "The growing disparity in numbers of white and coloured people in a democratic age means the inevitable decline of white power; while the former prestige of the white race has been undermined by its own beneficent rule." [27]

Despite the popularity of this genre, many demographers remained skeptical about the threat posed by non-white population growth. The American biologist Edward East and the British sociologist Alexander Carr-Saunders continued to insist that Asian and African populations were limited by racial and environmental factors.[28] However, other scholars including Harold Wright, George Knibbs, and the American sociologist Warren Thompson challenged this view. They emphasized the limits to food production and the potential for non-white population growth to threaten the interests of Western nations.[29] Warren Thompson, a demographer trained at Columbia, was the pivotal figure in this shift, and his books *Danger Spots in World Population* (1929) and *Population Problems* (1930) found a wide audience. He became a major figure in demography, publishing a series of popular texts and heading the Scripps Institute for Population Studies.[30]

Thompson argued that industrialization allowed Europeans to escape Malthusian limits to population and to expand rapidly. This expansion in turn led to a "swarming" of European peoples throughout the world. At the same time, prosperity encouraged a decline in Western births rates as a higher standard of living created expectations of continued improvements in that standard.[31] As Western growth rates fell, however, those of non-Western peoples accelerated. This trend resulted from the adoption of Western ways, as in Japan, or from the lowering of death rates because of Western attempts to end warfare and famine and attack disease through medical and sanitary measures. The result of these divergent trends would be ever-increasing demands by non-white peoples for the concession of territories and resources, particularly those areas outside Europe only lightly settled by Europeans. He saw Japan, China, India, and the East Indies as increasingly overpopulated, while East Africa, Australia, New Zealand, and southern Africa remained underpopulated.[32] Europeans could no longer maintain the belief that sheer numbers conferred entitlement and that the white race would inevitably expand. Population pressure, previously on the side of Europeans, now appeared to work against them and could undermine their dominance of the world system.

Asia represented the principal object of these new Malthusian concerns. Studies of Japan, China, and India suggested that previous assumptions about Asian backwardness and stagnation might no longer be correct.[33] Scholars agreed that Japan was experiencing explosive population growth, but there was considerable uncertainty about population trends in India and China.[34] Japan's industrialization and its adoption of Western technology produced higher standards of living and lower death rates, but India and China remained peasant societies. Many demographers continued to repeat Malthus's view of these societies as overpopulated but stagnant.[35] This tendency was reinforced by the poor quality of demographic data for China and to a lesser degree India. Political disorder and the lack of official data produced widely varying estimates of Chinese population.[36] In the case of India, views began to change in the 1930s as new census data showed an acceleration of population growth.[37] Despite the limits of demographic knowledge, demographers asserted the potential threat posed by population growth, especially through demands for Western nations to allow higher levels of Indian and Chinese emigration.[38]

While concerns about population growth in Asia appeared in the interwar period, demographers continued to focus on the problem of underpopulation in Oceania and Africa. This view dated back to the late nineteenth century, when Darwin and others argued that primitive peoples in these regions suffered from population losses in the wake of Western contact, as exemplified by the extinction of the Tasmanians.[39] Academics, missionaries and colonial officials raised the issue of depopulation in Oceania.[40] They highlighted the physical and psychological impact of Western culture upon the peoples of the region, as disease and deculturation led to a steep fall in the population in the late nineteenth century.[41] Activists called for a variety of governmental and private initiatives to halt the threat of depopulation.[42]

Most observers held a similar view of African populations.[43] Alexander Carr-Saunders believed that Africans, like other "primitive races," were isolated from the main stream of human civilization and showed little evolutionary progress. Given their limited innate endowments and the harsh environment they inhabited, Africans tended to stagnate at a low level of population, which they controlled through a variety of social and cultural practices. When faced with European competition, they suffered depopulation as a result of disease and warfare.[44] Julian Huxley, in *Africa View*

(1931), saw Africa's population as either stationary or in decline as a result of disease, native customs and "the strange distaste for living or conferring life which seized upon various primitive peoples . . . on being brought under the influence of an alien and incomprehensible culture."[45] The South African scholar William Macmillan's 1938 book, *Africa Emergent*, echoed Huxley's notion of an unstable African population pulled into the modern world by the work of Europeans. Macmillan portrayed Africa as a place where "nature has continued to dominate man."[46] Citing the familiar litany of hostile environment, native culture, and disease, Macmillan argued that a lack of population represented the primary roadblock to African development. Like Huxley, Macmillan believed that whites would have to direct Africans to ensure their progress through the provision of scientific medicine, agricultural improvement, and mass education.[47]

Such arguments echoed those made by Malthus more than a century earlier, but they rested on shaky empirical grounds. As was the case in discussions of Asian populations, demographers possessed little concrete information about population trends in African and the southwest Pacific.[48] The growing concern with population trends outside Europe and the Americas led to an increased awareness of the limitations of colonial demographic information. The desire for better demographic information would led to a call to reform colonial statistical operations and for the application of new demographics methods to non-Western populations. Such demands led to the creation of new subfield of demography that specialized in populations in Asia, Africa, and other parts of the colonial world.

THE BIRTH OF COLONIAL DEMOGRAPHY

The emergence of colonial demography reflected the convergence of concerns about colonial populations and changes in demographic method in the twentieth century. The new analytical tools developed in the interwar years transformed how demographers analyzed and understood European and American population trends, and many experts in the population movement hoped that these methods could be extended to colonial populations. While the debates over environment and heredity that drove the development of demography prior to 1914 would continue into the 1920s, the consolidation of demography as a discipline resulted from a fundamental shift in method.[49] A group of scholars carved out a separate field of demography and achieved some success in obtaining financial and institutional support. At the core of the new field lay an emphasis on quantitative studies and the development of more rigorous techniques of analysis that allowed data to be compared across time and place. The evolution of quantitative demography resulted from the intersection of older quantitative traditions with new forms of statistical analysis that took root in medicine, biology, and population studies in the first half of the twentieth century.[50]

The emergence of demography as a field with its own methods and theory was not a straightforward process. Demography remained an eclectic discipline in the 1920s. Students of population came from a variety of disciplines, including geography, statistics, economics, and biology, all of which offered alternative models for population research. Following in the wake of the biometric work of Karl Pearson, a number of scholars continued to search for fundamental biological laws of human population.[51] Raymond Pearl, a biologist at Johns Hopkins who worked with Pearson early in his career, made the most systematic attempt to create a biological model of human population behavior. Pearl believed that human populations, like those of other animals, fluctuated in accordance with environmental factors like density.[52] Although Pearl's quantitative work in demography established him as a leading figure in American population studies, his approach failed to gain acceptance from others in the field.[53] Contemporary critics accused him of ignoring the psychological and social dimensions that distinguished humans from other species and failing to construct a predictive model of human population.[54] Pearl's repudiation of his own arguments in 1939 signaled the collapse of efforts to build a purely biological model of human demography.[55]

Geographers also explored the environmental determinants of human population growth. The American geographer Ellsworth Huntington was the foremost proponent of this approach; he influenced a number of other scholars, including Edward East and Carr-Saunders. His most important work, *Civilization and Climate*, focused on the effects of race and climate in the development of civilization.[56] Several geographers expanded on Huntington's work in the hope of creating a geographic science of population. They divided up the world into climatic zones and developed elaborate maps of climate and resources in an attempt to explain the distribution and size of different populations.[57] While geographers concentrated on determining the limits of population growth through the analysis of climate and agriculture, their ability to predict population trends remained limited.[58] Like biologists, geographers were criticized for creating deterministic models that neglected the social factors that influenced demographic behavior.

The failure of efforts to build a biological or environmental model of human population dynamics coincided with a significant shift in demographic technique. While the biological approach of Francis Galton and Pearson, embodied in the work of their biometric laboratories, played a role in debates about evolution, their work became less significant for demographers.[59] Instead new mathematical techniques for measuring demographics rates, including component analysis and stable population theory, would come to the fore. These methods, pioneered by Alfred Lotka, Louis Dublin, and P.K. Whelpton in the United States, transformed the analysis of population characteristics.[60] They built upon earlier attempts to work out techniques for understanding the contribution of fertility to growth rates and to correct for compositional factors in demographic trends.[61] These developments helped lay the groundwork for a more rigorous mathematical approach to demography. British demographers were certainly aware of these developments in method. Major Greenwood, a leading medical statistician, in a paper given to the Royal Statistical Society, praised the work of Lotka and Dublin, and several discussants, including Carr-Saunders and R.A. Fisher, echoed his comments.[62] Despite the significance of these new methods, demographic techniques remained imperfect, as the exaggerated claims made about population decline demonstrated.[63]

The shift in techniques was accompanied by new models of explanation. Rather than linking demographic changes to underlying natural laws, demographers began to assert the significance of social forces for population trends, particularly fertility. In one sense, this represented the reemergence of the environmental approach of the vital statistics movement of the nineteenth century. The 1911 Fertility Census, which linked marital fertility to occupation, sought to demonstrate the role of social class in fertility. T.H.C. Stevenson would use this study to create his diffusion model of fertility decline, which argued that decline began among the better-off and diffused downward to other social groups. This model would gain wide acceptance among population scientists and reflected the prevailing consensus among demographers that fertility decline result from the conscious choice of couples to limit the number of children and grew out of social forces that shaped those choices.[64]

The diffusion model was assimilated within a larger theoretical construct that tied changes in demographic behavior to social and cultural development advanced by a number of scholars in the interwar years. This argument would be the core of demographic transition theory, which emerged in the post–World War II era as the central paradigm of population studies.⁶⁵ The linkage between social development and population trends led to a reappraisal of what constituted modern demographic behavior. Increasingly, observers pointed to the ability to limit population growth as an attribute of modernity. Older strictures about social norms in Asia and elsewhere that contributed to demographic stagnation were now portrayed as causes of excess growth. Thus, early and nearly universal marriage for women, previously seen as a cause of high infant and maternal mortality, could now, when linked to improvements in life and health brought by Western contact, be viewed as a cause of excess growth.

The importance of American researchers to the development of these new methods and models reflected the more rapid development of demography in the United States. As in Britain, population studies attracted a broad array of groups and individuals. Margaret Sanger and other birth controllers joined with eugenicists like Frederick Osborn as well as demographers to create the Population Association of America in 1931. American demographers enjoyed higher levels of funding and more academic opportunities than their British counterparts. The Scripps Foundation for Research in Population Problems, founded in 1924 at Miami University, was the first demographic institute in the United States. Warren Thompson became the institute's first director, and P.K. Whelpton remained there for the rest of his career. In addition to the Scripps Foundation, the Carnegie Corporation and the Rockefeller Foundation provided funding for demographic research in the United States and Britain. The Milbank Memorial Fund, funded by the Carnegie Corporation, became a significant contributor to the development of American demography. Its journal, the *Milbank Memorial Quarterly*, became an important outlet for demographic research. The fund created the Office for Population Research at Princeton University in 1936, with Frank Notestein as its director. The office established the first graduate training program in demography and published the *Population Index*. By the 1940s, it would become the center for international demographic analysis through its connections with the League of Nations and the U.S. government.⁶⁶

By contrast, demography in Britain remained a more marginal discipline. The interwar years saw a decline in the status of state agencies concerned with demography. The previous center of state demographic analysis, the General Register Office (GRO), was subsumed within the Ministry of Health. Under the leadership of Sylvanus Vivian, the GRO became less innovative and was seen as incapable of sophisticated analysis. His refusal to involve the GRO in the study of declining fertility created frustration among population activists.[67] The Ministry of Health and the Government Actuaries Office, while they pursued their own specialized forms of inquiry, failed to provide an overall direction for demographic work.[68]

Given the weakness of state demography and limited state support for social science research, the development of British demography depended on private efforts.[69] Two institutions—the Eugenics Society and LSE—proved critical in this process. The Eugenics Society's interest in demography went back to the debates over differential fertility prior to 1914. A number of important figures in statistics and demography, including Alexander Carr-Saunders, G. Udny Yule, and Major Greenwood, began their careers working in Karl Pearson's biometric laboratory.[70] Yule, who helped develop regression analysis, served as president of the Royal Statistical Society.[71] Greenwood became the driving figure behind the development of medical statistics and epidemiology in interwar Britain and helped direct the Medical Research Council.[72] Ethel Elderton, a longtime member of the Eugenics Society, worked in Galton's biometric lab and produced an earlier study of the decline of fertility in northern England.[73] All of these figures would contribute to demographic debates in the interwar era over methods and the adequacy of existing statistical arrangements in England.[74]

The Eugenics Society, under the leadership of C.P. Blacker, played a key role in the expansion of population research in the 1930s. In 1936, it created the Population Investigation Committee (PIC). The PIC was intended to be an independent group that could pursue demographic studies without being directly linked to the society. Blacker used the society's ties to private donors in Britain as well as the Rockefeller Foundation and the Carnegie Corporation to fund the PIC and to support promising new researchers.[75] The Eugenics Society also helped forge links between the PIC and the academic establishment, most notably LSE. The role of the LSE reflected its status as the leader in the social sciences in this era.[76] Efforts to establish population studies at LSE began during William Beveridge's tenure as director from 1928 to 1936. Beveridge hoped to achieve a fusion of the biological and social sciences and recruited Lancelot Hogben to serve as the first chair of social biology in 1930. These hopes faded after a series of academic and personal conflicts involving Hogben, who left the school in 1937.[77]

Despite the failure of social biology at LSE, Hogben played a critical role in establishing demography as a discipline at the school. He assembled a group of demographers including his wife Enid Charles, David Glass, and Robert Kuczynski, who served as Hogben's research assistant. He pursued a broad program of demographic research, as indicated by his edited volume *Political Arithmetic*, which featured the work of his group at LSE.[78] After Hogben's departure and Beveridge's replacement by Carr-Saunders, demography flourished at the school. Carr-Saunders created a readership in demography, the first such appointment at a British university, a position filled by Robert Kuczynski until 1941.[79]

Kuczynski's arrival in 1933 solidified the status of the new demographic methods in Britain. His reputation as a quantitative demographer predated the First World War. He lived for several years in the United States, and much of his early work appeared during his time as a researcher at the Brookings Institute in the 1920s.[80] He helped popularize the net reproduction rate first developed by Richard Bockh of the Berlin Statistical Institute, which became widely used in the interwar years.[81] Charles's work on depopulation relied on Kuczynski's work in fertility analysis and he weighed in with his own studies of declining fertility.[82] From his position as reader in demography he exerted a significant impact on the development of population studies in Britain and would come to be seen as the foremost demographer in Britain.[83]

While at LSE he helped advance the career of a number of scholars, most significantly David Glass. Glass, who graduated with a degree in geography from LSE, worked as an assistant to Beveridge and became a researcher for the PIC in 1937. In the 1930s he produced a series of highly regarded population studies on his own and in cooperation with others.[84] He took a research fellowship at the Rockefeller Foundation that was interrupted by the war and served briefly as the deputy director of the British Petroleum Board in Washington, D.C. After succeeding Kuczynski as the reader in demography at LSE in 1945, Glass became a pivotal figure in postwar demography and played a central role in the expansion of population studies at LSE.[85] In addition to his academic appointments, he served on the Royal Commission on Population and as the British representative to the United Nations Population Council.

LSE served as a crucial nexus for the development of demography for the next three decades. Demographers at LSE came into contact with a wide range of activists and intellectuals who constituted the political and social elite of the capital. The discipline's emphasis on data collection as an essential part of efficient and rational planning proved amenable to many on the left in the 1930s.[86] The policy research group, Political and Economic Planning (PEP), enjoyed close links with the population movement and LSE. A number of important figures in demography and the social sciences contributed to the work of PEP, including Julian Huxley, Alexander Carr-Saunders, and Richard Titmuss, who became a leading figure in social administration and a professor at LSE.[87] Relationships also flourished through informal channels. Tots and Quots, a dining club founded in 1931, attracted many of the major figures in demography and the population movement. Its founder, Solly Zuckerman (later Lord Zuckerman), gained fame for his work with primates, research funded in part by the Eugenics Society. During the war he would served on the Scientific Advisory Council and in the postwar years was the most prominent advocate for international population control within the British government. The club included Hogben, Huxley, and Max Nicholson, a well-known ornithologist and a close friend of Huxley's, who was the guiding figure behind the launch of PEP and an important figure in the conservation and population movements in the postwar era. Many of its members were part of a left-leaning cadre of scientists who hope to use science to address social issues in this era.[88] With the outbreak of the war, its members published the book *Science and War*, which called for greater integration of science into planning for war and postwar reconstruction.[89]

This web of connections proved crucial to the creation of colonial demography. It would be the Eugenics Society, acting through the PIC, that supported Kuczynski's new work on colonial populations. The origins of Kuczynski's interest in non-European populations are unclear. He wrote that in 1935 Lord Hailey contacted him to prepare material on demography for the project that would become *The African Survey*.[90] Most likely Kuczynski came to the notice of Hailey because of his relationship with members of the Eugenics Society. Julian Huxley, who knew Kuczynski, served on the committee that helped select the scholars who contributed to the *African Survey*.[91] In any event, his work with Hailey spurred a new interest in non-European, particularly African, demography. In 1937 he published a short study of colonial population statistics under PIC sponsorship.[92] Two years later Kuczynski produced a longer work on the population statistics of the Cameroons and Togoland that formed part of a larger study of sub-Saharan Africa as well as the chapter on population in *The African Survey*. As his work on colonial population drew notice, the society helped him find additional support. The PIC approached the Carnegie Corporation for a grant to expand his study of colonial population. The grant called for Kuczynski to complete his overview of colonial demography and then turn to a study of the West

Indies. Carr-Saunders and Huxley persuaded the Colonial Office to back the proposal and to give Kuczynski access to its library for his work.[93]

While a number of more sophisticated studies of non-European populations appeared in the 1920s and 1930s, they tended to be more narrowly focused.[94] Kuczynski's work was the first systematic examination of the underlying evidential basis of colonial population statistics. He was unsparing in his opinion of the work done by colonial officials. He dismissed most of their work as hopelessly confused and based on unscientific methods. As he argued in the introduction to *Colonial Population,* "Because the problem is not how to improve the existing colonial statistics. The problem is rather how to convince colonial offices is that what is needed in most colonies is a new departure. The population statistics of most colonies are today in a condition similar . . . to that of population statistics of most European countries 150 years ago. . . . Our ignorance of colonial population of the world will not be lessened essentially unless a fresh start is made."[95]

Kuczynski's critique exposed the ramshackle nature of the colonial state's statistical and demography services. He zeroed in on the lack of investment in statistical infrastructure and the absence of trained personnel among colonial governments. After his intervention it was no longer possible to cite official statistics without examining how they were collected and their limitations. His masterwork, the three-volume *Demographic Survey of the British Colonial Empire,* published posthumously in 1948, became the standard reference work for demographers interested in imperial populations.

The influence of Kuczynski and the new demographic methods can be seen in the work of Carr-Saunders, the best-known British demographer of the interwar era. Trained as a biologist at Oxford, his popular book, *The Population Problem,* published in 1922, attempted to unite evolutionary theory and population studies. Carr-Saunders drew primarily on the writings of anthropologists, geographers, and historians and provided little in the way of quantitative evidence or original research. By contrast, his 1936 book, *World Population,* relied heavily on quantitative data and focused on questions of differential fertility and growth rates on a global scale. This new emphasis on quantitative data included an acknowledgment of the inadequacy of colonial population statistics. Given that Glass served as his research assistant and Kuczynski prepared the tables in the text, the extent of Carr-Saunders's contribution to the book remains open to question. Nevertheless, Carr-Saunders interest in the differences between European and non-European peoples, especially so-called primitive peoples, remained central to his work. However, he abandoned his evolutionary model and instead explained population dynamics in social and cultural terms.[96]

Yet Kuczynski's work was not without its detractors. P. Granville Edge, who worked with Major Greenwood at the London School of Hygiene and Tropical Medicine, disagreed with Kuczynski's assessment of colonial statistics. Edge, who focused primarily on medical statistics, produced a series of studies of colonial vital statistics in the 1930s and 1940s.[97] He defended the efforts of colonial officials and attacked those commentators whom he saw as armchair critics. His review of Kuczynski's book on Cameroon and Togoland drove his point home: "However expert as a professional statistician an investigator may be, if he is entrusted with the critical examination of data relating to primitive peoples in remote places, yet lacks personal knowledge of the territories concerned, their peoples, their social organization and other features characterizing their way of life, his criticisms and conclusions may prove both unfair and misleading."[98]

This criticism, leveled by a respected medical statistician, represented the first shot in a war that would rage for the next two decades between critics of the colonial state's demographic and statistical services and their defenders. The former would call for officials to adopt the new standards of demographic analysis and census enumeration in order to provide accurate information for social and economic planning, while the latter invoked the importance of local information for proper administration. The old guard in the Colonial Office and local colonial officials often found themselves in conflict with the new generation of London-based officials and experts who called for a thorough reform of administrative practices and a more active approach to colonial administration. Many of the officials who supported colonial demography saw themselves as progressives attempting to modernize the empire in order to better serve the interests not only of Britain but of its colonial subjects. This strand of imperial thought, embodied in the work and writings of Leonard Woolf and the Fabian Colonial Society, sought to create an more humane and efficient empire, not abolish it outright. Its emphasis on planning and intervention mirrored the ideas of many on the left in Britain in the 1930s who embraced demography as part of this process.[99]

However, colonial demography meant more than simply reforming the demographic infrastructure of the colonial administration. Despite the claims of Kuczynski and others about the scientific nature of population studies and Kuczynski's own focus on technical issues, demographic debates remained politically charged. While many in the discipline opposed eugenics and tended to be left-wing in their political views, the relationship between colonial demography and an ideologically motivated group of population activists shaped its development.[100] The people who pushed for the integration of demographic factors into colonial administration hoped to draw attention to what they viewed as unfavorable racial trends and, just as important, to formulate a response that would reduce the threat posed by the changing composition of the world's population. The convergence of race, eugenics, and demography that characterized Britain occurred in other countries as well. In the United States, domestic fears about race, ethnicity, and immigration stood at the center of population concerns, although empire began to play a role with the addition of new protectorates in the Caribbean and Pacific.[101] In France, colonial demography focused on the need to ensure larger and healthier indigenous populations for economic development and military service.[102]

In Britain, colonial demography became one of a number of academic disciplines that were harnessed to the imperatives of the imperial state. This relationship provided some professional rewards. Demographers enjoyed greater support for their work in the empire than in Britain, where a lack of funds and entrenched political interests limited their options.[103] As advisors and experts, they participated in policy discussions at the Colonial Office to a degree unthinkable in the domestic ministries. In exchange, demographers served the interests of the colonial administration. They defined and described colonial populations in order to improve the efficiency and effectiveness of the imperial state, a process that tended to highlight (and justify) race and ethnicity as fundamental units of analysis.[104] They also became complicit in the efforts of officials to shift responsibility for poverty and social unrest from the colonial state to population trends.

The dilemma of colonial demographers mirrored that of other population experts in the Europe and North American in the interwar era. The implementation of involuntary sterilization policies in Canada, the United States, and Scandinavia demonstrated the darker side of the link between eugenics and demography.[105] Even more disturbing was the willingness of demographers in authoritarian states to serve the new regimes, thus enhancing their own power and prestige.[106] In the most extreme case, the National Socialist regime relied on the work of demographers to target populations for extermination.[107] Such measures represented a qualitatively different level of violence and abuse of power that exceeded those seen in other societies, even in the colonial world, but they served as a reminder of the complications encountered by ambitious experts who sought to advance themselves by allying with the state. Such dilemmas would multiply in the postwar era, as growing political unrest would embroil population experts in counterinsurgency campaigns.

EUGENICS AND THE POPULATION MOVEMENT

The role of the Eugenics Society in launching colonial demography reflected its dominance of the British population movement.[108] The society used its greater resources and the prominence of its members to support birth control work and the establishment of demography as an academic discipline. Despite its influence, it often coexisted uneasily with other groups in the population movement. The emergence of the Eugenics Society as a key player in the population movement was the work of a new generation of reform eugenicists who revised the strict hereditarian views of conservative eugenicists. The reformers believed that environmental factors could affect racial characteristics, and they embraced some social welfare measures as a way of improving the overall quality of the English population. They hoped to expand eugenics' appeal by softening its message and reaching out to other organizations for joint projects.[109] These initiatives allowed the society to reach a broader spectrum of the British elite, not simply those on the political right.[110] Imperial population issues became an important area of concern for reform eugenicists and provided a new way to promote eugenics at the national and international level. This success contrasted sharply with the controversy generated by the other major effort of the society in the interwar years, the push for voluntary sterilization of "defectives."[111]

The increased emphasis upon international and imperial population began a shift away from eugenics' prior concentration on class. The lessening of class differentials in fertility, coupled with fears of depopulation, played a part in this change. Increasingly debate in Britain focused on the overall health and size of the population. Eugenic ideas of "quality" persisted, but they competed with environmental arguments and proposals for improved conditions.[112] While hereditarian understandings of domestic population trends often contained an implicit idea of race, an explicit focus on the issues of race and racial difference characterized the new imperial eugenics and the broader population movement.[113] This change occurred despite the emerging critique of scientific racism in the 1930s.[114] However, the growing concern about global population depended less on racism than a racially constructed view of population that linked power with the relative size of superior and subordinate groups.

The views of Julian Huxley illustrate this aspect of imperial eugenics. Huxley, although a key member of the Eugenics Society, associated himself with the attack on scientific racism by scientists and intellectuals. Yet he remained convinced of the gap between Europeans and other races, though he tended to focus on differences in cultural or social development.[115] Critically, race remained central to his understanding of demographic trends. In a 1943 letter to Oliver Stanley, the secretary of state for the colonies, Huxley discussed the question of future African population growth in such terms, arguing that "the population (of Africa) will start shooting up just when all the white people (except the USSR) will be starting to go down."[116] While not racist in the conventional sense, this statement placed demographic concerns within a racially defined context. This construction of demographic knowledge lay behind the new mobilization around population issues in private and public circles in the interwar years.

C. P. Blacker, who became general secretary of the Eugenics Society in 1931, was a leading figure in the reshaping of the British eugenics movement. His support for social reform and birth control allowed him to establish new links to other organizations put off by the reactionary views of pre-war eugenists. He hoped these links would garner a more mainstream audience for the society. A number of prominent intellectuals and scientists were affiliated with the society during Blacker's time as secretary, including Julian Huxley, Solly Zuckerman, John Maynard Keynes, William Beveridge, Alexander Carr-Saunders, and R. A. Fisher. This group also included more prominent members of the English elite, including Lord Horder, the king's physician, and Sir Bernard Mallet, the former registrar general of England. Such support helped the society grow in influence and size at a time of greater public opposition to eugenics.[117]

The Eugenic Society's involvement in the population movement was part of Blacker's new strategy. Blacker used his own contacts and those of society members to advance the aims of all three branches of the movement. In the course of the 1930s, Blacker expanded the commitment of the society to birth control, which began in 1927 with the formation of the Birth Control Investigation Committee (BCIC), to foster contraceptive research. The society also played a key role in the creation in 1930 of the National Birth Control Association (NBCA), an umbrella organization that united existing birth control groups.[118] It provided financial support, published notices and furnished office space for BCIC, the NBCA, and the Birth Control International Information Centre (BCIIC). In addition to supporting birth control organizations and demographic studies, Blacker found ways to fund scientific research. In 1934, he persuaded the Rockefeller Foundation to support the work of John Baker at Oxford on the development of the spermicide Volpar, which was intended to be a cheap, easily usable contraceptive. The society also backed the work of Solly Zuckerman on the menstrual cycle of baboons in order to further research into the possibility of hormonal contraceptives.[119]

Blacker's interest in international population issues shaped the direction of the Eugenics Society. This interest must have come in part from his extensive contacts with foreign population activists, like Margaret Sanger, with whom Blacker carried on a long correspondence.[120] As a founding member of the International Medical Committee on Birth Control in 1927 and the medical advisor to the BCIC, he regularly came into contact with organizations in other countries. Once he became secretary of the society in 1931, Blacker established links with the Rockefeller and Carnegie Foundations.[121] These contacts allowed Blacker to keep abreast of developments abroad and to offer advice and support to a variety of groups and individuals interested in global population.

Blacker used the *Eugenics Review* as a platform for his interest in global population and demography. While the *Review* continued to devote attention to issues of heredity and domestic fitness, the journal increased its coverage of international population issues. A series of articles published in the *Review* in the 1920s and 1930s raised the issue of the falling birth rate and its possible implications for Britain and its empire. In addition to articles on world population trends, a reader of the *Review* would have encountered reviews of the work of population experts like Robert Kuczynski, George Knibbs, and Warren Thompson, as well as the work of more inflammatory authors like Edward Ross.[122]

Blacker expressed his own views about population in his 1926 book *Birth Control and the State*, which tied support for birth control and social reform to the future of the empire. Like many in the population movement, he linked population pressure to war and called for an international system of regulated population to prevent future conflicts.[123] At home, he believed that the state should intervene to ensure the future of the British race. He called for "state support for conception" to encourage the better-off to have children, but also supported increased access to birth control, which he believed would reduce the numbers of the poor. He linked this expansion of birth control with a call for environmental reforms to improve the lives of the lower classes.[124] This potentially smaller but healthier population would be more capable of sustaining the empire.

Blacker's vision of a revived imperial race appealed to many members of the Eugenics Society. Already in the 1920s, the society spoke of the need to preserve "the racial composition of the Empire" through guided migration and the encouragement of "parenthood on the part of the better stocks within the Empire."[125] Although this view echoed eugenics' long standing concern with the "quality" of the British population, in an imperial context this phrase evoked other images and anxieties. Concern about the future of the British race played an important role in the Eugenic Society's transformation into a supporter of international population work. "Britishness," the belief in the fundamental unity of areas of British settlement throughout the world, remained central to the analysis of imperial population. Late nineteenth-century observers portrayed overseas settlements as part of a "Greater Britain" that spread British customs and institutions across the globe.[126] The creation of white-only reserves in Africa and the acquiescence of the British government to race-based immigration policies in the Dominions helped ensure that these areas would be populated by migrants of "British stock."[127]

The need for a steady supply of British people of sufficiently high quality united metropolitan and Dominion interests. To a greater or lesser degree, the Dominions encouraged British emigration, higher settler birth rates and efforts to improve the white population. In the interwar years, new fears emerged about the future of the British world. Concerns about depopulation cast doubt on Britain's ability to supply migrants to the Dominions, even as these territories experienced a decline in their birth rates.[128] Many observers saw the falling birth rate as an indication of a loss of virility and power among previously vigorous and sturdy settler societies. In the words of one commentator, "If we do not become strong and self-reliant we shall be overwhelmed and enslaved by a more virile nation."[129] For residents of Australia and New Zealand, who expressed growing alarm over the expansion of Asian populations, the demography of settlement seemed increasingly precarious.[130]

The problems of immigration in the interwar years added to these concerns. In the wake of the war-time interruption in migration, the British and Dominion governments launched a number of assisted migration schemes, including one that targeted ex-servicemen.[131] Like many organizations in Britain, the Eugenics Society supported these programs as a way of strengthening the empire. The society's endorsement of these programs created a dilemma for its members, who worried about the drain of young people abroad after the war.[132] The more rigorous screening program for subsidized migrants created by the 1922 Dominion Migration Act increased these anxieties, because many eugenicists believed that only the more ambitious and capable members of society would qualify. In the face of such concerns, advocates of subsidized immigration argued that Britain's loss would be the empire's gain and that only by looking at the larger picture could Britain survive in the long run.[133] However, despite government subsidies and public support, immigration to the Dominions slowed dramatically in this era.[134] This trend reflected the difficulties of Dominion economies, which encountered the problems of declining prices and shrinking markets that plagued other countries dependent on the export of primary products.[135]

In addition to concerns about immigration and declining fertility, commentators in Britain and abroad expressed doubts about the quality of the white population. Many observers believed that Europeans in warmer climates suffered from poor health and over time degenerated, passing their reduced abilities onto their descendents.[136] Eugenicists feared the impact of climate upon British settlers and worried that close contact with other races could lead to miscegenation.[137] Such arguments formed part of a eugenic discourse that focused on the alleged deficiencies of poor whites and united British and Dominion eugenicists. The emergence of eugenics movements in Australia, New Zealand, South Africa, and Canada in the early twentieth century reflected the growing anxiety about racial fitness. In New Zealand, the Eugenics Education Society, founded in 1911, supported the Mental Deficiency Act of 1928, which sought to isolate the handicapped and ensure "proper" reproduction.[138] In Canada, eugenicists, concerned about increasing non-British migration and the reproduction of the "unfit," supported legislation that led to the sterilization of thousands.[139] Australian eugenicists formulated a program of mental and physical hygiene that sought to invigorate the white population, while attempting to isolate non-whites and unfit members of society.[140] The desire to solve the "poor white problem" provided an additional motive for the British Eugenics Society's support for birth control research. The society sought a simple and cheap contraceptive that would be suitable for both colonial peoples and poor whites, which were thought to present similar problems of ignorance and improvidence.[141]

Fears of degeneration took on a particular saliency in Africa, where British settlers represented a small percentage of the total population.[142] In South Africa, which possessed a sizable European community, commentators devoted considerable time to the discussion of the "poor white problem."¹⁴³ Public and private organizations called for measures to limit the reproduction of the poor and improve the general heath and conditions of the white community.¹⁴⁴ This problem appeared more urgent because of the rapid growth of the indigenous population of South Africa. The missionary John Oldham called this situation a tragedy in the making, arguing that if the situation continued, these "blind natural forces" could lead to the collapse of the European civilizing mission and a descent into chaos.¹⁴⁵

Concern with the "poor white problem" lessened as fears about depopulation grew in the 1930s. In his 1935 Galton lecture, Carr-Saunders noted the trend and called on eugenicists to pay attention to the issue of quantity as well as quality.¹⁴⁶ Like other organizations supporting birth control, the fear of population decline produced a crisis for the society; it tried to emphasize the positive benefits of what came to be called "family planning," as opposed to "birth control."¹⁴⁷ Fear of decline also affected how many activists viewed global population trends. As Blacker noted in his 1935 memo on a proposed Institute of Family Relations, the specter of depopulation might lead to new concern over birth rates overseas, "Many cries will be raised. One will be heard throughout the whole of Western Europe—that the races of this region are failing to replace themselves while those of Eastern Europe, the Slave Races of Poland and Russia, are still increasing, while behind them swarm the hordes of Asia with even greater powers of multiplication."¹⁴⁸ The image of a declining imperial people threatened by the swarming masses of Asians and other non-white peoples became a potent symbol of the demographic problems facing Britain in the 1930s. Anxieties about this threat formed the backdrop to the Eugenics Society's support for overseas birth control efforts.

The message of the society resonated because of its perceived expertise in population studies.¹⁴⁹ The lack of a clear disciplinary authority within demography allowed eugenists and other population activists to establish themselves as experts. Beyond the central triumvirate of Blacker, Huxley, and Carr-Saunders, eugenicists helped define the debate over population in the interwar years. Popular writers like Harold Cox and J. W. Gregory belonged to the society and participated in its conferences and events. C. V. Drysdale, former president of the Malthusian League, reviewed population books for the *Eugenics Review* and participated in Edith How-Martyn's 1933 conference on birth control in Asia, as did Dr. Binnie Dunlop, another neo-Malthusian stalwart who worked in the Scottish Office of the Registrar General. J. P. Brander, a retired Indian Civil Service officer who belonged to the society, worked with birth control groups and corresponded prolifically with newspapers and journals. Members of the society, most notably Huxley and Carr-Saunders, appeared in public events and radio programs that highlighted population problems.[150]

The acknowledged expertise of the society in demographic issues stood in stark contrast to other projects pursued by the society in the interwar years. Debates over sterilization and "problem families" roused far greater political controversy. The uncertainty about the nature of heredity and the existence of alternative scientific models of inheritance undermined eugenicists' claims to expert status. The seemingly scientific findings about imperial and international population provoked far less public concern. Just as important, addressing the issue of imperial population did not require rallying public or parliamentary support. Instead, activists needed to persuade permanent officials, especially those in the Colonial Office. This task required a lobbying campaign better suited to the strengths of the Eugenics Society, which could rely on the social prominence of its members for entrée into the world of officialdom. Over time, the society evolved into the political arm of a growing population movement, forging close links to officials and overseas organizations.

THE BIRTH CONTROLLERS

While eugenicists encountered growing opposition to hereditarian ideas and sought a new role in population work, the birth control movement flourished. The Neo-Malthusian League, the most public advocate for birth control in the nineteenth century, faltered. Its focus on family size as a cause of poverty limited its appeal, and the league disbanded in 1927. In its place, a new set of organizations, often led by women and affiliated with the feminist movement would appear. Beginning with Marie Stopes's clinic in 1921, private birth control facilities developed throughout Britain in the 1920s. The Ministry of Health's decision in 1930 to allow contraceptive advice within public health facilities marked the success of a prolonged campaign by activists, although state support for birth control would take longer to achieve.[151] In a broader cultural sense, birth control triumphed, as it became widely acknowledged that an ever-larger proportion of couples made use of contraception. Indeed, the continued debate about falling fertility and depopulation usually started with the assumption that the root cause laid in the voluntary choices of men and women.[152]

If the revitalization of eugenics turned on the issue of race, the success of the birth control movement brought gender to the center of the debate about population and empire. The leaders of the campaign came from the feminist and suffrage communities that predated the First World War. However, the birth control movement, like the broader feminist movement in the interwar years, remained in flux. Birth control work represented one part of the proliferation of feminist organizations in this period that possessed overlapping membership and goals. With full suffrage won in 1928, women's organizations turned to issues like protective legislation, family allowances, and birth control.[153] Most activists linked birth control to women's and children's health, though some radicals emphasized women's control of their sexuality and reproductive choices.[154]

Given the role of eugenics in the population movement, the question of the relationship among feminism, birth control, and eugenics takes a prominent place in the literature.[155] Recent work on the movement has highlighted the eugenic sympathies of many of its key proponents, including Margaret Sanger and Marie Stopes.[156] The membership of feminist leaders like Eleanor Rathbone in the Eugenics Society as well as the important role played by feminists like Cora Hodgson and Eva Hubback in its operations raises the question of whether eugenicists and birth controllers made an alliance of convenience or shared core values about issues of class and race.[157] Certainly, there appear to have been mixed feelings on both sides. Edith How-Martyn, one of the leaders of the movement, noted in a letter to Margaret Sanger, "My uncompromising feminist and democratic views are far too pronounced for many people. . . . Nearly all the men connected with the last Conference (Geneva) come into that category."[158] She amplified those remarks in a letter to a non-white friend in the movement in which she wrote that members of one birth control organization had "an authoritarian, if not to say, Fascist outlook."[159]

The birth control movement rested on a broader idea of the shared bonds of women not only in Britain but in the empire and beyond. It constituted part of a larger imperial feminism that dated back to the nineteenth century and the campaign for slave emancipation.[160] Victorian British feminists cited the need to improve status of women in the empire as evidence of their potential to shape the empire and as a justification for being granted suffrage.[161] This effort continued in the interwar years in what Susan Pedersen refers to as imperial feminism's "Maternalist moment."[162] The presence of women members of Parliament lent strength to the movement, as did the growth of new organizations that provided opportunities for women to intervene in imperial concerns.[163]

Activists saw birth control as one component of a campaign to improve the lives of women. Edith How-Martyn extended this justification to her work abroad, arguing "Motherhood knows no frontiers."[164] The focus on the health and welfare of women and children helped birth control activists reach out to a variety of groups in the empire. Helen Beck, a birth control activist in Singapore who claimed support in the local Chinese community, spoke of "the intolerable burden which motherhood imposes on the very poor, the unemployed and the extremely unhealthy" and argued that "among hard-working peasants it would be a definite alleviation of much distress, and the means of eliminating much inevitable crime and cruelty."[165]

This belief in the universal bonds of womanhood coexisted with ideas about race and culture that portrayed non-European women as backward and in need of aid from their more advanced British sisters. The racial and hereditarian ideas of some participants in the birth control movement coexisted with humanitarian motives that animated their work.[166] The encounter between activists and colonial peoples could uncover these attitudes, as in the case of How-Martyn, who revealed her dismay at what she witnessed in India.[167] In a letter to Sanger she wrote, "How humanity breeds here. No registration of deaths, so infanticide, abortion and stealthy murders can go on unchecked. Sanitation they will not understand. Cows and other animals wander almost everywhere unmolested. They bathe in, wash clothes and drink from the dirty Ganges. Yet for the most part they attractive, good looking, quiet and have the animal's unquestioning acceptance of life as it is and its surroundings."[168]

Despite the ambivalent roles of race and class in their campaigns, birth control activists challenged the prevailing gender narrative of colonial demography. Population writers going back to Malthus argued that the improper family lives and sexual behavior of the poor, particularly single mothers, created the excessive fertility that doomed them to poverty.[169] Such argument were extended to "primitive" or "traditional" peoples, whose failure to conform to civilized behavior lay at the root of their demographic problems. In particular, the failure of women to adhere to these norms lay behind many demographic problems. Marriage patterns, women's labor, child-rearing practices, sexual behavior, birth control, and breast feeding all came under scrutiny in this era.[170] Arguments about the negative impact of polygamy and child marriage fell into this category, as did the presumed contribution of West Indian promiscuity to population growth.[171] The officials and scholars who made these arguments used as their model of correct behavior their assumptions about gender and sexual behavior among members of the British middle class. Demography contained an implicit set of standards that should be followed by workers at home and natives abroad in order to correct population problems.[172]

Birth control activists by contrast turned their attention to the failings of men and the poverty and misery of working-class and colonial women. Their demand for increased access to birth control at home and in the empire rested upon a belief in the ties among women of different races and classes. They asserted that the shared burdens of women's social, political and economic disadvantages, as well as the common experiences of child birth and child rearing united all women. While birth control activists claimed the right to speak for indigenous women and often portrayed them as the victims of colonial men, they also asserted the impact of poverty and poor health upon their lives. Their implicit critique of colonial rule challenged prevailing notions that the behavior of colonial peoples alone created population problems. This emphasis on the shared problems of women contrasted with the patriarchal and paternalist attitudes of others in the population movement, especially eugenists. The efforts of feminists to highlight the disabilities of women and their role in population problems dovetailed with efforts by activists like Eleanor Rathbone for family allowances at home and reform of perceived male abuses abroad.[173] Birth controllers insisted that the problems of gender were central to any attempt to construct effective responses to demographic problems.

British birth control advocates focused on building a set of imperial and global organizations to further their objectives. Three of the major birth control organizations; Marie Stopes's Society for Progressive Birth Control, the BCIIC, and the NBCA began overseas work in the 1920s and 1930s. The rapidity with which these groups moved from domestic to overseas work suggests a broad consensus within birth control circles on the importance of such work. Their efforts, particularly in the case of the NBCA, the forerunner of the Family Planning Association (FPA), resulted in the creation of a network of affiliates and clinics by the end of the 1930s.[174]

Marie Stopes relied upon her reputation as a pioneer to exert influence abroad. She received thousands of letters from overseas correspondents seeking personal advice and assistance in creating birth control clinics.[175] Stopes failed to build a centrally directed organization, but her advice and supplies of contraceptives proved crucial to birth control groups in places like South Africa and India. In the long run, however, Stopes's difficult personality and insistence on strict adherence to her methods of birth control and clinic organization limited her influence over overseas activists.[176]

BCIIC, founded in 1930 by Margaret Sanger and Edith How-Martyn, emerged as a major contributor to the international birth control movement.[177] From its inception, BCIIC aimed for an international audience and tried to advance the cause of birth control outside of Europe and the United States. In a letter to C. P. Blacker in November 1935, Sanger outlined her goals for the organization: "In my coming campaign I hope to do the preliminary work for realizing two aims: first, to bring to the poorer and biologically worse-endowed stocks the knowledge of birth control that is already prevalent among those who are both genetically and economically better favored: and secondly, to bring the birth rates of the East more in line with those of England and the civilizations of the West."[178]

Sanger worked with the veteran English feminist Edith How-Martyn, who ran the Centre's London headquarters. While historians have written about Sanger's part in the story, the contribution of How-Martyn is less well known.[179] Before joining with Sanger to run BCIIC, How-Martyn enjoyed a long career in the suffrage and birth control movements. She served as honorary secretary of the Women's Social and Political Union and joined the Malthusian League in 1910.[180] She met Sanger during the latter's visit to England in 1914 and formed a close working relationship with her during the next twenty-five years. Her letters to Sanger in the late 1920s showed an eagerness to expand birth control work overseas. In 1929 she wrote, "I am hoping you will have some big new ideas on the world problem of birth control for I do feel the whole question is stirring."[181]

Once BCIIC began its work, How-Martyn worked tirelessly to advance birth control outside of Britain. Between 1933 and 1939, she traveled to Asia, the Middle East, and the Caribbean, undertaking four tours of India and also visiting Ceylon, Egypt, and China.[182] During her travels How-Martyn made local contacts, encouraged the establishment of clinics and tried to generate support for birth control through speeches and public appearances.[183] Her trip to Egypt in 1934 coincided with rising concern about Egyptian overpopulation and she met several Egyptian officials and physicians sympathetic to her message.[184] How-Martyn used this same combination of British expatriates, indigenous social activists, and semi-official support throughout the 1930s. By the end of the decade, she assisted with the establishment or operation of birth control clinics in the West Indies, China, Ceylon, India, and Malaya.[185]

Her visit to the West Indies in 1939 typified her mode of operation.

She went to Jamaica at the invitation of Amy Bailey, an Afro-Caribbean feminist who wrote to How-Martyn and told her that "Jamaica needed the help of a feminist birth controller."[186] While there she received the support of the honorary secretary of the Jamaican branch of the British Medical Association and the Women's Liberal Club, to which Bailey belonged. Although she arrived during a general strike, How-Martyn encountered no difficulties and toured the island in a car provided by Jamaica Welfare Limited, an agency sponsored by two fruit companies and headed by the nationalist leader, Norman Manley. She helped cement the fledging birth control movement on the island, which dated back to the mid-1930s, and after her visit a Jamaican branch of the FPA opened.[187] In Jamaica, the push for the establishment of birth control clinics involved a coalition of feminists, colonial doctors, the fruit industry, and Afro-Caribbean nationalist leaders. How-Martyn became sufficiently well known for her work in Jamaica to be called to give evidence before the Moyne Commission, created in 1938 to examine the roots of social and political unrest in the region.[188]

In addition to her work abroad, How-Martyn remained involved in birth control circles within Britain. In 1933, she organized a conference on birth control in Asia, which brought together experts and activists from England and China, Japan and India. The meeting, which received coverage in the *Journal of the British Medical Association* and whose proceedings appeared as a book in 1935, focused on overpopulation and the possibilities for birth control in the Far East. In addition to demographers like Alexander Carr-Saunders and Robert Kuczynski, the conference also featured prominent activists from the birth control and eugenics movement, including Eleanor Rathbone, Marie Stopes, Harold Cox, Lord Horder, Helena Wright, and Frida Laski.[189] While in London, she attended the meetings of population activists. However, she expressed frustration about the lack of activity generated by these conferences. In her account of a 1937 meeting of the BPS, she commented, "The proceedings seemed to me pitiful and the talks I had with some of the people there made me feel how little practical help and guidance come from academic people towards solving the world's problems."[190]

The financial and administrative difficulties of running a stand-alone organization led BCIIC to merge with the NBCA in 1938. The collapse of the BCIIC came after a long series of struggles within the organization. As early as 1935, How-Martyn wrote of her desire to quit touring and of the interference with her work by what she termed the "Beaconsfield clique."[191] She argued that they knew nothing of the difficulties of fieldwork.[192] Upon her return to England in 1936, How-Martyn resigned from BCIIC and established Birth-Control World Wide, which published a newsletter and sought to create its own institutional and financial base.[193] Despite limited finances, How-Martyn continued her work, including her trip to Jamaica. She remained active before leaving on another tour in 1940. While on that tour, she decided to immigrate to Australia and ceased active work in the movement.

The merger of BCIIC with the NBCA solidified the latter organization's position as the leading birth control organization in Britain. The NBCA, created in 1931 by the amalgamation of several birth control groups, became the dominant private British organization in overseas population work, first as the FPA (1939) and then in collaboration with the International Planned Parenthood Federation. In its early years, the association struggled financially and relied on assistance from the Eugenics Society. Its membership and directors represented the elite of the birth control movement in England, including Marie Stopes, Helena Wright, Julian Huxley, and Lord Horder. The NBCA established branches and clinics overseas and lobbied officials for support of birth control work abroad. It devoted considerable attention to India and supported the work of a number of societies in the subcontinent. The Jamaican Birth Control League, formed in 1939 after How-Martyn's visit, became an affiliate of the FPA, as did clinics in South Africa and Hong Kong.[194]

Beyond the formal organizations and their leadership, a number of individuals, including several current or retired colonial officials, became activists for their own reasons. Individuals who lived and worked in India seemed particularly interested in the topic. London-based retirees often attended meetings of the East India Association, where several lectures in the 1930s focused on Indian population growth. Sir John Megaw, former chief of the Indian Medical Service, became one of the best-known spokesmen on the topic. He raised the issue while still in India in the 1920s and upon his return to England lectured and wrote articles on the threat of Indian population growth and the problem of world food supplies.[195] J. P. Brander, another retired Indian Civil Service officer, became an enthusiastic supporter of birth control. Brander focused in particular on India and championed the work of Megaw. He toured eastern and southern Africa for BCIIC in 1936 to assess the possibility of expanding its operations. Brander represented the type of freelance activist attracted to the movement in its early days and remained active until his seventies.[196]

Officials serving abroad also lent a hand to birth control organizations.

In Hong Kong, Robert Forrest, secretary for Chinese affairs, collaborated with the Hong Kong Eugenics League in its efforts to set up a birth control clinic, while Helen Beck, the wife of the police superintendent of Singapore, played a leading role in the Straits Settlements movement in the late 1930s.[197] The wife of the governor of Ceylon, Lady Stubbs, was supportive of a birth control clinic established in 1937.[198] In Bermuda, the initiative came from the government itself, as the health department provided birth control advice as part of its maternal and infant health clinics.[199] Officials and expatriates living abroad provided the critical link between activists in England and the populations they wished to reach. Often a two-way traffic existed in ideas. For example, Helena Wright, who became an important figure in the British birth control movement, became interested in the topic while working in China in the 1920s. Upon her return to England, she became an activist in the NBCA.[200]

Birth control organizations tried to cultivate a close relationship with colonial elites. In a number of countries, emerging nationalist elites proved willing to embrace their ideas. Doctors and other medical professionals in the West Indies, China, Egypt, and India collaborated with the birth control movement as part of a larger approach to questions of health and poverty.[201] The desire to preserve and strengthen the nation motivated politicians and social activists in colonial territories.[202] However, other nationalist politicians proved less receptive. In India, both British and Indian feminists encountered resistance to their birth control work from the Indian National Congress, particularly Gandhi.[203] In Jamaica, despite Norman's Manley support for family planning and the endorsement of his stance by the *Daily Gleaner* newspaper and the Women's Federation of Jamaica, other nationalists proved less supportive. Adam Bustamante, Manley's rival and leader of the Jamaican Labor Party, attacked birth control as an attempt by the British to avoid giving the West Indies more financial support for development.[204] This argument resonated with many on the island, who opposed the work of British activists for both political and religious reasons.[205]

CONCLUSION

The resistance of some nationalist elites to the work of birth controllers exposed the tensions that underlay the population movement. Many in the population movement viewed colonial elites, especially those with Western educations, as their natural allies. Colonial students, professionals, and politicians were seen as the best hope for persuading their fellow subjects to change their behavior and many of them participated in the population movement, forming local societies, pursuing academic training, and staffing clinics. However, the vision of cooperation articulated by activists encountered the racial, class, and gender categories that divided the empire. The British, both at home and abroad, constituted the core group of the empire and observers often spoke of Britishness as a force for melding the empire together. While Britishness involved a shared set of social and cultural values, its principal marker remained race. Other groups within the empire were ranked in relationship to this core group on a scale that encompassed economic development, culture, political order, and skin color.

The focus of the population movement on the "British race" and the future of the British Empire produced a curious myopia. The colonial subjects of the empire, whose demographic behavior became increasingly important in this era, lacked a substantial presence in the literature and programs of the movement. Activists lumped Asian, Caribbean, and African peoples together as primitive and backward, differentiated by race or religion but possessed of common characteristics that impeded their advance toward modernity. Superstitious, oversexed, disorganized, and mired in poverty, they required outside intervention to make progress and even to understand the basics of birth and child rearing. The vast majority of colonial subjects remained faceless and nameless, existing only to be counted and classified.

While some colonial elites sought alliances with population activists, as long as this contact occurred within the imperial context, their status remained subordinate to that of metropolitan activists. The desire to influence the colonial state placed the population movement squarely on the side of empire, offering its services to assist a system under increasing strain. This imperial bias contradicted the international and universal language activists used in their campaigns and underlined the limits to constructing a movement across racial and ethnic boundaries. Race and a privileged position within the imperial system remained fundamental dividing lines in the years before 1939.[206]

The population movement succeeded in constructing colonial demography as a field of study and as a subject for political action. By uniting birth control and demography, the movement gained new creditability and public support for its work. The key to the success of the movement, however, lay in its ability to influence public officials and to obtain support for its initiatives. They were able to accomplish this goal in large part due to their ability to connect signs of population growth in the empire with fears about depopulation in Britain.²⁰⁷ Activists could use the widespread awareness of the issue among politicians and officials to transform their eugenic and racial concerns into issues of broader significance. While population activists found only a limited public audience, they alerted the British government to the need for greater attention to colonial demography.²⁰⁸ Their lobbying efforts proved quite successful and allowed activists to shape how the Colonial Office understood imperial population issues and the solutions officials crafted to these perceived problems.

2 The Colonial Office and the Population Question, 1918–1939

The emergence of colonial demography occurred as the British Empire faced a series of new economic and political challenges in the interwar years. The acquisition of new mandates in the Middle East and Africa after World War I brought British rule to its greatest extent. Yet the growing resistance of colonial peoples stretched the resources of the colonial system. At a time of budget cuts and economic slowdown, it proved difficult for the British government to meet its many obligations, leading to reductions in colonial personnel and military expenditures. The collapse of the global economy in the late 1920s only exacerbated these problems, as colonial economies faltered in the face of falling commodity prices. Faced with domestic and international criticism of Britain's colonial record, the Colonial Office embraced a series of institutional reforms that sought to make colonial administration more efficient and responsive to the needs of imperial subjects. These reforms were accompanied by a shift in philosophy within the Colonial Office, as officials began to abandon older ideas of colonial governance for a more interventionist approach. The rejection of laissez-faire and the dual mandate slowly gathered steam in the interwar years, as the limits of these ideas to address problems of poverty and development became clear. The publication of *The African Survey* in 1938 and the widespread West Indian unrest of that year helped build support for the new departure.

This chapter examines the role played by colonial demography in the transformation of the imperial state. It begins by sketching the structure of the colonial state at the end of the First World War. The colonial service proved ill prepared for the new challenges it would face in the interwar years. It was under strength, lacked sufficient specialist staff, and relied almost exclusively on locally generated revenues. Its statistical and census operations were uncoordinated and depended on untrained local officials and indigenous assistants to gather and report information. The colonial state relied on private economic interests for development and private agencies like missions to provide education and medical services to colonial peoples. Despite its limited capacities, the colonial state affected population trends through its actions in public health, agriculture, labor policies, and immigration. The officials who pursued these policies often expressed beliefs about colonial populations that justified their actions, whether underpopulation in Oceania or overpopulation in East African native reserves.

These demographic constructs would be contested in the interwar years, as changing economic and social conditions forced officials to rethink their ideas. Even more important, demographic experts and population activists called into question the accuracy of colonial population statistics and official views of demographic problems. In particular, the focus on labor shortages and underpopulation would be replaced by a growing belief in overpopulation as the central demographic problem facing the British Empire. In the absence of a centralized imperial demographic agency, demographic ideas and knowledge remained disputed. Many local colonial officials continued to defend their views and methods of information gathering in the face of challenges from London-based officials and experts.

Colonial demography was one of the disciplines that helped push the colonial state to shift its practices. Demography generated changes, especially in the realm of quantitative social analysis, but the field was also pushed forward by the changes in the colonial state, most important the creation of expert bodies and research grants. Other areas of knowledge like anthropology and the biological sciences enjoyed a similar relationship. The colonial state embraced expert knowledge because it felt the need to solve problems, but the deployment of expert knowledge depended on the networks of activists, experts, and officials. In demography the presence of a core group of experts in the capital and at the London School of Economics, many of whom were also activists with close ties to officialdom, shaped how the discipline was perceived and the experts who were selected by officials to assist them. This can be seen in the lobbying campaign launched by population activists. This campaign persuaded the Colonial Office to recognize the weakness of its statistical and census operations and institute reforms. More important, activists hoped to alert the British government to the threat posed by non-white population growth and of the need for a coordinated response to the problem.

Although officials responded to this lobbying effort, they also responded to demographic concerns that appeared in the course of events. The value of expert knowledge lay in its potential to help official address new problems of colonial governance. The issue of migration, especially in Palestine and the West Indies, raised questions about demographic changes, controls over movement, and the capacity of local economies to support larger populations. Concerns about colonial agriculture and nutrition intensified in the 1930s even as the new Colonial Agricultural Service launched a series of initiatives intended to make indigenous agriculture more productive. Finally, controversies over the clinics established by birth control activists in the empire made the Colonial Office consider their legality, the role of colonial governments in such schemes, and the problems of maternal and child health. By the outbreak of the war, officials recognized the need for a more systematic approach to demographic issues that would include improved population data and an effort to define the scale of imperial population problems as well as any potential solutions. Officials remained leery of blundering into an area that brought issues of race and sexuality to the forefront and could subject them to criticism from all sides.

THE COLONIAL OFFICE AND THE CHALLENGES OF TWENTIETH-CENTURY EMPIRE

Although most people viewed the British Empire as a monolithic whole, the reality in the early twentieth century was far more complex. No single institution governed the empire, and its territories possessed their own constitutional and political links to Britain. India was governed by its own ministry based in London and a viceroy in Delhi. In areas of so-called white settlement, autonomous governments directed their own affairs under an umbrella of British sovereignty. From 1907, the British Dominions Office handled relations with these states. A third group of dependencies fell under the authority of the Colonial Office in London. In theory, the Colonial Office exercised control over these colonies, but in practice its power was limited. Some colonies, such as Jamaica or Bermuda, claimed their own special relationships with Britain as well as their own versions of the "ancient constitution." This gave them the right of redress to the governor and London as well as limited representative government. A large number of dependencies, mostly in Africa, lived under more or less direct rule from London, mediated by the role of local colonial officials and indigenous rulers.

Before the First World War, the Colonial Service was divided into eight geographic organizations that were grouped under three assistant secretaries of state based in London. Overseas officials remained the employees of their respective colonies and the colonial secretary of state enjoyed a limited amount of patronage in his appointment of officials. The Colonial Office formed part of the Home Civil Service, recruiting its London-based officials through the examination system. In these circumstances, the number of officials overseas and in London remained limited.[1] The colonial service attracted the generalists produced by the universities and the Civil Service Examination system.[2] The British placed great faith in the ability of such men to master the diverse conditions and circumstances found in the empire. Colonial Office personnel based in London tended to concentrate in one particular region, while in the colonies officials prided themselves on their local knowledge and awareness about the lives of "their people." There existed little need for specialists beyond a bare minimum in fields such as law, medicine, and accounting.[3] The Colonial Office took a fairly consistent laissez-faire stance, leaving economic development and social welfare to private actors. Officials in London focused primarily on financial and fiscal matters, insisting on balanced budgets and well-serviced loans. Within the world of Whitehall, the Colonial Office was a relatively weak ministry, lacking the clout of the Treasury and the Foreign Office.[4]

Although the First World War forced the British government to exert greater control over colonial economies and manpower, the war resulted in limited institutional changes.[5] The British acquired new territories in Africa and the Middle East as mandates from the League of Nations but simply incorporated them into the existing system. This expanded empire faced a series of new challenges in the interwar years. The growth of Indian nationalism proved to be the most formidable one, but the British also faced insurgencies in the Middle East. The empire suffered from the effects of a global slowdown, exacerbated in the colonies by the collapse of commodity prices. In the 1930s, political unrest in the West Indies and West Africa brought new attention to the economic and social conditions of colonial peoples. The Colonial Office and colonial governments faced these challenges with a bureaucratic organization inherited from the nineteenth century. Prior to the 1930s, the institutional structure of the colonial service worked against the formulation of systematic policies, especially in the areas of social and economic development.[6]

The weakness of colonial administration extended to imperial statistics and censuses. Despite efforts over the previous eighty years to create a unitary imperial census on a common plan, each territory continued to devise and implement its own census, often relying on incomplete information and estimates. As a consequence the British government lacked basic demographic information for most of the empire.[7] The deficiencies of imperial statistics led to calls for reform, culminating in the Imperial Conference on Statistics in 1920. Despite vigorous debate and proposals to create an imperial statistical bureau, the situation remained unchanged.[8] The censuses conducted in 1921 remained poorly planned and inaccurate.[9] The onset of the Great Depression, which reduced colonial revenues, meant that the 1931 censuses either failed to take place or were greatly reduced in scope. The limitation of official demographic knowledge constituted a serious obstacle to interwar efforts to manage colonial populations, one that would not be addressed until the late 1930s.

While the British colonial state remained fragmented and lacked basic demographic information, officials in London and abroad adopted policies with important demographic consequences. The pursuit of development under the notions of the dual mandate and trusteeship justified the creation of migration, labor, agriculture, and public health policies that influenced the demographic characteristics of subject peoples. Many of these policies rested on widely held assumptions about indigenous populations. These ideas often reinforced one another, as concerns about underpopulation rationalized forced labor, migration schemes, and public health measures. This de facto policy of population control expanded in the interwar years, as economic dislocation and political unrest led the British government to pursue a more interventionist path.

MIGRATION AND POPULATION IN THE INTERWAR EMPIRE

Attempts by British officials to control imperial migration represented the most significant effort to shape colonial populations prior to 1945. These policies dated back to the nineteenth century and the creation of an indenture system that brought South Asian workers to the West Indies after the abolition of slavery. In the years before the First World War, officials sought to tap the "surplus" labor of Asia for economic development, facilitating the movement of Indian and Chinese workers throughout the empire. The indenture system provided workers for the sugar industry of the West Indies and the mines of South Africa and led to the establishment of substantial South Asian and Chinese communities in eastern and southern Africa, the West Indies, Malaya, Fiji, and

Mauritius. Increasing criticism within India, as well as changing labor markets, led to the abolition of the system in 1922, although migration from India and China continued, especially to Southeast Asia.[10]

The transfer of indentured labor constituted only one part of a larger flow of people inside and outside the empire. British emigration in the nineteenth century created significant white populations in South Africa, Australia, New Zealand, and Canada. While this flow of people peaked in the early twentieth century, the British and Dominion governments attempted to revive migration in the interwar years.[11] At the same time, millions of Asian workers followed their own migratory patterns in southern and eastern Asia, as the global economy mobilized new workers for the mines, cities, and plantations of the region. This larger stream of migrants often fell outside the direct control of the British, although they attempted to regulate migration to and from British colonies.[12]

These policies, which sought to ensure a supply of labor for development and settlers for colonization, forced officials to confront questions about the size and distribution of colonial populations as imperial migration patterns changed in the 1920s. New immigration laws, particularly in the United States, disrupted existing patterns of migration. At the same time, the slump in colonial commodity prices in the interwar years, exacerbated by the Depression, disrupted labor markets and movements throughout the empire. Even in the Dominions, older patterns of migration shifted and Britain experienced a net inflow of returning migrants.[13]

These circumstances led the Colonial Office and colonial governments to exert greater control over migration. As different groups contended with each other and the imperial state for control over land and resources, the British faced increased pressure to allow intercolonial migration and to broaden access to British-controlled territories. These demands required the Colonial Office to confront the relationship among population, migration, and economic development. The issue of migration also raised questions about the nature of citizenship and rights in the British Empire. It remained unclear the extent to which all imperial subjects enjoyed the same rights to travel and settle throughout the empire. Concerns about the status of foreign workers led to the Alien's Seaman's Registration Act in 1925, which forced non-European migrants to register with local authorities, despite their nominal right to travel freely to and within Britain. In essence, the act created a two-tiered system of entry and citizenship in Britain and the empire.[14] British rejection of the idea of a unitary imperialism citizenship led to a variety of limits upon the movement of African, West Indian, and Asian subjects within the empire.

However, because the British government feared a negative response to its actions, it relied upon administrative measures rather than legislation to impose these restrictions.

The West Indies took a prominent place in discussions about migration in the interwar years. The restriction of immigration to the United States and the decline in sugar prices altered long established patterns of labor migration. West Indian workers, unable to work abroad, suffered from high rates of unemployment.[15] By the mid-1930s the Colonial Office worried about how to deal with the problem. Concerns about the West Indies increased in the wake of the disturbances in the region, which peaked with widespread rioting in Jamaica in 1938. Both officials and experts repeatedly asserted that this "surplus population" needed to find an outlet in order for standards of living to improve. In the late 1930s, officials proposed sponsored immigration of West Indians to other parts of the empire and Dominions. These plans mirrored the existing programs of sponsored settlement in Australia and other Dominions. However, they encountered the roadblock of restrictive immigration policies in those countries. Plans for a transfer of Afro-Caribbean residents of the West Indies never got beyond the preliminary stage, given that that Australia would not welcome non-white immigrants.[16] Officials even mooted the idea of sending West Indians to East Africa, a suggestion quickly dismissed by colonial administrators in Africa.[17]

Closer to home, the Colonial Office and West Indian governments promoted settlement in British Honduras and Guiana.[18] The idea of using immigration to foster development in both colonies dated back at least to the 1920s, when Sir Frederick Lugard raised the possibility of settling Italian and Maltese migrants in British Guiana, which in his words, was "clamoring for a white population of any kind."[19] This proposal, like others in the interwar years, ran afoul of the difficulties of finance and the economic problems of both colonies.[20] The Colonial Office also encountered resistance from the West Indian governments, which imposed their own immigration controls even while they wished to find new outlets for their own migrants.[21] Commenting on the problem in Barbados, one official argued, "Barbados could not hope to get rid of her 'scallywags' by dumping them in other colonies and emigration would not . . . result in any net reduction of the population."[22]

While the problems of the West Indies increasingly occupied the attention of colonial officials, concerns about unemployment and migration surfaced elsewhere in the empire. In the Federated Malay States and the Straits Settlements, officials dealt with the consequences of their efforts to promote labor migration and Malay dominance.[23] This multiethnic Malaya, codified in the censuses of 1921 and 1931 that used race as their central organizing principle, faced new problems in this era.[24] As tin, rubber, and plantation agriculture slumped during the 1930s, unemployment among migrants and Malays rose.[25] The British imposed controls over Chinese and Indian migrant labor through the Immigration Restriction Ordinance of 1928, which allowed the governor of the Straits Settlement to restrict immigration and repatriate unemployed migrants.[26]

Other colonial governments faced similar dilemmas over migration. In Hong Kong, the Sino-Japanese War produced a flow of refugees, which led the government to restrict their entry into the colony.[27] Even in Africa, colonial governments limited population movements. East African governments wanted to restrict South Asian migration into the region, and they resisted attempts to allow West Indian and other groups to settle there. When questioned on this policy, they asserted the necessity of maintaining racial balance in the colonies, as well as the need to provide maximum opportunities for Africans to obtain more skilled work.[28]

The question of Jewish migration in this period reveals the concerns of the Colonial Office and how its efforts to control the movement of people in the empire forced it to address demographic issues. From the beginning of the British mandate in Palestine, the Colonial Office faced the issue of Jewish migration and its potential to destabilize the region. Given the porous borders and the limited resources available to the Mandatory government, considerable illegal immigration existed. Efforts to limit this flow floundered in part on the commitment to allow Jewish settlement, which complicated the process of enforcing controls. While Jewish migration caused political tensions in Palestine in the 1920s, the coming to power of Adolf Hitler and the subsequent influx of refugees contributed to a rapid deterioration of the political situation, climaxing with the Arab Revolt that began in 1936.[29]

The immigration crisis forced the British government to devise guidelines to regulate Jewish settlement. The High Commissioner for Palestine and the Colonial Office resorted to the concepts of optimum population and carrying capacity developed by demographers during the interwar years. Both concepts related population to the resources of a territory in order to assess the limits of its population.[30] The British government attempted to assess the economic capacity of Palestine, particularly in the critical area of agriculture.[31] It then used these estimates to determine levels of Jewish migration and to suggest destinations for migrants.[32] The High Commissioner Sir Arthur Wauchope defended the system in the face of requests for higher levels, arguing that such an increase would violate the principal of regulating immigration in accordance with the absorptive capacity of Palestine.[33]

Throughout this period, Jews and Arabs used demographic arguments to bolster their claims to land and the right to settle in Palestine. In order to sort out these claims, the British government attempted to track population trends within the two communities. In the mid-1930s, as the British struggled to control immigration, they discussed the possibility of maintaining a stable ratio between the two communities, with the Jewish population comprising between 30 and 40 percent of the whole.[34] Implementation of this policy required an accurate census as well as a detailed assessment of Arab and Jewish vital rates. The man charged with this task, Eric Mills, the commissioner of migration and the census, trained as a mathematician and statistician at Cambridge and possessed the necessary quantitative skills to undertake the work. However, the politically charged nature of the topic complicated his efforts considerably. While officials saw the 1931 Census as accurate, they doubted whether it could be duplicated.[35] Arabs and Jews viewed any census with suspicion, and officials noted that any measurement of population would require legalization of the status of all residents to be successful.[36] In the end, unrest and financial constraints led to the cancellation of the proposed 1936 census.[37]

In the absence of a census, it fell to Mills to provide estimates of population size and vital rates, which proved to be as controversial as the census. Mills produced a series of technically sophisticated reports on migration and birth rates that the high commissioner intended to use to bolster his attempts to limit Jewish immigration. Despite their neutral tone, the reports provoked numerous complaints. The Jewish Agency's research arm claimed that the higher growth rate of the Arab population provided circumstantial evidence of illegal Arab migration. Mills found that a higher Arab birth rate, as well as a falling death rate, explained the growth of the Arab population. At the same time, he noted the lower birth rate of the Jewish community, which he attributed in part to the use of birth control.[38] Given this information, officials faced a dilemma. If they attempted to factor differential fertility into their deliberations about migration, they risked further politicizing the census and vital statistics registers, because both communities would have new incentives to falsify their vital rates and evade enumeration. Some officials even speculated that the Jewish population would abandon birth control in the event of immigration restriction.[39] Despite attacks upon his estimates,

Mills defended his work.⁴⁰ In its White Paper of 1939, the British government imposed a limit of 75,000 upon Jewish migration to Palestine over the next five years, which triggered a fierce political debate.⁴¹

By the end of the 1930s, colonial officials began to grasp the scale of migration within the empire. A review ordered by Malcolm MacDonald, the colonial secretary of state, in 1938 found that 600,000 aliens immigrated into the empire during the previous five years. Although 400,000 Chinese immigrants to Malaya and Borneo constituted the majority of migrants, 168,000 Jewish migrants went to Palestine.⁴² Faced with this increase, the Colonial Office emphasized the right of the British government to impose controls over the movement of peoples into and within the empire. This policy mirrored that of the British government at home, which used administrative procedures to restrict non-white migration into the country.⁴³ To preserve this right, the Colonial Office resisted efforts by the International Labor Organization (ILO) to regulate migration, arguing that intercolonial movements and native workers did not fall under its jurisdiction.⁴⁴ The Colonial Office also asserted its right to veto migration plans emanating from other government departments. Even within the colonial service, geographical departments tended to resist the immigration schemes of other departments. The policy that emerged in the interwar years focused on a decentralized system of controls, relying on local legislatures and governors to enact restrictions and shying away from uniform regulations. In Cyprus, the local colonial government used such methods to limit migration by Greek Cypriots into England.⁴⁵ Although officials could restrict the movement of people within the empire, the possibility of using migration as a tool to solve problems of poverty and unemployment remained limited. Increasingly officials saw population growth as the core problem whose solution remained elusive. This situation led them to consider new ways to control population in a rapidly changing political environment that placed a premium on the well-being of the colonial subject.

LABOR AND DEVELOPMENT IN THE INTERWAR EMPIRE

While colonial migration policies were often premised on the need to supply labor for economic development, colonial regimes also pursued labor polices that sought to regulate and control the supply of workers. These policies often began with the belief that certain parts of the empire were underpopulated and that labor shortages hindered development. In Africa and the Pacific, British officials expressed frustration with the difficulty of obtaining sufficient labor, which led to the use of coercive measures like forced labor.[46] Officials argued that the demographic weakness of indigenous peoples and their reluctance to engage in wage labor justified such measures.[47] In the case of Africa, the perceived link between underpopulation and labor shortage reflected demographic ideas about the continent that predated the Scramble for Africa in the 1880s. Many Europeans argued that sub-Saharan Africa suffered from a lack of available workers, caused by the unwillingness of Africans to take on wage labor, slow population growth and ill-health, a situation made worse by deaths from warfare and epidemics during the colonial conquest.[48] African colonial governments resorted to the use of forced labor, particularly for large-scale infrastructure projects, a practice that continued into the twentieth century.[49] However, forced labor only exacerbated the problem of obtaining sufficient workers and undermined European claims that "free labor" would bring benefits to indigenous peoples.[50] The practice proved disastrous for many African populations, as the mortality of European work sites, the disruption of African agricultural life, and the alteration of disease environments through migration led to sharp rises in death rates and perhaps declining birth rates.[51] Contemporary observers raised similar concerns about the relationship between labor demands and population decline in the Pacific.[52]

The recognition of the problems with existing labor systems reflected the changing politics of empire in the interwar years. Britain and other colonial powers faced growing criticism by missionaries and political activists about their labor practices. A campaign to reform the labor practices of Western colonial powers led to the Forced Labor Convention of the ILO in 1930.[53] Colonial governments hoped that greater state regulation of labor, combined with improved sanitation and medical treatment, would blunt attacks on colonial regimes and help to ensure an adequate supply of labor.[54] In addition, the British and French believed that health and welfare programs would create a larger, more efficient labor force, in the pursuit of what the French termed *mise en valeur*.[55]

These concerns led to the appointment of Major Granville Orde-Brown as the first labour advisor in 1938. Orde-Brown, whose work was supported by the Institute of African Languages and Culture, enjoyed a reputation as an expert on Africa based on his book *The African Labourer* (1933) as well as his work in the Copperbelt of northern Rhodesia. His appointment came as labor unrest in the West Indies and West Africa highlighted the need for a new approach to labor problems. Orde-Browne, like other officials, believed that trade unions could play a vital role in the creation of a modernized workforce in the empire and could channel political grievances into more acceptable channels. He traveled throughout the empire in the late 1930s and 1940s to report on labor conditions and to push for the establishment of labor departments by colonial governments.[56]

PUBLIC HEALTH, MEDICINE, AND COLONIAL REPRODUCTION

Concerns about labor shortages and regulations raised larger questions about the reproduction of indigenous populations. While migration and labor policies sought to rationalize labor and move it from areas of surplus to areas of shortage, many in the colonial establishment argued that a more comprehensive approach was needed to address the root causes that impeded the development of colonial societies. One critical part of this new approach lay in the area of public health. Officials hoped by attacking endemic disease and addressing the causes of high mortality they could produce healthier and larger colonial populations. This led them to pursue a series of initiatives in Oceania, Malaya, Ceylon, the West Indies, and Africa during the interwar years.

In Africa, private observers and public officials drew similar conclusions about the link between population and underdevelopment. The missionary J.H. Oldham argued that the continent as a whole suffered from a low population density and asserted that outside one or two colonies, the population of British Africa was either stationary or in decline. He attributed this situation to disease, malnutrition, and poor child care practices, as well as the impact of European colonization.[57] The solution to this problem lay in the expansion of medical care and research, better nutrition through the improvement of African agriculture, child and maternal welfare services, universal education, and limits on labor demanded by European interests.[58] Africans should not be "left to stagnate in their reserves but under the guidance of sympathetic administrators helped forward on the path of industrial and social progress."[59]

Colonial administrators accepted this analysis of the demography of Africa and its implications for the continent's future development.[60] In 1925, Leo Amery, the secretary of state for the colonies, declared at the Imperial Social Hygiene Conference, "The problem of development in Africa, is in the main, a human problem: it has got to be carried through by the people of the country themselves. At the present moment the people of Africa are neither in numbers nor in physique or intelligence capable of coping with the great task that lies before them in the development of Africa. The duty of statesmanship lies in the physical, moral and intellectual development of those people, and the physical side is the foundation of it. We have got to cope—and we are increasingly realizing that very foundation of successful administration in Africa lies in that—with the health problems of that great continent."[61]

W. Ormsby-Gore, parliamentary undersecretary for the colonies and a future secretary of state for the colonies, offered a similar assessment of the African problem in his 1926 address to the Geography Section of the British Association. He argued that most of tropical Africa suffered from a severe labor shortage as a result of underpopulation. Only by addressing the poor condition of the natives and the low standards of health and hygiene through increased production, improved transportation, and the expansion of public health could this problem be solved.[62] Like Amery, Ormsby-Gore embraced intervention in African societies as a means of fostering African development.[63] This solution reflected prevailing notions of trusteeship and the dual mandate, which called colonial regimes to advance Africans within the context of their own traditional societies.

While Africa represented the principal focus of official concerns, the link among population, imperial health, and development presented the British government with a larger dilemma in the 1920s. Despite their awareness of the problems of indigenous health, officials lacked the resources to transform a system focused principally on the needs of the government and the European population of the colonies as well as epidemic diseases such as smallpox. The passing of what David Arnold terms the "heroic age" of Western imperial medicine left a skeletal infrastructure of health care, whose flaws became evident in the weak response of colonial governments to the flu pandemic of 1918–19.[64]

To address these problems, the British government expanded its funding of medical research during the interwar years. The British hoped to harness the potential of scientific medicine to combat endemic diseases like sleeping sickness and malaria. In Africa, research into sleeping sickness accounted for almost half of all research expenditures, as scientists searched for new approaches to contain the disease and its vector of transmission, the tsetse fly.[65] These efforts involved not only medical and ecological research but also forced resettlement of African villages in an attempt to slow the spread of the disease.[66] Support for medical research helped foster the growth of tropical medicine as a specialty, centered in the colonial medical departments and the metropolitan institutions of the London School of Hygiene and Tropical Medicine (LSHTM) and the Liverpool School of Tropical Medicine (LSTM). LSHTM, endowed in 1924 by the Rockefeller Foundation, became a center for the new scientific medicine, with its emphasis on clinical research and statistical analysis.[67]

Despite the growth of tropical medicine and imperial medical research, officials increasingly recognized the limitations of scientific medicine in the colonies. The "turn toward social medicine" reflected the view that an expansion of medical services to colonial subjects was a necessary part of ensuring development in the empire.[68] The threadbare nature of the colonial medical infrastructure made it difficult to realize that ambition, despite the reorganization of colonial medical services in the interwar years.[69] The Colonial Office and local colonial governments turned to private agencies such as missionary societies and foundations in an effort to expand medical services.[70] To combat rising rates of venereal disease, colonial regimes worked with the British Social Hygiene Council. Founded in 1914, the council expanded its operations overseas after the war, establishing branches in a number of colonies, including Singapore and Hong Kong.[71] In the West Indies, the Rockefeller Foundation, beginning with a campaign against hookworm in the 1920s, launched a series of health programs in the islands and other parts of the empire with the blessing, albeit sometimes grudging, of the Colonial Office.[72] In areas with greater resources, such as Ceylon and Malaya, more ambitious efforts could be launched to help ensure the continued stability of the labor force in the lucrative plantation and mining sectors.[73] Yet even these programs could service only a fraction of the total population and remained unable to cope with public health crises like the malaria pandemic of 1934–35 in Ceylon.[74]

Officials and private agencies often attributed the slow growth of indigenous populations to the high mortality of mothers and children. Consequently, maternal and infant health became an important area for medical intervention. These initiatives dated back to the prewar era, and they expanded throughout the empire in the interwar years. Using models originally devised for working-class families in late nineteenth-century Europe, health workers created programs to improve maternal and infant health by encouraging the adoption of European methods of childbirth and child rearing. These programs sought to regulate and marginalize indigenous local midwives and encourage hospital delivery when possible. They also tried to persuade mothers to adopt new infant care practices, including early weaning and bottle feeding. This advice reflected the beliefs of physicians, missionaries, and European settlers about the inferiority of indigenous mothers and their seeming indifference to their children. Such attitudes rationalized the creation of maternal and child welfare programs in the empire in order to reform maternal behavior and instill British norms of family life. The provision of health care sought to ensure colonial reproduction and enhance the authority and legitimacy of the colonial state.[75] Not surprisingly, these efforts encountered resistance from indigenous women who refused to cooperate with colonial initiatives.[76]

Programs for maternal and child health relied not only on the efforts of colonial medical officers but also the work of activists in Britain and the colonies. In the West Indies, health workers received training in Britain and in local clinics organized along British lines. Both white and Afro-Caribbean women promoted the cause and staffed the agencies that provided services.[77] In Ceylon and Malaya, similar coalitions of local elites and the wives of colonial officials assisted with the establishment of maternal and child clinics.[78] While such efforts often reflected prevailing ideas of race and class, they succeeded in creating the beginnings of a system of health care for indigenous populations. The clinics created in the interwar years would play a key role in the work of birth control activists, who used them as a base of operations.

While the expansion of maternal medical service reflected the imperatives of the colonial state, it was also a response to domestic and international criticism. The growing internationalization of medicine in this period made it difficult for the British to escape scrutiny of their colonial medical policies. The interwar years witnessed the expansion of international health on an unprecedented scale. The work of medical researchers reached beyond national and imperial frontiers and new networks of scientists emerged in tropical medicine and public health.[79] The Rockefeller Fund and other private foundations facilitated this process with their support for research and health programs across the globe. One expression of this new international health community was the League of Nations Health Agency (LNHA), which sought to encourage application of public health practices across national borders and began to track global patterns of disease and health.[80]

While these agencies and networks lacked the power to compel governments to act, their presence forced the Colonial Office to defend its actions. The publication of a League of Nations survey on malnutrition in 1933, which included a section on colonial regions, led to the formation of the Committee on Nutrition in the Colonial Empire to study the problem.[81] The British faced another dilemma working with private foundations. While they welcomed the funds the foundations provided, they were uncomfortable with the access that researchers and physicians gained as a result. Local officials sought to control outside experts while still enjoying the extra resources they provided.[82] The presence of foreign doctors in colonial territories made it difficult for the British government to limit the flow of information about colonial populations given the public nature of their work and the presentation of their findings to foundations and international conferences.

The Colonial Office also faced domestic pressure over colonial health polices. In 1930 a group of members of Parliament (MPs) sent a series of questions about the health of colonial populations.[83] In response Lord Passfield (Sydney Webb), the secretary of state for the colonies, sent a circular letter to African and Pacific colonial governments asking about the status of maternal and child health.[84] Officials worried about releasing the full replies they received, which contained damaging information about conditions in the colonies.[85] In his final response Lord Passfield had to acknowledge the low level of medical services in the colonies and the need to improve them.[86]

Maternal and child health also attracted the interests of women's groups. In May 1932, Gertrude Horton of National Union of Societies for Equal Citizenship contacted the Colonial Office to request information about the condition of "coloured women" in the colonies. This led to a meeting with secretary of state for the colonies, Samuel Cunliffe Lister, and a delegation of women's activists headed by MP Eleanor Rathbone that included Eva Hubback from the Eugenics Society.[87] During the meeting, Rathbone argued in favor of increasing the number of women working in the colonial services as one method of improving medical services.[88] Such encounters reflected the expansion of imperial feminist campaigns in the interwar years into areas like child marriage, prostitution, female circumcision, and birth control.[89] Despite predictable complaints by Colonial Office officials about interference by "busybodies" from the "shrieking sisterhood," they felt compelled to respond to their concerns and in some cases offer assistance.[90]

Pressure for improved services also came from within the colonial establishment. Medical officers like Dr. Henry Wilkinson, director of medical services in Bermuda and a supporter of birth control work, used his position to press the Colonial Office for the expansion of medical services in the colony.[91] Dr. Mary Blacklock, a medical officer in Sierra Leone and the wife of the director of LSTM, was a central figure in such efforts. As the first female member of the Colonial Medical Advisory

Committee, she carried on a campaign in the 1930s and 1940s to persuade the Colonial Office to expand the provision of maternal and child health. She worked with outside groups, especially women's organizations, and obtained the support of the Women's Medical Federation. Her tour of several colonies in 1935 produced a report critical of their maternal and child services. While she agreed that indigenous customs and practices contributed to the problems, she also blamed limited expenditures, the lack of female personnel, and the poverty of colonial subjects.[92] The Colonial Office forwarded her report to colonial governments, but many officials remained unhappy with her criticism.[93] In particular her call for the employment of more women in the colonial service encountered the entrenched opposition of the colonial establishment to women serving in senior positions.[94] Her recommendations, toned down for official consumption, would be considered by Lord Hailey's Committee on Post-War Reconstruction in 1942.[95]

LAND, FOOD, AND POPULATION

During the interwar years, students of colonial policy highlighted the relationship among reproduction, labor, and resources in the empire. For many experts, the solution to the problems of poverty and malnutrition they associated with both over- and underpopulation lay in changes in agriculture practices.[96] This call for agricultural reform reflected the growing interest in scientific agriculture in the British Empire.[97] In Britain, concerns about the food supply dated back to the late nineteenth century, when commentators called attention to the nation's growing dependence on food imports.[98] Scholars emphasized the interconnected nature of food production in Britain, the Dominions, and the empire.[99] Discussions about migration and population often included estimates for the potential agricultural output of the Dominions, especially Canada and Australia. Most experts assumed that a larger population in these countries would be necessary to expand agricultural production to meet the needs of Britain and the world. Attention also focused on potential areas of increased food production in the empire, especially temperate regions of Africa. As with the Dominions, experts made the link between directed British and European migration and higher agricultural output.[100] In other parts of the empire, the focus remained on the question of shortages and the possibility of famine.[101]

Officials hoped that the creation of tropical agricultural research stations in Trinidad and elsewhere would address problems of plant and animal disease that hindered colonial agriculture and lead to increased output. The Colonial Advisory Council on Agriculture (CACA), created in 1929, served as a central body for imperial agriculture; Sir Frank Stockdale, the head of the Ceylon Agricultural Service, became the first agricultural advisor for the Colonial Office.[102] This was followed by the establishment of the Colonial Agriculture Service (CAS) in 1935.[103] The CAS focused on research and the practical application of farming techniques. Many agricultural specialists believed that improved methods could allow colonial peoples to improve their general standard of living, while at the same time creating more economic activity in the empire. Research initially focused on ways to expand the output of export crops, but by the mid-1930s attention turned to ways to increase the production of food crops. British farming practices, especially mixed-use farming, provided the model for this work despite the difficulties of transplanting such methods to the colonies. Agricultural specialists attempted to persuade farmers to adopt new styles of plowing, cropping, and land use to improve yields. This campaign coincided with an initiative to address soil erosion in arid regions like East Africa that drew on the work of U.S. agricultural specialists in the wake of the Dust Bowl.[104]

Stockdale toured throughout the empire in his capacity as chief agricultural advisor. Like other agricultural experts he voiced concerns about population pressure in the 1930s. Agricultural specialists and geographers had been among the first to call attention to the limits of agricultural output and the possibility of pressure on food supplies in some regions.[105] In the 1930s, despite surpluses in much of the Western world, attention focused on food shortages in tropical regions like the West Indies. Many observers saw land reform as a possible solution to hunger and unemployment. While Stockdale recognized the problems in the region's focus on export agriculture, he doubted that land redistribution would solve the problem, citing the backwardness of the people. In his words, "The West Indian small holder requires some measure of supervision if his lands are to be maintained in a high degree of fertility and production."[106] The Moyne Commission devoted considerable attention to the question of agriculture in its report, calling for the expansion of local food production to help address the problem of poverty.[107]

Worries about food production also existed in East Africa, where the forced settlement of Africans within reserves aggravated what many experts saw as the inefficient and destructive system of indigenous agriculture.[108] The Colonial Office and local governments attempted to persuade African cultivators to take up British methods of mixed cultivation.[109] These efforts coincided with a growing perception of overpopulation in the region.[110] Administrators argued that population pressure in the reserves would lead to overuse of the land and erosion. A number of experts expanded upon this theme. E. B. Worthington, in *Science in Africa*, produced as part of *The African Survey*, linked shifting cultivation and overpopulation on reserves to erosion and soil exhaustion.[111] Sir A. Daniel Hall, a prominent agricultural scientist, went further, saying, "Now the increase in population in Africa has become very marked since the advent of European government, and in many tribes land hunger has developed already to an alarming degree. It is the fundamental cause of political unrest and threatens disastrously to break down tribal organization and native agriculture."[112]

The focus on scientific agriculture dovetailed with new concerns about nutrition. The advances in nutrition science in this era found their way into the debate over food and population in the empire. One of the central figures, Sir John Boyd-Orr, who directed the Rowett Research Station and served on the CACA, kept a foot in both areas of research. In the mid-1920s, along with John Gilks, he conducted a pioneering study of nutrition in East Africa, which concluded that poor soil and primitive agricultural practices impaired the health of the natives and reduced their efficiency.[113] Boyd-Orr tied malnutrition to overuse of the land and poor soil management, a view endorsed by other agricultural specialists like Hall and Worthington.[114] The identification of nutrition as a problem linked health to the content of a diet, as opposed to the quantity of food consumed. By the 1930s, however, attention focused on malnutrition as a feature of poverty, not simply ignorance of nutrition, a point raised by the LNHA's study of malnutrition. A circular distributed to governments by the Committee on Nutrition in the Colonial Empire asked them for information on the problem of malnutrition in their colonies. A number of these reports acknowledged the role of poverty in malnutrition, although they also cited lack of knowledge of nutrition. The committee's summary report, issued in 1939, shied away from the conclusion that absolute shortages of food rather than poor nutrition represented the largest problem.[115] However, the report made an explicit linkage between malnutrition and population growth. It noted, "Another factor which is of greatest importance nutritionally in some Dependencies is the rapid increase in population that is at present occurring. In Malta, Ceylon, Basutoland, and some of the West Indian colonies this problem is in varying degrees acute, for it is obvious that unless an increase in population is accompanied by a proportionate increase in the wealth of the community the result must be decreased wealth on the average head of population.... The problem is likely to become more serious as infantile and general mortality decrease."[116]

Elsewhere in its report, the committee cited the behavior of parents as a key problem, noting in particular the negative impacts of early weaning on the nutritional status of children. The report failed to mention the efforts of maternal and child health advocates in the empire to encourage that behavior in the name of faster population growth and infant health.[117]

EXPERTS, LOBBIES, AND THE NEW COLONIAL STATE

The increased concern with demographic issues occurred at the same time as significant changes within the colonial service. Many officials came to believe that the existing approach to administration no longer sufficed. Two works, W. M. Macmillan's *Warning from the West Indies* (1936) and Lord Hailey's *An African Survey* (1938), crystallized this sentiment within the Colonial Office.[118] Both authors made clear that poverty and the slow pace of economic development presented a serious challenge to the future of British rule.[119] Political unrest within the empire, especially the West Indies, reinforced these arguments. By the late 1930s, faced with domestic and international criticism, the Colonial Office accepted the need to foster economic development and social welfare in order to preserve the empire.[120] This new emphasis highlighted the significance of demographic trends for colonial rule. Increasingly, poverty and political unrest could be seen as by-products of overpopulation, an argument reinforced by the lobbying of population activists. This emphasis on overpopulation deflected attention from the failures of colonial policy and toward the behavior of colonial peoples.

The new approach to imperial governance necessitated a reshaping of the colonial service. Its reorganization in 1930 ended the formal division of the central and overseas branches of the service, placing all overseas officials into a single Colonial Service. In theory, all officials above a certain grade appointed from London formed one organization, although in reality, most remained tied to local governments. To create closer links between the Colonial Office and the overseas service, from the mid-1930s officials from the colonies served two-year periods in London, earning the name "beachcombers," and some officials from London served in positions abroad. The new approach also required expertise in the natural and social sciences that the traditional geographic departments lacked.

In an effort to foster such expertise, the Colonial Office created subject departments that focused on particular areas of knowledge, such as administration (1932), medicine (1934), and agriculture (1935).[121] This change allowed the Colonial Office to bring together specialists previously scattered throughout the organization and to offer specialists the opportunity for career advancement throughout the entire colonial establishment. These specialists served both in London and in the colonies, and it was hoped that their work would remain free of the regional particularism of existing departments.

Of equal significance was the role played by outside experts. The increased investment by the British government in colonial research gave the Colonial Office access to these experts and their work. The new departments recruited them to work on particular projects or to serve on advisory committees.[122] While the bulk of research funding went to medicine and the natural sciences, the colonial state showed interest in the social sciences as well. The Social Services Department, created in 1938 to deal with issues of social welfare in the empire, became the department most directly involved in population issues and with social science research. In addition to demography, anthropology became closely affiliated with imperial administration in this era. This reflected in part the influence of Bronislav Malinowski, the LSE anthologist who forged a relationship with colonial administrators and had a profound impact on how they viewed indigenous peoples. His associate Audrey Richards, who studied at LSE, would be one of the first female principles at the Colonial Office. She was instrumental in the creation of the Colonial Social Science Research Council and the East African Institute for Social Research.[123] As was the case with demography, ties among academics, officials, foundations, and activists, in this case missionaries like John Oldham, facilitated the assimilation of anthropology into the colonial administration. Beginning in the late 1920s with support from the Laura Spellman Rockefeller Fund, LSE ran training courses for overseas colonial officials. This relationship, which expanded in the late colonial era, exhibited tensions similar to those generated by colonial demography. While many officials in London embraced a more "scientific" approach to their work, many officials overseas resisted the use of anthropological research in administration and rejected the restructuring of knowledge about indigenous peoples.[124]

The ties between experts and the colonial state forged in the 1930s reflected the evolution of social policy and the role of experts in the interwar years, a period that until recently received little attention from histo-

The Colonial Office and the Population Question, 1918–1939 / 69

rians. In the standard narrative, the British state, bound by laissez-faire and Treasury control of expenditure, embraced intervention only under the pressures of the Second World War.[125] This intervention deepened in the postwar years as a consequence of the creation of the welfare state and its expansion after 1945, reaching a peak in the 1960s and 1970s before retreating under the Conservative government of the 1980s.[126] Studies of the role of experts in the formulation of social policy follow a similar timeline.[127] Historians note that the British state made little investment in social science research or training before 1945 and that such support remained limited before the 1960s.[128] Recent historical works focus on the role of private organizations and individuals in promoting the use of social science research in the formation of state policy in the interwar years.[129] Martin Bulmer uses the term "intermediate institutions" to describe the mix of groups that attempted to influence government officials by claiming expert knowledge.[130] Shared political and intellectual interests tied pressure groups with university departments, philanthropic foundations, and individual researchers. Such intermediate institutions often sponsored or forwarded research to government departments through informal channels. The Carnegie Corporation, which funded *The African Survey*, and the Rockefeller Foundation, which invested heavily in medical research, were crucial to colonial studies.[131]

This informal system functioned because of several key features of British policy formation in this era. First, senior civil servants enjoyed a high degree of autonomy and influence over policy making. Selected through a meritocratic, yet socially exclusive system, these civil servants served for long periods within their departments. Although the politicians who served as ministers bore overall responsibility for their departments, these same politicians necessarily relied on permanent civil servants to provide continuity and expertise. Such continuity made civil servants capable of shaping policy initiatives over the long term despite the coming and going of politicians.[132] Second, government offices and political life remained highly concentrated in London, largely within the administrative district of Whitehall and the political orbit around Westminster. This metropolitan concentration allowed senior officials to live and work within a social world that linked them to others of similar background and training in British society.[133] Unlike the United States, with its more diverse university system and relatively diffuse system of government, the British system, focused on London and Oxbridge, created a compact social and intellectual elite that tied officials to their peers outside government and provided ample opportunities for informal contacts and networks. By tapping these networks, pressure groups and experts could directly influence the policy-making process.[134]

The existence of core groups of experts in the social sciences contributed to a growing confidence in the potential benefits of greater state involvement in social life. Towering figures like John Maynard Keynes and William Beveridge, both of whom took a keen interest in demographic issues, helped fashion an alternative to the prevailing laissez-faire approach, often functioning as advisors to Labour and Liberal politicians who were out of power during the long years of Conservative Party dominance during the 1930s.[135] A belief in the need for intervention developed in the Colonial Office, where permanent officials, often in advance of their political masters, embraced a more activist colonial policy in the late 1930s and relied upon a growing array of experts to plan and implement these policies.[136] A new generation of colonial officials emerged in the interwar years, often better educated than the prewar generation, many of whom escaped the rigors of the exam system. Men like Andrew Cohen and Philip Rogers embraced the new ethos of colonial rule and formed relationships outside the traditional Conservative and Oxford networks of the colonial service. Closer to the world of Labour and the left, they saw themselves as part of a new generation of progressive imperialists who would restructure and modernize the empire to ensure its survival and promote the well-being of colonial subjects.[137]

While changing attitudes within the Colonial Office help explain the emergence of new policies, part of the reason for the new initiatives lay in the work of metropolitan activists. Colonial pressure groups like the Anti-Slavery Society dated back to the nineteenth century and the campaign for the abolition of slavery. Humanitarian initiatives, linked to groups such as Aboriginal Protection Society and the Congo Reform Association, continued in the late nineteenth and early twentieth centuries even as the empire reached its peak.[138] By the interwar years, a variety of groups attempted to raise public awareness about imperial issues and to lobby politicians and officials. In addition to the Anti-Slavery Society and missionary groups, more secular agencies like the Social Hygiene Council and women's organizations agitated on behalf of "native peoples." The period also saw the growth of more overtly political lobbies on the left, such as the League of Coloured Peoples and the Friends of Africa. The most influential lobbying group, the Fabian Colonial Bureau, founded in 1940, emerged from the milieu of 1930s activism and academic life, enrolling a number of important academics and politicians, including Arthur Creech Jones, the secretary of state for the colonies during the postwar Labour government.[139]

The efforts of the population movement to influence the Colonial Office grew out of this environment. Their lobbying campaign relied on the prestige of individual activists and the social networks that linked these activists to politicians and civil servants. The first contact occurred in 1928, when the British Population Society (BPS) requested Colonial Office help in gathering information about colonial populations. More sustained contacts began in the 1930s, as the National Birth Control Association (NBCA) and the Birth Control International Information Centre (BCIIC) attempted to gain official backing for their work overseas. The manner in which these organizations approached the government demonstrates how metropolitan activists employed informal methods to gain entrée to the Colonial Office and local colonial officials. The BPS, in large part made up of members of the Eugenics Society, used Sir Bernard Mallet, the former registrar general of England and president of the BPS, to smooth the way with the Colonial Office.[140] When the NBCA wanted to approach the Colonial Office to discuss the work of its affiliate in Hong Kong, it relied on Baron Horder, the king's physician and president of the Eugenics Society, to contact Malcolm MacDonald, who arranged for a meeting between a delegation headed by Margaret Pyke and senior officials in June 1938.[141]

While reliance upon prominent persons ensured easier access for activists, in the long run, sustained contacts between permanent officials and activists proved to be a more important method for influencing the formation of policy. Officials and activists shared ties dating back to university days. In particular, the number of Oxford graduates within the Colonial Office would prove important for the population movement. The London School of Economic, a less ancient but equally significant school, also linked activists and officials. In addition to housing the Population Investigation Committee (PIC) and employing a reader in demography, its graduates also served in a variety of government posts. Sir Sidney Caine, head of economic development at the Colonial Office in the 1940s, graduated from LSE in 1922 and served as its director after his retirement from government service.

Common residence in the London metropolitan region played a role in facilitating contact between officials and activists. Politicians, activists, officials belonged to overlapping social networks and organizations. Clubs, the quintessential home of the English establishment, allowed members to mingle behind closed doors in a more informal setting. The activists Julian Huxley, David Owen, and Max Nicholson all belonged to the Athenæum, where they mixed with officials and politicians like Sir Eric Pridie, the chief medical officer of the Colonial Office, Andrew Cohen, architect of African decolonization and later permanent secretary of the Ministry of Overseas Development, and Lord Moyne, secretary of state for the colonies for 1941–42.[142] Other clubs like the Reform Club and United Oxford and Cambridge Club provided additional arenas for contact between officials and activists.

Julian Huxley, C. P. Blacker, and Alexander Carr-Saunders played a lead role in lobbying efforts. By the 1930s Julian Huxley already enjoyed a considerable reputation as a scientist. His writing on science for a general audience and his position as director of the London Zoological Society made him a public figure.[143] His years at Oxford as a student and a professor placed him in contact with many future politicians, including William Ormsby-Gore, the secretary of state for the colonies from 1936–1938. He enjoyed personal ties with other colonial secretaries, including Malcolm MacDonald and Oliver Stanley. His writings on race, as well as his account of his travels in Africa, *Africa View*, gave him a high profile as a commentator on empire. Huxley's contacts with the Colonial Office dated to the 1920s, when he traveled to East Africa as a delegate for the Advisory Committee on Native Education, headed by Ormsby-Gore. His status as an advisor grew in the 1930s, when *Africa View* became required reading in the Colonial Office. Along with a group of other experts, including Margery Perham, he helped select Lord Hailey to head the project that became the *African Survey*. In 1939 he participated in the Carlton Hotel Conference convened by Malcolm MacDonald, the secretary of state for the colonies, to discuss the future of the African colonies in the wake of the publication of Hailey's work. There he met with senior officials, as well as Lord Hailey, William McMillan, Margery Perham, and J. H. Oldham.[144] Huxley's position as a scientist and advisor gave him the ear of senior officials and politicians.

While less well known than Huxley, Alexander Carr-Saunders and C.P. Blacker both enjoyed considerable status as public intellectuals. Carr-Saunders's reputation as a social scientist and a demographer, built in large part on his highly regarded book *The Population Problem*, made him a sought-after advisor on population issues.[145] He served as a member of the Economic Advisory Council's Committee on Migration in 1930–31 and advised the Overseas Settlement Board of the Dominions Office in the late 1930s, appearing before the board with the registrar general, Sylvanus Vivian, to discuss future population trends.[146] During the war, Carr-Saunders headed the committee whose work led to the establishment of the CSSRC.

Blacker was known for his leadership of the Eugenics Society and his publications such as *The Family and the State*. A decorated war veteran and a prominent psychiatrist in London, Blacker fit easily into the social and political world of the capital. His launching of the PIC in the mid-1930s, his editorship of *Eugenics Review*, as well as his book, *Population and the Future* (1937), cowritten with David Glass, established him an expert on population. He would serve as an advisor to the Colonial Office and the Ministry of Health on issues of population prior to his work with the International Planned Parenthood Federation and the Simon Population Trust after World War II.

All three men stood strategically placed to link the broader population movement with government officials. In April 1937 Carr-Saunders wrote to Ormsby-Gore to discuss the interest of the PIC in colonial population issues and to ask for assistance from the Colonial Office. The PIC wanted to expand on Robert Kuczynski's *Colonial Population*, an overview of colonial population published in 1937 with the assistance of the PIC. They asked the Colonial Office to support their application for a grant from the Carnegie Corporation to fund this project.[147] Although officials initially balked at the request, they were willing to consider the idea. As one noted, "It would hardly be possible to exaggerate the importance of the subject which this Committee is investigating and it is composed of very distinguished persons."[148] Although unwilling to directly support the grant application, the Colonial Office agreed to express sympathy with the project if contacted by the Carnegie Foundation.[149]

While the grant application gave Carr-Saunders a reason to approach officials, he also wanted to offer assistance to the Colonial Office on demographic matters. As he stated in a 1937 letter, "[We] are most anxious that our project should be of use to those concerned with the administration of the Colonial Empire."[150] After a meeting between C. P. Blacker, David Glass, Robert Kuczynski, and officials at the Colonial Office in July 1937, Kuczynski gained access to the Colonial Office Library for his research.[151] While conducting his research Kuczynski was approached by officials seeking his advice about population issues. His work was considered important enough that in 1940 the Colonial Office intervened to prevent Kuczynski, a German exile, from being interned as an enemy alien.[152] After his retirement from LSE in 1941, he served as an unofficial advisor to the Colonial Office and received a further £500 for his research from Colonial Development and Welfare funds.[153] In 1944, he was formally appointed as demographic advisor, a position he held until his death in 1947. In that role he worked closely with his mentors from the Eugenics Society, Julian Huxley and Alexander Carr-Saunders, both of whom were involved with the new Demography Group of the Colonial Research Council.

While officials had previously turned to outside experts like Granville Edge for assistance on specific problems, Robert Kuczynski served as the first full-time demographic consultant.[154] Officials recognized the value of his expertise and hoped to he could help address their woefully incomplete knowledge of colonial populations.[155] Several official reports had already called attention to this problem in the 1930s. Colonial Office officials, in the course of assisting the Moyne Commission, noted that existing personnel in the West Indies produced inaccurate and incomplete demographic information.[156] In the view of the Moyne Commission, "It is not very easy to measure accurately the size of the population, since the Census of 1931 . . . was omitted in most colonies owing to the spirit of public economy that then prevailed, and it is necessary, therefore to calculate on the basis of the 1921 figures, the accuracy of which moreover is in many cases open to considerable criticism."[157]

Kuczynski pointed out that colonial governments possessed only the roughest estimates of overall population size or vital rates and that there had never been a simultaneous census of the empire that employed a uniform methodology.[158] With a few exceptions, such as the Office of the High Commissioner for Palestine, the Colonial Office and colonial regimes lacked basic information about colonial populations and the staff to gather such information. This situation forced the Colonial Office to look outside its own ranks for demographic experts and to plan for the expansion of its statistical services, a process that began in earnest during the Second World War.

THE COLONIAL OFFICE, RACE, AND POPULATION IN THE INTERWAR EMPIRE

The recognition that demographic information needed to be improved was only one fruit of the lobbying efforts of population activists. This campaign help persuade colonial officials of the need for a more systematic approach to imperial population issues. This process revealed their increasing concern about population growth as well as the underlying notions of race, class, and gender held by officials who shared many of the ideas about population prevalent in the early twentieth century. Like their counterparts in the population movement, colonial officials saw population issues in part in racial terms. Their views ran the gamut, with relatively liberal attitudes mixing with paternalist and dismissive assessments of the capabilities of colonial peoples. Beyond such individual views of race, officials tended to see the empire as an environment made up of distinctive racial groups who occupied specific positions in the imperial system due to their innate abilities or cultural practices. Officials expressed a hierarchy of class and race that shaped their understanding of population and the causes of poverty and underdevelopment.

Yet these views evolved during the interwar period. Although the upper levels of the colonial service remained exclusively white and male, older ideas of race came under increasing scrutiny. The attack on scientific racism forced the abandonment of explicitly racial arguments about development and population. The work of scientists like Julian Huxley and the examination of race in *The African Survey* brought home the new thinking to the colonial establishment.[159] At the same time, views about population changed, as mounting evidence of population growth undermined older ideas about the fragility of non-white races. Despite both of these changes, however, race retained its central role in the interpretation of demographic trends. The significance of higher growth rates among non-white populations lay in their potential to destabilize the existing racial balance within the empire and to undercut efforts at economic development. Although officials used race to frame their demographic views, they recognized the political difficulties that would ensue should population policy be seen as racially motivated and constructed.

The issue of migration in particular revealed how ideas of race, ethnicity, and class influenced population policy. The treatment of Jewish and non-British migrants contrasted markedly with that of British migrants to Australia and other areas of "white settlement." Officials continued to justify the use of subsidies to encourage British migration as a means of encouraging the spread of British influence throughout the world. Senior official officials supported the idea of maintaining "British stock" at home in order to provide "a sufficient reservoir from which migration can take place."[160] Yet this British stock itself constituted an unstable category. Many officials differentiated between the characteristics of the middle class and the more questionable qualities of poor whites at home and abroad. While British officials wished to increase the white population of the empire, they feared that the growth of a poor white component might weaken the British race, a view shared by Dominion and colonial governments.[161] Thus while officers and other representatives of the middle class could be suitable migrants, other groups faced greater scrutiny. A plan to transfer poor whites from Barbados to Australia floundered on the reluctance of the Australian government to accept migrants of "dubious racial stock."[162] Sir Frank Stockdale made clear his views of this group: "The community is pure white and they took a pride in remaining so. . . . But one must not suppose that they would be recognized by the uninitiated as white. They are by generations of life under tropical conditions 'red.' . . . The very young are not bad, but after seven years of age they are the most unreliable people that I have ever come across. If they are sent direct to Australia . . . the emigrants would be little better that the 'bushman'. The only difference would be that they had a red skin instead of a black one."[163]

While questions of class figured heavily in how officials constructed the poor white community, gender and sexuality also played important roles. Malcolm MacDonald in his comments on the poor whites of Barbados noted, "It appears doubtful whether the female stock which is available from among the poor white community would reach the standards set by the Commissioner of Australia."[164] Such comments highlighted the assumptions that informed official attitudes about this community and others like it. The presumed promiscuity and improper behavior of women lay at the heart of fears of racial degeneration and miscegenation.[165]

Officials also associated the sexual behavior and family practices of colonial peoples with population problems.[166] They linked population growth in the West Indies to promiscuity and irregular family life. One official claimed that a leading physician in Bermuda told him that in forty years of practice he had encountered only two "coloured virgins."[167] This view persisted in the Colonial Office into the 1950s, when it was debunked by social researchers.[168] Yet, as the responses to Lord Passfield's circular of 1930 made clear, many governments also believed that indigenous social and health practices often injured women and children and reduced population growth.[169] In Oceania, officials believed that the desire for sexual intercourse led women to limit fertility through practices "inimical to motherhood."[170] Officials held similar views about Africa and argued that polygamy, native midwives, taboos against intercourse, and the incidence of venereal disease contributed to slow population growth.[171]

The West Indies proved to be the critical region for discussions of race and population. As officials dealt with the consequences of high unemployment and low living standards, a number of them made a connection among population, poverty, and unrest. E.J. Waddington, a colonial official in Bermuda, linked unemployment to overpopulation in a letter to the Colonial Office in 1934. In his words, "The island is rapidly becoming overpopulated. In the past the surplus coloured population has had an overflow into the US but since they have tightened up the Immigration laws in the USA, there is no outlet. They breed rapidly and I hesitate to think what the position will be twenty years."[172]

Sydney Caine made a similar argument in a discussion of William Macmillan's *Warning from the West Indies*. He argued, "From the economic point of view I should have thought that the trouble in the West Indies is primarily one of overpopulation."[173] The labour advisor, Major Granville Orde-Brown, who traveled to the West Indies in the wake of the riots in Jamaica to assess the general conditions of life and labor in the region, linked the problem of unemployment to the increasing population of the region.[174] Other officials echoed these sentiments, reflecting an emerging consensus within the Colonial Office that overpopulation was the underlying cause of problems in the West Indies.[175]

The perception that higher birth rates among non-European peoples constituted an important problem for the empire found its way into official deliberations in the late 1930s. While the Overseas Settlement Board dealt extensively with the question of British and Dominion birth rates as it discussed the future of overseas migration it also focused on the potential of non-European population growth to affect these plans.[176] While concerns about overpopulation first appeared in areas with limited resource bases and changing patterns of immigration, such as the West Indies, Singapore, Malta, and Hong Kong, over time these fears would be generalized to most of the empire.

The work of the Moyne Commission, created to investigate the political and social problems of the region in the wake of the West Indian riots of 1938, cemented the linkage between population and unrest in the official mind. The commission, named for its chairman, Lord Moyne, a future secretary of state for the colonies, gathered information from private individuals like Edith How-Martyn as well as colonial officials.[177] The commission's report, completed in 1939 but not published in full until after the war for political reasons, cited population growth as a critical issue for the future of the West Indies. Although the commission discussed the need for a reduction in the birth rate, it stopped short of embracing a specific solution.[178] It also linked the issue to a broader set of concerns: "High birth rates are not a West Indian peculiarity; birth rates about as high prevail as far as statistical evidence enables us to judge in Africa, in India, in the East generally and throughout the whole tropical and subtropical world. The sharp contrast between the present birth rates of tropical peoples and those of most people of European stock is indeed a phenomenon of the most profound importance, with far-reaching implications."[179]

The positioning of non-white population growth as an imperial problem fed upon a deep-rooted sense of the importance of the relative size of racial groups for the balance of power within the empire and the world at large. Even those officials with relatively liberal views on the subject of race acknowledged the implications of racial differentials in fertility.

While officials recognized the importance of population growth for the future of the empire, there was no clear consensus on what should be done. Although officials embraced controls over migration and efforts to expand food production as possible solutions, they believed that such initiatives addressed the symptoms rather that the root causes of the problem. Yet the obvious answer to some, the promotion of birth control among colonial peoples, generated considerable controversy within and outside of the colonial service. Despite the reluctance of the Colonial Office to confront the issue, it would be drawn into this controversy in the late 1930s as private organizations established birth control clinics in a number of British colonies. As a result of discussions over these clinics, the Colonial Official devised a policy that emphasized local control and voluntary effort and sought to avoid the appearance of racially motivated population control.

The earliest discussions concerned Bermuda. Already in the early 1930s, medical officers in the colony contacted BCIIC to obtain information about birth control. In 1934, E.J. Waddington corresponded with the Colonial Office about the desire of the Board of Health to offer birth control on the island. The medical advisor to the Colonial Office replied, stating that the issue was a new one, but that "we may have to face it." He sent pamphlets on birth control and suggested that Waddington contact the BCIIC.[180] Events moved quickly in Bermuda, in part due to the role played by Henry Wilkinson, the chief medical officer. Wilkinson, who held relatively progressive views of race, believed that birth control could help reduce poverty and improve women's lives. After the legislature approved funding for the clinics in 1935, he moved to establish clinics for white and Afro-Caribbean women.[181]

The question of Bermuda's population provoked a series of controversies over the next few years that landed in the lap of the Colonial Office. In 1935, the Legislative Council, as part of its program to promote birth control, proposed a bill that would authorize the sterilization of black sex offenders and the parents of illegitimate children. The proposal prompted Lady Astor, a Conservative MP, to write Malcolm MacDonald in protest.[182] Even as this controversy faded, the remarks of the new governor, Reginald Hildyard caused a fresh uproar. Upon on his arrival in December 1936, Hildyard spoke of "the necessity of checking the growth of the coloured population of the island."[183] Such comments led to protests from both British and West Indian sources, and the newspaper *Negro Worker* castigated Hildyard for his remarks, arguing that he desired the sterilization of the black population.[184] Despite this criticism Hildyard arranged for a visit by Margaret Sanger in 1937 at government expense to foster support for birth control.[185]

The controversy in Bermuda revealed the complicated politics of population the Colonial Office encountered in ensuing years. Proponents of population control in Bermuda's legislature and government focused exclusively on the "coloured population" in their proposals. This bias led Lady Astor to attack them. She noted, "We seem to be facing a period of depression and unemployment, and the oligarchy who have in our days of prosperity imported labour for their needs are now frightened that they may have to face the financial responsibility of unemployment and are putting all the emphasis on over-population and suggesting these brutal methods (abortion and sterilization) of population reduction."[186]

The Colonial Office feared that any linkage between race and the concept of overpopulation would open the British government to attack from Afro-Caribbean nationalists in the West Indies. To forestall such attacks, the Colonial Office tried to maintain a delicate balance between white elites and the Afro-Caribbean majority. In Bermuda, the Colonial Office refused to give official endorsement to birth control, despite support among some officials, leaving the issue in the hands of local officials and the legislature.[187]

The issue also arose in 1936 and 1937 when Lord Fitzalan, head of the Catholic Union of Great Britain and a former MP, wrote to the Colonial Office to complain about birth control efforts in Hong Kong and the West Indies. In particular he protested the involvement of Robert Forrest, secretary for Chinese affairs in Hong Kong, in the birth control activities of the Hong Kong Eugenics League. The league ran a weekly Maternal and Child Clinic in the government's Violet Peel Health Center, which in addition to mother craft and child welfare advice, offered information about contraception. Fitzalan took issue with Forrest's role as an officer of the league and the use of the health center by a birth control organization. He claimed that such activities contradicted Chinese government policy and that the league intended to expand its work to southern China.[188]

Fitzalan's letters sparked a debate within the Colonial Office over the propriety and wisdom of such initiatives. Much of the discussion revolved around religious issues and the question of official sanction for birth control work. His complaints invoked a hostile reaction from some officials, who saw them as religiously motivated. One official described them as Catholic propaganda, while another spoke of his "extreme distaste for Catholic dictation in any form."[189] Other officials disputed his claims about the Chinese government, noting that chemist's shops in southern China sold contraceptives and that at least two hospitals in Canton provided birth control advice. One official doubted the sincerity of Fitzalan's complaints, arguing, "South China is only a stick to beat a dog with."[190]

Even as officials discussed this case, the subject came up again, this time in the Straits Settlements. Helen Beck, the wife of the police superintendent, who served on the visiting committee of the government hospital at Malacca, wrote to Malcolm MacDonald to urge the establishment of a birth control clinic there. Beck also wrote Edith Picton-Tuberville, a Labour MP and feminist reformer, to ask for her help.[191] She enclosed a petition from a local group of mostly Chinese businessmen that supported the idea of a clinic and claimed the backing of G.R. Sykes, the resident councilor. She asserted that she had "made it her business for many years past to ascertain, whenever possible, what opinion is held about birth control among Asiatics of both sexes, and is convinced that amongst the educated classes there is sufficient sympathy for such a reform to be welcome."[192] It was her belief that "if the government would foster birth control and give a lead there would be no lack of followers."[193]

These requests presented officials with a dilemma. On one hand, many of them expressed sympathy for the idea of family planning. The head of the Eastern Department, H. R. Cowell, said, "I feel convinced that, if the present increase of population goes on in the east, as the result of the improvement in the mortality rates which our administration has affected, we are heading for a major disaster of famine, pestilence or war, a sad termination to the efforts of generations of self-sacrificing officials."[194]

In reference to Hong Kong, Philip Rogers argued, "The activities of the League generally raise larger questions which are to some extent a matter of personal sympathy, and if I may venture to say so, my own opinion is in agreement with Sir G. Northcote, (the Governor of Hong Kong) that the League's efforts can do little but good in the present conditions."[195]

Yet officials tempered their support for birth control with the recognition that it might lead to political embarrassment for either local governments or the Colonial Office. These concerns led officials to rebuke Beck for using an official address in her letter and for bypassing normal channels. They also insisted that Forrest no longer use his official address in his work as the treasurer of the Hong Kong Eugenics League.[196] Such niceties reflected the go-softly approach that characterized the actions of the Colonial Office regarding family planning during the next twenty-five years. William Ormsby-Gore in his reply to the governor of the Straits Settlement, gave local governments limited freedom of action as long as their efforts conformed to local law and public opinion. In his words:

> I do not enter into the question of birth control except to say that, as we all know, it is a subject on which widely divergent opinions are held. Bermuda had its own problems to face, and has to face them in its own way. Having regard to the ancient constitution of Bermuda, if the policy of making this small grant is carried by the local legislature, I hardly think that the matter is one in which any Secretary of State for the Colonies could be justified in interfering. . . . While there may be no objection to voluntary action, I do not think any colonial government would be well advised to take the initiative or to propose the expenditure of any public funds in connection with the establishment of birth control clinics unless and until there was ample evidence of a wide spread demand from the community for such measures.[197]

This policy, affirmed a year later by Malcolm MacDonald, Ormsby-Gore's successor, gave groups like NBCA and BCIIC a green light to operate within the empire, as long as local governments consented. By the end of the 1930s, a small but growing network of such clinics existed.

CONCLUSION

The Colonial Office faced a number of new challenges in the interwar years. Concerns about migration, unemployment, and political unrest gave demographic issues greater visibility among members of the colonial service. This greater visibility produced at least two important shifts. Officials increasingly recognized the significance of population for colonial policy and the limitations of official knowledge about numbers. It also became apparent to many that overpopulation, rather than underpopulation, represented the critical feature of imperial population trends. Despite these changes and the growing emphasis on a more activist colonial state, officials for the most part remained reactive and policies continued to be ad hoc. The need to manage the consequences of growth in some regions in the short term overshadowed the formulation of a policy for the longer term. Thus, immigration policy remained decentralized and controlled by local colonial governments according to their own needs. In the same way, the permissive policy toward private family planning work permitted the government maximum freedom for maneuver between supporters and opponents of birth control and gave final say to local officials. At the end of the 1930s, the Colonial Office lacked a systematic approach to population questions and the infrastructure needed to assess adequately demographic trends within the empire. Only in the early 1940s, as the Colonial Office expanded and mobilized under the press of war, would this change.

Although officials acted upon their own perceptions of colonial events, the work of population activists and the growing significance of colonial demography as a field of study provided officials with access to information and expertise sorely lacking within the colonial establishment. The population movement, particularly the Eugenics Society, used its social connections to lobby officials on the need for a new approach to demographic issues. Their efforts led to the Colonial Office to employ Robert Kuczynski as an advisor as part of a larger reorganization of census and statistical operations. The hiring of Kuczynski was the first step in a process that saw activists move to the center of policy decisions. During and after the Second World War, Julian Huxley, C. P. Blacker, and Alexander Carr-Saunders would help construct a population policy for the empire as advisors to the Colonial Office. Their efforts would bring support for colonial demography as a field and help place it at the heart of the postwar imperial state.

3 War, Population, and the New Colonial State

The outbreak of the Second World War brought dramatic changes to the British Empire and its system of governance. The need to mobilize the resources and manpower of the colonies to support the war effort required a far more interventionist state, particularly in economic affairs. At the same time, the political issues raised by the war and the need to portray the war as a struggle for freedom against tyranny complicated the management of colonial affairs. Both of these trends gave greater impetus to the drive to enhance social and economic welfare that emerged in the late 1930s. To expand the scope and aims of government, it became necessary to increase the numbers of specialists and experts who worked with the Colonial Office and local colonial regimes.

These circumstances formed the context within which officials expanded their reliance on demographic analysis. Prior to the war, interest in colonial demography was limited to activists and sympathetic officials in London. However, the need for improved population data for logistics and planning raised the profile of demography. The forecasting techniques developed in the interwar years would be taken up by a number of ministries, including the Colonial Office. At the same time, official views about population issues continued to evolve. By the end of the war, most of the London-based officials concerned with planning and development accepted that overpopulation represented the principal demographic problem facing the empire, one that threatened the drive to improve colonial social welfare. Yet the effort to formulate a response remained tentative at best. Continuing doubts about the accuracy of demographic information made it difficult for advocates of population control to persuade skeptics of the urgency of the problem. Although the colonial state continued to use resettlement, agricultural policy, and controls over migration to shape colonial populations, British officials remained divided about the use of more direct techniques of population control like family planning services. Opponents of direct government support for birth control raised moral and political objections to a program that would be aimed principally at non-white imperial subjects. They warned of the consequences if colonial subjects viewed population policy as racially motivated during a period of uncertainty about the loyalty of imperial peoples and increased international scrutiny. In light of these concerns, ministers proved unwilling to alter the status quo, which allowed local governments and private groups to act, but without official support from London. The caution displayed by officials about family planning contrasted sharply with their more aggressive stance toward economic and military problems and their use of compulsion to force colonial subjects to work for and deliver resources to the imperial state.

THE GEOPOLITICS OF POPULATION

Although the pressures of wartime highlighted the importance of demographic information for planning, the British government had begun to account for population trends in the interwar years. The depopulation panic of the 1930s coincided with strategic conflicts in Europe that included a demographic component. Authoritarian regimes in Germany, Italy, and the Soviet Union seemed to be growing at a faster pace than Britain and the Dominions, which many in Britain saw as an ominous trend and a destabilizing factor in international relations.[1] Other observers linked Japan's growing population to its expansionist ambitions in the western Pacific, which threatened British interests in the region.[2]

Even before the war, the Foreign Office tracked demographic trends in authoritarian states. Concern about Italian population growth dated back to rise of Mussolini in the early 1920s. In 1926 the British Embassy at Rome wrote to the Foreign Office about a scheme to sponsor Italian migration to British Guiana. The official who wrote the letter admitted that the rapidly increasing "surplus population" of Italy constituted "rather an obsession with me, as I see in it the germ of future trouble."[3] Another official agreed, pointing out that limits on immigration into the United States and South America made Italian population problems more acute and that it seemed "inevitable that Italy's difficulty (would) assume large proportions and become an important and disturbing factor in Italian foreign policy."[4] The Foreign Office's concern with Italian population continued into the 1930s and the Embassy in Rome forwarded information on Italian vital rates to London. An official, commenting on a reported increase of more than 400,000 people during the "great demographic drive of 1937," argued that such increases made it difficult to see how immigration alone could reduce population pressure in Italy. In his words, "Sending 20,000 colonists to Libya and a few to Abyssinia is not going to do much to relieve overpopulation in Italy."[5] The Foreign Office also tracked Japan's demographic trends, relying on reports from the embassy in Tokyo. Officials noted the general decline in the birth rate and rising death rates in the period, as well as calls for the Japanese government to expand social and medical services to offset such trends. In the view of embassy officials, these trends undercut Japanese arguments in favor of expansion and could be used to counter Japan's territorial demands.[6]

The outbreak of the Second World War seemed to confirm the fears of activists and officials. British experts assumed that excessive population growth in Italy, Germany, and Japan played a role in the origins of the war and that future growth could destabilize these countries in the postwar era. Population became part of a larger assessment of strategic and geopolitical conditions. As the British government devoted increased attention to logistics and planning, demographic projections became more important. One critical area lay in estimating civilian populations and their food needs. Both the Foreign Office and the Colonial Office attempted to provide improved statistical information for military and civilian planners to facilitate a more efficient use of resources.[7] The Lord President's Committee oversaw the organizations and ministries that controlled the allocation of labor and resources to ensure proper coordination of their efforts.[8]

The needs of the war led to the creation of a series of regional organizations that coordinated the use of resources and manpower among military forces, foreign powers, and colonial governments. In the Middle East, responsibility for this work rested with the Middle East Supply Centre (MESC). The MESC, which grew out of the efforts of the British government to control shipping and the distribution of goods, came to enjoy a broad authority over the region and its population of 100 million people. The MESC gathered demographic data for the Mediterranean and Middle East to assist in the planning of food and materials distribution and established a statistical operation in Cairo.[9]

Although the principal focus of the MESC remained the allocation of resources, it also developed research and advisory capacities that analyzed agriculture and industry in the Middle East. These research efforts became more important as the war wound down and attention turned to postwar issues.[10] MESC sponsored a series of conferences that focused on increasing agricultural output by improving cultivation techniques.[11] In 1943, the British and American governments created a Scientific Advisory Mission attached to MESC. The mission consisted of three men—B. A. Keen, an agricultural scientist, E. B. Worthington, author of *Science in Africa*, and H. B. Allen, director of the Near East Foundation of New York. Their work attempted to summarize the state of knowledge about scientific and technical topics in the region and was intended to lay the groundwork for postwar planning.[12] While their survey ranged broadly, the authors included a section on the demography of the Middle East.[13] In their summary report, they noted "the importance of population pressure as a basic factor in the future economy of the Middle East." They went on to add, "Great importance is attached to maintaining a balance in development between the many subjects and factors, which lead toward improvement in the standard of living. But it is emphasized that an increase in standard of living and education, though it may ultimately lead to stable populations, has a long intermediate stage when it tends to increase rather than decrease the rate of increase. Some countries in the area, notably Egypt and Palestine, which are already heavily populated, will therefore have to face a critical stage during the next half century."[14]

The creation of population estimates and forecasts by regional groups like the MESC provided a source of information for officials in London. The Foreign Office possessed a number of departments that assessed this information. Demographic analysis began in the regional offices that collected diplomatic information and intelligence. These regional work groups could also draw upon the expertise of the Foreign Office Research Department (FORD). FORD began as a group of experts from the Royal Institute of International Affairs, organized by Arnold Toynbee and housed at Balliol College in Oxford. After the outbreak of the war, the group affiliated with the government under the name the Foreign Research and Press Service. Its semi-official status ended in 1943 when the government made FORD a branch of the Foreign Office.[15] FORD's establishment reflected the growing emphasis upon collecting information to assist policy making in the Foreign Office, and it relied upon academic volunteers from a number of disciplines. It employed several demographers and other social scientists, among them T. H. Marshall, a well-known sociologist associated with the population movement in the interwar years. Marshall used his academic contacts to bring in experts, such as Alexander Carr-Saunders, to assist in the creation of demographic estimates. The Foreign Office asked the Royal Commission on Population, which began work during the war, for help with population forecasting. Officials also turned to the United States, where Frank Notestein headed up a group of demographers at Princeton working on similar topics for the U.S. government and the League of Nations.[16]

During the war, researchers focused on population trends in the three Axis powers—Italy, Germany, and Japan—in order to forecast food supply and manpower reserves.[17] As the outcome of the war became certain, attention turned to postwar relief and reconstruction. The Foreign Office required accurate estimates of population and vital rates in order to make reasonable assumptions about future economic and political trends. Officials expressed considerable interest in these estimates. As one argued, "I myself think that population figures give much the best approximate index to the potential military power of a modern industrial state and that in considering the menace which Germany might represent in fifteen or thirty years from now it would be useful to have an estimate of the population at that time to work on."[18]

These reports emphasized the necessity of controlling population growth and finding outlets for excess people if these countries were to be reintegrated into the Western bloc. Researchers contended that these countries suffered from relative, if not absolute, overpopulation that would make the task of reconstruction more difficult. They also suggested possible ways to limit population growth in Germany, including population transfers and the wider provision of birth control, which required the repeal of Nazi-era statutes. Behind these suggestions lay the belief that for the foreseeable future Germany's population would exceed its available resources and that this situation threatened the stability of Europe.[19]

The Foreign Office also tracked long-run population trends outside of Europe and Japan.[20] Its researchers used the work of Princeton demographers like Notestein and Ansley Coale to forecast potential changes in the U.S. population. In addition, the Foreign Office discussed the population estimates produced by the MESC Scientific Advisory Committee. In response to public concern that Christians would be persecuted upon the withdrawal of French and British forces from Syria and Lebanon, the Foreign Office asked for estimates for the population of religious groups in those countries.[21]

WAR AND POPULATION IN THE COLONIAL OFFICE

For the Colonial Office, the war provided a dramatic challenge to the existing organization and led to a significant expansion of the specialist groups within the London-based establishment. The interventionism of war built upon the foundations laid by the forward policy of the Colonial Office in the late 1930s.[22] The passage of the Colonial Welfare and Development Act in 1940 and the publication of the recommendations of the Moyne Commission committed the British government to a far greater role in promoting colonial welfare in the future. This commitment took on more significance when linked to the need to defend the empire from its foreign and domestic critics. Officials hoped to promote imperial patriotism among colonial subjects, who were promised rewards in exchange for their loyalty and sacrifices.[23] The portrayal of the war as a people's war contributed to support for a more interventionist domestic state that would provide a higher level of social services and employment in the postwar years.[24] This promise, embodied in a series of proposals such as the Beveridge Report, created a new political environment to accompany the changing intellectual one.[25] As Joanna Lewis's work on Kenya demonstrates, efforts to improve the lives of colonial subjects relied on British ideas of social welfare and models of bureaucratic organization. Yet significant differences existed within the colonial sphere that would affect the implementation of this policy. One critical issue was the fragmented nature of colonial governance. The growth of a modernizing cadre of officials in London left untouched a more traditionalist colonial service abroad that prided itself on local knowledge and the wisdom of established practice.[26] Officials and experts in London could propose policies but could not ensure their acceptance and implementation.[27] Within the Colonial Office, a newer generation of officials faced an older group of officials, selected outside the examination system, who dominated the higher ranks of the service.[28]

Despite support for a more active colonial state, planning efforts in the Colonial Office lagged behind those of the domestic ministries. Lord Hailey's Committee for Post-War Planning enjoyed a brief period of ascendancy in 1942–43, but it quickly encountered resistance from officials in the empire and London. The shunting aside of Hailey left permanent officials in charge of postwar planning.[29]

Their views, while more sympathetic to calls for modernization than overseas officials, tended to be more conservative and paternalist than those of outside experts. The failure of the economist W.A. Lewis's efforts to foster a more systematic approach to development planning while serving on the Colonial Economic Advisory Council grew in large part out of the unwillingness of officials like Sidney Caine to cede control over policy to experts or to embrace more progressive ideas about colonial governance. The course of events during the war also favored the triumph of conservative ideas within the Colonial Office, as production and regulation replaced welfare as the central aims of state intervention.[30]

Such generational and ideological differences provide only part of the answer. The authoritarian and paternalist traditions of colonial administration stifled the emergence of a civil society that might have participated in the new initiatives. In Britain, the vogue for planning and intervention emerged from an unprecedented mobilization of resources for the war effort. Yet this mobilization remained tempered by the existence of political and legal safeguards within metropolitan society. In the empire, the war led to a number of significant new interventions in the lives of colonial peoples. The stepped-up recruitment of soldiers and civilian workers and the need for resources, which increased after the fall of Southeast Asia, produced a dramatic expansion of state power.[31] Colonial subjects, however, enjoyed few of the protections offered to British citizens. Intervention and social welfare grew out of the imperatives of a colonial system that imposed its decisions on colonial subjects. At the same time, the empire possessed far fewer resources than the metropole, as demonstrated by the government's inability to maintain the Colonial Service. Even as the domestic civil service expanded dramatically, the overseas establishment shrank due to war losses, the collapse of recruitment, and the calling-up of officials for military service.[32] The remaining officials become overstretched as they took on new tasks related to the war, a situation that continued until the postwar era brought a wave of fresh recruits and resources. Although the London establishment of the Colonial Office expanded after 1939, it too faced shortages of personnel, especially in the upper administrative ranks, that affected its ability to function.[33] In these circumstances, the immediate needs of war often took precedence over planning for postwar development.

These circumstances shaped the response of the Colonial Office to the demographic problems brought by the war. A lack of resources and personnel often led to ad hoc solutions by local colonial governments. Hong Kong, before its occupation by the Japanese, experienced a refugee crisis. This influx, which dated back to the mid-1930s, increased as the Sino-Japanese War intensified, with the population doubling to nearly 2 million by 1940. Officials in Hong Kong and London discussed various ways to deal with the problem. They decided to move the refugee camps outside the defense perimeter on the Kowloon Peninsula, to impose limits on junk and steamship passenger traffic, and to require a permit for entry into the colony. These proposals, embodied in the Immigration Control Ordinance of 1940, continued to be applied after reoccupation, although their legality remained in question.[34]

Immigration controls appeared in other regions during the war and would continue after 1945. In Palestine, the Colonial Office and other British ministries struggled to enforce the limitations on Jewish immigration imposed by the White Paper of 1939. Given the scale of the tragedy facing the Jewish populations of Europe and the flood of refugees seeking safety, a great deal of unauthorized migration occurred.[35] The Colonial Office attempted to measure the scale of this immigration to assist in its efforts to formulate a new policy. David Glass and Robert Kuczynski became involved in these discussions, working to produce estimates of population and illegal migration in the absence of a census.[36] As was the case before the war, such statistical work contained obvious political overtones in Palestine. Proposals for a census or compulsory registration floundered in the face of communal resistance and lack of funds.[37]

The British compounded the harshness of their hard line on Jewish immigration to Palestine by refusing to consider seriously the prospect of settling refugees within the Dominions and the empire. The Dominions, despite repeated official and private appeals, only provided sanctuary to a limited numbers of refugees. As in the case of intercolonial migration, authorities refused to modify their restrictive policies and viewed non-British migrants as undesirable.[38] Given this response attention turned to the dependent empire. Politicians and private groups suggested potential areas for refugee settlement in Africa, the Mediterranean, and the West Indies. In 1939 Sir Hugh Emerson, the high commissioner for refugees of the League of Nations and Max Nicholson of the policy group Political and Economic Planning approached the Colonial Office about the possibility of allowing Jewish refugees to settle in the colonies.[39] Nicholson, who later became a key figure in MESC, saw Malaya, East Africa, the Gold Coast, and Jamaica as potential sites for refugees.[40] The Colonial Office dismissed this list, arguing that a lack of space and resources made them unsuitable for resettlement.[41] A number of people, including Winston Churchill, saw the West Indies, especially the mainland colonies of British Guiana and British Honduras, as a promising destination.[42] The Colonial Office entertained the idea but refused to endorse mass migration to the region, citing its backwardness and low level of economic development. West Indian colonies, already suffering from high unemployment, had erected barriers to immigration in the 1930s.[43] Ironically, a number of officials in London and the West Indies previously supported migration to address poverty and unemployment in Barbados, Bermuda and Jamaica.[44] The issue of Jewish migration created considerable tension within the Colonial Office. British officials remained highly critical of Jewish desires to settle in Palestine, despite their inability to assist refugees through settlement in the empire. J. G. Hibbert, who handled the issue for the Colonial Office, argued that Jewish organizations wanted to settle only in Palestine "regardless of the fact that that small territory cannot possibly absorb more than a limited number of people." After meeting with Jewish representatives, including Sir Robert Whaley Cohen, about settling refugees in British Guiana in 1939, Hibbert wrote that he "never again would . . . be a party to anything done to assist these people in the Colonial Empire."[45] In the end the Colonial Office refused to allow any large-scale resettlement of refugees, confining itself to small experimental schemes such as the creation of a small colony of German Jews in Kenya under the auspice of the Council for German Jewry.[46]

Despite the anti-Semitic overtones of Hibbert's remarks and the tragic consequences of the British government's refusal to allow large-scale migration to the empire, the treatment of refugees conformed to the pattern established by British colonial authorities in the interwar years. Even before the refugee crisis reached its peak, the Colonial Office imposed limits over settlement within the empire. Its response to West Indian migration schemes in the 1930s resembled the one given to refugee advocates and relied upon the same rationales: the attitude of Dominion governments and the lack of room in the empire. The tightening up of migration controls seen in Palestine occurred elsewhere in the empire. In East Africa, the war saw an expansion of state regulation of migration. Already in the prewar period, attention focused on the difficulties raised by South Asian immigration to the region. During the war, the governments of Kenya, Uganda, and Tanganyika imposed limits on Indian immigration. Rather than risking public disapproval for such measures, the legislatures empowered the governors of these territories to use administrative means to accomplish the same ends.[47] Although officials justified such rules as a product of wartime conditions, the desire to limit South Asian influence in the region constituted the principal motive for the restrictions. Sir Charles Dundas, governor of Uganda, worried about potential problems between Indian and African populations and argued,

"It is from this point of view that restrictions on Indian immigration may not only be justified but seen as imperative."[48]

The issue of West Indian migration continued to vex colonial officials during the war. The Colonial Office became involved in plans to import West Indian labor into Britain for military and industrial purposes.[49] Despite the need for labor, many officials expressed doubts about the suitability of West Indians as migrants to the United Kingdom and linked racial prejudice in Britain to the behavior of West Indians.[50] Some 6,400 West Indians served in the Royal Air Force, while more than a thousand civilians worked in Britain.[51] The use of West Indian labor for the war effort failed to change official attitudes about migration. In 1943, in response to a request from the governor of Bermuda, the Colonial Office again took up the issue of West Indian migration. The governor, reacting to the creation by the legislature of a Select Committee to investigate the problem of overpopulation, inquired about the possibility of emigration to imperial or Dominion destinations for islanders. As they had before the war, these governments and officials in London rejected the idea of large-scale migration as a solution to overpopulation.[52]

While migration remained restricted for West Indians, the war brought a significant increase in funding for development and welfare projects. The West Indies' position as "the British shop-window to the USA" and its role as a forward base for U.S. naval power made it the subject of considerable attention before and during the war.[53] The West Indies received a disproportionate share of the initial £1 million promised by the Colonial Development Act of 1940. Sir Frank Stockdale, the colonial agricultural adviser, became the comptroller for development and welfare for the region in 1940 and oversaw the expenditure of the new funds.[54] However, much of the promised funding never materialized and the West Indies actually transferred funds to Britain in the early stages of the war. At the same time, unemployment and shortages caused by the war led to increased political unrest in the islands, including riots on several islands in the summer of 1942.[55]

Although the war disrupted existing patterns of migration, many of the ruling assumptions about migration remained intact. The vulnerability of the Dominions, underscored by Japanese military successes in 1941–42, reinforced the desire of officials to restart the flow of migrants as soon as possible. The Overseas Settlement Board argued that the continued fall in Australian fertility made migration to the region necessary to maintain the vitality of the population.[56] A number of prominent politicians shared this belief, including the dominions secretary and future prime minister, Clement Atlee.[57] In 1943 he wrote a memo in which he predicted continued support by the government for British migration.[58] The desire to expand immigration faced several difficulties, including fear of a population drain from Britain and the continued reluctance of Australia and the other Dominions to admit large numbers of non-British migrants.[59]

Although local officials usually controlled migration, the Colonial Office and other ministries undertook a more systematic review during the war. In 1941, in response to a Foreign Office request, the Colonial Office asked Sir Alan Pim to review the prospects for European settlement in the empire. Pim, a retired Indian Civil Service official, previously worked with the Colonial Development Advisory Council and served on several commissions and boards in the 1930s.[60] He traveled widely in the empire and published several works on economic and agricultural issues.[61] Pim's study, completed in 1942, concluded that only Africa might offer opportunities for European settlers. Even there, he rejected European settlement as too costly and politically difficult, except in southern Rhodesia where a relatively large settler population already existed.[62] The Colonial Office agreed with Pim's general argument and would use the report to defend its refusal to cooperate with plans for refugee resettlement in the postwar era.

LABOR AND RESOURCES DURING THE SECOND WORLD WAR

Although migration remained a central demographic issue for the Colonial Office, the requirements of war focused attention on other population problems. The need to control resources and manpower gave further impetus to planning and demographic analysis within the colonial establishment. Although the MESC represented a London-based (and later Washington-based) initiative, the Colonial Office created its own agencies to mobilize resources for the war effort and to coordinate its efforts with other ministries, military forces, and foreign governments. The Eastern Group Supply Council undertook this work in India and southeastern Asia, while in Africa regional groups like the West African Produce Control Board and the West African War Council came into existence. A senior representative from the Colonial Office normally headed such agencies in order to ensure effective communication among London, local officials, and military staffs.[63]

The importance of African resources made the continent an arena for increased state intervention during the war. To replace tin, rubber, and other strategic materials previously supplied by Asian territories officials expanded production in areas like the Jos Plateau in Nigeria, which became the empire's principal source of tin during the war.[64] Allied countries became more dependent upon African supplies of cobalt, copper, and chromium, as well as more mundane articles like cocoa and sisal. In addition to meeting their own food requirements, African colonies became suppliers of food products for the Allied forces in Africa, the Middle East, and South Asia. Government agencies used production quotas as well as wage and price controls to mobilize African peasants and workers. These efforts, while successful at delivering products for war use, imposed severe hardships upon African consumers as the result of inflation and shortages.[65] Essential commodities like maize and firewood became more difficult to obtain, a situation aggravated by the presence of foreign troops and drought in parts of the continent.[66]

The military and civilian sectors increased their demand for African labor during the war. By one estimate, at least 500,000 Africans served in imperial military units from 1939 to 1945, the vast majority of them as laborers and construction workers.[67] Although the conditions of service were better than during the First World War, when thousands died as a consequence of disease and poor treatment, British officials faced widespread evasion and resistance to recruitment.[68] In addition to military conscription, colonial authorities also engaged in forcible recruitment of civilian labor for private enterprises. The most massive of these projects, the tin mines of the Jos Plateau, absorbed 100,000 laborers, of whom 10,000 died. Widespread recourse to forced labor also occurred in Tanganyika, Kenya, as well as in northern and southern Rhodesia, where private and public employers conscripted as many as 100,000 Africans.[69]

These tactics resembled those employed during the First World War but went considerably further in their scope.[70] The scale of demand for labor and the use of coercion to ensure its supply revived concerns about African population. Already in the interwar years, British officials came under increasing scrutiny regarding labor policy from both domestic and international groups. Many observers, including Lord Hailey, made a connection between forced labor and the demographic problems of Africa. At the outbreak of the war, Margery Perham, an expert on Africa and a central figure in the work of the *African Survey*, expressed concern about the potential impact of wartime programs on African populations, arguing that "war may lead to even more wasteful use of the docile African humanity."[71] Despite such concerns, many officials continued to view African populations through the lenses of prewar notions of shortage and surplus. Thus, areas like Nyasaland and Kenya could be viewed as labor reserves for the larger war effort, despite evidence of local labor shortages as recruitment and conscription increased during the war.[72] To allay concerns about labor problems, Major Granville Orde-Brown, the Colonial Office labour advisor, toured the empire to examine labor conditions. Despite the problems he noted with wartime conditions, especially in East Africa, Orde-Brown's assessment remained upbeat and his recommendations focused on the need for greater attention to regulations and procedures.[73]

DEMOGRAPHIC INFORMATION IN THE COLONIAL OFFICE

Although the Colonial Office recognized that its migration and labor policies could have demographic consequences, it lacked the ability to accurately measure them. The Colonial Office acknowledged this problem in the interwar years, but the war increased the pressure on the Colonial Office to reform its statistical and census operations. The principal justification for improved demographic analysis lay in its link to planning, which became more important as attention turned to postwar reconstruction after 1942. The emphasis on planning reflected the momentum of changes already underway in the late 1930s as well as the new commitment to colonial social welfare embodied in the Colonial Development Act of 1940. Officials hoped to understand how demographic issues, especially population growth, might affect efforts to improve colonial social welfare. During the war, the Colonial Office reviewed existing policies and created advisory groups to assist officials in formulating new demographic procedures.

When the war began, the Colonial Office turned to Robert Kuczynski, who was already familiar to officials through his work in the department's library. He served as an informal advisor before his retirement from the London School of Economics (LSE) in 1941 and then worked full time with the Colonial Office until his death in 1947.[74] Even as Kuczynski began his work, the Colonial Office cancelled the imperial census planned for 1941.[75] The logistical and personnel problems experienced by colonial governments made it impossible to conduct the census in the short term, and Kuczynski instead set about reviewing previous censuses to prepare for a postwar count. He noted the failure to hold censuses according to a single set of criteria or even on the same day and argued that the situation had deteriorated over time.[76] Up to 1891, governments produced Blue

Books with reasonably comparable demographic information. From 1901 on, however, London allowed local officials to gather whatever information they thought important, which made an empire-wide census impossible. In 1931, the Colonial Office left the decision on whether or not to conduct a census up to local governments, which meant that many colonies decided either not to hold one or conducted inadequate ones. As a consequence, the censuses carried out since 1922 accounted for only 22 percent of the imperial population. Much of the demographic information consisted of group counts or estimates of population based on tax and other administrative data. Kuczynski placed the margin of error at +/– 15 percent for three-quarters of the empire and +/– 20 percent for half of the empire. This inaccuracy, combined with the lack of comparability, made the figures "of little practical value."[77] He pointed to the weakness of a system in which untrained officials relied upon low-paid, indigenous enumerators or local informants for most of their information[78]

Kuczynski's review demonstrated the consequences of the decentralized, laissez-faire administrative system of the empire and pulled him into the minutiae of each colony's particular circumstances. In the West Indies the state of demographic information remained spotty at best. Several colonies, including the largest, Jamaica, failed to hold censuses in 1931, citing financial problems. Driven by heightened concern about population growth, as well as a desire to document the need for colonial development funds, several West Indian colonies sought permission to hold special censuses during the war. These colonies included Bermuda (1939), Barbados (1941), Jamaica (1942–44), and the Bahamas (1943). Kuczynski consulted on these projects and traveled to the West Indies to help design the 1946 Census.[79]

Kuczynski's analysis of imperial censuses highlighted the limitations of demographic information, a topic that would receive closer attention as the Colonial Office expanded its commitment to research and formed expert bodies to advise it on specialized subjects. The provision of £500,000 per year for research in the Colonial Development Act of 1940 provided the resources necessary to fund new initiatives in imperial studies. However, the emergency circumstances of the first few years of the war delayed the implementation of this program, and it lay dormant until June 1941 when Lord Moyne reactivated it and asked for proposals from researchers. Despite this call, the Colonial Office failed to act on these proposals until the creation of the Colonial Research Advisory Committee (CRAC) in June 1942.[80]

Much of the initial concern of the CRAC focused on the hard sciences, where support for research in agriculture, tropical medicine, and veterinary science predated the war.[81] However, the role of the social sciences in this effort remained uncertain. A proposed colonial research group at Nuffield College, Oxford, revealed the ongoing discussions among officials about the role of social science and experts in the formulation of policy. The debate began in 1939 when Margery Perham wrote to the Warden of Nuffield College suggesting a study of demographic impact of labor migration in Africa. She called for a joint project involving Professor Reginald Coupland of Oxford, Orde-Brown, and Lord Hailey. Orde-Brown expressed support for the project, noting, "The outstanding need is for publications which will appeal to the people who need them, i.e. the busy government official and the employer. Serious scientific works of bulk are ignored by such men, not because they would not be interested, but because they have neither the time nor the energy to read them after a hard day's work."[82] F. J. Pedler, Hailey's assistant on the *African Survey* and a member of the Committee in Post-War Problems, argued, "It is an outstanding illustration of the need for a central fund from which investigations can be financed into sociological subjects affecting Africa as a whole."[83]

Although the war led to the cancellation of the proposed labor survey, Perham succeeded in establishing a colonial research unit at Nuffield College during the war that would eventually become the Institute for African Studies.[84] However, colonial officials continued to question the value of such efforts. In part this reflected the hostility within the colonial service to Perham. One official contended that "Miss Perham is a self-advertising person," while another agreed on the need to keep her "in her place."[85] However, they also objected in general to turning over control to academic researchers. As one official argued, "While admitting that it would be a good thing that somebody should be 'researching' into matters on which a post-war policy will be needed, I am by no means certain that the most authoritative people to do this 'researching' are academics who use the written word as their raw material and have no experience of the actual responsibility of administration. It seems to me that if the Government accepts financial responsibility for this sort of thing, it will be extremely difficult for it to take a detached view of the results."[86]

Other officials expressed greater sympathy for Perham and her work. C. Eastwood rejected the idea that only those with administrative experience could do research and argued, "Miss Perham herself, whatever her flaws, cannot be accused of lack of experience."[87] In the end, the CRAC and officials accepted the need for imperial social science research. Officials spoke of "the necessity of obtaining, through research, information essential for that coordinated postwar development which is so desirable."[88] In order to do this, officials turned to Audrey Richards, an anthropologist with well-established ties to the Colonial Office.[89] Richards, appointed as a temporary principal at the Colonial Office in 1941, presented a summary of needed research to Lord Hailey's Committee on Post-War Problems in July 1942. She consulted with Carr-Saunders, who wrote a memo that discussed the state of knowledge in the various fields as well as the institutions most involved in social science research.[90] They suggested that teams of experts in relevant areas should assemble to examine how to proceed in each field. In the end, the CRAC created eight groups, each headed by a convener, including one in demography. Six of the eight reported back by October 1943. Carr-Saunders, who headed the Sociology Group, used the reports as the basis for recommending the creation of the Colonial Social Science Research Council (CSSRC), which came into existence in July 1944.[91]

The Demography Advisory Group, created in mid-1943, formed one of the core research groups of the new CSSRC. J. H. Hutton, commissioner of the Indian Census of 1931 and professor of anthropology at Cambridge, was the convener. Kuczynski and Carr-Saunders were original appointees, and Julian Huxley would be invited to join them in late 1943. With the addition of Huxley, the Demography Advisory Group contained two of the central figures from the population movement of the interwar years with close ties to government officials. In addition, Theodore Culwick, a colonial official and his wife G. M. Culwick, an ethnographer, who cowrote a series of groundbreaking studies of African population, became members. The group also enrolled members of the Colonial Office staff working on the West Indies and Africa. In addition to assisting officials, it stood ready to offer advice on population issues to other groups in the Colonial Research Council, such as the Medical Advisory Committee and the Advisory Council on Agriculture.[92]

The initial meetings of the group focused on Kuczynski's plans to standardize the process of census taking and to improve the training of officials. His proposals, and the responses of local colonial officials to them, illustrate the problems faced by the Colonial Office in its efforts to modernize the administration of the colonies and to reorganize its statistical and census operations. Kuczynski insisted that each census be an actual count, performed simultaneously by a uniform methodology throughout the empire. He rejected the use of ad hoc procedures or estimates based on tax rolls or other official categories.[93] He believed that officials exaggerated the difficulties of obtaining information from colonial subjects and argued that only trained personnel could conduct a proper census. In the long run, he envisioned either a separate Demographic Service or the creation of training schemes in demography for officials at British universities.[94]

Colonial officials disagreed vigorously with Kuczynski's plans. They objected to the cost of an actual census and asserted the superiority of local knowledge, arguing that only those with practical experience could design a survey and interpret the statements of the "natives."[95] Traditional administrative officers remained wedded to the idea of the generalist, attuned by experience to local conditions.[96] Even more progressive officials, such as Eric Dutton, the acting British resident in Zanzibar, believed that local officials, who understood the "native mentality," should take the lead.[97] Despite his support for Kuczynski's plans, Sir George Gater, the permanent undersecretary of state, sided with local officials. As he noted, "Few candidates for such employment would have personal acquaintance with conditions in tropical conditions and scarcely any could be expected to have experience of dealing with the peoples with whom they would come into contact or to speak their language. . . . There are risks to allowing inexperienced staff to handle matters of this kind among colonial people, some of whom . . . are likely to regard a census with no little suspicion and distrust."[98]

This unwillingness to press colonial governments led to further delays in the planned imperial census. In November 1944, Sir George Gater wrote to all colonial governors and said that an empire-wide census would occur within six years and urged them to proceed with interim counts in the meantime. Despite this request, the secretary of state remained reluctant to force the issue given staff shortages.[99] As a consequence, a number of colonies failed to conduct counts or performed only partial ones. The final round of colonial censuses would not be completed until the late 1940s. Thus the British government still lacked much of the crucial demographic information it required, even as it geared up for postwar development in the empire.

THE COLONIAL OFFICE AND OVERPOPULATION

As efforts to improve demographic information proceeded, senior officials began to give greater weight to demographic issues in their policy discussions. The perception that imperial population growth represented a fundamental problem took root in the Colonial Office in the early

1940s. This shift represented an important change in official views. Prior to the war, concerns about overpopulation appeared in areas with limited resource bases and changing patterns of immigration, such as the West Indies, Singapore, Hong Kong, Fiji, Mauritius, and Malta.[100] During the war, however, key officials expressed increased concern about overpopulation in other regions, including, surprisingly, Africa. Although officials in 1943 dismissed Julian Huxley's concern that falling mortality in Africa would lead to population growth, by the end of the war his concerns received more attention.[101] In 1945 Andrew Cohen, a central figure in postwar Africa, discussed a lecture by P. A. Buxton of the London School of Hygiene and Tropical Medicine that warned that the introduction of DDT would dramatically lower death rates from malaria and potentially lead to higher growth rates.[102] Reports of population growth in Africa reinforced this warning. In 1944, the CSSRC concluded that population pressure existed in parts of the continent and would lead to an expansion of private land holding.[103] In Kenya, where much of the indigenous population lived in native reserves, settlers and the government worried that population growth among Africans would increase economic and political discontent. One official estimated that East African population growth had increased from 1 to 1.5 percent per year in the 1930s to as high as 2 percent a year in the early 1940s.[104] Such estimates alarmed the settlers and calls for encouraging birth control among Africans began to be heard.[105]

Such reports led officials to express concern about the potential impact of population growth upon postwar plans. They linked poverty, welfare, and population in the debate over development. In the words of Sidney Caine: "In many dependencies, the natural poverty and/or the over-population is such that it is very doubtful whether any economic development will ever be able to maintain the inhabitant in anything like the standard at which we are now aiming."[106]

Dr. Archibald Smart, a medical advisor to the Colonial Office, placed the issue in a global context, arguing, "The problem is of course one of great importance and the question ... that looms large is how to deal with the large surplus populations in parts of the West Indies and elsewhere.... The same difficulty is occurring all over the world and confronts the Government of Japan and especially the Dutch in Java, and the question must be faced."[107]

The connection between development and population was also raised by A. V. Hill, a biologist and future president of the Royal Society after a visit to India.[108] In a series of lectures as well as a letter to the *Times of*

India in June 1944, he portrayed population control as central to India's future development.[109] He contacted the Colonial Office about the issue, which passed his memo on to the Demography Group. Although Andrew Cohen believed Hill expressed a "rigidly Malthusian view" about population, he agreed on the importance of having information about long-term population trends.[110]

These statements expressed an emerging consensus within the Colonial Office that overpopulation would be the dominant demographic problem in the postwar era. Although officials agreed on the significance of population growth, they failed to agree on what to do about the problem. Birth control activists continued to push their case for direct government support for family planning. In August 1940, Edith How-Martyn and Eileen Palmer visited Frank Stockdale at the Colonial Office. In a meeting interrupted by an air raid warning, How-Martyn reported on her work with Birth Control World Wide and urged the government to include birth control information as part of any plan for maternal welfare in the West Indies.[111] That same year, J. P. Brander, a retired Indian Civil Service Officer and population activist, wrote to Lord Lloyd, the colonial secretary, about the need for birth control in the empire.[112] Finally, in 1943, Julian Huxley wrote to Oliver Stanley, one of Lloyd's successors, to raise the question of birth control in Africa.[113]

Despite a willingness to listen to outside activists, officials remained divided about the morality and efficacy of birth control. They also worried about the potential political problems that could accompany government support for family planning. The release of the Moyne Commission Report, which highlighted the problem of overpopulation in the West Indies, triggered a debate within the Colonial Office about whether the British government should become directly involved in providing birth control services. The debate revealed the political, religious, and racial attitudes of the participants as they ranged over a variety of topics tied in the official mind to population.

In December 1939, Sir Alan Burns, a senior civil servant who had served as governor of British Honduras, wrote to Sir Cosmo Parkinson, the permanent undersecretary of state, to voice his concerns with the report. In particular, he objected to the commission's argument that a reduction in the birth rate would be an essential part of any solution to the problems of the West Indies. Burns, a Catholic, saw a number of problems with the idea, stating, "I can quite imagine the local agitators and the Press making capital of the argument that the Commission's method of solving the problem of unemployment, which now exists, is to limit the numbers of the next generation. With a more or less ignorant audience such an argument would be effective, more especially as it would probably be twisted into a campaign against the forcible reduction of the black race."[114]

Burns, whose previous postings included Nigeria, believed that people of African descent would reject birth control, arguing, "Again the Negroes of the West Indies, like those of Africa, are very fond of children and like to have a number of them around. They would agree with the attitude of the churches in denouncing birth control. Finally I am quite certain that the majority of the people would not understand what birth control really is. They would probably regard the suggestions as an attempt to deprive them of one of the few pleasures of the poor."[115]

Burns appealed to Parkinson to persuade the secretary of state not to endorse birth control. A number of officials remained skeptical about endorsing government-funded birth control services. Some of them agreed with Burns, who believed that "the natural carelessness and lack of forethought of the people would prevent any birth control campaign from being successful."[116] As Dr. Smart argued in a 1943 minute, "I don't think that in the present state of things in Africa amongst indigenous populations much attention would be paid to advice on birth control. . . . Amongst ordinary folk in Africa, children are very valuable property, the girl on account of the dowry she commands, and the boy because he is a labour asset. I don't know what method Dr. Huxley has in mind, but I am sure that primitive people would find it very hard to absorb the technique of this.[117]

Opponents of birth control also believed that support for family planning would increase racial tensions and exacerbate political problems in the empire. More than one colonial official argued that nationalists in the empire, especially in the West Indies, would seize on birth control as "a trick of the white races to destroy the coloured peoples."[118]

Supporters of birth control, while recognizing the difficulties presented by official endorsement of family limitation, argued in favor of making some effort to reduce the birth rate. Some, like Frank Stockdale, argued that opponents exaggerated the possibility of a backlash among colonial peoples and pointed to the work of private groups in the West Indies as proof that birth control would be welcomed.[119] Officials with experience in the West Indies proved to be most vigorous proponents of birth control. They argued that without population control, giving development aid would simply be, as Sidney Caine put it, "pouring money down a bottomless sink."[120] The governor of Jamaica, in a dispatch to the

Colonial Office in February 1940, said, "The somber fact emerges that with the continuation of the present birth rate there is no policy, long or short, which will not be submerged by the rising tide of population," a view echoed by his labour advisor.[121] Such statements led one official to argue, "The growth of population is the principle and at present possibly an insuperable obstacle to any real increase in standards of living, except ultimately at intolerable cost to this country. It may be that a really extensive and courageous propaganda drive in favour of birth control would be the best contribution we could make in those colonies."[122]

Philip Rogers, a younger official who had served in the West Indies, emerged from these debates as the most vocal advocate for birth control within the Colonial Office. He cited the impact of population growth upon social problems and called limiting growth an issue of "real urgency in the West Indies."[123] He acknowledged the potential opposition of churches and other groups but felt that the government must do something to support family planning. Rogers remained an advocate of population control and supported the establishment of population programs in the postwar era. Despite his views, he rose quickly in the Colonial Office, becoming an assistant undersecretary of state in 1953 and playing a major role in imperial policy in the 1950s. He would be knighted in recognition for his service and ended his career as the permanent secretary of the Department of Social Security and Health with responsibility for more than 90,000 employees.[124]

Although advocates of family planning never produced a formal plan of action, the outline of a plan can be discerned from their statements. First and foremost, they wanted the British government and local colonial governments in affected areas to acknowledge the problem of overpopulation and conduct an education campaign for the general public, which would also include information about birth control. Officials were unclear about how to deliver birth control services, but some argued in favor of government-run clinics.[125] Although these goals were modest, it is unclear to what extent they could have been implemented had the government chosen to adopt a more aggressive policy. Even in Britain, which possessed a reasonably advanced medical and public health system, many people lacked access to medical services. Family planning services remained in the hands of private groups like the Family Planning Association, though local governments could offer assistance. In the West Indies, Africa, and Asia, medical services, especially for the poor, remained rudimentary. No trained corps of nurses and doctors existed to staff clinics nor did a substantial health infrastructure exist outside urban areas. In such circumstances, colonial governments could have worked with private groups and foundations, as they did in other public health initiatives. Certainly access to public funding would have expanded the reach of these programs, but in the absence of a major investment in health care and birth control technology, the impact would have been limited.

Supporters of birth control appear to have embraced it as the only possible solution, even in the face of considerable uncertainty about how a program would be designed and implemented. They also expressed doubts about the potential for birth control to limit population growth. E. J. Waddington, a future governor of Barbados, doubted the efficacy of birth control, even as he argued in favor of it. He made his views known in the mid-1930s in reference to Bermuda: "My doubt is whether birth control clinics will do more than defer the problem for a few years and the danger lies in lowering the general standard of the population by providing information which will be utilized mainly by the more intelligent. The answer to this criticism is that the majority of the more intelligent—black and white—practice birth control already and the answer to the charge of inducing immorality is the statement of a leading medical practitioner that in 40 years practice in Bermuda he has only seen two coloured girls who are virgins."[126]

Such accusations of sexual immorality and "disorganized family life" became common among officials discussing West Indian birth rates, or what one official termed, "the torrent of babies."[127] Major Orde-Brown, during his visit to the region in 1938, drew attention to the high level of illegitimacy as one source of the population and labor problems of the islands.[128]

Despite such reservations, advocates of birth control hoped that this debate would lead to a review of policy by higher authorities. As J. J. Paskin, the head of the Social Services Department, noted in 1942, the question of birth control had never been "systematically considered as a matter of policy in the Colonial Office, though various aspects of it have been dealt with, ad hoc, from time to time."[129] F. J. Pedler, who was sympathetic to birth control, helped move the issue onto the agenda of Lord Hailey's Committee on Post-War Problems.[130] The committee took up the issue in March 1942 but refused to endorse a more aggressive policy. This approached accorded with the views of Lord Cranborne, the secretary of state for the colonies, who hoped to avoid any political controversies during wartime. He followed the policies laid out in the 1930s by his predecessors and ruled out direct support for birth control for "moral and political reasons."[131] Cranborne expressed doubts about the wisdom of promoting family planning, arguing, "Nor frankly, am I convinced of the desirability of His Majesty's Government supporting a policy of birth control in the colonies or anywhere else. There seem to me to be immense potential dangers in one nation artificially restricting or even reducing the population of its territories in a world where other nations are not doing the same things."[132]

Although in the postwar years senior politicians would come to accept the argument that population growth represented a serious problem, they would remain cautious about pursuing a more direct policy to limit that growth.

CONCLUSION

The Second World War proved favorable to the supporters of a more "forward" policy in the British Empire. The needs of wartime produced a dramatic increase in the powers of the colonial state. The explicit commitment to economic development and social welfare by the Colonial Office in 1940 led to the growth of planning and research within the colonial establishment, which in turn raised the profile of demographic issues. By the end of Second World War, the Colonial Office began to operate on the assumption that the empire stood on the brink of a population crisis. This view would be expressed to others within and outside the British government. Following a meeting with Colonial Office officials about European settlement in the empire, one Foreign Office official described the Colonial Office's view of the situation as "a general picture ... of increasing population, overcrowding and unemployment."[133] Although such sentiments could be used in the bureaucratic turf fights between the Colonial Office and other ministries for the control of imperial policy making, they also formed the rationale for sustained improvement in the quality of demographic information within the Colonial Office.

Despite these changes, there remained a great deal to be accomplished. Fields that affected population trends, like health, labor, and migration, remained under the control of local colonial governments, despite London's attempts to create centralized specialty departments and advisory bodies. Demographic information, though improved, continued for the most part to be gathered in a haphazard, incomplete manner. No one department was responsible for compiling or disseminating demographic information for the ministry as a whole, and no central population policy group existed. More important, officials like Philip Rogers failed to persuade senior officials and politicians to endorse population control measures like birth control or consider an integrated approach to managing population growth. Supporters of such a policy inside and outside the government hoped that in the postwar period these shortcomings would be addressed.

4 Population and the Postwar Empire

In 1944, as the Second World War drew to a close, Robert Kuczynski, the demographic advisor to the Colonial Office, called for an imperial census in the immediate postwar period, arguing, "The most fundamental demographic fact which must be known for planning of any kind is whether and to what extent the population is growing."¹ Senior officials like Sir George Gater, the permanent undersecretary of state, and Sidney Caine, the head of economic affairs at the Colonial Office, agreed about the importance of adequate demographic information for future development activities. This linkage between population and development provided the rationale for the continued expansion of demographic analysis by the Colonial Office and colonial governments after 1945. Demography, like other social sciences, benefited from the growth of state support in the postwar era, as the British government deployed expert knowledge in its drive to foster colonial development. These initiatives constituted part of what historians term the "Second Colonial Occupation," when the British government increased the flow of money and manpower into the empire in an attempt to revive and sustain it.²

Efforts to improve demographic analysis also reflected the concern that the empire faced a population crisis. Officials pointed to evidence of population growth in parts of the empire and argued that it threatened to undercut efforts to improve the lives of colonial subjects. These concerns led the colonial state to expand its efforts at population control. As in the interwar era, officials relied on resettlement, the regulation of imperial migration, and efforts to increase agricultural production. The desire to exert control over imperial populations faced many obstacles. A shortage of funds and trained personnel hamstrung efforts to track demographic trends, which meant that the Colonial Office lacked accurate population information for large parts of the empire. More important, the colonial state remained fractured, as officials in London and the colonies disagreed about how to proceed. The option endorsed by experts and a number of officials, state support for family planning services, remained politically charged. Ministers and officials feared that overt support for birth control would open them to accusations of restricting colonial populations for racial reasons. As a result, the British government continued the policy it developed during the interwar years. It cooperated with private population groups and allowed colonial governments to offer birth control services but refused to endorse family planning as an official policy.

However, the limited achievements of British population policy resulted not just from a fear of potential criticism or an unwillingness to employ racially constructed policies but from the place of demographic concerns within the colonial system. In private, officials and ministers discussed colonial population trends in racial terms. Such thinking reflected the continued importance of race and ethnicity in the postwar empire. Officials constructed political frameworks around racial and ethnic categories, playing groups off one another. The squeamishness of colonial rulers about birth control did not prevent them from using resettlement and movement restrictions to control populations and as a counterinsurgency tactic despite criticism from the outside world. Demographic concerns never attained a high level of significance in an empire facing successive political and economic crises. The weakness of medical and social services in the colonies would have made any plans for providing birth control to the general public difficult to implement. The long-run nature of population programs and the immense cost of a serious effort at population control made it far easier to postpone a commitment to the future. By the time the British government began to develop a systematic population policy in the late 1950s, most of the empire was on the verge of disappearing. Its collapse in the 1960s left the work of officials and experts to the new international agencies that inherited the unfinished projects of imperial rule.[3]

DEVELOPMENT AND THE COLONIAL STATE IN THE POSTWAR ERA

The end of the Second World War found Britain and its empire in a dramatically changed environment. The Labour government's commitment to a comprehensive welfare state and full employment created a new domestic political atmosphere. At the same time, the British economy faced severe dislocation in the wake of the war as well as a legacy of crushing debt.[4] The rise of the United States and Soviet Union left Britain's future as a great power in doubt; it found itself torn among Europe, the empire, and the "special relationship" with the Americans.[5] In these circumstances, the future of the empire appeared uncertain. During the war, the United States pressured the British to reform the empire, which it saw as at odds with the rhetoric of a war for freedom and self-determination. Although this demand brought a defensive response from British politicians and officials, it provided justification for increased spending on colonial development.[6] However, with the onset of the Cold War in the late 1940s, the United States proved more willing to accept the continuation of the empire in order to assist its goal of containing the Soviet Union and limiting its influence in colonies and newly independent states. Although U.S. pressure decreased as a result of the Cold War, American officials still pushed their British counterparts to advance self-government in order to limit the appeal of communism among disgruntled nationalists.[7] The need to satisfy aspirations for self-government while still maintaining control over events shaped imperial politics in the postwar era.[8]

Despite the political problems associated with the empire, the British remained committed to its survival. The Labour government hoped to use the empire to assist Britain's recovery and to bolster its claims to great power status.[9] To accomplish these aims, the British government renewed its commitment to encouraging economic and social development in the colonies, signaled by the passage of a new Colonial Development and Welfare Act in 1945. The British government sought to foster closer ties between the metropolitan and colonial economies while countering demands for greater autonomy or independence for dependent territories.[10]

The elevation of development to a central aim of imperial policy necessitated an increased level of planning and intervention by colonial regimes. It also entailed greater control from London, in order to break down the resistance of local colonial governments to change and to oversee the use of new resources provided by the metropole. Colonial officials could draw on the experiences of domestic planners who oversaw the creation of new ministries and government functions as well as the dramatic increase in the number of central government employees.[11] Yet colonial officials also drew on their own experiences with planning before and during the Second World War. After 1942, officials had engaged in long-range planning about the future of the empire. In Southeast Asia these plans focused on the restoration of British control in areas conquered by Japan, while in India, attention turned to the transition toward self-government.[12] In the West Indies and Africa, planning for economic development began during the war, when the Colonial Office pushed governments to submit proposals. In the initial stages, the West Indies received the bulk of the attention and available funds, channeled through the new colonial development agency headed by Frank Stockdale.[13]

Officials hoped that concrete development plans, backed by £120 million in new funding, would placate political activists and international critics, who saw colonial underdevelopment of as indicative of the broader failings of the empire.[14] Officials also believed that economic development would form part of a broader modernization of colonial societies that would move them along the path to self-rule.[15] Although London-based officials could create plans, implementing them in the colonies proved more difficult. The confused and coercive efforts of officials, particularly in Africa, often failed to achieve their objectives.[16] Like other developmentalist colonial regimes, the British often faced resistance or evasion from the erstwhile subjects of development that revealed the limits of their power.[17]

The scope of development plans varied widely. Plans for India and Burma faced an uncertain future, as independence proceeded at a more rapid pace.[18] In resource-rich areas like Malaya or Brunei, the British government hoped to reestablish prewar production levels and then use colonial commodities to earn badly needed dollars within the sterling area.[19] Officials attempted to align colonial development with British economic needs, especially the management of currency reserves.[20] In less developed parts of the empire like Africa, officials tried to maximize the output of local commodities to meet British needs and to expand state revenues. Despite the promise of development aid, British policies, especially controls on imports and exports, prevented colonial societies from benefiting from the increased output of their economies. The need to assist British recovery while fostering economic growth in the colonies created an ambiguity in the idea of development. Colonial development policy never served either end exclusively, and the emphasis shifted several times in the postwar era.[21] U.S. loans eased, but did not eliminate, the currency problems experienced by Britain after 1945. Even with Marshall Plan aid, Britain needed to manage the sterling area in order to maximize dollar earnings and minimize dollar imports.[22]

The Colonial Office tried to create a planning and development infrastructure to implement its vision of a new colonial order. In order to obtain funding, colonial governments submitted plans to London, where the Colonial Economic and Development Council (CEDC) reviewed them and forwarded them to the Treasury. Given the limitations of local administration, these plans often failed to provide an adequate framework for future action. Even the West Indies, which possessed its own development agency, fell short of the mark.[23] Arthur Lewis, the West Indian economist who served on the CEDC, disparaged the plans, arguing, "Most colonial administrators have not yet even begun to recognize the nature of their most important economic problems, let alone to make provision for dealing with them."[24] The CEDC itself failed to develop a consensus about planning and the limits of state power in its own discussions and split between more conservative officials like Sidney Caine and experts like Lewis, a conflict that dated back to the Second World War.[25] Problems with allocating resources and materials between the colonies and Britain led to the creation of a Colonial Development Working Party in 1947 to improve the process.[26] Despite efforts to bolster the CEDC, its value remained limited and it was dissolved in 1951.

Notwithstanding the difficulties of planning, the British government increased the level of funding provided through successive Colonial Development and Welfare (CDW) Acts. In 1956, the British extended the CDW Act to 1960, adding an addition £80 million to the roughly £140 million allocated from 1946 to 1956.[27] Further extensions of £95 million and £75 million in 1959 and 1964 brought the total allocated to £344 million from 1946 to 1970. The Colonial Development Corporation and the Overseas Food Corporation pursued their own projects, sometimes with disastrous results, such as the infamous Tanganyika groundnuts scheme. In addition, loans raised in London by colonial governments totaled some £283 million from 1948 to 1970. Last, revenues from colonial governments constituted the largest proportion of funding for development projects, peaking at 56 percent of the total for the period 1955–60.[28]

As development funding increased, so did the administrative capacity of the British colonial system. The postwar era witnessed the proliferation of advisory boards and experts. These advisors vetted research proposals in their areas, helping to distribute the £500,000 per year allocated for research by the CDW Acts of 1940 and 1945.[29] The expansion of advisory capacities occurred against the backdrop of an intensified recruitment campaign by the Colonial Service. Additional staff was needed to restore control to areas conquered by the Japanese during the war and to supplement colonial establishments diminished by personnel losses during the Depression and the war. This buildup of the colonial administration continued until the mid-1950s and facilitated the creation of a more interventionist colonial state.[30] The Colonial Office staff experienced a similar expansion, increasing from 460 officials in 1938 to approximately 1,200 in 1947.[31]

Although the British increased their development funding, the United States became the principal contributor to international assistance schemes.[32] With the end of the war in Europe, the United States provided billions in short-term aid to European economies through the United Nation Relief and Recovery Administration. The announcement of the Marshall Plan and the establishment of the European Recovery Program (ERP) in 1947 dramatically expanded the resources available and established international agencies to oversee its distribution.[33] The Americans also extended assistance to the colonial territories of the European powers through the Economic Cooperation Administration. Part of the rationale for this aid lay in the hope that increased dollar earnings by these colonies would supplement the dollar reserves of their colonial rulers, thus reducing the need for American aid. President Harry Truman's announcement of the Point Four Program in 1949 boosted aid to current and former colonies as part of an effort to forestall communist gains in the less developed world. Although this funding was in theory separate from ERP aid, American and British officials consulted with each other to avoid duplication of effort.[34] Although relatively modest, these programs would grow in the 1950s and received a boost with the establishment of the Agency for International Development (AID) in 1961.[35] It would be under the auspices of AID that the dramatic expansion of population programs occurred in the late 1960s.[36]

In addition to British colonial programs and U.S. aid, the 1950s saw the creation of international development programs. The Colombo Plan provided aid for Asian members of the Commonwealth as well as other states in Asia. Established in 1951, it included Britain, Australia, and Canada, as well as newer members of the Commonwealth. Britain and Australia hoped that increased aid to South Asia would stabilize the region and slow the advance of communism. Despite an initially lukewarm response, the United States agreed to help finance the plan after the outbreak of the Korean War.[37] The United Nations also provided assistance. In addition to the work of its Food and Agricultural Organization (FAO), the United Nations created agencies for technical assistance and development aid, culminating in the creation of the UN Development Programme in 1966.[38]

POPULATION AND THE NEW COLONIAL ORDER

The expansion of planning and development work formed the context within which population concerns received a more systematic examination by the colonial state. Social and economic development planning required accurate demographic information. To accomplish this goal, officials continued the effort to improve statistical and demographic services that began in the 1930s. Attempts to reform the system, begun by Robert Kuczynski, made only limited headway during the war due to limited budgets and a lack of personnel. The turbulent situation in parts of the empire after the war continued to present an obstacle. In Palestine, the refugee crisis forced the Mandatory Authority to cancel a planned census and instead rely on population estimates.[39] In Malaya, the problems of restoring a functioning government complicated the census mandated by the Long-Term Policy Directive on Social Welfare.[40] Kuczynski assisted officials in the West Indies, Southeast Asia, and Africa as they conducted new censuses. He also continued work on his multivolume study of imperial population. However, his illness and subsequent death in 1947 left the project unfinished. The Royal Institute of International Affairs published his study posthumously after his daughter agreed to help the Colonial Office produce a final version.[41] David Glass and W. F. Searle, the new chief statistician, assisted in the final preparations for publication.[42]

Kuczynski's death left the Colonial Office without a demographic advisor. David Glass, in part, filled the vacuum, serving as the UK representative to the United Nations Population Commission from 1946 to 1950 and assisting the Colonial Office. However, his burgeoning academic career at the London School of Economics (LSE) prevented him from taking on a full-time role in government service. The work of building a cadre of specialists thus fell to officials in London, especially W.F. Searle. Searle, a graduate of LSE, worked as a statistician for the Ministry of Food and the Ministry of Fuel and Power during the Second World War. He served as chief statistician at the Colonial Office from 1948 to 1961, after which he moved to the Department of Technical Cooperation.

Searle oversaw the final round of colonial censuses that followed the war. By 1950, this task largely accomplished, he focused on the expansion of the demographic and statistical capacity of the Colonial Office and overseas colonial governments. Having rejected Kuczynski's proposal for a separate Demographic Service, officials called for the creation of short training schemes in demography, modeled on programs offered by Oxford and LSE to members of the colonial service, the so-called

Devonshire schemes.[43] In addition to providing quantitative training to colonial officials, Searle expanded the recruitment of college graduates with statistical and mathematical degrees. Yet officials doubted if enough recruits could be persuaded to accept postings of 12–18 months in West Africa and up to four years in Hong Kong and Malaya, despite reasonably generous salaries.[44] Facing eighteen vacancies in the existing establishment, officials intended to send recruits directly to the colonies. Searle worried about sending out newly minted graduates who would soon encounter "the problems to be faced in practice, which are often very different from the selection made by text book writers preparing students for examination."[45] Even if these recruits succeeded, the question arose: What to do with them next? London-based officials knew that colonial governments would dislike bearing the cost of training such experts only to see them transferred to other duties or other colonies.[46]

The costs of training and retention also created difficulties. Many colonial governments could not afford to employ full-time statistical staff, and only larger colonies could maintain statistical departments. The quality of staff still varied widely. The East African Statistical Department (EASD) employed a number of qualified men, including its director, C. J. Martin, who published articles on African demography in the 1940s and 50s. The EASD held its own conference in the early 1950s and undertook a large-scale exploration of population and living conditions in cooperation with the Royal Commission on East Africa.[47] Yet small colonies were often understaffed. The West Indies departments remained fragmented and inefficient, and only those in Jamaica and Trinidad reached a reasonable standard; Searle felt that senior officials in the region displayed a limited interest in demographic and statistical information.[48]

Conferences in London in 1949 and 1953 brought together statisticians from throughout the empire to share their expertise and lay plans for future work.[49] The most important issue remained the colonial censuses. Although most colonies conducted counts from 1943 to 1950, only a handful planned to do so again before 1960. Some officials saw population sampling as a possible solution to the problems of conducting censuses.[50] Searle hoped to regularize the census process so that colonies would come into line with the recommendations of the United Nations Population Commission. Yet demographic information remained spotty at best, especially in British Africa. The expansion of statistical work competed against a number of demands for resources, and many governments failed to give it a high priority. By the end of the 1950s, the

British government still lacked an adequate machinery to assess demographic trends.

In addition to expanding the statistical services within the colonial establishment, the Colonial Office also increased its support for research by outside experts. From 1940 to 1946, the government spent a total of £6,310 on demographic research and a further £13,500 on experts' salaries.[51] In the postwar years, the Colonial Social Science Research Council (CSSRC) reviewed future research needs and argued for increased attention to population studies. To accomplish this task, it funded demographic projects by independent and government researchers. This work benefited from the expansion of regional research groups, such as East African Institute of Social Research and the South Pacific Commission Research Council.[52] The latter sponsored a demographic survey of the South Pacific by Dr. N.R. MacArthur of the Australian National University in the early 1950s.[53] In East Africa, officials made plans to bolster demographic research in the region, requesting £200,000 over five years and seeking advice from outside experts.[54]

The Colonial Office, through the CSSRC and the Statistical Department, developed demographers within its own ranks. T.E. Smith, an official from Singapore, worked with the Colonial Office and the Department of Technical Cooperation.[55] He published a study of the population of Malaya in 1954 and served as a lecturer at the Institute for Commonwealth Studies. In 1959 the CSSRC considered a proposal to give Smith £6,000 to undertake a two-year study of African population trends that would update Kuczynski's survey.[56] William Brass, who served in the East African Statistical Department from 1948 to 1955, became an important figure in African demography and in the 1960s helped create the Centre for Overseas Population Studies at the London School of Hygiene and Tropical Medicine.[57] Another colonial official, G..W. Roberts, also became a well-known demographer of the West Indies. Originally an official in British Guiana, in 1949 Roberts became an assistant to L.G. Hopkins and then served as vital statistics officer for the CDW organization in Barbados and a professor at the University of the West Indies.[58]

One reason for this increased interest in demographic research lay in the realization that the issue of population growth represented a far more complicated issue than originally thought. In addition to their desire for improved demographic information officials wanted to understand the social and economic forces behind population trends. This new focus led the CSSRC to support research into family life and attitudes. In 1945, the CSSRC discussed the work of T.S. Simey, Charles Booth Professor of Social Science at the University of Liverpool and the Social Welfare Advisor to the West Indian Development and Welfare Organization from 1941 to 1945. Simey's 1946 book *Welfare and Planning in the West Indies* linked the economic problems of the region to population growth. He paid particular attention to the nature of family life and its relationship to the problems of the West Indies and argued that only a reconstruction of West Indian society along lines suggested by rigorous social analysis would allow the region to escape its social disorganization and poverty.[59] The Development and Welfare organization of the West Indies also supported the LSE anthropologist Edith Clarke's study of peasant family life in the West Indies.[60] Clarke published her book, *My Mother Who Fathered Me*, in 1957.[61]

The largest project of this kind, the Jamaican Family Life Survey, examined attitudes about family life and birth control in Jamaica. The study, based on a similar project in Puerto Rico by the American demographers J. Mayone Stycos, Kurt Black, and Ruben Hill, began in 1954 as a pilot project funded by the Conservation Foundation, which approached the Colonial Office in 1956 about expanding the study.[62] The Colonial Office, the Conservation Foundation, and the government of Jamaica cooperated in its design and implementation. The project received £7,000 in funding through the CSSRC and CDW funds, £10,000 from the Nuffield Foundation, and a further $25,000 from the Conservation Foundation.[63] Jamaica's governor, Sir Hugh Foot, worked with the Jamaican leader, Norman Manley, a longtime supporter of birth control, to ensure that no political problems ensued.[64] To lessen potential criticism, a local committee called the Population Research Foundation, which included twenty-two prominent Jamaicans, sponsored the study. In addition, the project called for training research workers at the University of the West Indies.[65] Although the full study would not be published until 1961, a preliminary report of the results in 1957 argued that Jamaicans would be receptive to efforts to encourage family planning.[66]

The Colonial Office sought outside funding because of its limited resources. Of the £605,000 allocated for research for 1955–60, only £15–20,000 remained, forcing officials to look elsewhere for research funds.[67] In some cases officials proved willing to accept funds from UN agencies like UNESCO, WHO, and the FAO despite the unease that they felt about an increased role for the United Nations in colonial issues.[68] Officials also hoped to tap private resources as during the interwar years, when foundations like the Rockefeller Foundation and the Carnegie Corporation funded colonial research. The Colonial Office continued to rely on these foundations after the war and also approached the Ford Foundation for support of population projects.[69] Although this reliance on American foundations necessitated some discussion of the limits to American influence, both countries increasingly cooperated in population policy and research.[70]

The Colonial Office sought support for social science research from private sources in the United Kingdom. It worked with the Nuffield Foundation from its formation in 1943 and hoped to persuade Lord Nuffield and his foundation to support colonial research.[71] As one official put it, "I understand from other sources that Lord Nuffield is as yet by no means colony conscious . . . . His Foundation could be of great use to us in many ways in the future if his enthusiasm could be aroused."[72] The Colonial Office developed a close relationship with the foundation's director Leslie Farrar-Brown, who served on the CSSRC. In addition to funding the Jamaican Family Life project, the foundation gave scholarships to overseas colonial officials and funded a study of West Indian immigrants in Britain.[73] From the early 1950s onward the foundation expressed greater interest in world population issues and increased its support for demographic research.[74]

POPULATION AND SECURITY IN THE POSTWAR WORLD

Even as the Colonial Office expanded its demographic services after 1945, other ministries followed suit. The Foreign Office Research Department (FORD) produced a series of assessments of the populations of Japan, Germany, and Italy.[75] This work involved creating accurate population estimates for the occupation authorities, which needed to plan the supply of food and other resources for the immediate future. The researchers also devoted considerable effort to producing long-range population estimates for the defeated powers, as well as for Europe as a whole. They expressed concern over the rapid expansion of population of the western zone in Germany and argued that excess population represented an obstacle to German development. In an effort to avoid such problems, they raised the possibility of sponsored immigration and examined the potential barriers to birth control posed by existing laws in Germany.[76]

The postwar occupation of Japan provoked a similar discussion. Officials believed that Japan faced an imminent population crisis. Given the difficulties of the food situation in Japan, much of the initial debate revolved around the impact of malnutrition upon population growth. In the short term, emigration seemed to provide the only possible solution, but officials recognized that Western governments would not open their doors to large numbers of Japanese migrants. Researchers focused on the possibilities of raising food output, including more intensive settlement of the northern island of Hokkaido. For the British, the best solution seemed clear; the systematic provision of birth control. Researchers cited historical evidence that birth control had been widely used before the Meiji Era and saw no fundamental religious or cultural barriers to its the reintroduction.[77] After the adoption of the Eugenic Protection Law of 1948, which legalized abortion and eased access to birth control, Japanese fertility began a steep decline. This decline, as well as the dramatic expansion of the Japanese economy, eased worries that a Malthusian crisis in Japan could lead to political turmoil.[78]

The Foreign Office also spent considerable time examining the demographic situation in Italy. Observers argued that Italy suffered from overpopulation, which they linked to high unemployment.[79] British officials believed that birth control would not be acceptable in Italy and instead focused on plans to foster economic growth and encourage emigration to relieve population pressure. Apparently the Italian government shared this view; in the words of one official, "De Gasperi [the Italian Prime Minister] [was] obsessed with the population pressures in Italy which he felt could be solved only by encouraging emigration."[80] Some suggestions were nonstarters, such as the proposal to settle large numbers of Italians in the Middle East using American capital and British managers. Other plans existed for relocating Italian workers in eastern and central Africa to supply a labor force for development. This transfer of surplus workers would relieve pressure on the Italian government and help forestall the coming to power of the left.[81] Officials felt that the program also served to reassure Italians about the intentions of the British government, especially in light of the unsettled question of former Italian colonies in the region.[82]

These plans, like those for Germany, formed part of a larger Organization for European Economic Cooperation (OEEC) effort at reconstruction. Researchers emphasized the necessity of controlling population growth and encouraging emigration to assist the integration of these countries into the Western bloc. FORD researchers discussed the feasibility of large-scale immigration schemes. Much of their attention focused on possible destinations for European migrants. In addition to Africa, officials also considered the United States and other developed regions.[83] These discussions found some support in the work of the Intergovernmental

Committee for European Migration, which received financial backing from the United States in the 1950s.[84]

The Foreign Office also tracked global demographic trends.[85] The onset of the Cold War naturally focused attention on Eastern Europe and China.[86] Even before the communist victory in 1949, British officials monitored the size and activities of the overseas Chinese populations in Hong Kong and Malaya.[87] After the establishment of the People's Republic, officials in London and China kept an eye on demographic trends. The rapid growth of China's population generated anxiety, leading one observer to argue that "population, like water, if it rises above a certain point it may spread over the surrounding land."[88]

EMPIRE, POPULATION, AND MIGRATION IN THE POSTWAR YEARS

As during the interwar years, migration represented a central demographic issue in the postwar era. The creation of an Afro-Caribbean community in Britain in the 1950s represented a dramatic shift in British life and portended the influx of other ethnic groups in the 1960s and 1970s.[89] For the Colonial Office, West Indian migration formed one part of a larger effort to manage migration. Race and ethnicity played a central role in how officials viewed migration and the solutions they constructed, even as their policies generated racial and ethnic tensions.

The Colonial Office and the British government continued to encourage British settlement in the empire and Commonwealth. During the war, politicians like Clement Attlee spoke of the need to ensure the flow of settlers to these areas and made plans to resume financial support for such schemes as soon as conditions allowed.[90] This policy prevailed despite Sir Alan Pim's study of the prospects for white settlement in the empire, which concluded that the colonies offered limited opportunities for migrants.[91] Officials offered a variety of rationales for supporting immigration programs. Many believed that these initiatives would foster a shared "Britishness" in the empire and Commonwealth.[92] Select migration, especially to areas "suitable" for British settlement, would increase the flow of capital and skilled labor to colonial economies. Others pointed to the vulnerability of the Commonwealth and the need to bolster its population. As Viscount Addison, the secretary of state for the Dominions, argued in 1945, "We are in agreement that the right policy for the United Kingdom government is to do all that is practicable to assist Australia (and any other Dominion) to build up their population as quickly as possible and to do so from British stock." He went on to assert "the overriding importance of a better distribution of population within the British Commonwealth on Defence and other grounds."[93]

The desire to shelter Britain from future attack and to strengthen the Commonwealth found its most far-reaching expression in a plan for a large-scale dispersion of British population and industry throughout the empire. First raised in November 1947 by the Home Defence Committee, it was supported by H. T. Tizard, the chief scientific advisor to the government, who argued, "in the atomic bomb age . . . a better distribution of population . . . especially of British stock in Africa and Australia would not only greatly ease our Home Defence problem, but would be a great source of strength in war."[94] Tizard suggested the possibility of the migration of entire communities, while one official recommended a minimum of 3 million to as many as 15 million migrants over a twenty-five year period.[95] The cabinet debated the idea before shelving it for fear of political fallout should the plan become public.[96]

Although rejecting mass emigration, the Labour government committed itself to a goal of at least 25,000 British migrants a year despite labor shortages. Although officials supported British migration, they feared that "undesirable" groups might demand the right to migrate to Great Britain, the "white Dominions" and the empire. Colonial workers and soldiers were in theory eligible for overseas settlement schemes or foreign worker programs that brought badly needed labor to Britain. Officials hoped to exclude colonial subjects like the West Indians and the Maltese from these schemes by requiring participants to have resided in the United Kingdom before 1938. As one official pointed out, "It would be embarrassing if all these (colonial ex-servicemen) were made eligible and if the Dominions were then to reject coloured applicants, as it would be impossible to conceal the fact that they were rejected on grounds of colour."[97] At the same time, the British government recruited European refugees to fill positions in the United Kingdom.[98] These policies, along with British acquiescence to the racially exclusive immigration policies of the Commonwealth countries, opened the British to criticism from colonial nationalists and newly independent states.[99]

Despite this criticism, the British continued to differentiate between racial and ethnic groups in their management of population movements in the empire. Officials justified such policies by the need to maintain the proper balance of ethnic and racial groups within individual colonies and the empire as a whole.[100] In the immediate postwar period the Colonial

Office maintained existing limits on imperial migration. In Palestine, the Colonial Office struggled to retain control in the face of massive illegal immigration and growing communal strife that ultimately overwhelmed the Mandatory government.[101] In Southeast Asia, Chinese immigration into Malaya, Singapore, and Borneo led the government to consider severe limits on this flow for political and security reasons.[102] The presence of large numbers of refugees complicated the reoccupation of Hong Kong and raised the specter of a flood of refugees in the event of a Nationalist defeat.[103] The British government continued the limits on free movement imposed during the war, ignoring Chinese protests.[104] These restrictions failed to halt the flow of Chinese refugees into the colony, despite the Hong Kong government's refusal to provide adequate services for the rapidly expanding population. Only in the wake of international attention to conditions in Hong King in the 1950s would British authorities take a more active role in settling these refugees, in conjunction with NGOs, the United Nations, and the United States.[105]

The contradictions of this race-based migration policy became evident in East Africa. Despite claims of race neutrality and an official policy that placed African interests first, the British favored the European settler community and sought to secure its place in the region. The war produced a boom for settler farmers and enhanced their political position in Uganda, Tanganyika, and Kenya. The settler community in Kenya, the largest and most important in the region, pushed for higher levels of white immigration, particularly from Britain, to bolster their position. Despite the failure of official settlement schemes, the European community in Kenya grew substantially after 1945, reaching a peak of 61,000 on the eve of decolonization in the early 1960s.[106]

The Colonial Office faced several challenges to its pro-settler policy. One came from the Foreign Office, which hoped to settle European refugees and Italian workers in East Africa.[107] The Colonial Office, which exercised an effective veto over plans involving colonial territories, balked at these plans. Colonial administrators argued that African colonies could not absorb large numbers of Europeans without provoking economic and political difficulties. Andrew Cohen and other officials cited the Pim report to support this view and invoked the need to protect native interests.[108] Foreign Office officials characterized such arguments as disingenuous and rejected colonial administrators' claims of impartiality. As one said, "The Colonial Office are out to protect the interests of British settlers—both present and future—from Italian competition, but there is another side to the question."[109] Another official argued, "We must cut out the pious explanation to the effect that our sole motive is concern for the welfare of the native populations."[110] The Foreign Office saw the policy of reserving territories for British settlers as unsustainable in the long run. As one official noted, "Personally I doubt whether in face of the ever growing economic and demographic needs of Europe we shall be able to indefinitely maintain the policy of protecting the natives against European immigration."[111]

Plans for Italian immigration drew only tepid support from British settlers, who questioned their suitability. The Colonial Office expressed apprehension about the character of potential Italian settlers and feared that Italians would become a poor white class in East Africa.[112] They also worried that communist troublemakers might be imported into East Africa, concerns heightened by reports of unrest in labor camps in Kenya.[113] Although Italian POWs and workers participated in small-scale schemes in Kenya, the more ambitious ideas of the Foreign Office never came to fruition. In the end, the Foreign Office accepted that East Africa could not absorb large numbers of European settlers.[114]

The question of South Asian immigration to East Africa proved to be a thornier issue. In the interwar years, it had provoked political controversy in East Africa, especially Kenya. Wartime controls had further limited migration, but with the end of the war, the South Asian community pushed for an end to these restrictions. The East African Indian National Congress raised the issue and drew support from the subcontinent. In 1946 the head of the organization argued, "The White Races have taken good care to shut the doors of almost all new countries to them." Letters from dignitaries such as the Aga Khan reinforced this demand for reopening East Africa to Indian immigration.[115] After 1947, the Indian government took up the issue through its External Affairs Department and its Protector of Emigrants, as well as the Office of the High Commissioner.[116]

Officials resented this pressure and accused Indians of using the charge of racism to bully the British government.[117] In private, they attacked the Indian government for encouraging migration.[118] As one official argued, "The Government of India has never bothered to conceal their view of British East Africa as a suitable area for the accommodation of India's surplus population."[119] They also questioned the political tendencies of the Indian community, portraying them as anti-European and likely to combine with the Africans against the white community. Given the politically sensitive nature of the subject, the Colonial Office moved cautiously in public. Officials denied any desire to discriminate against South Asians and couched their defense of restrictions in terms of political stability and the interests of the African population.[120]

Philip Rogers dismissed economic arguments against restrictions, pointing out that Africans could compete for jobs and that a shortage of skilled workers impeded economic development in the region. Instead, he emphasized political considerations, most important the desire to foster the growth of a European community. Since Europeans already feared being swamped politically and socially by Africans, "The main aim of our policy is to give him [the European] security for the future and to reassure his fears to a degree which will induce him to let the African come forward.... I submit therefore that a restriction of the present rate of Indian immigration into East Africa is on balance desirable in the interests of the East African territories, including of course the interests of the Africans. That view is, I am sure, shared by senior officers in the East African Governments. It is widespread among the European communities and I am sure among Africans who think about it."[121]

Other officials agreed with Rogers. One official argued that "the operation of a form of logistical Gresham's Law had already shown signs of beginning to take effect as the increased numbers of Indian immigrants are matched by the rise in European emigration figures."[122]

The problem, as Andrew Cohen argued in June 1950, was how to stop Indian migration without seeming overtly discriminatory.[123] The passage of the 1948 British Nationality Act further complicated the issue by bestowing on Indians certain rights of residence within the empire. According to J.S. Ward, "It is and will be necessary to get around the provisions of Section 6(1) of the British Nationality Act if Asian Immigration into East Africa is to be effectively controlled.... We know that India is looking for 'lebensraum' in Africa for her surplus population and Asian immigration must be kept down to reasonable level."[124] The Colonial Office advised colonial governments to avoid using legislative action such as quotas or outright bans on Asian migration. Instead, it suggested that governments employ administrative methods, allowing local officials broad powers of discretion over the entry and residency of nonnative migrants. Officials pointed to procedures in Malaya and Singapore "designed ... at restricting Chinese immigration into Malaya without saying so."[125] East African governments used similar procedures to exclude unwanted immigrants.[126] They relied on temporary work permits, combined with strict limits on residency, as well as financial and other requirements that favored European migrants. At the heart of the system was the individual officer, empowered to deny access to anyone considered undesirable. Despite these measures, the Asian population of East Africa reached some 350,000 by the 1960s, in large part due to a high rate of natural increase.[127]

POPULATION AND EMPIRE UNDER LABOUR

Although migration forced officials to consider demographic questions as a matter of day-to-day administration, the British government moved haltingly toward a more systematic approach to population. Many officials in the Colonial Office recognized the need to take a longer-term view of population. The proliferation of advisors to the Colonial Office increased the flow of information to officials and ministers; demographic issues formed part of that flow. However, although advisory groups considered population trends relevant to their work, discussions of population policy by senior officials and ministers occurred in a more irregular fashion. During the Labour Government's term in office from 1945 to 1951, no one body within the Colonial Office or the government was responsible for tracking demographic trends or formulating a population policy. The actions of local governments remained uncoordinated, and most activity occurred at the regional level.

After 1945, advisory groups within the Colonial Office moved toward a comprehensive approach to population. They linked food production, population growth, medical services, and development and called for the Colonial Office to take all of these factors into account when planning for the future. In 1948 the Colonial Advisory Council on Agriculture (CACA) and the Colonial Medical Advisory Council (CMAC) considered imperial population trends. Discussions in the CAAC about future trends in imperial food production led to a debate about the impact of population growth on agriculture. Several members argued that population pressure was beginning to affect some regions, especially more arid ones, and could force a shift away from stock-rearing to grain production. Dr. Norman Wright, who had previously served on the Scientific Advisory Mission to the Middle East, suggested a central body to study the relationship between food supplies and population pressure.[128] Soon afterward the Colonial Office created a Working Party on Food Supplies and Communism to examine the relationship between hunger and political unrest in the empire. The group stressed the importance of increasing food supplies to meet the needs of a population larger than previously thought.[129]

Under the leadership of the new medical advisor, Eric Pridie, the

CMAC focused on the relationship between medical policy and population.[130] In early 1948 CMAC members discussed a memorandum by T. H. Davey of the Liverpool School of Tropical Medicine that reviewed population trends in the empire and warned about the possibility of rapid growth as a consequence of medical advances. He argued that in the short term, production of food must be increased through the adoption of more efficient agriculture, a point amplified by J. H. Seddon, who called for the expansion of plantation agriculture and industry.[131] CMAC also worried about the impact of population growth on medical policy. Members feared that if improvements in public health led to falling mortality and population growth, the standard of living might fall.[132] Such circumstances could lead colonial governments to reconsider the wisdom of increased spending on medical services.[133]

Like CAAC, CAMC called for an integrated approach to the study of population trends. As one official noted:

> This subject brought forward by Professor Davey is one of great importance and one which must have exercised the minds of all who think seriously of colonial problems and it would . . . be a very good thing to have it brought into the open and fully discussed. . . . The salient point to my mind is that there must be far more integration between the various departments of Government. . . . If by the endeavors of medical departments we increase the expectation of life, reduce the death statistics and by child welfare and maternity work ensure that the heavy loss in infant life is materially reduced, and yet do not, at the same time, take steps to produce a concomitant improvement in economic standards, it is at least arguable that the final stage will be worse than the first.[134]

Despite such suggestions, divisions remained over how to respond. Some officials proposed the creation of a separate body to study the issue, while others hoped to use the existing advisory councils. They all saw the difficulties of proceeding given the limitations of current knowledge, and several suggested that a team of researchers and experts should undertake a review of the problem.[135] Although some officials urged immediate action, others argued that population pressure would only become a real threat in a decade or more, giving the British government time to make plans.[136] In the face of this uncertainty, senior officials maintained the status quo and left it to the advisory groups and regional departments to continue their discussions.

The absence of a central body responsible for tracking and analyzing imperial demographic trends reflected the limitations of the new postwar imperial state. Although senior officials were aware of the possible impact of population growth on imperial plans, the responsibility for action on issues with potential demographic consequences like migration and agriculture remained in the hands of colonial governments. The Colonial Office tried to create an overall policy toward such matters, but its powers to compel action were limited. For Labour ministers, the concerns of experts about population competed with a series of crises that demanded their attention—independence for South Asia, the collapse of the mandate in Palestine, the insurgency in Malaya, the victory of the communists in China, the Korean War, and the shaky condition of Britain's finances. In such circumstances, long-term demographic planning remained at best a secondary concern. An aggressive population policy, with its potential for political controversy, must have seemed unpromising.

One consequence of this situation was the embedding of demographic concerns in the local politics of empire. Population issues could not be abstracted from the social and political context of individual colonies. Although experts at the center might see birth control, migration controls, and agricultural modernization as objective responses to the obvious problem of overpopulation, for colonial administrators and subjects they touched on aspects of everyday life, from marriage to land use, which raised larger issues of political and social power. In the postwar era, no one outside the colonial establishment saw the British as impartial actors. Efforts to manage populations inevitably acquired the political baggage of empire and thus remained either ineffective or overtly coercive. Only after the transfer of power, when new colonial elites gained power, could population control be repackaged as development aid from neutral parties.

THE WEST INDIES AND LABOUR'S POSTWAR POPULATION POLICY

For the Labour government, the West Indies represented the most pressing example of imperial overpopulation. Concern about West Indian population dated back to the 1930s. The Moyne Commission report, although not publicly released until 1945, linked the region's problems of poverty and unemployment to population growth. The Colonial Development Act of 1940, passed in the shadow of the West Indian riots and the outbreak of the war, directed a disproportionate share of resources to the islands.[137] The situation in the West Indies remained tense, which the inability of the British government to deliver on its financial promises exacerbated.[138]

Even with the expansion of development funding under the Colonial Development and Welfare Act of 1945, officials remained pessimistic about the long-term prospects of the region, in part due to continuing population growth. The beginning of mass migration from the West Indies in the late 1940s made the issue increasingly significant and triggered a search for a solution that accelerated under the Conservatives in the 1950s.[139] However, despite growing concern about overpopulation, the Colonial Office failed to persuade West Indian governments to pursue a more aggressive policy.

In the immediate postwar era, officials again focused their attention on migration as a possible solution to population pressure. Calls by the West Indian Conference of the Anglo-American Commission on the Caribbean and the Fabian Colonial Bureau for the resettlement of islanders to the mainland colonies of British Honduras and British Guiana prompted the colonial secretary, Arthur Creech Jones, to create a commission to study the proposal.[140] The Evans Commission, in its report issued in November 1948, argued that 25,000 workers, or a total of 100,000 people including families, could be resettled in the two colonies. The commission envisioned the creation of large-scale plantation enterprises, funded by a mix of private and public capital, with the governments of the West Indies and the Colonial Development Corporation holding a majority of the shares. Despite the publicity generated by the commission and subsequent discussions among officials and governments, its recommendations were not pursued. As with previous plans for mass migration in the region, the costs and political difficulties involved proved too great. Officials also recognized that even a plan that accommodated 100,000 people would not reduce population growth.[141]

The inability to find a regional solution led the Colonial Office to consider alternative destinations. It faced pressure from West Indian activists, who complained about the coexistence of unemployment in the region with the recruitment of European labor in Britain.[142] In response, the permanent undersecretary of state, Sir Thomas Lloyd, approached Sir Godfrey Ince at the Ministry of Labour about the possibility of employing "surplus" colonial labor, especially West Indians, in Britain. Ince responded that European migrants enjoyed a special status as displaced persons and that the cold climate and racial prejudice against West Indians made them unsuitable candidates for employment in Britain.[143] However, Ince and Lloyd agreed that an interdepartmental committee drawn from the Home Office, the Ministry of Labour, and the Colonial Office should study the problem, and the Working Party on the

Employment of Surplus Colonial Labour began meeting in the summer of 1948.[144] Despite attempts by Colonial Office staff to obtain support from other ministries, the Working Party's final report in June 1949 recommended against any large-scale program to bring West Indian workers to Britain. Ministry of Labour officials and others repeatedly referred to the problems of housing and employing black workers in the country. They also cast doubt on the skills and motivation of "lazy and unreliable" West Indians and questioned the need for their labor. The report linked overpopulation and unemployment in the West Indies. It rejected emigration as a solution given the rapid increase in population and the limited ability of other countries to absorb migrants. Instead it argued that only slower population growth would address the problem.[145]

The Colonial Office rejected such arguments. As A. J. Fairclough noted in 1950, "I cannot help feeling that the real difficulty is the colour question and although the problems that this can cause are certainly genuine ones, they can be overemphasized."[146] Fairclough restated a point made by Colonial Office officials during the Working Party's deliberations: increasing numbers of West Indians were arriving and jobs existed for them. This reality shaped official responses to colonial migration throughout the 1950s.[147]

Despite disagreements with other ministries, the Colonial Office had already accepted the need to address West Indian population growth. In 1948, at the request of Creech Jones, W. D. Sweaney prepared a memorandum on overpopulation in the region. Sweaney linked overpopulation to unemployment and underemployment, arguing, "The high birth rate is undoubtedly the greatest menace to the standard of living of both present and future generations."[148] He argued that birth control represented the only viable solution. Sweaney called for a campaign to convince the public of the necessity of birth control, which he hoped would allow for the creation of clinics similar to those provided in Britain by local authorities. Creech Jones echoed these arguments in a memo for the Cabinet Commonwealth Affairs Committee and a dispatch to West Indian governors in early 1949.[149]

Creech Jones's endorsement of Sweaney's memo reflected the agreement among London-based officials about the demographic situation in the West Indies. During the late 1930s and early 1940s proponents of birth control like Philip Rogers clashed with critics of birth control like Sir Alan Burns. By the late 1940s, this opposition faded, and discussions increasingly focused on the political and practical obstacles to family planning. In London the case for population control seemed clear. As the minister for state, Lord Listowel, argued in a letter in 1949 to Sir Hubert Rance, the comptroller of development and welfare for the West Indies:

> Those of us who deal with the West Indies, including Arthur Creech Jones and myself, have been extremely concerned about the annual excess of births over deaths, which doesn't appear to have diminished since the Moyne Commission reported.... Of course it is easy to see if population doubles in the next thirty years ... the moment will come when the present miserable standard of living will begin to fall. Thereafter the money poured into the West Indies by the British taxpayer will simply serve to prevent standards falling as low as they would otherwise do. What we don't know is whether it is possible to take any action now to prevent this disaster from happening.[150]

For officials, the solution for what one referred to as the "cancer" of overpopulation lay in the provision of birth control. Yet they acknowledged the potential problems created by official support for a campaign of population control aimed at a primarily working-class Afro-Caribbean population. Creech Jones understood the political difficulties involved. His brief statement in the House of Commons in February 1949 in support of family planning in the West Indies provoked a negative response from the opposition and politicians in the West Indies.[151] West Indian governors argued that no government could advocate birth control, despite their private belief that it would be necessary in the long run. They cited strong religious objections and the potential for racial and class divisions about the subject. The governor of British Honduras argued that efforts to promote family planning might be seen as an "Attempt at racial strangulation and a subtle design by the white man to keep the rising power of the black man in check.... It will be argued that the black man is made to sweat out his life in the West Indies in order to produce cheap crops to enable the white man to live, not only in social security, but in a way which encourages him to increase the size of his family and thus to maintain his racial dominance."[152]

The governors also noted that poorer members of the community, the source of the problem in their minds, would not be swayed by arguments in favor of birth control. As the governor of Trinidad stated in his reply to Creech Jones, "The majority of the people are too ignorant, feckless and poverty stricken to be capable of practicing these methods even if they could be persuaded to try."[153] Other governors and officials in London shared this view of West Indians, arguing that their sexual behavior lay at the root of the problem. They believed that little could be done to improve the situation as long as the attitudes of the poor remained unchanged. In their minds, the prevalence of illegitimacy contributed to overpopulation by encouraging "reckless reproduction." Only by regularizing family life could the problem be addressed. To accomplish this end, the governors called for legal reforms to discourage illegitimacy, especially stronger bastardy laws.[154] Ironically this assertion would later be shown to be false by two colonial officials from the West Indies, G. W. Roberts and Dora Ibberson.[155]

Many officials focused on the need to persuade West Indians of the severity of the problem. They argued that most West Indians still believed that emigration and more development spending could alleviate the problem. As Sweaney noted, "Many people in the West Indies do not recognize that there is any population problem. They take the line that, if only HMG would do more to encourage the development of secondary industries and economic development generally, there would be plenty of jobs for all."[156] To counter these views, West Indian governors and the Colonial Office agreed in late 1949 to produce a pamphlet to raise public awareness about overpopulation.[157] Yet this effort foundered over fears about how West Indians would respond. Officials felt that only more "intelligent members" of the community would understand, not "the man in the cane field."[158] It also proved difficult to discuss population growth without suggesting a solution. The obvious solution for officials, birth control, might not be so obvious to others. As one economist observed, the pamphlet failed to answer the question why more investment would not solve the problem.[159] The project was abandoned, and efforts to address West Indian population growth would have to wait for several more years.

THE CONSERVATIVES AND POPULATION POLICY IN THE 1950S

The coming to power of a Conservative government in 1951 had little impact on the evolution of population policy in the Colonial Office, despite the party's differences with Labour over the empire. The Conservatives, who ruled from 1951 to 1964, took a more cautious view of colonial reform and offered greater support for settler regimes in Africa. While they presided over the decolonization of much of the empire, they also prosecuted counterinsurgency campaigns in several territories, most notably Malaya and Kenya. The acceleration of decolonization in the late 1950s radically shifted the focus of the Colonial Office, which began to plan for the transition to independence.[160] These events led to the virtual dismantling of the colonial service and the transfer of development projects to the newly independent states. For much of the 1950s, however, the Conservatives continued to support colonial development, while the permanent officials with an interest in population remained in place. The rapid increase in West Indian migration raised the visibility of demographic issues and generated interest at the highest levels of government. This interest led to a systematic examination of imperial and global population by the Advisory Council on Scientific Policy (ACSP), which was created in 1947 to advise the cabinet on scientific matters. This review was the genesis of British efforts to devise a global population policy in the 1960s and 1970s. The Conservatives maintained Labour's agricultural, migration, and resettlement polices but remained hesitant to acknowledge their desire to control colonial populations. They offered tacit support for private family planning efforts and permitted colonial governments to support birth control agencies but refused to allow central government funding for such services. Frustrated officials could only fume and press for a change in policy.

Like the Labour government that preceded them, the Conservatives took notice of demographic issues in large part because of West Indian immigration to Britain. Surprised by the rapid growth of the West Indian community, the government created an interdepartmental Working Party on Colonial Immigration and Employment to consider the scale of the problem and possible responses. The home secretary, in a brief to the cabinet, estimated that 10,000 West Indians entered Britain in 1954 and projected that the number could rise to as many as 20,000 in 1955. Officials set about to devise a way to restrict this flow without appearing overtly discriminatory or provoking a negative response from the West Indies.[161]

It fell to the Colonial Office to devise a plan to limit West Indian immigration. Officials dismissed the idea that control could be imposed at the source, given the scale of the movement, its complexity, and the limited resources of West Indian governments. They also reminded other ministries of the possible political fallout from legislation aimed only at nonwhite migrants. White Commonwealth residents and Irish citizens were allowed free access to Britain; any effort to differentiate among migrants by race would conflict with the nominally equal status of all migrants from the Commonwealth and empire.[162] Although initially reluctant to impose restrictions, officials changed their minds as West Indian immigration increased. Some officials suggested that the techniques employed in the empire to control migration without legislation might offer a solution. The use of the discretionary powers by governors and immigration officials in East Africa, Fiji, the Seychelles, and Hong Kong showed the potential for control without legislative action.[163] As one official argued in 1955, "Commonwealth immigration into the UK and Asian immigration into Tanganyika are presenting similar problems. It may well be that administrative and legislative methods to control the former will have the desired effect on the latter."[164] As concern over immigration increased in the 1950s, the British government relied on similar practices to control migration prior to the enactment of legislation in 1962.[165]

Supporters of population control in the Colonial Office used the concern about West Indian migration to push for a more forward policy. Philip Rogers put it this way: "It will in my view do no good service to the future of the Colonies in question if they remain under the impression that they can solve their own population problems by uncontrolled immigration to the UK."[166] In 1956, Thomas Lloyd called attention to the "truly alarming increase in West Indian migration" and argued, "Whilst full employment remains it is a comfortable solution to Jamaica's overpopulation problem, so comfortable in fact that little or nothing is being done to advance family planning which is the only real solution. Even if Jamaica is not prepared to face up to the truth we surely must."[167]

The connection made by the Colonial Office among migration, overpopulation, and family planning proved to a persuasive one. As the home secretary R. A. Butler put it in 1958, "The Home Office is, of course much interested in this subject [family planning], because it is largely as a result of population pressure in the Colonies that we are having to cope with the very embarrassing flow of colonial immigrants to this country. We would, therefore, welcome any steps that could properly be taken to ease the pressure; and I am interested in what is said in the memorandum accompanying your letter about the work already done in Jamaica."[168]

Despite the efforts of Rogers and other officials and the growing interest of ministers, the Colonial Office refused to change its position. This stalemate led Rogers to advise West Indian governments about how they could encourage family planning efforts and still remain in compliance with official policy. He recommended that governments, after consulting with prominent members of the community, should encourage voluntary groups to provide information and birth control services and pointed to the work of the International Planned Parenthood Federation (IPPF) as an example.[169] West Indian governments took his advice, and by the end of the 1950s, a network of mostly private clinics existed in the region.[170]

However, such programs had little effect on overall growth rates or emigration from the West Indies.

The linkage between population growth and migration led to a renewed attention to demographic issues. In 1953 the ACSP began a review of global population trends. The leading figure in this process would be Solly Zuckerman, the council's deputy chair. After preliminary discussions in 1953, the ACSP decided to take an in-depth look at the subject and asked Zuckerman produce a report on methods of population control.[171] Zuckerman's report provided an overview of world population trends and work being done in the United States, especially studies of the social aspects of population growth.[172]

The ACSP also requested that the Colonial Office report on demographic trends and population policy in the empire. In November 1955, Philip Rogers and several other officials met with Zuckerman to discuss how to proceed.[173] The preparation of the report gave officials who supported population control an opportunity to voice their opinions on the topic. As one of them argued, "After this immediate exercise is over, I hope that the population question may be looked at afresh. The subject of birth control, has in my opinion, been treated with excessive caution in the past.... Some of the points made in Mr. Kendall's paper [about population trends] present a challenge... which should not be evaded any longer. That they have been evaded in the past is I think undeniable."[174]

The report, finished in early 1956, reviewed growth rates in the colonies and offered predictions for future growth and its impact on economic development. It rejected the idea that migration could relieve overpopulation and discussed birth control efforts in the empire. The report stressed the problem of a white government recommending population control for non-white populations and emphasized that the Colonial Office's role was limited to publicity, social research, and encouraging local governments to act. It also suggested that programs of social development, by encouraging changes in employment and family structure, might help initiate changes in the birth rate. This latter approach, termed the "indirect approach" by Zuckerman, reflected the influence of demographic transition theory on the discussions.[175]

By early 1957, ACSP members were in general agreement about the importance of the issue. As the minutes of one meeting noted, "The population problem in Colonial Territories was probably even more urgent one than the provision of technical assistance."[176] The council recognized the political problems involved and focused on the need to change public attitudes about family planning. This belief led it to support the Jamaican Family Life project, which Zuckerman helped shepherd to completion. Zuckerman, a friend of Robert Snider, the research director of the Conservation Foundation, also maintained a close relationship with Henry Fairfield Osborne, the president of the foundation and son of a prominent American eugenicist. Zuckerman used his contacts in the Colonial Office, most notably Philip Rogers, and his connection to the Nuffield Foundation to secure funding and political support for the study. The fact that the head of the Nuffield Foundation, Sir Alexander Todd, served as chair of the ACSP, made Zuckerman's task easier.

Zuckerman and the advocates of population control in the Colonial Office saw these modest advances as significant. After a meeting with senior politicians on the subject of family planning in late 1955, Zuckerman wrote, "The prairie's on fire!"[177] For Rogers, the growing interest in population vindicated his support for a more aggressive stance by the Colonial Office. As Sir John Macpherson wrote to Rogers in 1956, "I have read these files with much interest—right back to the battle you lost in 1942!"[178] Rogers and Zuckerman used this flurry of interest to push for a more vigorous population policy. Senior officials called for the creation of a committee of officials and outside experts to "examine facts about population pressures in the Colonial Territories and to secure expert advice on methods of control with a view to advising the Secretary of State on the policy which he should adopt in relation to them."[179] Officials hoped that demographic research would serve as the "handmaid of development policy."[180] Although the colonial secretary, Alan Lennox Boyd, agreed that population growth was a serious matter, he rejected the recommendation and instead relied on Zuckerman and the ASCP for advice.[181]

The British government continued its policy of indirect assistance for population control. Officials encouraged local governments to assist private family planning groups, particularly the IPPF. In the words of one official, the IPPF provided "much useful assistance both to the Colonial Office and to colonial territories, in the formation of voluntary associations and the establishment of birth control clinics."[182] Of equal importance, the IPPF stayed out of politics. As an official noted in reference to its Berlin Conference in 1957, "No delegates were disposed to take the opportunity of casting reflections upon the colonial powers."[183] As a result the federation played an ever-greater role in the work of the Colonial Office, and its representatives carried out inspection tours and attended conferences with government support.[184] The IPPF also expanded its family planning network, establishing clinics in fourteen territories by the late 1950s.[185] Several colonial governments, including Hong Kong, Malaysia, and Singapore, funded this work.[186]

POPULATION AND DEVELOPMENT IN POSTWAR AFRICA

Although London-based officials tried to grasp the dimensions of imperial demographic problems and formulate a coherent response, for officials on the ground demographic issues were not easily separable from concerns about economic and social development. This proved to be the case particularly in postwar Africa. Sub-Saharan Africa, with its mineral resources, agricultural commodities, and vast size, appeared to be the logical starting point for a renewed empire if its riches could be tapped.[187] To accomplish this goal, the British increased development funding and expanded the colonial administration.[188] As in other parts of the empire, officials expressed concern about the possible impact of population growth on these plans. However, considerable uncertainty existed about African demographic trends. Robert Kuczynski argued that he lacked sufficient information to make reliable estimates of African populations, but new evidence appeared to confirm impressionistic accounts of population growth.[189] Postwar colonial governments pointed to signs of population growth in British Africa, a viewed endorsed by independent researchers.[190]

Experts and officials rejected the idea that all of Africa was experiencing population growth. Instead, they argued that population pressure was a regional or local problem. This view placed population in the context of long-running debates about African land use, farming, and environmental practices. Colonial regimes saw African behavior as the source of social and economic problems that could only be addressed by the intervention of colonial authorities.[191] Officials increasingly linked these problems to overpopulation and argued for an integrated approach to reshape African life. Family planning appears not to have been seriously considered as a possible solution until very late in the colonial era. As a result, officials continued to rely on resettlement programs and changes in agricultural practices to address population pressure. Given their reluctance to acknowledge the role played by colonial policies in creating these conditions officials remained convinced of the need to change Africans societies even if it required the use of compulsion. This approach encountered increasing resistance from rural populations and fed support for nationalist movements.[192]

Despite reports of population growth in other parts of British Africa, including the Gold Coast, Nyasaland, southern Rhodesia, and northern Nigeria, East Africa, particularly Kenya, generated the most concern.[193] In Kenya, the white settler elite, created by the displacement of part of the African population into native reserves in the early twentieth century, began to worry about the expansion of the population of the reserves by the early 1930s. Settlers portrayed African population growth as the cause of environmental degradation and a threat to the stability of the reserve system. These claims found a sympathetic audience in the Colonial Office and East African governments.[194] Sir Phillip Mitchell, the governor of Kenya, called African population growth a critical issue for the future of East Africa.[195] However, the Royal Commission on East Africa in its report in 1955 failed to endorse this view, speaking only of overcrowding and primitive agricultural methods[196]

Resettlement was the most visible effort to address such concerns in postwar Africa. Building on the experience gained from tsetse fly control efforts in the interwar years, the British launched a number of schemes in the 1940s and 1950s.[197] Officials transferred populations from overcrowded areas to reduce local population pressure and bring lands they perceived as underutilized into production.[198] The governments of Nyasaland (1942), Uganda (1944), Swaziland (1945–46), Nigeria (1946), and Tanganyika (1947) launched resettlement programs.[199] These projects involved thousands of settlers and considerable sums of money.[200] The need to provide infrastructure like roads and water as well as the desire to create model settlements using erosion controls and new farming practices increased their cost.[201] Although some of these schemes were voluntary, colonial governments also relied on compulsion. Resettlement overlapped with efforts to control access to land. Kenya and southern Rhodesia forcibly removed ten of thousands of "squatters" from areas reserved for whites.[202] In other cases, conservation schemes led to forced removals, as in the Jos region of Nigeria, where African farmers were moved so that a forest reserve could be created.[203] Forced removals generated evasion and resistance.[204] Some of the resettled attempted to return home, while neighboring groups might occupy the now unoccupied land. In the case of the Jos forest reserve, officials tried and failed to enforce a ban on settlement, despite fines and the use of local authority courts.[205]

Kenya saw the most comprehensive use of resettlement as a means of population control.[206] Colonial administrators hoped that resettlement would forestall calls for redistribution of land to Africans and improve indigenous agriculture. As a 1951 report noted, "In Kenya, where the pressure of population is 'beyond the present, and in some cases the possible future carrying capacity of the land'; a more adequate redistribution of the African population through resettlement has been adopted as one of the main objectives of economic development."[207] As elsewhere, Kenyan officials resorted to forced removals to resettle Africans and to expel squatters from the "White Highlands." Despite the great cost of these efforts and the growing tensions they generated, the British governments continued these programs, even after the outbreak of the Mau-Mau insurgency.[208]

Colonial officials saw resettlement as one part of a larger project to transform African agricultural practices.[209] Efforts to change indigenous farming practices dated back to the interwar years and sought to eliminate what the British saw as inefficient and destructive techniques.[210] They argued that overuse of the land and soil erosion threatened to reduce food production even as populations increased.[211] In the postwar era, the British used the incentives and compulsory powers at their disposal to force Africans to accept British methods of cultivation. Yet these programs failed to advance the interests of African cultivators.[212] Despite the ability of African peasants to increase their output of maize and other cash crops during the Depression and the Second World War, officials continued to see well-capitalized European farmers as the basis of economic modernization. This distrust of African farmers reflected a larger debate about tradition and modernity in Africa.[213] Many British officials remained committed to sustaining "traditional" African society as the best guarantee of stability. They remained uncomfortable with Africans who appeared to embrace modern ways, whether market-oriented peasant cultivators or urban workers.[214] Some officials argued that the spread of cash cropping and individual land tenure would accelerate overuse of the land. Other experts and officials, however, embraced what they saw as the rise of the market and individualism. They argued that such changes would spur innovation in land tenure and farming practices, leading to increased productivity.[215] Although some experts recognized the value of indigenous knowledge and the skills of African farmers, no one proposed allowing them to control their own destinies.[216] Both sides agreed that rural populations still required British assistance in order to make progress.

Experts and officials concerned with demographic issues followed these debates. Under the influence of demographic transition theory, they argued that the adoption of modern attitudes was an essential precondition for population control. As long as African families remained within traditional social institutions they would have no incentive to reduce their birth rate. As mortality fell, Africans would continue to have large families, leading to rapid population growth. As J.K. Greer, a Colonial Office agricultural specialist, argued in 1948, "The utterances of Governors make it appear that most East Africans are incurably lazy and industrialization and plantations will be possible up to the point at which the few exceptional members of the community who are willing to do regular work have all been absorbed. The rest will continue to live a shiftless existence, surrounded by swarms of children."[217]

These concerns led demographic experts to argue that the solution to the agrarian and demographic problems of Africa lay in expanding the scope of the market and the spread of individualism.[218] In the words of one official, "A voluntary limitation of families will only come when the people have been educated to more sophisticated wants—bicycles instead of babies, furniture instead of families."[219] These arguments, which sounded convincing in London, proved more difficult to work out in practice. Colonial regimes had to balance long-range plans to transform African societies with the more pressing need to satisfy the economic and political demands of a more assertive African public. By the mid-1950s, the rapid pace of political change made such plans unrealistic.[220] The drive to "Africanize" local colonial services reduced the power of the Colonial Office to control events.[221] As the pace of decolonization increased, the Colonial Office planned for the transition to independence, winding down development projects and making arrangements for the transfer or redundancy of colonial officials.[222] The dismantling of the colonial state put an end to the dream of a comprehensive imperial population policy. Instead attention would turn to the remaining fragments of empire and the transition to a postcolonial development regime that included population programs.

APPLYING THE LESSONS

Even as decolonization accelerated, the British pursued population control in their remaining territories, using their experiences in the West Indies to guide their work. As one official said, "It is now up to us to make the best use of this experience by continuing the work in the West Indies and by applying it elsewhere, especially in Mauritius, Singapore, and Fiji, where it is most required."[223] In the mid-1950s the Colonial Office turned its attention to the island territories of Mauritius and Fiji.[224] Both colonies had agricultural economies and a history of labor migration from South Asia. As in East Africa and Southeast Asia, population concerns reflected ethnic and racial tensions.[225] Philip Rogers took the lead in efforts to deal with the demographic situation in these colonies.[226] He made use of the new statistical services and worked closely with voluntary groups like the IPPF. Officials hoped to frame the debate to avoid overt political problems while persuading governments of the need to establish a population control policy.

In Mauritius population growth had accelerated after 1945. Given the campaign to eradicate malaria on the island, observers feared that overpopulation would become a problem.[227] The legislature debated the issue in the early 1950s but divided over the issue of birth control. As in the West Indies, officials explored the possibility of emigration, but the preferred options of Madagascar and Australia proved to be dead ends.[228] The assertion by some residents of their "pure European descent" provoked misgivings among officials, who alluded to the "delicate question of race" in Mauritius.[229] Differences among whites, creoles, and South Asians hampered attempts to create a family planning program. Many in the Catholic and South Asian communities opposed this initiative. Health clinics affiliated with the Sugar Welfare Committee offered birth control advice, and officials attempted to interest the IPPF in working in the colony. In 1957 a local commission called for the creation of a family planning policy. The Mauritius Family Planning Association, created in the wake of the report, established twelve branches and a clinic in its first year. Officials cheered this development, arguing, "If it [the MFPA] can consolidate its early achievements it will be an important force making for stability and economic development in Mauritius. The real difficulty will come, administratively and politically, when the Mauritius government moves into the field and begins to spend the Roman Catholic taxpayer's money on family planning."[230] Despite this opposition, the government developed a "strong birth control policy" by the early 1960s.[231]

In Fiji, the topic of population proved even more controversial, pitting indigenous Fijians against the descendants of South Asian migrant workers.[232] As in Mauritius, concerns about population growth in Fiji surfaced in the early 1950s. A study by the English geographer Eila Campbell argued that a reduction in the birth rate was the only way to prevent overpopulation.[233] In late 1952, a white member of the Fijian legislative council noted the potential impact of population growth on the colony's racial makeup. The governor, Sir Reginald Garvey, called for a Commission of Inquiry to investigate "the danger of the Indian population completely swamping and dominating the Fijian in all fields of life."[234] Many European residents and officials shared this view. As one report argued, the "more astute Indian leaders are content to let things take their course feeling certain that pressure of population will give them or their successors political power."[235] A Commission of Inquiry, headed by Sir Alan Burns, issued a report in 1960. The period during which the commission worked saw the rise of interethnic tensions, and most of its recommendations focused on how to foster development in the colony. However, the commission also called for the establishment of government-run birth control clinics. Burns, a Catholic and opponent of birth control, dissented from this recommendation. Nevertheless, the government soon established clinics, with seven in existence by mid-1960.[236]

THE POLITICS OF POPULATION CONTROL

Within the Colonial Office, supporters of population control forged ahead.[237] They expressed their frustration with the caution of the Colonial Office given the changing political environment. Calls by members of Parliament for forceful action on population issues, as well as newspaper articles and letters in support of family planning, led some officials to argue that public opinion was moving in favor of population control. They discounted religious and political opposition to family planning and argued that the Colonial Office should directly fund clinics and publicity efforts.[238] Despite these appeals, the British government refused to change course. Successive colonial secretaries would not support birth control for fear of alienating public opinion at home and abroad. Ministers and senior officials cited a number of reasons for their caution. One issue remained the attitude of religious groups. Although the Anglican Church's acceptance of family planning in 1958 lessened religious objections within England, the continued opposition of the Catholic Church remained a cause for concern. The government, which needed support from Catholic states within the United Nations, feared alienating Catholic opinion.[239] Catholic opinion within the empire also needed to be considered. The existence of Catholic populations in the West Indies, particularly Trinidad, made politicians hesitant. They displayed a similar hesitation in Fiji, the Seychelles, and Mauritius. In 1958, John Profumo, secretary of state for the colonies, noted his reluctance to acknowledge receipt of a letter in favor of family planning in Mauritius despite "the considerable importance of this work."[240] The opposition of conservative Protestant clergy also presented a problem. Throughout the West Indies many Anglicans, including the bishop of Barbados, continued to oppose birth control. As one official argued, "We must not commit the Secretary of State to anything that looks like encouragement of 'family planning.' This is too controversial a subject in the West Indies and even in Barbados the public opposition of the established Church has been aroused. The Secretary of State must be kept out of this."[241]

Although religious sensibilities raised concerns, race remained the critical factor in population policy. Ministers and civil servants remained sensitive to the charge that population control was racially motivated. Even Philip Rogers, the most forceful advocate of population control, acknowledged this perception, which he characterized as dishonest. Such fears led the Colonial Office to deny a request by the Family Planning Association for £3,000 for a training conference for colonial health workers in 1959. Lennox Boyd endorsed the idea and sought backing from other ministers, who were willing to support the idea "if the Colonial Secretary is satisfied that there is a demand for such action from the coloured peoples of the Colonies themselves."[242] However, they feared accusations of racism. As Lord Hailsham noted, "For a 'white' colonial power to go in for birth control in a 'coloured' colony contains political dangers of misrepresentation quite distinct from the familiar moral and theological arguments. We should be very careful about this."[243] Lord Holme echoed this concern, saying, "It would be awkward if it could be said that the aim was to limit population increase only among coloured races."[244]

The lengths to which politicians and officials went to deny racial motives contrasted with the views they expressed in private. The attitudes of officials toward their colonial subjects remained at best paternalistic and at worse racist. Belief in the inferiority and incapacity of colonial peoples persisted, even as overt expressions of racism became politically unacceptable. Time and time again in their discussions of family planning, officials disparaged the intelligence and culture of colonial peoples. Solly Zuckerman listed ignorance, squalor, and poverty as factors inhibiting the spread of population control, asserting, "Most are too ignorant or too resigned even to take the trouble to understand the simple facts involved in human reproduction."[245] Officials hoped that the development of new contraceptives suitable for "primitive" peoples might overcome this problem.[246]

Although the attitudes of officials played a role in the racial politics of population control, their understanding of population in racial terms proved more important. Zuckerman, much as Julian Huxley had thirteen years earlier, divided the world into black and white zones. Calling attention to the fact that growth appeared concentrated in "backward areas," he argued "that the vast disparities which already exist between the numbers of white and other peoples will continue to grow."[247] The racially constructed view of population held by officials could be seen in their defense of race-based immigration policies. Their support for British migration to the Commonwealth in the postwar era was the last gasp of a policy based on a belief in the inherent superiority of the British. The Colonial Office's conversion to restrictions on non-white immigration in the 1950s represented a fundamental departure from its stance of neutrality on the issue. It coupled this shift with an unwillingness to challenge the racially discriminatory policies of white Commonwealth countries, despite increasing pressure to do so. Even Grantley Adams, an ally of the British government on family planning, came under attack when he raised the issue at the Commonwealth Parliamentary Conference in 1959. Officials at the Commonwealth Office attempted to silence him by asking the Australians to make a quick negative reply.[248] The Colonial Office gave a similarly perfunctory answer to the high commissioner for the West Indies in the early 1960s after he raised the question of West Indian migration to Australia, New Zealand, and Canada.[249]

A reliance on racial and ethnic categories as a tool of colonial governance constituted the other side of this worldview. Many of the areas targeted for population control were riven by racial and ethnic divisions. In the West Indies, the politics of birth control became enmeshed in the divisions of religion, class, and race that characterized the region on the eve of independence.[250] Most supporters of birth control came from the white elite or the educated, better-off mixed-race community. Eddie Burke, chair of the Population Research Foundation of Jamaica, made clear these social divisions when he argued that "classes with modern enlightenment are often strangers in their own land" and spoke of the "inconvenient fecundity of the poor."[251] Some West Indian politicians, like Norman Manley of Jamaica, had long supported family planning programs. In Barbados, Sir Grantley Adams and his government gave a grant of $5,000 to the Barbados Family Planning Association.[252] The British allied themselves with these moderate nationalists, while other politicians remained hostile to family planning. British officials worried about the political consequences for Manley and Adams of supporting family planning, given both men's support for the new West Indian Federation.[253] Manley contended with the opposition of Adam Bustamante, his cousin and principal political rival. Bustamante rejected claims of overpopulation and argued that the rich wanted to control the numbers of the poor.²⁵⁴ Adams, who received an award from the IPPF in 1958, faced criticism from the archbishop of Barbados and the *Barbados Advocate*, which argued in 1959, "The people who come to the Caribbean to introduce Planned Parenthood must like the West Indies so much that they do not want to see too many West Indians."²⁵⁵

In addition to class divisions within the Afro-Caribbean community, racial divisions influenced the construction of family planning programs. In much of the West Indies, a white minority clung to power more than a hundred years after the emancipation of the Afro-Caribbean majority. Yet colonial officials tended to view this elite as a natural ally in their campaign to gather support for birth control, even when this alliance reinforced nationalist claims about the racial orientation of population programs. Robert Kirkwood, a wealthy planter and a member of the Legislative Council, received a sympathetic hearing from the Colonial Office to his call for action on overpopulation in the late 1940s.²⁵⁶ Kirkwood, an opponent of universal suffrage, founded the Farmers' Party in the 1950s to protect the interests of white planters.²⁵⁷ In Bermuda, where the government funded family planning clinics, support came from similar circles. One official called the Bermuda legislature "more progressive than the Legislatures of the over-populated British West Indian islands, which, so far as I am aware, have not attempted to face up to this complicated problem."²⁵⁸ However this legislature, which Philip Rogers described in 1955 "as . . . among the angels" on the subject of birth control, proposed the sterilization of "irresponsible" parents in the early 1950s, an echo of its attempt to link birth control and sterilization in the 1930s.²⁵⁹ Bermuda's willingness to fund family planning stemmed from the racial politics of the island. As one official noted in 1952, "Their views seem on the whole to represent the rather unimaginative reactions of a dominant white community towards a subordinate coloured community."²⁶⁰ W.D. Sweaney put it more bluntly when he said, "It seems that the whites may wish to curtail the numbers of blacks."²⁶¹

Similar calculations appear to have existed in Mauritius and Kenya, where white minorities endorsed family planning programs at an early stage. In Kenya, support for birth control came initially from the settler community. In 1945, Dr. H.L. Gordon, a leader of the Kenyan eugenics movement, raised the question with the Colonial Office.²⁶² The English writer, Elspeth Huxley, and the former director of the Kenyan Medical Service, A.R. Patterson, pointed to the high birth rate of Africans and suggested that improved education and health services might transform African attitudes and encourage family limitation.²⁶³ Although several clinics appeared in Kenya and elsewhere in East Africa by the mid-1950s, a lack of medical facilities made it impossible to reach the rural population, the presumed target of family planning.[264]

Such alliances undermined the assertion by colonial officials that population programs served the broader community and were racially neutral. Officials interested in population control saw these programs through political lenses. Philip Rogers, who defended the white minority in Kenya and supported resettlement, enjoyed a reputation as a hardliner on Malaya, Kenya, and British Guiana and served on an interdepartmental security committee in the 1940s.[265] The gap between the stated aims of population policy and its operation in practice appeared most starkly in those colonies in which the Colonial Office used population control to manage multiethnic societies. In the interwar years, the Colonial Office used migration and resettlement to try to control the ethnic balance in Palestine, East Africa, and Southeast Asia. After 1945, the British took sides in a series of ethnic and racial conflicts. Two of these conflicts, Malaya and Kenya, demonstrated how population control became a weapon in the hands of colonial administrators.

Malaya, whose mineral wealth made it the largest earner of foreign exchange in the empire, was crucial to British plans for postwar Asia. Prior to the war the colonial government limited Chinese and Indian migration to help bolster Malay dominance.[266] The outbreak of the insurgency in 1948 fed ethnic tensions and led to targeted population control, as officials employed the tools of population management primarily against Chinese guerrillas.[267] The military displaced and restructured local populations to isolate and control guerrilla forces, relying on techniques that resembled those used since the 1930s to reorganize peasant agriculture.[268] The British linked this tactic with rural development schemes to improve rural life. The defeat of the insurgents settled the ethnic balance of power in favor of ethnic Malays, an outcome cemented by the terms of independence in 1957.[269]

In Kenya, a similar mix of ethnic and racial conflict erupted in the 1950s. Discontent over land lay at the heart of the Mau-Mau insurgency. Mau-Mau forces found support among displaced squatters and others on the margins of Kikuyu society, a base increased by crackdowns on militants and squatters during the Emergency. Alongside detention camps that housed more than 70,000 people, the British forcibly resettled rural populations into controlled villages to isolate rebel forces. The new villages reduced the floating population of the native areas while providing a labor force for improvement projects.[270] The British used detainee labor for these projects in violation of international law.[271] The Swynnerton Plan, launched at the height of the insurgency in 1953 and funded with £5 million from the Colonial Development Fund, tried to foster a landowning peasant class that would grow cash crops on consolidated land holdings using new agricultural methods. The British used these schemes to reward loyalists by granting access to land and cheap labor. British tactics fueled conflict within the Kikuyu community and between other ethnic groups in Kenya. As in Malaya, the defeat of the insurgency left a legacy of ethnic discord.[272]

CONCLUSION

The limitations of population policy in the postwar empire reflected the problems of colonial governance in an era of rapid political and social change. The integration of demographic concerns into colonial development gave population issues a greater prominence but failed to guarantee the creation or implementation of a coherent policy. A lack of administrative and financial resources inhibited population policy. Despite its efforts to upgrade its statistical operations, the Colonial Office still lacked sufficient staff in the late 1950s. Colonial governments, particularly smaller ones, lagged farther behind. Population initiatives competed with other projects for funding within the social services, which formed only a portion of development funding. Even if viable projects could have been created and funded, colonial governments lacked the health infrastructure to reach more than a fraction of their populations, particularly in rural areas.

The political constraints upon population policy proved to be as significant as the structural ones. Politicians and officials understood the difficulty of defending an aggressive population policy aimed at colonial peoples. The coexistence of appeals for increased white birth rates alongside public apprehension about non-white birth rates highlighted the racially constructed nature of the problem. Officials and politicians sought to distance themselves publicly from accusations of racially motivated demographic policies even as they agreed in private on the need to reduce imperial population growth. Such caution frustrated activist officials in London, who already faced the problems of persuading local colonial officials of the urgency of the problem. Religion provided another flashpoint for ministers worried about the political complications of population control. Religious objections to birth control affected the calculations of British officials into the 1960s. The combination of race and religion helps explain the reluctance of politicians to embrace population control publically or fund family planning programs.

The combination of limited resources and political worries meant that by the end of the 1950s imperial population programs remained embryonic. Aside from a few family planning schemes launched by colonial governments or newly independent states, most population work in the empire remained the province of private organizations, most notably the IPPF. Despite this modest record, some important strides were made. Demographic information and the infrastructure needed for its collection improved in this era, aided by the growth of academic demography and international organizations like the United Nations. These accomplishments would prove their worth in the 1960s and 1970s as demographic statistics in Africa and elsewhere became more reliable. The concern of the British government with demographic issues found an echo among experts and the public. The debate about global population shifted the focus from the colonial world to a broader "Third World" of less developed states. The end of colonial demography coincided with emergence of a global discourse of population in the 1960s, centered on the theory of the demographic transition. This discourse and the public concern it generated helped rationalize the development of international population programs under UN and U.S. sponsorship. Even then, the British legacy persisted. The reliance of these programs upon British experts, officials, and private agencies gave them, and the broader development community, a distinctive British accent.

5 Population in a Postcolonial World

As the British Empire expanded and then contracted in the postwar era, the British population movement underwent its own evolution. The movement navigated the decline of eugenics and the empire and positioned itself at the center of the international campaign for family planning, especially through its relationship with the International Planned Parenthood Federation (IPPF). Its leaders maintained their close relationship with the British government, acting as advisors and experts for the Colonial Office, its successors such as the Department of Technical Cooperation (DTC), as well as for international organizations. Despite the achievements of the British population movement after 1945, it was increasingly overshadowed by developments in the United States. The willingness of the Rockefeller and Ford Foundations to fund American population activists allowed them to expand their work at home and abroad dramatically. By contrast, British foundations and donors possessed far fewer resources than their American counterparts. Even the British-led IPPF relied heavily on private American donors in its early years. The most significant product of this funding, the Population Council, became the principal population organization in the postwar era. American demography experienced a similar expansion, benefiting from increased government funding and the rapid growth of university positions. By the 1960s, the U.S. population movement dominated the international population movement.

American demographers and activists would be central to the transformation of the global debate about population growth and its consequences. They played a leading role in the elaboration of a new intellectual paradigm, demographic transition theory. This theory, which drew on social science concepts like modernization, linked demographic trends to the level of social and economic development. While this model could be used to understand current population trends in the West or those of historical populations, its application to the less developed nations of the "Third World" would be critical to how activists and governments understood global population. For its adherents, the slowness of modernization in the former colonial world led to explosive growth as birth rates remained high, even as medical and economic advances led to lower death rates. The need to quickly close this gap provided the rationale for international family planning efforts.

The general acceptance of transition theory by British demographers and activists signaled the end of colonial demography as a distinctive field and its incorporation into a global model of population dynamics. This shift reflected the impact of decolonization and changes in how the British understood their own population trends. While the postwar baby boom put an end to fears of depopulation, many of the concerns of the interwar population movement persisted. Activists called for higher white birth rates and migration to the empire and Commonwealth. As the empire unraveled in the 1950s and 1960s, this imperial focus would give way to a global perspective that concentrated on the need to control the growth of non-white populations. Environmentalism would influence how British activists and demographers portrayed Britain's demographic future. The environmental movement in Britain focused attention on the impact of continued population growth in a country already suffering from high density and ecological degradation. At the same time, immigration from former colonies raised the prospect of a dramatic shift in the ethnic and racial composition of Britain, which many saw as threatening its identity. This recasting of demographic concerns as threats to the integrity of Britain represented the domestic side of the new postcolonial demography.

BRITAIN'S POSTWAR POPULATION DEBATE

In the immediate postwar years, declining fertility continued to be a staple of population debates in Britain. During the war, activists and demographers produced several assessments of future population trends. David Glass and Robert Kuczynski emphasized falling birth rates and the likelihood of a decline in Britain's population in the near term.[1] More popular works like Richard Titmuss's *Parents Revolt* (1942) and Sir Roy Harrod's *Britain's Future Population* (1943) presented similar arguments for a broader audience. These studies played a part in the debate over postwar reconstruction. The belief that an impending decline in population required state intervention became widespread during and after the war. The Beveridge Report gave a prominent role to demographic issues, calling for a larger, more vigorous population to ensure Britain's future.[2] Its focus on family-based assistance reflected the belief that "obstacles to parenthood" needed to be reduced in order to revive the birth rate.[3] Enid Charles, who popularized the idea of population decline in the 1930s, predicted that Britain's population would begin to decline by 1970, despite the upturn in fertility rates during the war.[4] Charles, like many among the left in Britain, argued that unregulated capitalism lay at the root of the problem of declining fertility and that only the expanded provision of state benefits could reverse what Titmuss called the "biological failure of capitalism."[5] Writers influenced by eugenics took a somewhat different approach. Harrod, while agreeing with the need for a comprehensive program of family allowances, argued for a graded scale of benefits to induce middle- and upper-class-families to have more children.[6] In 1947, Eva Hubback, a prominent feminist and a member of the Eugenics Society, published a best-selling book, *The Population of Britain*. Hubback, who worked with Eleanor Rathbone on the issue of family endowments in the 1930s, continued her call for state funding of parenthood but also raised the issue of "quality."[7]

The creation of the Royal Commission on Population in 1944 gave population activists an opportunity to make their arguments to a broader public.[8] The Eugenics Society, the Fabian Society, and the policy group Political and Economic Planning (PEP) gave information to the commission and published their recommendations. In 1945, the Fabian Society's Committee on Population's pamphlet *Population and the People* called for Britain to increase its birth rate in order to maintain its economic and political power. It argued, "We cannot maintain our military position as a Great Power and the centre of the British Commonwealth with a net reproduction rate below unity."[9] The report predicted a continued need for large-scale migration to the Commonwealth and empire and called for an expansion of state planning and provision to accomplish these goals. Other groups agreed with the Fabian Society's arguments. In 1948, PEP published *Population Policy in Great Britain*, which called for the coordination of social welfare measures to ensure a stable and healthy population. Although less alarmist than interwar assessments, it saw Britain and other European nations as entering a period of falling growth and even possible decline.[10] Not surprisingly given the presence of a number of prominent eugenicists on the committee, the report raised the issue of population "quality."[11]

While most commentators agreed about the need to increase fertility rates over the long term, considerable uncertainty existed about British population trends. Some activists and politicians argued that given continued shortages and rationing Britain's present population could not be sustained; other observers spoke of the "crowded island."[12] Only through falling birth rates and massively increased emigration could Britain hope to escape this problem. In the words of Winston Churchill, "Of 48,000,000, one quarter will have to disappear in one way or another, after enduring a lowering of standards of food and comfort inconceivable in the last 50 years. Emigration, even if practiced on a scale never before dreamed of, could not operate in time to prevent this melancholy decline."[13]

While Churchill used this argument to attack the Labour government, his views expressed a widely held belief about the future of Britain's population. The Fabian Society and other organizations discounted this view by arguing that unemployment and shortages reflected temporary conditions or a lack of adequate planning, not overpopulation.[14]

The debate over emigration occurred as the government considered and rejected a proposal for sponsored mass migration on strategic grounds.[15] A series of publications called for increased emigration. While recognizing the limitations imposed by labor shortages and lower fertility, writers like George McCleary argued that the strategic and political advantages would outweigh any difficulties for those left behind.[16] However, other commentators argued that Britain could no longer be the "reservoir of empire."[17] This view led Brinley Thomas to propose a limit on emigration until the birth rate increased and to call for the recruitment of European migrants for Britain and the Commonwealth.[18]

Despite the uncertainty about British population trends, population activists continued to press for increased British emigration which they saw as crucial for maintaining the racial balance between Britain, the empire and the Commonwealth. Activists called for continued government subsidies and increasing emigration to 125,000 per year.[19] Sensing a lessening of government support for their goals, supporters of Commonwealth migration formed the Migration Council in 1950. The tenor of the council's work can be gauged in part by the presence of Air Marshall Whittle as president and by the focus on European migration as the essential issue. As Dudley Barker argued in his pamphlet for the council, "The British Commonwealth is in danger. This danger, which threatens whether the future brings war cold war or peace, springs from the ill-distribution of white people and industries in the Commonwealth. . . .

The nearly 11 million coloured people who also inhabit these countries, most of them in South Africa and Southern Rhodesia, do not materially redress this ill-balance of population, since most of them are agricultural workers and scarcely affect the mal-distribution of industry."[20] He then contended that white migration would benefit "not only Britain and the Commonwealth, but the whole world. It would vastly strengthen the security of the Western democracies; it is the most obvious way of ensuring that increase in the world's wealth, by developing under-developed areas, which is most likely to pacify the nations of the earth by feeding the hungry."[21]

The council kept up a steady stream of propaganda and met with ministers and officials in an effort to gain greater government support. It also argued that only large-scale European migration could ensure the development of Africa; a task that one writer argued would require 100 million European immigrants.[22] The destinations for these migrants would be areas like Rhodesia and Kenya, where white settlement already existed. Despite private support from ministers, the council made little headway and complained of a lukewarm response from the government.[23] Nevertheless, the level of emigration from Britain to the Commonwealth remained high from the late 1940s through the early 1960s. Some 1.5 million migrants left Britain for Australian, South Africa, New Zealand, and Canada at a cost of some £7 million to British taxpayers.[24]

The expansion of emigration in the late 1940s coincided with declining fears of depopulation.[25] Estimates of fertility produced during the war, most notably the 1942 White Paper, *The Current Population Trend*, called into question the more extreme predictions of decline.[26] In 1947 John Hajnal demonstrated that interwar demographic estimates reflected the skewed age structure of Britain in the 1930s, caused by the First World War and migration, and relied too heavily on the maternal reproduction rate, which overstated the fall in fertility.[27] The Royal Commission on Population, which supported Hajnal's research, accepted his argument but still considered the declining birth rate a potential problem.[28] Demographers like Frank Notestein, commenting on the report, noted that higher rates of marriage, the diminishing impact of the First World War on sex ratios, and the stability of family size suggested continued, albeit slow, growth.[29] By the mid-1950s, depopulation disappeared from public discourse and the British government instead worried about the consequences of population growth.[30] Many in the population movement distanced themselves from what C. P. Blacker in 1951 referred to "as certain arbitrary projections."[31]

The fading of claims about imminent depopulation undercut much of the rationale behind the appointment of the Royal Commission on Population. Its report, issued in 1949 generated a limited response from the public. The creation of a welfare state made many of its recommendations unnecessary, and attempts to highlight eugenic concerns failed to gain traction in the postwar political environment. However, the Royal Commission's discussion of Britain's place in the world raised questions that increasingly concerned activists and officials. Members of the commission worried about the differences in birth rate between Britain and the rest of the world. As its report argued:

> The drift of world affairs is giving a new emphasis to the conception of Western civilization as an entity possessing reality and value. This lends significance to the fact the modern fall in the size of the family towards and often below replacement level is a phenomenon common to most the peoples of Western civilization and virtually confined to them. Their rate of increase has markedly declined while that of Oriental peoples has markedly accelerated. The establishment or continuance of size of family below replacement might accentuate a change in relative numbers as radical as that which occurred between France and Germany in the 19th century and might be as decisive in its effects on the prestige and influence of the West. The question is not merely one of military strength and security: it merges into more fundamental issues of the maintenance of and extension of Western values and culture.[32]

This focus on differential racial fertility reflected a broader shift within British population discourse after 1945. While population activists raised the issue of non-white population growth in the interwar years, in the postwar era it became the central issue. As one writer argued, "As far as Great Britain is concerned, they regard the Malthusian Devil as still chained up and out of sight. But in the world at large, in Asia and the Middle East, he is on the prowl."[33] Observers focused on the implications for Britain and its empire of higher non-white growth rates. References to the "swarming millions of Asia" reflected the belief that Britain faced a demographic struggle that showed little signs of abating. Estimates of future American and Russian population growth added to the sense of foreboding felt by many British population activists.[34]

The increased importance of non-European population trends can be seen in the work of PEP. Its 1948 report on British population gave only sketchy coverage to the issue and projected little potential for growth outside of Asia.[35] However, in less than a decade, PEP reversed its view.

Its 1955 report, *World Population and Resources*, which appeared as West Indian immigration accelerated, focused on the relationship between global population trends and political unrest. It linked population growth to colonial problems, arguing, "Would thousands of sun-loving Jamaicans emigrate each year to Britain . . . but for the extreme population pressure in their islands[?] . . . Would the peaceful Kikuyu have embraced the great terrorist conspiracy Mau-Mau had not their population increased rapidly during this century alongside an immigrant population which itself increased substantially in the same period?"[36]

PEP called on governments and international organizations to recognize the scope of the problem and make greater investments in economic development and population control. It viewed increased use of birth control as the only solution to the problem. The report compared those who wished to ignore the issue to the appeasers of the 1930s and urged governments to abandon their squeamishness about the topic. As it noted:

> Under-developed countries have been left, for the most part in the dark except for the efforts of a few enthusiasts and specialists. They have not been enabled to appreciate that to catch up economically with the West; they must reduce their birth rates much faster than the West, so as to match the quickly falling death rates. These countries are left under the impression that reduction of birth rates is a distasteful measure, which no Western government would press upon its own people. Such a measure is held to involve discriminating between under-developed and advanced countries, rather than adopting an essential element in Western progress.[37]

Like most population activists, the members of PEP's population committee called for the development of a cheap, safe contraceptive "suitable for use by illiterates in difficult climatic or social conditions."[38]

One feature of postwar demographic debates was the increased participation of the scientific community on both sides of the Atlantic. Biologists, physicians, agricultural scientists, and ecologists analyzed human population dynamics and offered solutions for what many observers presented as an impending crisis.[39] Their work enhanced the credibility of the population movement by endorsing its goal of population control. While presented under the mantle of science, many of these scientists echoed the eugenic and racial themes found in other population writing. British biologists like Julian Huxley took a leading role in discussions of population growth. G. C. Bertram, a longtime member of the Eugenics Society, wrote about the impact of population growth, especially in Asia, upon food supplies, while A. V. Hill, a future president of the Royal Society, focused on the rapid growth of India and the need for a dramatic increase in agricultural productivity to prevent a disaster.[40] Hill attacked what he saw as the backward social and religious customs of India and discounted the ability of industrialization or social modernization alone to address the problem.[41] He went on to argue, "The same problem of overpopulation exists in other parts of Asia, notably in China and Japan, and the same conclusion would be arrived at by considering any other part of the world for the possible reception of emigrants. Irresponsible reproduction indeed can only be countered in the end by Nature's crude method of want, famine and pestilence, or by civilized man's methods of conscious and deliberate control."[42]

American biologists also weighed into this debate. The Harvard botanist Karl Sax wrote a series of popular works on population. In his best-known work, *Standing Room Only* (1955), Sax offered a vigorous defense of Malthusian population theory and attacked those who opposed the widespread use of birth control.[43] Garrett Hardin achieved greater fame for his more extreme stance on population control. Best known for his 1968 article "The Tragedy of the Commons," Hardin argued for a revolution in human morality to avoid the looming disaster of overpopulation and environmental collapse.[44] His call for a coercive approach to human reproduction echoed the language of the earlier eugenics movement; his text, *Biology: Its Human Implications*, first published in 1949, contained an extended discussion of the virtues of eugenics.[45]

The British medical establishment also weighed in on the subject. The medical journal, *The Lancet*, became an advocate of population control. Its lead editorial in June 1952 called attention to the potential consequences of global population growth and proposed birth control and expanded food production as the answer. The editorial argued for "the spacing of children by birth control as a method of keeping the human farmyard from being overstocked."[46] *The Lancet*'s position was unsurprising given the role played by physicians in shaping demographic debates. Among the most prominent was Sir John Megaw, the former director of the Indian Medical Service, who had first raised the question of Indian and global population in the 1920s.[47] In 1947, in conjunction with the British Social Hygiene Council, he published *Overpopulation as a World Problem*, which focused on the imbalance between population and food supplies. He examined India and Puerto Rico as examples of the disastrous consequences of public health initiatives that reduced mortality without affecting the birth rate. Although he shied away from outright advocacy of family planning, he made clear its role in solving what he saw as a looming catastrophe.[48]

Like biologists and physicians, agricultural scientists in the United States and Britain feared that shortages in the immediate postwar era presaged a Malthusian subsistence crisis. Concerns about food supplies led Western governments, foundations, and businesses to sponsor agricultural research that laid the groundwork for the Green Revolution of the 1960s.[49] While this research could be applied to Western farming, it also focused on agricultural modernization in Asia and Africa. Britain's long engagement with colonial agriculture made it a leader in this field.[50] Two British scientists, Sir John Boyd-Orr and Sir John Russell, enjoyed international reputations for their work.[51] Originally trained as a physician, Boyd-Orr made his mark as a nutritionist, including his work in East Africa in the 1920s.[52] He directed the Rowett Research Institute, headed the Food and Agricultural Organization (FAO) of the United Nations from 1946 to 1948, and won the Nobel Peace Prize in 1949. Russell served as the director of Rothamsted Experimental Station from 1912 to 1943 and was credited with the revival of agricultural science in Britain. Both men reached a broader audience with their work and became advocates for scientific agriculture and population control.[53]

Boyd-Orr's *The White Man's Dilemma* (1953) and Russell's *Population and World Food Supplies* (1954) argued that a widening gap between food production and population growth threatened the world with potential disaster. Both books called on Western governments to assist less developed countries develop scientific agriculture and family planning services. Despite their agreement about the problem and its solution, Boyd-Orr and Russell differed in their views about colonialism and race. Despite the title of his book, Boyd-Orr argued against ideas of racial difference and spoke of the "common brotherhood of man." A committed pacifist and internationalist, Boyd-Orr called upon the Western powers to devote more resources to develop the economic potential of Asia and Africa, even if this increase led to a loss of Western ascendancy.[54]

In contrast to Boyd-Orr's expansive view of human nature, Russell took a dim view of the intellectual and cultural abilities of non-European peoples. He linked the problems of food supply to the backwardness of Asian and African peoples. In particular, Africa lacked "great civilizations ... comparable to those of Europe and Asia." Its "agriculture was primitive and never progressed far."[55] Russell defended British colonialism as a force for progress, citing the example of Kenya, where "British farmers ... by their own resources and at no cost to the British taxpayer converted a wilderness that Africans could never tackle into productive farmland."[56] He feared that decolonization would lead to the collapse of these efforts, thus he called on newly independent states to allow Western experts to continue their work "in peace and security."[57]

While Russell's and Orr's work grew out of their experiences within the British imperial system, it also reflected the influence of American population writers whose work centered on the ecological consequences of population growth. Henry Fairfield Osborn's *The Plundered Planet* and William Vogt's *The Road to Survival* invoked the limits to global resources to justify comprehensive programs of population control. Osborn, the head of the New York Zoological Society, possessed a long record as a eugenicist and population activist. His book ranged widely over human history and painted a picture of a planet driven to the brink of collapse by the overexploitation of resources and population growth.[58] Osborn called for the rebalancing of nature and humanity, which implied the need for limiting human numbers. The linkage between environmentalism and population dated back to the earliest days of the environmental movement in the United States and would become a staple of population discourse in the postwar era.[59]

As was the case with the British environmentalist Max Nicholson, Vogt's interest in environmentalism grew out of his work as an ornithologist. While he agreed with Osborn's conclusions, he provided a considerably more detailed analysis. He argued that the world already faced a severe environmental crisis that presaged the exhaustion of its resources and a global Malthusian crisis. Vogt believed that neither industrialization nor advanced agriculture could be sustained indefinitely and only a combination of conservation and population control could prevent a collapse. He saw Europe and Britain as living beyond their means and potentially threatened by famine.[60] Vogt saved his harshest assessment for Asia, which he portrayed as mired in poverty and overpopulation, caused in large part by improved health and security brought by Western imperialism. He laced his book with remarks about the backwardness of various peoples. He linked India's problems to "untrammeled copulation" and called the high death rate of Chile "one of its greatest national assets."[61] For Vogt, global population growth threatened America's well-being, as overpopulated regions demanded assistance from the United States. He spoke of "the high cost of policing parts of overpopulated Europe and Asia" and argued that aid should be tied to population control. In his words, "Until they (India and China) adopt a rational population policy these nations . . . have no right to expect aid from the rest of the world."[62]

The popular and often sensational tone of Vogt's and other writers' work reflected their desire to raise public awareness and to reach a broader audience. Activists recognized that before the war most people ignored global population trends. The flood of books and articles on the subject helped bring the topic to the attention of the general public. In Britain and the United States, newspapers and general circulation periodicals carried articles on the emerging population crisis from the 1940s onward.[63] Letters and editorials in British newspapers like the *Times*, the *Daily Telegraph*, and the *Observer* reflected this public concern. In addition to public lectures by prominent figures like John Megaw, Julian Huxley, and C. P. Blacker, BBC radio offered opportunities for activists to spread their message, as in the series of talks in 1952 for the Overseas Service on population and food.[64] Much of this work echoed the apocalyptic tone of Vogt and Russell and culminated in the "population explosion" literature of the 1960s, exemplified by Paul Ehrlich's *The Population Bomb*. By the late 1950s, Julian Huxley could look back and say, "In 1927 I attended the International Population Conference in which Margaret Sanger played a leading role; and I have remained deeply interested in the problem. Much has happened in the 32 years that have elapsed since then. Public interest in the problem of population has grown in an astonishing way."[65]

This focus on global overpopulation influenced how the British viewed their own population. The environmental movement's concern with global population growth found a responsive audience in Britain. Julian Huxley, Solly Zuckerman, and Max Nicholson played major roles in the movement.[66] Huxley explicitly linked the two in his own work. His conservation work in Africa in the 1960s solidified this view, and he argued that population control was a necessary part of any effort to preserve wildlife on the continent.[67] The creation of the Conservation Society, the leading environmental group in Britain in the 1960s and early 1970s, was inspired in part by an article on overpopulation by Julian Huxley in *Playboy*, and the Society made population growth one of its central issues.[68] Publications like *Blueprint for Survival* portrayed Britain as a society dependent on food imports and intensive agriculture and poised on the verge of ecological collapse.[69]

Immigration from former colonies also affected British population debates. The rapid expansion of immigration from the West Indies and South Asia raised fears that the British could be swamped on their own island. While this perception built on complex social and cultural currents within Britain, for those concerned about population growth, immigration represented the consequence of uncontrolled growth abroad. Already in the mid-1950s, PEP linked immigration to overpopulation at the source. This understanding of immigration informed government discussions of the topic from the late 1940s onward and would provide a rationale for more aggressive measures of population control in the 1960s and 1970s. Fear of the domestic political consequences of uncontrolled immigration would result in increasingly restrictive measures enacted after 1962.[70]

EUGENICS AND THE POPULATION MOVEMENT IN THE POSTWAR ERA

The close relationship between the work of British and American population writers reflected the growing interconnectedness of academic and organizational life in the two countries. In the interwar years, Britain, by virtue of the prestige of its academic institutions and its imperial networks, played a leading role in the international population movement. In the postwar era, however, leadership of the movement shifted to the United States. Many in the movement saw it as a natural consequence of the United States' global leadership. However, activists in the United States still looked to Britain for support and guidance in this new era. As William Vogt noted in the preface to the British edition of his book, the British possessed a sense of global needs and "if Britain could help bring this problem before the United Nations and develop an action program that would cure the malady, there is little doubt but that other nations would follow her lead."[71] The continued importance of British activists and institutions allowed the British population movement to play an important role in the expansion of private and public population control programs even after the collapse of the empire undercut Britain's claim to special status in the colonial world.

The population movement struggled to recover from the disruptions brought by the war. The difficulties of life in wartime as well as the dispersal of many activists outside London and to national service made it difficult for the organizations that comprised the movement to sustain their work.[72] At the same time, the renewed public debate about population during the war offered the movement a new opportunity to find official and public support for its work. The creation of the Royal Commission on Population raised hopes among activists and a number of them, including Alexander Carr-Saunders, David Glass, Robert Kuczynski, C.P. Blacker, and Julian Huxley joined in its deliberations. Yet the commission proved to be a dead end, because it failed to generate any significant debate about the future of Britain's population. The movement, particularly its central organization, the Eugenics Society, faced a very different political and social environment in the postwar era.[73] The association in the public mind between eugenics and the crimes of the Nazi regime placed the society in a precarious position. While its leaders rejected such an association, the charge held some legitimacy.[74] The society's support for voluntary sterilization of "defectives" took on a more sinister tone after 1945 with the revelations of the German regime's treatment of the handicapped and mentally challenged, a problem exacerbated by the support expressed for Nazi social polices by many eugenicists in the 1930s.[75] Such support reflected not a murderous disposition toward "inferior" groups, but rather a more general elitism and belief in their own social superiority. Despite backing postwar social welfare measures, the society and its leading members—Blacker, Huxley, and Carr-Saunders—remained committed to the idea of raising the "quality" of the population. Even William Beveridge supported this goal. His largely favorable review of the Fabian's Society's *Population and the People* criticized its failure to address the question of population quality.[76] Such views lay behind the society's continued support for studies of intelligence and "social problem" groups.[77]

Even as many of the cherished proposals for "improving" Britain's population became irrelevant, the imperial and demographic aspects of the society's work offered new opportunities for influence. As during the interwar era, work on migration, birth control and demography linked eugenicists to other population activists. The Eugenics Society still relied on the prominence of its members and its journal, *Eugenics Review*, to reach a broader audience. *The Eugenics Review* maintained its focus on "population quality," but increased its coverage of world population trends and family planning work, covering the work of the IPPF, which received support from the society.[78] It also maintained its backing for the Population Investigation Committee (PIC), whose new journal *Population Studies* became a leading journal of academic demography.

C.P. Blacker, who led the Eugenics Society until 1952, devoted more time to questions of imperial and global population. In the late 1940s, Blacker expanded his contact with population activists at home and abroad, attending the International Union for the Scientific Study of Population meeting in Geneva in 1947, the Cheltenham Conference on World Population in 1948, and the World Population Conference in Rome in 1954. He also remained an advocate for a more forward position by the British government on population issues, as in his call in 1950 for an Imperial Demographic Institute to track population trends and foster the development of the discipline in Britain.[79] This commitment led him to further involvement with PEP and its World Population Committee. Blacker, long a proponent of selective British migration, became an active member of the Migration Council and wrote several public letters in support of its work.[80] He also played a central role in the founding of the IPPF, participating in the committee that wrote its rules and constitution in 1952. Blacker served as an officer for the federation and attended its conferences in Bombay and Tokyo. Because of his long-standing contacts with the Colonial Office, officials consulted him about IPPF involvement in voluntary family planning work.[81]

In 1957 Blacker helped create the Simon Population Trust and served as its director until 1969. The trust, founded by Lord Simon, an industrialist and Labour Peer who previously had headed the BBC and the Royal Commission on Population, concentrated on threats to global peace from overpopulation and nuclear weapons. Blacker contacted Simon in 1952 after hearing of his interest in population from Max Nicholson. Blacker carried on a correspondence with Simon, hoping to raise his level of awareness and interest.[82] Simon became enthusiastic about the topic. After a visit to Barbados in 1954 he published *The Population and Resources of Barbados*, which called for the establishment of birth control clinics as a necessary step toward solving the problems of the island. The pamphlet drew considerable attention to Simon and Barbados. Philip Rogers of the Colonial Office sent copies to West Indian governors in 1955 as part of his effort to alert them to the issue of overpopulation. Simon also chaired PEP's committee on World Population and Resources. Housed at first with the Eugenics Society in Eccleston Square, the Simon Population Trust shared quarters with the IPPF at Sloane Square and then Lower Regent Street.[83] The two organizations shared members, including Blacker and Vera Houghton. In addition the trust played a central role in changing the legal climate for voluntary sterilization, particularly vasectomies.[84]

Blacker reputation as a demographic expert continued to grow. His relationship with the *Eugenics Review* allowed him to publish and stay current with new demographic research. Much of his work echoed that of American demographers and linked population characteristics with social development, as in his 1947 article "Stages in Population Growth."[85] He became a sought-after speaker on population issues and addressed the Bombay Conference of the IPPF, the NATO Defense College, and the Royal Naval Institute in addition to speaking tours aimed at more general audiences.[86] He served as an advisor to the Ministry of Health and worked as a consultant for the Colonial Office and the Advisory Council on Scientific Policy[87] In the late 1950s, the Colonial Office considered using the Simon Population Trust to help centralize its population work.[88]

Despite his new role as a demographic expert, Blacker retained his close ties with the eugenics movement and continued to believe in the central tenets of eugenics. In 1951 he argued, "The present trend of differential fertility diminishes the nation's fund of intelligence."[89] He linked such ideas to his interest in global population, noting in a letter to Frederick Osborn in 1958, "As you know, I hold that, within a couple of centuries or so at most, world conditions are all too likely to deteriorate to a condition where the death control of natural selection will again become the control of human populations, and by then there will be little chance for eugenics to do much."[90] Such views fit his belief in the fundamental differences between the races. In another letter in 1958 he argued:

> I personally agree with your standpoint—that the African Negro south of the Sahara does not find it easy to make a success of what is called the western way of life; and that because this mode of life will unavoidably spread throughout the world, he will need some cosseting and would benefit from some probation before being pushed off on his own. But these views are highly unpopular just now, partly because of the influence of UNESCO (see its Statement by Experts in Race Problems 1950) and partly because of the influence of Jews (who wield much influence on international organizations, UNESCO's experts not excluded) who, though doctrinally wedded most firmly to the view that the Jews are a chosen people, nowadays make out that all races are equal in the sense of being mentally similar. This I regard as nonsense.[91]

For Blacker, racial differences made immigration a threat to Britain's future. Noting the "swelling boat loads of Jamaicans (that) arrive at our ports," he wrote, "Unless our immigration policies are drastically revised the increasing population of other parts of the world—especially those tropical and sub-tropical areas where death-control has been most effective—will result in the emigrants from this country being quickly replaced by coloured people accustomed to lower standards than ours. Instead of a quantitative reduction of our population there will take place a qualitative change, which despite dogmatic pronouncements to the contrary by UNESCO will almost certainly be for the worse."[92]

Blacker's work in population also brought him into contact with more overtly racist members of the population movement, most notably Clarence Gamble and R. Ruggles Gates. Gamble, best known for his aggressive advocacy and funding of sterilization, mainly in the American

South, hoped to expand his work overseas in the postwar years.[93] In 1954, Margaret Sanger and Blacker discussed Gamble's plans and worried that he might antagonize prominent supporters of birth control outside Europe. Blacker pointed out, "The plain fact seems to be that some people are afraid that Dr. Gamble might use the women in undeveloped countries for unauthorized experiments."[94] At the same time, they noted his experience and financial resources, which made him useful. In the end, they decided to use him, but to try to make him work as an individual rather than as a representative of the IPPF.[95]

Alexander Carr-Saunders remained engaged in population debates even after his retirement from the London School of Economics (LSE) and still carried weight in the small world of demography. He served as chair of the Statistical Committee of the Royal Commission on Population.[96] Both during and after the war, the Colonial Office turned to him for guidance on integrating the social sciences and demography into policy making and consulted him about colonial population issues.[97]

Blacker's former teacher and mentor Julian Huxley achieved an even more prominent place in the postwar population movement. Huxley garnered international attention while serving as the first director general of UNESCO (United Nations Educational, Scientific and Cultural Organization) from 1946 to 1948. His advocacy of population control generated considerable controversy during his tenure as director. He raised the profile of the issue and helped lay the groundwork for the World Population Conference in 1954.[98] After his departure from UNESCO, Huxley continued his campaign for population control, publishing and traveling extensively. Like Blacker, Huxley saw control of non-white populations as a matter of preserving the "quality" of population on a global scale. As he noted in a radio appearance, "Quantity is the enemy of quality."[99] He also linked population control to immigration in Britain, arguing, "The problem of coloured immigrants can never approach a solution until something is done, officially, and on a large scale, to encourage birth control in their overcrowded homelands."[100]

While Blacker and other eugenicists became acknowledged experts in global population, the influence of the Eugenics Society reached much further. Eugenicists played an important role in social policy networks, which helped them to shape postwar debates about population policy. Prominent academics like Richard Titmuss, David Glass, and Francois Lafitte had benefited from their relationship with the society, even if their views about eugenics often diverged from those of Huxley and Blacker. Lafitte, the son of Havelock Ellis, served as secretary of the Population

Policy Committee, directed PEP, and became a professor of social policy at Birmingham University. He would be an influential figure in public policy circles and the family planning movement, although he severed his ties with the society after 1945.[101]

Richard Titmuss, who received a chair in social administration at LSE in 1950, remained actively involved in population issues. His work in the 1930s and 1940s on fertility decline established his reputation as a population expert, and he worked with the government and private groups after the war on various projects. A longtime member of the Eugenics Society, he helped edit the *Eugenics Review* in the 1940s and worked with PEP and the PIC.[102] The Colonial Office employed him as a consultant, and he served as a member of its Social Development Committee. He also participated in the review of population policy initiated by the Advisory Council on Scientific Policy in the late 1950s. In 1958, at the request of the Colonial Office, Titmuss undertook a study of the population of Mauritius. His study, published in 1961, recommended a broad-based program of social welfare for the colony, including a comprehensive family planning system.[103]

The most significant relationship for the Eugenics Society would be with PEP. Created in 1931, PEP remained closely affiliated with the Eugenics Society and the PIC, with whom it shared a number of members. In 1938, PEP and PIC formed a joint population policy committee that included Glass, Blacker, Carr-Saunders, and Max Nicholson.[104] The committee continued to function throughout the war, though at a reduced level. It published a series of broadsheets and pamphlets, most notably *Population Policy in Great Britain* in 1948. In the early 1950s, PEP formed a committee to study world population trends. Prominent eugenicists, including Blacker, Nicholson, Carr-Saunders, and Huxley, again comprised much of committee, which Lord Simon chaired and which also included David Glass and Solly Zuckerman. The result, *World Population and Resources*, appeared in 1955. In addition to the population committee, a number of PEP members influenced population policy as activists and officials. Richard Terrell, a Colonial Office official, advocated government support for family planning in the 1950s. Richard Symonds worked for the United Nations' development agencies and helped shape the UN population program in the late 1960s, while Geoffrey Wilson headed the Colombo Plan's Bureau of Technical Cooperation in the early 1950s and served as the permanent secretary of the Overseas Development Ministry from 1968 to 1970.[105]

The PEP report marked the emergence of Solly Zuckerman as an important figure in the population movement. Zuckerman, a South African-born physician, trained under Julian Huxley at Oxford, but his professional life and work concentrated on the anatomy and physiology of primates.[106] Early in his career he studied the hormonal cycle of baboons at Oxford with financial support from the Eugenics Society. He maintained a wide circle of friends and colleagues, including prominent politicians, and became a well-known scientist and intellectual. During the Second World War he served as deputy science advisor to Sir Henry Tizard. After the war, while a professor of anatomy at Birmingham University, he continued his work as a scientific advisor, becoming chief science advisor to the Ministry of Defense in 1959, before serving as chief science advisor to the government of Harold Wilson from 1966 to 1970. In the 1950s, Zuckerman developed an interest in population issues. As he wrote to Julian Huxley in 1955, "A visit to Japan and India have [sic] terrified me."[107] Despite his interest in the topic, Zuckerman knew relatively little about demography in the early 1950s. Zuckerman relied upon his American friend Robert Snider, director of research for the Conservation Foundation, as well as Huxley for guidance. Notwithstanding his lack of experience and intellectual credentials, he became the leading population expert within the British government in the 1950s and 1960s. He delivered a paper at the World Population Conference in Rome in 1954 and became a regular participant in population conferences, including the Caribbean Commission Conference on Demography of 1957, during the next decade.[108] Zuckerman claimed that officials placed a lot of weight on the conference and that they wanted him to "get the matter of population control, i.e. birth control, into a much more powerful context than it is now and one which obviates the political difficulty which prevents anything being done on a big scale."[109]

In addition to his work with the government and private agencies, Zuckerman published a number of articles in newspapers and magazines.[110] Zuckerman also advised the government and private organizations about contraception. His research on baboons helped lay the groundwork for the development of oral contraceptives, and his position as editor of the *Journal of Endocrinology* gave him an important role in the field. He remained pessimistic about the possibility of developing a hormonal contraceptive and believed it would not be a practical alternative in the short run.[111] However, in 1956, faced with a flood of inquiries about the possibility of an oral contraceptive, Zuckerman conceded that the Americans seemed to be on the verge of success. Yet he argued that the necessary testing and controls seemed to be lacking and noted,

"Despite possible dangers, an authoritative American view was that it was unnecessary to wait until a pill had been proved 100% effective. It was reasonable to suppose that the 'pill' would, in fact, be launched prematurely, before there was full knowledge of side-effects."[112]

THE EMERGENCE OF FAMILY PLANNING

In addition to their work in social policy circles, eugenicists continued to be involved in the burgeoning fields of demography and family planning. British activists were central to the creation of the IPPF, which became the principal international family planning group in the postwar era.[113] The IPPF was one of a number of British NGOs that played an important role in international development after 1945. Oxfam, Save the Children, and other organizations shifted their focus to Asia and Africa as decolonization proceeded.[114] They joined an array of British missionary organizations that survived the end of colonial rule and continued to operate in former colonies.[115] Given the lack of facilities in newly independent states and the absence of large numbers of trained population experts in Western governments, private family planning groups often represented the best option once governments decided to fund international population programs. Despite the prominent role played by British nationals in the organization and its close association with the British colonial state, the IPPF enjoyed a quasi-governmental status and received substantial government and UN funding for its work.

The postwar era witnessed a steady expansion of family planning services and dramatic changes in birth control methods, most notably oral contraceptives. After 1945, the principal birth control organization in Britain, the Family Planning Association (FPA), expanded its operations and attempted to find an accommodation with the newly formed National Health Service (NHS). The government remained reluctant to fund family planning and only authorized prescriptions for birth control through the NHS in 1967.[116] The FPA reestablished ties to its colonial affiliates and forged connections with family planning groups in other countries. In 1948 it sponsored the Cheltenham Population Conference, which led to the creation of the International Planned Parenthood Committee. The committee organized a conference in 1952 in Bombay that resulted in the founding of the IPPF.[117] The FPA continued its domestic activities, but its international work transferred to the IPPF. Like its predecessor, the IPPF possessed close ties to the Eugenics Society. Vera Houghton, its first secretary, belonged to the society, and C.P. Blacker and Julian Huxley became prominent in the new organization, which occupied rooms in the Eugenics Society's headquarters.[118]

In its early years, the IPPF struggled financially. Lord Simon and George Cadbury provided funds for setting up offices and work abroad.[119] Cadbury, a Canadian who studied economics at Cambridge, served as the head of the Technical Assistance Administration of the United Nations and as an advisor to several former colonies, including Jamaica. A leader of the Canadian birth control movement, he served in a variety of capacities in the IPPF. Oliver Bird, the heir to a food processing fortune, gave £10,000 in 1956 and established the Oliver Bird Trust to support contraceptive research.[120] However, the bulk of the money came from the United States. The Dorothy Brush Foundation provided $9,000 to set up the headquarters in London and provided another grant for a monthly newsletter.[121] Beyond its headquarters and regional organizations, the IPPF relied upon the energies of local activists. The IPPF inherited a chain of FPA affiliates, including organizations in Hong Kong, India, Jamaica, and Singapore. From the early 1950s onward, the IPPF expanded the number of birth control clinics in the colonies and newly independent states of the Commonwealth, which constituted the bulk of overseas affiliates in the first years of the federation. India, with its well-established movement, constituted one of the critical locations for IPPF work.[122]

The IPPF tried to expand its presence in Africa. The London office corresponded with physicians and officials in eastern and southern Africa who expressed interest in family planning activities. In 1956 Edith Gates, the East African and Far East field representative of the Committee on Maternal Health, set up the IPPF field organization in Africa with a proposed budget of £11,000. Her visit to Kampala, Uganda, in 1957 led to the creation of a family planning committee in the city staffed principally by South Asian volunteers, as would be the case in much of eastern Africa. In 1959, the IPPF appointed the wife of a Colonial Medical Service officer as its regional field organizer for East Africa to work with affiliates in Nairobi, Mombassa, Dar es Salaam, Kampala, and Zanzibar. Work also began in Nigeria, Ghana, and Sierra Leone.[123] In southern Africa, both Rhodesia and South Africa allowed the establishment of clinics aimed at the African population.[124]

The IPPF's experience in the West Indies facilitated family planning efforts among West Indian migrants in Britain. The FPA reported that its Islington Clinic attracted a large number of West Indians and proposed a separate clinic for West Indians in the area. The FPA cooperated with the head of the British Caribbean Welfare Service, Ivo De Souza, to provide birth control information to migrants before their departure for Britain and after their arrival.[125] De Souza's work with the FPA in Britain and the West Indies led to his involvement in international efforts in the region.[126] The High Commission of the West Indies also worked with the FPA as part of its migrant welfare services in Britain.[127]

In addition to its work with affiliates, the IPPF trained health care workers to run overseas clinics. It ran training courses in London; building on the work begun by Edith How-Martyn's Birth International Information Centre in the 1930s and continued by the FPA.[128] By the mid-1950s, several dozen overseas nurses and doctors took the course, which involved lectures and clinic work.[129] The IPPF established links with the Empire Medical Advisory Bureau, which brought health workers from the empire to Britain for training with support from colonial governments.[130] It also collaborated with the Oliver Bird Trust, which wanted to create a Medical Institute in London to train overseas medical staff in birth control techniques. In addition the IPPF organized training conferences for overseas health care professionals in Britain.[131] The first one, held in Edinburgh in November 1958, involved 180 participants drawn from the colonies and the non-white Commonwealth. However, the conference encountered problems. As one observer noted, "Certain of the students appeared to resent population control as an aspect of Colonialism and a discussion of it tended to raise political issues."[132] To avoid this problem in the future, officials decided to emphasize the medical and humanitarian aspects of the IPPF's work.

The IPPF funded research into new contraceptive methods. For most population activists, the future success of the family planning movement abroad required development of a simple, inexpensive contraceptive. In the interwar years, this led the Birth Control Investigation Committee, one of the forerunners of the IPPF, to support the development of the spermicide Volpar.[133] Despite long-standing questions about its safety, the IPPF continued to rely on Volpar, distributing it to its clinics in Africa and Asia.[134] The reliance on Volpar and "foaming powder" for African and Asian clients reflected a consensus view that "simple" methods might be best for less sophisticated peoples and that "any method is better than no method."[135] This lack of concern with the potential risks of contraception characterized much of the population movement in this era.[136]

The IPPF Medical Committee, set up in 1955, tested and approved of spermicides and "rubber devices."[137] In 1957, the IPPF created the Council for the Investigation of Fertility Control, funded by a £30,000 grant from the Oliver Bird Trust.[138] Many population activists believed that a hormonal contraceptive would be the best solution, a view echoed by the Colonial Office. The development of an oral contraceptive in the 1950s by the American Gregory Pinkus capped a thirty-year campaign of research.[139] Yet even as testing proceeded, Eleanor Mears argued that the expense of the pill, its side effects, difficulty of use, and unknown long-term effects made it a unsatisfactory solution. She expressed a preference for something simpler, nonhormonal, and less expensive.[140] Her reservations proved accurate; oral contraceptives, despite their widespread use in the United States and Europe, made less impact in other parts of the world.[141]

The IPPF's work abroad required a close relationship with the Colonial Office. Vera Houghton, who moved from the FPA to the IPPF, corresponded with officials about its activities, and requested assistance on several occasions. Houghton, a veteran of interwar birth control work, was married to Douglas Houghton, a Labour member of Parliament, who became a prominent supporter of family planning in Parliament. In 1967, as chairman of the parliamentary Labour Party, he would help shepherd through the bill legalizing abortion in Britain.[142] The Colonial Office came to treat the IPPF as an extension of the government, even allowing IPPF members to attend meetings as official delegates. As one official said, "In view of the interest being shown by certain colonial governments in the possibility of official support for birth control clinics in their territories, our relations with the IPPF are likely to become closer."[143] While unwilling to fund family planning work, the Colonial Office encouraged the IPPF and local colonial governments to cooperate in the creation of birth control clinics.[144] As Sir John Macpherson, the top civil servant in the Colonial Office, noted:

> The pressure of population growth in many of our overseas territories, particularly in the islands, is a cause of serious concern to us. The Family Planning Association has set up voluntary efforts in Hong Kong, Singapore, Tanganyika, Kenya, Northern Rhodesia, Bermuda, Jamaica, Barbados, and Mauritius .... It has been considered that it would not be politic for the Colonial Office to assist the movement directly, but we have for some years maintained close and friendly relations with the Family Planning Association in this country and with the IPPF. Indeed the growth of the movement must be attributed very largely to the practical assistance given by these two bodies.[145]

Despite this relationship, the government refused to fund IPPF programs, even turning down a request to subsidize its training activities in Britain.[146] Only in the 1960s, as the British moved away from colonial development toward bilateral and international aid programs, would this policy change.

DEMOGRAPHY AS A POLICY SCIENCE

Demography also saw its fortunes advance in the postwar period. The need for improved population information for planning purposes during the war underlined the importance of demography. The growth of the welfare state and economic planning led to a dramatic increase in the amount information collected by the British government. This expansion necessitated the employment of larger numbers of experts, including demographers, to gather and analyze this data.[147] In the immediate postwar years, demographers and other population activists looked to the Royal Commission on Population to provide guidance. In addition to its findings about British population trends, the Royal Commission also recommended changes to the General Register Office (GRO), including increasing the number of statisticians and appointing a statistician as registrar general.[148] Such changes helped trigger a long-running dispute between the GRO and the Government Actuary's Department, which produced competing estimates of future population for use in planning for housing education, family allowances, and the health service.[149]

Academic demography benefited from the expansion of state demography. Its rise in the postwar era mirrored that of other social sciences, which saw an increase in funding and university positions.[150] The center of the discipline remained LSE. David Glass, appointed as reader in demography in 1945, oversaw its expansion at the school, which added a concentration in demography within the sociology program. Glass, who became a chair in sociology in 1948, stayed at the school for the rest of his career. His replacement as reader in demography, Eugene Grebenik, became an important figure in demography as well.[151] Although population studies became a formal program only in 1965, the school attracted a number of students from Britain and abroad who wished to study demography, including Sripati Chandrasekhar, who studied at LSE in the 1950s on a Nuffield Fellowship and later became India's minister of health and family planning.[152] The formal move of the PIC to LSE in 1946 improved the status of demography at the school. LSE provided space and ancillary services to the PIC, and the reader in demography served as its secretary. The PIC flourished due in large part to its ability to secure funding from outside sources. Starting in 1945, the Nuffield Foundation gave £5,000 a year and funded *Population Studies* as well. The PIC, which also received support from the Rockefeller Foundation, the Population Council, and the Simon Population Trust, became an internationally recognized leader in demographic research.[153]

The institutional development of demography was accompanied by the consolidation of a new intellectual paradigm, the theory of the demographic transition. The idea of a demographic transition dated back to the interwar era and the work of scholars like Alexander Carr-Saunders and Warren Thompson, who spoke of stages of population growth and linked changes in population trends to changes in social organization. In the postwar era, American demographers like Davis and Notestein refined the concept; the previously loose association of social and demographic variables became a well-defined sequence of steps undertaken by all societies in the process of modernization.[154] In their model, population growth occurred as traditional societies industrialized and quickly reduced their death rates while birth rates remained high. As a society reached socioeconomic maturity, its values and social system encouraged the emergence of small families and the practice of birth control on a wide scale, thus allowing population stabilization. While subject to further elaboration by later demographers like Ansley Coale and considerable criticism from other scholars, demographic transition theory proved remarkably durable. It remained the cornerstone of demographic analysis and policy initiatives on both sides of the Atlantic.[155]

Demographic transition theory gave demographers a tool to link population trends across historical and social boundaries and thus unified the field in a new way. In particular, the theory explained the central demographic issue of the postwar era, the dramatic growth of non-European populations. The "population explosion" resulted from the unintended consequence of Western medical and technical advances, which lowered death rates by providing modern medicine and infrastructure well before traditional societies in Asia and Africa achieved the social and economic changes that would lead to lower fertility. The idea of a demographic progression toward modernity shared common elements with the idea of modernization elaborated by sociologists like Talcott Parsons. It also echoed the emphasis on economic development in British imperial policy and American foreign policy after 1945.[156]

The emergence of demographic transition theory accelerated the decline of colonial demography as a field. American demographers attacked colonialism and called for an international approach to demographic problems. In their view, the British and other European powers bore much of the responsibility for the emerging crisis because the conquest and exploitation of colonial societies unbalanced their demographic systems. Improved health, administration, and infrastructure led to lower mortality, while fertility remained high. The reliance of colonial economies on agriculture and raw materials delayed the growth of industry and urban life, which left fertility to be determined by traditional social customs. The insistence of colonial governments on the need to protect traditional society from outside influences exacerbated this situation and led to the persistence of high fertility.[157] To break this cycle would require replacing imperial rule with new international organizations capable of monitoring demographic and social trends and encouraging modernization.

The onset of the Cold War made the growth of non-Western populations a more pressing problem. During the Second World War, American demographers warned that Asia and much of the non-Western world stood on the brink of a dramatic increase in population, even as Western population growth would continue to be slow.[158] Demographers and officials feared that overcrowded poor nations would be vulnerable to communist subversion, a point reinforced by the victory of the communists in China in 1949. At the same time, demographers worried that population growth and the problems of economic development in Asia and Africa might prevent or slow down the economic and social modernization necessary to achieve demographic stability. This concern led to an emphasis on increasing access to contraception rather than waiting for social change to generate fertility decline. As a consequence, population control rather than the elimination of poverty became the principal goal.[159]

The widespread acceptance of transition theory reflected the growing dominance of America in population work. The willingness of the Rockefeller Foundation, Carnegie Corporation, and the Ford Foundation to fund demographic research and family planning organizations was central to American success. As in Britain, however, the development of an American population movement took place against a backdrop of official caution and public reluctance to embrace family planning at home and abroad. American birth control activists faced a patchwork of state and federal laws that made it far more difficult for them to operate than their counterparts in Britain. Unlike British activists, they confronted the determined resistance of the American Catholic hierarchy, which retained considerable political influence at the state and local levels.[160] As a consequence, groups like Planned Parenthood made slower progress and continued to encounter legal obstacles until the mid-1960s, when several court rulings and new legislation transformed the legal environment. The political and social issues raised by birth control in America meant that direct support for family planning work remained limited.[161]

Despite this environment, private institutions were willing to fund demographic research.[162] The principal supporter of population work in the interwar years, the Milbank Memorial Fund, derived much of its financial backing from the Carnegie Corporation. In addition, the Rockefeller Fund took a greater role, spurred in large part by the interest of John Rockefeller III in the topic.[163] The creation of the Ford Foundation would provide an even greater impetus to the movement; its role expanded throughout the 1950s and 1960s.[164] Alongside these well-known foundations, other groups and individuals provided funding, including the Brush Foundation, associated with Dorothy Brush, and the Pathfinder Fund, created by Clarence Gamble. Notestein, Kingsley Davis, Frank Lorimer, and other demographers made use of such funding to build an institutional base for the discipline, displaying the entrepreneurial behavior characteristic of social scientists in the postwar era. Their efforts made possible the rapid development of demography in the 1960s and 1970s, when government funding increased dramatically. By contrast, funding for British demography remained considerably more modest.[165]

Notestein and other demographers, while acknowledging the importance of private support, hoped to distance their work from its previous association with eugenics and racism and hoped the professionalization of the discipline would assist in this process.[166] This desire led Notestein to block the appointment of William Vogt to a position at Princeton University because of his extreme views.[167] However, much of the funding for Notestein and other demographers came from organizations and individuals whose motives remained problematic. Gamble, an heir to the Proctor & Gamble fortune, displayed an eagerness to support the sterilization of African Americans and "defectives" that provided a chilling reminder of the eugenic roots of the population movement in the United States.[168] Demographers and activists continued to talk about the "quality" of both the U.S. and non-Western populations. While Notestein spoke of constructing a new "social demography" appropriate for a mass democratic society, he retained distinctions between social classes based on innate attributes. The persistence of these ideas reflected the continued presence in the population movement of convinced eugenicists like Frederick Osborn, who headed the Population Council.[169] In addition to social class, America's racial and ethnic diversity, as well as its colonies in Puerto Rico and the Philippines, made race central to demographers' understanding of American population trends.[170]

American activists hoped for government support for their work. By the late 1940s, demographers already enjoyed a close relationship to the U.S. government. During the war, the Office of Population Research at Princeton provided assistance to U.S. and international agencies. It produced a series of population estimates for postwar Europe for the League of Nations Economic Division. Demographers at Princeton also provided forecasts of Asian populations for the Geographic Section of the State Department.[171] This close relationship continued after the war. In 1948, Notestein and Irene Tauber headed a group of demographers who traveled to East Asia to review the region's population prospects. In spite of General MacArthur's reluctance to raise the issue of population control, they met with officials in Japan and elsewhere in Asia.[172]

For many inside and outside of government, concerns about population growth reflected the emergence of the United States as the dominant Western power. With the coming of the Cold War, the United States dramatically expanded military and development assistance, first in Europe and then in the wider world.[173] One rationale for these programs was their promise to reduce poverty and inequality. Many observers argued that if such conditions persisted, communists and other radicals would take advantage of them and foment unrest.[174] Population growth presented a problem for policy makers, because it seemed to threaten the peaceful transition of power from colonialism to independence and undermine efforts to increase the global standard of living.[175]

Despite sympathy for the ideas of population activists, the U.S. government, like that of Britain, remained wary of the potential political problems involved in open sponsorship of population control. Although officials considered population a significant factor in American policy, political leaders remained reluctant to make family planning a part of foreign aid. The Draper Committee, formed in 1959 to advise the U.S. government on foreign aid programs, characterized population growth as a major concern for U.S. foreign policy and recommended that the government offer assistance to countries requesting family planning aid. The ensuing public controversy led President Dwight Eisenhower to repudiate its conclusions, although he later questioned his decision. While many politicians and officials endorsed the idea, the U.S government did not act until the mid-1960s.[176]

Although the U.S. government refused to play an active role, the American population movement expanded during the 1950s. The Ford Foundation, with its aggressive approach to funding population work, helped break the logjam of public caution in the early 1950s and provided millions of dollars to support research and population programs. In addition to the Conservation Foundation, which took an increasing interest in population issues under the leadership of Henry Fairfield Osborn, the formation of the Population Council in 1952 provided a new focus for U.S. population work. The Population Council, funded by the Ford Foundation, the Carnegie Corporation, and the Rockefeller Foundation, became a major sponsor of demographic and biomedical research.[177] The council provided funding for the establishment of university-based population studies centers, thus boosting the discipline's academic standing. Even before the onset of widespread government support for demographic research and family planning programs, U.S. foundations and organizations created an infrastructure of research and specialists that far surpassed those available to British activists.[178]

British organizations also benefited from the expansion of private grants for population work. The IPPF relied on American support, and the LSE and the PIC depended on the Rockefeller Foundation for much of their early funding. Such funding also facilitated cooperation between public and private organizations in birth control work. In addition to the Jamaican Family Life Project, funded by the Conservation Foundation and the Population Council, Americans provided assistance to family planning services in Barbados.[179] By comparison to the Americans, British foundations offered limited funding. The most important British institution, the Nuffield Foundation, gave a total of £60,000 from 1945 to 1960, a substantial sum, but only a fraction of the amount contributed by American foundations. In addition, the Simon Population Trust and the Oliver Bird Trust contributed to the training and administrative costs of the IPPF.

The willingness of American foundations to fund British organizations reflected the close ties that existed between American and British demographers and population activists. C. P. Blacker worked with Margaret Sanger and William Vogt as well as Frederick Osborn. David Glass, who spent a year at the Rockefeller Foundation in 1939 and lived in Washington, D.C., during the war, enjoyed close ties with American demographers. He worked with Frank Notestein at the United Nations, and the two of them met with the Nuffield Foundation trustees in March 1954 to encourage the foundation to support population research, particularly the PEP report on world population.[180]

Solly Zuckerman played a critical role in using these relationships to bring the American and British governments together on population policy. As a representative of the British government, he knew how to reach out to officials to gain support for population initiatives, as his work on the Jamaican Family Life Project in the mid-1950s demonstrated. His personal ties to American activists like Robert Snider and Henry Fairfield Osborne made him the natural choice to approach the Colonial Office and the Nuffield Foundation to obtain backing for the project. These ties also allowed him to make connections with American foundations and officials. Zuckerman urged closer cooperation between the two countries and argued that the British should welcome such assistance. In his words, "The US would like to feel that their work in a British territory is done in co-operation with British workers and resources."[181] Initially this cooperation involved private efforts funded by American foundations like the Carnegie Corporation and the Ford Foundation. Zuckerman believed that such assistance would increase if the British proved receptive. As he noted in a letter to the colonial secretary of state, Alan Lennox Boyd, "The way things are moving, however, I have little doubt that American Foundations are likely to help in the future more than they are already doing."[182]

The work of British and American population activists, although more public and substantial in the postwar years, remained limited in effect through the 1950s. More progress required support from national governments. In Britain the decline of the empire altered the political environment for population work and led to government funding for international family planning programs in the 1960s. The British also supported American efforts to establish an international population program under UN auspices in the mid-1960s. The work of the United Nations, along with U.S. support for overseas family planning services, led to a dramatic increase in funding for population programs that began in the early 1970s. These efforts marked the end of the colonial era in population policy and a transition to an international regime of population control dominated by the United States.

The emergence of international population programs in the 1970s also affected the fortunes of the groups that made up the population movement: eugenicists, birth controllers, and demographers. The last enjoyed unprecedented opportunities within the population establishment and academic life, as the need for trained experts expanded rapidly. The retrenchment of the 1980s still left an impressive infrastructure of university departments, international organizations, and professional journals. Birth control campaigners experienced considerable success as well. The development of new contraceptives, the growing acceptance of birth control, and its easier accessibility through state and private channels fulfilled one of the central objectives of the movement. The upsurge in women's political activity gave feminist birth control activists far greater power within the population movement than in previous decades. However, many feminist remained critical of the methods used by population programs and their marginalizing of women's concerns, despite attempts to reorient these programs toward the needs of women.[183] For eugenicists, the seeming collapse of the movement masked considerable continuity. The first generation of activists in the postwar international population movement could still trace their roots in the movement. Even after this generation faded from the scene, eugenic ideas retained a hold in both public discourse and scientific research. The controversies over race and IQ as well as debates over the hereditary nature of sexual orientation, poverty, and criminal behavior drew in part upon older ideas. Eugenics proved capable of refashioning itself and pursing its goals in the fields of medical genetics and sociobiology even as it functioned as a bogeyman to both the right and the left.[184]

6 British Population Policy in the Postcolonial Era

The dismantling of the empire left the British searching for a new global role. Even before the merger of the Colonial Office with the Commonwealth Relations Office in 1966, the British government transferred most of the aid and development functions of the Colonial Office, including population policy, to the Department of Technical Cooperation (DTC) and then to the Ministry of Overseas Development (ODM). New bilateral and multilateral aid programs, which included funding for family planning work, replaced the colonial development agencies created by the British in the 1940s. British officials, through contacts with successor governments, private agencies, and international organizations, established a framework for cooperation on population issues. With the Scandinavians and the Americans, they became leading advocates of a new regime of international population programs. In many ways, decolonization liberated the British from the constraints imposed by imperial politics and allowed them to pursue the more aggressive approach to population problems that many of these officials unsuccessfully advocated in the waning years of the empire. The provision of family planning aid and advice to successor states and the work of private activists ensured that Britain maintained an influential role in the formulation and implementation of postcolonial population policies. As in other areas of postcolonial engagement, Britain traded on its contacts and local knowledge to retain a place in a world now dominated by the United States, the Soviet Union, and new international organizations.

These programs emerged as decolonization compelled the British government to reorganize its aid policy. The desire to fund the remaining colonial governments as well as assist newly independent states complicated the allocation of aid.[1] To address this issue, the government created the Department of Technical Cooperation in 1961. The DTC represented a compromise among the three ministries that retained responsibility for overseas affairs—the Colonial Office, the Commonwealth Relations Office and the Foreign Office. The DTC reported to each of these ministries in relevant cases; control over capital expenditures and grants remained the prerogative of the ministries. In 1964, the new Labour government, which had promised to increase development funding, created the Ministry of Overseas Development, headed by the left-wing member of Parliament Barbara Castle.[2] The new ministry reflected the interest of the prime minister, Harold Wilson, in the subject, which dated back to the early 1950s and his association with Thomas Balogh, a well-known development economist.[3]

The transition from colonial development to international aid involved a redeployment of ideas and people. As the government reorganized its overseas ministries, the fate of more than 20,000 colonial officials became more pressing. Negotiations over the pay and pension of civil servants occupied considerable time, and officials expressed concern for the prospects of the members of the Overseas Civil Service.[4] While some found employment in the remaining British colonies, the vast majority had to look elsewhere. Some officials were absorbed by branches of the Home Civil Service, while a number transferred from the Colonial Office to the DTC. Most of the personnel employed by the new department came from the Colonial Office, including its director general, Sir Andrew Cohen.

The desire to establish a new role for Britain and to train officials for development work led the DTC and ODM to support the growth of development studies in Britain. Already in the 1950s, the Colonial Office had given £50,000 from the Colonial Welfare and Development fund to establish Queen Elizabeth House at Oxford, the forerunner of the Department of International Development.[5] In the 1960s, Cambridge University hosted a series of conferences on international development that brought together experts and government officials from around the world. Organized by Ronald Robinson, a historian and former Colonial Office Africa expert, they replaced the training courses for colonial officials established in the postwar era. These conferences allowed the British to offer their own experiences of development administration in a new framework of international aid, which paralleled the shift in aid functions from the Colonial Office to the DTC.[6] In 1966, ODM created the Institute for Development Studies (IDS) at Sussex University to train experts for its own agencies as well as for overseas and international institutions.[7]

Development institutes and agencies provided a new area of employment for the officials displaced by the end of the empire, as did the international agencies and nongovernmental organizations (NGOs) that replaced many of the functions of the colonial state. Both the IDS and the development studies unit at Cambridge relied upon former colonial administrators to staff their courses.[8] By one estimate, 10 percent of former colonial officials worked for the United Nations and international organizations after leaving government service.[9] The presence of these former colonial officials added the weight of practical experience to the new field of development studies, but it also allowed for many of the ideas and programs of the late colonial state to continue in the postcolonial era.[10] In agriculture, the programs of the Food and Agriculture Organization (FAO), the World Bank, and the UN Development Programme drew on British experiences, especially in Africa.[11] While much of the intellectual inspiration for international population programs would come from demographic transition theory, British officials had long made a connection between problems of development and population growth. This argument gained traction in the 1960s as experts assessed the failure of postcolonial aid programs.[12] The linkage among food, population, and development that emerged in the postwar colonial state would inform the new programs for development and ensure that British expertise remained in high demand.

It was in this new political environment that DTC began to reassess British population policy. Most of the officials who supported population control within the Colonial Office, including Philip Rogers, W.H. Chinn, and J.K. Thompson, occupied senior positions in the new agency. Almost immediately after its creation, the DTC addressed the subject of population control. In late 1961, the Pakistani high commissioner contacted the department to inquire about technical assistance for the newly established Pakistani family planning program. Officials, while expressing interest, remained unclear on how to proceed.[13] The DTC contacted the Colonial Office, which reported that it handed off such inquires to the Family Planning Association (FPA) and the International Planned Parenthood Federation (IPPF). As one official put it, "[The Colonial Office] acted as a post office in the matter, but certainly as a friendly one, with a desire to help. The Associations have done quite a lot to help in a number of dependent territories—including Barbados, Hong Kong, Singapore and Jamaica—with the knowledge, and tacit blessing, of the Colonial Office. The Colonial Office have, however, always acted in such a way as to be able to say that the matter was not one in which HMG had ever taken the initiative or played any active part."[14]

The appointment of Sir Colville Deverell as secretary-general IPPF in 1964 would bring the government and the federation even closer. Deverell, who retired from the colonial service in 1962, had served as governor of the Windward Islands and Mauritius, where he supported family planning programs. Once installed at the IPPF, he relied on old contacts to further the organization's agenda. Andrew Cohen, the secretary of ODM, described him as an old friend and met with him frequently.[15] In early 1965, Deverell served on a working party of experts and officials that recommended government funding for the IPPF.[16] In 1965, the ODM gave the IPPF a Colonial Development and Welfare grant of £7,625, which grew to £12,980 in 1966–67, including £6,000 for an IPPF regional office for East Africa at Nairobi.[17] This grant increased to £50,000 for 1967–68 and for 1968–69, with a further increase to £100,000 per year for the next two years.[18] While this decision grew out of the existing relationship between the IPPF and the British government, it also reflected the shortage of demographic and contraceptive specialists in Britain. The British government lacked the ability to offer much in the way of concrete assistance in the short term.[19] The ODM expanded its support for the IPPF as a way of bridging the gap.[20] This policy enhanced the status of the IPPF and laid the groundwork for the massive increase in its funding in the 1970s.

While the British government worked through the IPPF in the 1960s and 1970s, Cohen and others in the DTC expressed an interest in developing a more forward policy for the department. In 1963, after lengthy discussions, the DTC decided it should field requests from overseas governments for technical assistance with family planning, without announcing this shift publicly. Instead, the DTC sent a telegram to colonial and Commonwealth governments informing them of the change.[21] The creation of a bilateral program of family planning assistance, while politically significant, proved to be less important in practical terms. The decision not to provide capital grants or bulk supplies of contraceptives limited the impact of the new policy.[22]

The new stance of the British government increased the significance of population issues but also highlighted the bureaucratic infighting and confusion generated by the shrinking of the empire and Britain's role in the world. In theory, the creation of the ODM resolved the confusion over responsibility for aid programs, but the ODM quickly encountered problems. The foreign exchange crisis inherited by the Wilson government led to deep cuts in its budget.[23] It lost its place in the cabinet in 1967 and fought unsuccessfully to remain independent. Cohen and other officials tried to prevent the Foreign Office, previously uninvolved in population issues, from taking over population policy.[24] They argued that only ODM possessed the necessary expertise to deal with newly independent states.[25] As one official complained, "I do not know how we are going to make the Foreign Office take notice of what our experts think, instead of picking up the more tendentious American propaganda on the subject."[26] After reading a paper prepared by the Foreign Office, Cohen expressed misgivings: "We think the paper, if I may say so, is a shade too paternalistic. We are less expert in population questions than some of the developing countries. It is not so much a question of persuading them and showing them what to do, but of joining with them in tackling some of their problems and using our influence in suitable ways."[27]

An official with the Aid Department of the Commonwealth Office made a similar argument in a letter to an ODM official: "Indeed it is important to us in our dealings with the Commonwealth that our policy should be presented as a continuation and development of existing policy rather than as something new. In certain vital Commonwealth countries, such as India, we should, as you know, be preaching to the converted; but in other countries, especially in Africa, we should have to approach the question with considerable tact, as will no doubt be the case for you in, for example, many Latin American countries."[28]

Despite such arguments, in 1970 ODM became an agency within the Foreign Office and renamed the Overseas Development Administration (ODA). The Foreign Office, which absorbed the remnants of the Colonial Office and the Commonwealth Relations Office, emerged as the sole departmental representative of British interests overseas.

While the British government reorganized the structure of overseas aid, it began a fundamental reassessment of population policy. A general sense existed that the British needed to catch up to the United States and Sweden, which would require a considerable increase in resources and a more focused approach.[29] In March 1968, Harold Wilson created an interdepartmental Committee on World Population, headed by Solly Zuckerman.[30] The committee's report, issued in July 1969, reviewed global population trends and their possible impact upon Britain. It emphasized the potential for political and economic unrest within rapidly growing countries like Nigeria, Mauritius, Brazil, Indonesia, and Egypt. It also argued that population growth, by frustrating efforts at development, could lead to more aggressive external policies by some governments and help the spread of communist ideas in Asia.[31]

In order to forestall such problems, the report recommended an increase in funding for population control to £2–3 million per year.[32] Not surprisingly, this recommendation met with resistance, most predictably from the Treasury. However, even officials sympathetic to family planning programs worried about the difficulties of allocating increased funding at a time when donors appeared to be chasing a limited pool of projects, with the Americans, Swedes, and the United Nations hoping to fund similar initiatives.[33] As an official argued in a letter to Cohen, "Population control is now a fashionable subject and becoming more so, and everybody is going to try to promote their part."[34] Officials expressed doubts about the ability of voluntary groups to oversee large projects. As one ODM official noted, "Some of the FPAs ... are rather like duchesses at the garden party—in other words they are small outfits relying almost entirely on voluntary work and would need a good deal of administrative support to enable them to spend money more effectively."[35] Notwithstanding such concerns, the British government increased its support for population programs from £174,000 in 1969–70 to £1.3 million in 1972–73, including funds for capital grants and contraceptives.[36]

In order to bolster its population programs, in 1968 ODM created the Population Bureau.[37] Under the direction of David Wolfers, a demographer, the bureau functioned as a clearinghouse for information and encouraged the development of courses to train British personnel in demography and family planning.[38] It established close ties with the London School of Hygiene and Tropical Medicine and its Centre for Overseas Population Studies, founded in 1965. William Brass, a former colonial official who became an expert in African demography, played a key role in establishing the center, which offered a master's program in medical demography.[39] The bureau also worked with the IDS to create seminars on demographic issues and subsidized training schemes for overseas medical personnel along the lines of those carried out by the FPA and the IPPF since the 1950s.[40]

The willingness of the British government to support overseas population programs also reflected changing attitudes within Britain about population and family planning. In 1967 the British government finally authorized family planning services within the National Health Service. This decision removed a source of embarrassment for supporters of population control, who felt keenly the difficulty of arguing for programs abroad that would not be allowed in Britain.[41] In the early 1970s, following the liberalization of British abortion laws, David Wolfers raised the idea of providing support for abortions in recipient countries.[42] The embrace by the government of a more aggressive policy on birth control fit the mood of many in the government and the population movement about domestic population trends. While Solly Zuckerman raised concerns about Britain's and Europe's declining share of the global population, he also worried about the environmental impact of Britain's population.[43] Officials and activists discussed the impact of immigration from the former empire on Britain's future population. As one official argued, "The UK however has of course already experienced more of the effects of the world population explosion than most other countries because of its imperial heritage and relatively lenient immigration laws. Even though the latter have now been tightened, it seems to me that it would be appropriate to try to gauge the likely pressures to emigrate from our remaining colonial possessions and from those newly independent islands where the problem of overpopulation is already severe."[44]

Ironically, the increased interest of the British government in population planning at home brought an old colonial hand back into the discussion. As Sir Philip Rogers noted in a letter in 1970, "As you know, I have been interested in population questions for some considerable time, arising out of my early work in the Colonial Office. When I was in CSD [Civil Service Department], I was delighted to take part in discussions with Solly Zuckerman about the proposal to establish in the Cabinet Office a unit for the study of population questions. In my new job here [Department of Health and Social Services] I am of course inevitably concerned with such issues, and my Secretary of State is also anxious that this Department should be active in a number of fields which relate to population questions, particularly family planning."[45]

The decision to fund family planning services applied to the empire and former colonies. Hong Kong's family planning program, which dated back to the 1930s, received support from private and public sources. By 1962, the government provided a subsidy of HK$240,000 for the IPPF, which operated twenty-two clinics within government medical facilities.[46] Despite the fact that the colony enjoyed a "fairly easy wicket . . . compared with the West Indies," officials and activists worried about potential political problems and hoped for an official endorsement of their activities.[47] Yet the governor of Hong Kong argued that the real question was whether the clinics could address what one activist called the desperate situation in the colony. Governor Black noted that only 9,000 out of 600,000 women of childbearing age attended clinics and argued, "In light of these figures, one wonders whether, given any amount of official endorsement, the impact of the Association's present activities is likely to have any striking effect. If in due course, a cheap and effective oral contraceptive were available, without side effects, then the position may change radically, and the question of official endorsement will become a matter of moment."[48]

The Colonial Office also maintained its interests in the Pacific and Indian Ocean as well as the West Indies. In 1965 the Colonial Office, in consultation with the DTC, gave Mauritius £14,000 for family planning work and £7,000 for an IPPF project in the Seychelles.[49] Fiji, Tonga, and the Gilbert and Ellice Islands continued to receive aid up until independence.[50]

The DTC's shift in policy opened the door for family planning aid to independent states inside and out of the Commonwealth.[51] Efforts to include population programs in the Colombo Plan remained stalemated by the political caution of the British government. This stance frustrated Geoffrey Wilson, the director of the Colombo Plan's Bureau of Technical Cooperation, who supported population control.[52] In 1957, Solly Zuckerman contacted the high commissioner for India, Malcolm MacDonald, in an effort to generate a request from the Indian government for assistance with birth control research.[53] The Commonwealth Relations Office, despite being sympathetic to the idea, ruled out this approach for political reasons.[54]

The failure of a multilateral approach via the Colombo Plan led the Pakistani and Indian governments to request assistance directly from Britain, a move that precipitated DTC's endorsement of family planning aid. While initially limited to advice and training, the program expanded to provide capital assistance and supplies of contraceptives. In initial discussions in the mid-1960s, Indian officials hoped to obtain subsidized oral contraceptives and IUDs. Given the cost and greater complexity of these methods, the Indian and Pakistani governments also expressed interest in bulk supplies of condoms.[55] In 1960, the Indian government placed an order for diaphragms and condoms with two British firms, and in 1966 the Pakistani government received £25,000 worth of condoms from DTC.[56] This provision of condoms built upon the preference in Asia for Durex condoms from the London Rubber Company and helped solidify the position of this company in the marketplace. In 1969, the Indian high commissioner requested that the company consider expanding its manufacturing in India to help meet demand. The popularity of Durex and the alleged unwillingness of Asians to use American condoms led the ODA in 1974 to request that the Energy Ministry increase the power allocation for the condom maker to address a shortage of Durex products in Sri Lanka and elsewhere.[57] Officials also discussed other methods of birth control. Sterilization appealed to some officials because of its low cost. Yet, the scale required to achieve significant results caused them to hesitate. One official noted that although 400,000 sterilizations had already been performed in India, it would require 3,000,000 per year to affect population growth.[58] As part of its overall expansion of support for population programs in the late 1960s, the British government substantially increased funding for South Asia.[59]

Former colonies in Africa and the West Indies also requested assistance. In addition to assisting existing programs in Jamaica and Barbados, in 1967 the ODM supported a family planning program in Trinidad and Tobago.[60] In Africa, the ODM worked in concert with the IPPF to create a headquarters in Kenya.[61] The climate on the rest of the continent remained less welcoming. The government in Tanzania expressed an interest in increasing its population, and as one official noted in 1967, "The general impression in Africa is that the continent is under-populated, but few of the African countries have adequate demographic and other statistics to show whether their rates of growth are outrunning their capacity for economic growth."[62] Despite such feelings, by the early 1970s, a number of African countries received family planning aid from Britain.[63]

The creation of bilateral population programs fulfilled a central goal of officials and population activists. Yet this accomplishment represented somewhat of a pyrrhic victory, for the British government lacked the resources to make a significant contribution to population control on its own. The budgetary and foreign exchange problems of the government led to a decline in overseas assistance in real terms.[64] This decline complicated family planning aid, because recipient countries wished to avoid having such assistance counted as part of their total. While the British maintained their bilateral programs, they also recognized that given their limited resources, support for international programs offered the best opportunity for Britain to make an impact.[65] This view led the British to become partners with the Americans in an effort to create international population programs in the 1960s that laid the groundwork for a new approach to global population control.

BRITAIN AND THE EMERGENCE OF INTERNATIONAL POPULATION PROGRAMS

Although the British government launched its own bilateral family planning initiative, it also worked with the United States and other countries to sponsor international population programs. The scope of these programs far exceeded those of the British government and would have a far greater impact on newly independent states in Asia and Africa. British support for international population control grew out of Britain's evolving relationship with the United States and the United Nations. Even as the British signaled their willingness to fund population programs, the Lyndon Johnson administration in the United States dramatically stepped up its support for family planning work and made population control part of its foreign aid program. U.S. government assistance soared from $2.3 million in 1965 to $70 million in 1973.[66] Following this shift in policy, the British and American governments would lay the groundwork for an international population program under UN auspices. The breakthrough of the mid-1960s was the product of an Anglo-American agreement about the significance of population growth and the desire of both governments to work with the United Nations and other groups to create an international population policy.

Britain's willingness to work with the United Nations on population issues in the 1960s contrasted sharply with its stance in the immediate postwar years. The British government attempted to limit international scrutiny of its colonial territories, a concern that extended to demographic issues.[67] Although the British government supported the formation of a United Nations Population Commission, it resisted efforts to make colonial demography an area of UN concern. In the commission's early years, the British refused to allow international access to colonies and trust territories. The British government feared that other nations would use the issue of overpopulation to criticize the shortcomings of British colonial administration and to interfere in the work of local governments. As the Colonial Office argued, "The problems in which the Population Commission and other functional agencies of the UN are interested certainly arise in colonial territories as elsewhere, but are not inherent in or conditioned by the colonial status of the territories.... But the terms 'colonial' and 'backward' are by no means synonymous. There is already far too much tendency in international circles to concentrate on colonial questions in order to divert attention from conditions in their own territories."[68]

This line placed David Glass, the British representative to the commission, in an uncomfortable position. On one hand, the British lacked the ability to take accurate censuses in much of its empire, particularly Africa; on the other they refused to accept international offers of assistance. Glass's suggestion that the Population Commission study the demography of equatorial Africa led to a rebuke from officials.[69]

By the early 1950s, however, British officials began to see the advantages of cooperating with the United Nations. This shift occurred as the Colonial Office began to argue that population growth was undercutting its development programs. This view may have led officials to take a warmer attitude to multilateral discussions in part to deflect criticism of colonial governance by focusing on the demographic obstacles to progress. The new attitude can be seen in the response to the UN Committee on Land and Settlement Policy in Dependent Territories in 1951. Officials hoped to use the committee "to publicize the problems a colonial power has to face and to emphasize the success we are achieving."[70] The brief prepared by the Colonial Office for the UN delegation emphasized population growth, especially in East Africa, as the source of social and economic difficulties.[71]

Despite cooperating with the United Nations on demographic issues, the British remained reluctant to raise the issue of population control in the United Nations. British officials maintained a discrete silence about their own interest in family planning and their cooperation with the IPPF in colonial territories. In the absence of concerted effort by the major powers in support of population programs, it fell to Sweden and other Scandinavian countries to press for UN action.[72] A coalition of Catholic and communist regimes effectively blocked international work before the early 1960s, despite the hopes of British officials that the Catholic Church would change its mind about contraception.[73] In early 1961, the British UN delegation requested permission to "swim with the tide" on a proposal by the Swedes to allow UN agencies to provide technical assistance on family planning. In practice this meant that the British delegation would vote in line with the majority of developing countries.[74] The resolution in favor of UN technical assistance failed to gain a majority, despite British support.

In the mid-1960s, the stalemate over international population programs would be broken. In June 1964, the Foreign Office, which handled UN population issues prior to the creation of the ODM, entered into discussions with the United States about a joint effort to create a UN population program. It informed the Americans of the British government's new family planning policy but asked that it not yet be publicized.[75] That same year, the deputy medical advisor for DTC contacted the U.S. Agency for International Development (AID) to discuss plans for population programs.[76] The United States welcomed the British government's increased openness and its support for population programs in the United Nations.[77] This initiative would lead to the 1966 UN resolution that sanctioned assistance for family planning. The United States and Great Britain both contributed to the Population Trust Fund and its successor, the UN Fund for Population Activities, and became, along with Sweden, major backers of international family planning efforts.[78]

Britain's partnership with the United States in support of international population programs represented an important shift in British policy. While some officials remained skeptical of the United Nations and called for Britain to focus on its own bilateral program, those most involved in population policy, like Andrew Cohen, supported international efforts.[79] The recognition that Britain could no longer go it alone forced officials to recast Britain's international role. They hoped Britain's expertise and contacts would allow it to serve as a go-between for the United States and the United Nations with newly independent states. Officials felt that the presence of the British would prevent accusations of strong-arming or even genocide being directed at population programs by their opponents. They also argued that some nations would consider the British less domineering than the Americans, thus facilitating the acceptance of international assistance.[80]

While official efforts formed a one part of Britain's new role in international population programs, the work of private individuals and agencies provided another channel for British influence in the postcolonial world.[81] The British played a central role in the creation of the new regime of international aid that emerged in the postwar era, including population programs. Notwithstanding the coolness of the British government to what it saw as UN meddling, individual Britons filled key posts in the United Nations. Julian Huxley served as the first head of UNESCO (the United Nations Educational, Scientific and Cultural Organization), while Sir John Boyd-Orr headed up the FAO from 1945 to 1948. Both men used their positions to raise population issues on the global stage. From the onset of the United Nations, British and Commonwealth nationals, often from civil service backgrounds, helped construct its organizational framework. They filled important positions in the development agencies of the United Nations and oversaw their integration with population programs in the late 1960s. In addition to Boyd-Orr, Frank McDougall, an Australian economist who worked with a number of Commonwealth agencies in the interwar years, became a key FAO advisor and advocate for population control. George Cadbury, a Canadian population activist and a future president of the IPPF, became the first director of the United Nations Technical Assistance Administration (UNTAA). A Briton, Sir David Owen, was the co-administrator of the UNTAA's successor organizations, the United Nations Technical Assistance Board (UNTAB) and the United Nations Development Programmes from 1951 to 1969. Owen had previously acted as secretary of PEP before serving under Stafford Cripps during the war.[82] He took a keen interest in population issues and briefly served as president of the IPPF before his death in 1970. Owen played a central role in the initial roll-out of the UN population program and was responsible for hiring Richard Symonds at UNTAB in 1950. Symonds, who later taught at IDS, worked as a consultant for the UN Population Division and wrote an influential report on how to organize the United Nations' new population efforts.[83]

The creation of the United Nations, international agencies, and NGOs opened up new opportunities for British and Commonwealth administrators with imperial and international experience. This generation of international civil servants moved in a milieu of private organizations, policy groups, and government service similar to that which formed the British population movement. Perhaps the prototypical figure of this new breed was Sir Geoffrey Wilson. Wilson, a protégé of Stafford Cripps, served with the British government's United Nations department in 1945 and worked for thebefore becoming head of the Technical Cooperation Bureau for the Colombo Plan. After working for the World Bank from 1956 to 1966, he joined the ODM, becoming its permanent secretary from 1968 to 1970. Upon retirement in 1970, he became the chairman of Oxfam and a board member of the Overseas Development Institute and the IDS.[84]

In the decade of the 1970s, population programs expanded rapidly under the aegis of USAID and the United Nations Population Fund (UNFPA). The new international population regime rested on a consensus among Western elites about the threat posed by overpopulation to global stability and a new discourse of international development. On a purely quantitative scale, these programs enjoyed remarkable growth, with the UNFPA share of funding reaching some $500 million by 2004. At the same time, the growing sophistication of contraceptives and the programs used to distribute them expanded access to birth control to much of the world's population. Virtually every nation that wished could receive family planning assistance. In this new era, Britain continued to play a subsidiary role as both a donor and program manager, particularly in the area of family planning and aid work by NGOs. Given the political twists in American family planning policy since the 1980s, Britain and other Western nations could be viewed as more consistent supporters of population programs, with the British share reaching £65 million in 1995. In this postcolonial world, the practical experience and networks of the British, stripped of their colonial trappings, proved crucial to the new programs. The refashioning of British aid and population policy in the 1960s made this transition possible. The new ethos of development fostered in the ODM and academic programs proclaimed the neutrality of British efforts and a desire to assist former imperial subjects. As many in Britain had hoped, the end of the empire led not to the elimination of British influence, but rather to a redeployment of British energies within the new international organizations that carried out development and population work. Such systematic programs can be seen as the fulfillment of the dreams of two generations of activists and officials in Britain, though not in the context they originally envisioned.

Conclusion: Population and the Legacies of Empire

> It is no exaggeration to say that in power the English countries would be more than a match for the remaining nations of the world, whom in the intelligence of their people and the extent and wealth of their dominions they already considerably surpass.
> CHARLES DILKE, *Greater Britain* (1869)

> The sense of being a persecuted minority which is growing among ordinary English people in the areas of the country which are affected is something that those without direct experience can hardly imagine.
> ENOCH POWELL, "Rivers of Blood Speech" (1968)

A century separates the optimism of Charles Dilke's *Greater Britain* from the pessimism of Enoch Powell's "Rivers of Blood." While both turned on the question of race and power, Dilke wrote at a time when the British saw the power of numbers moving in their favor, while Powell expressed the fears of a Britain seemingly shrinking in the face of new challenges from abroad. These quotes embody the dramatic changes in how the British perceived themselves and their place in the world in demographic terms. The evolution of demographic ideas sheds light on changing beliefs about race, empire, and national identity in twentieth-century Britain, as the empire disappeared and a new postimperial Britain emerged. While much of the debate about imperial population remained confined to realm of ideas, the ideas of British demographers and population activists mattered because they influenced the policies of the world's greatest empire at a critical time in its history and would continue to be important even after that empire collapsed.

This book offers a cautionary tale about the limits of expert advice and technocratic government in the twentieth century and the ways in which the desire for control and power can shape seemingly objective science. Colonial demography emerged out of the intersection of the development of quantitative human sciences and the need of colonial governments for greater knowledge of indigenous societies. Demographers examined how the population dynamics of colonial peoples differed from those of Europeans and offered suggestions how these dynamics could be shaped by the imperial state. Population activists served as crucial intermediaries in this process, supporting the work of colonial demographers and lobbying the state about the demographic problems of empire. Given the current interest in the relationship between power and knowledge, what is most striking about imperial population policy is how often officials and activists got it wrong. Students of population persistently overstated the possibility of population decline in Britain, while stubbornly clinging to outdated ideas about non-European peoples. More fundamentally, even as officials began to grasp the dimensions of the demographic issues they faced, they proved unable to act effectively. Hamstrung by limited resources and political concerns, they could do little to create effective population programs.

This failure is all the more surprising in light of the officials and activists who pursued imperial population control. The outstanding private exponent of population control in the postwar era, Solly Zuckerman, possessed an international reputation as a scientist, had close ties to the left and the Labour Party, and held advanced views on issues like nuclear war and the environment. Civil servants like Philip Rogers and Andrew Cohen represented a new generation of colonial officials. Educated at elite schools and chosen through a rigorous examination system, they rose to the top just as the colonial system remade itself, placing a premium on specialist knowledge and administrative skills. They were given unprecedented authority and resources in an attempt to reform the empire. Politically, they believed themselves to be progressives and were close associates of left-wing pressure groups and politicians. These officials saw themselves not as reactionaries defending an outdated system, but the vanguard of an age of effective, constructive imperialism that would prepare colonial subjects for freedom while raising their standard of living. Despite their ideals and the advantages they possessed, their efforts failed. However, for many of them, the postimperial age would offer a second chance to pursue their ambitions in the new development agencies of the British government and international institutions like the United Nations.

The failure of colonial demography reflected the larger weakness and shortcomings of the British Empire in the twentieth century. For much of its history, the British Empire was administered "on the cheap," allowing the British to make only minimal investments in defense, economic development, and social welfare. The dual challenge of nationalist movements and new international rivalries put an end to that era and forced the British to make difficult choices about allocating resources and the nature of imperial governance. Yet such change encountered strict limits. As imperial population policy demonstrates, British elites clung to their belief in the fundamental differences between themselves and their non-white subjects. This meant a policy for whites that encouraged higher birth rates and immigration and another for non-whites focused on lower birth rates and strict controls over movement. Such a racially based policy made it difficult to persuade colonial subjects that population control served their interests. At the same time, the failure of the British to create an infrastructure of health services and education in the empire made the implementation of population policy at the local level virtually impossible. These twin failings prevented any meaningful progress on population control prior to decolonization.

The racial construction of imperial populations tended to lump all imperial peoples together as "primitive," despite the radical differences among colonial societies. This belief was deeply embedded in British ideas of population going back to the work of Malthus. Non-white peoples were thought to possess fundamentally different population dynamics from Europeans. While the justification for this belief switched from biological traits to social attributes, population activists and officials still viewed non-Europeans societies as backward. This belief lay at the core of British perceptions of the empire as a demographic system subdivided by race and level of development. It also led them to link the problems of poverty and underdevelopment to population rather than the failures of the British Empire to advance the interests of its subjects. The postcolonial world would inherit this approach to population. With the end of the empire, former colonies became the "Third World," and the problems of poverty and development came to be seen as characteristic of all these societies.

While the population movement flourished in the postcolonial era, the launch of postimperial Britain proved to be a rocky one. Despite its admission to the European Union in 1973, Britain remained uneasily perched between its own national identity and its ties to the United States and its former colonies. Alongside a fierce debate about the reasons for Britain's decline, another debate over the meaning of Britishness and Englishness raged in Whitehall, Parliament, and popular culture. Concerns about Americanization, the influence of Europe and the emergence of ethnic nationalism in Scotland, Wales, and Northern Ireland contributed to a growing sense of unease about British identity and its future.[1] The growth of a non-white population and the immigration that fed this growth coincided with this crisis of identity and became a visible sign of the transformation of Britain.[2]

The centrality of race and immigration in postimperial Britain reflects the intellectual and political legacies of empire, but also how those legacies came to be reinterpreted in the postcolonial era.[3] The emergence of a non-white minority within Britain challenged prevailing assumptions about the homogeneity and cohesiveness of British society, even if this view rested on a disregard of class differences and the experiences of ethnic minorities like Jews and the Irish in Britain since the nineteenth century.[4] The belief that migrants differed in values and behavior from "real Britons" provided a new way of defining national identity in terms of race and culture. This "racialization" of Britain rested in part on the domestication of attitudes and ideas about other races that operated within the empire.[5] Empire provided a set of images and ideas about these new Britons to assist in understanding these "strangers"—ones that could induce fear and suspicion. Thus Elspeth Huxley, who wrote of East Africa for British audiences and warned of the danger of African population growth, also wrote about New Commonwealth immigrants.[6] As was the case in the empire, notions of difference often focused on sexuality, gender, and domesticity.[7] The belief that West Indian men sought out white women in Britain built on stereotypes about African and Afro-Caribbean men that possessed a long history.[8] Such ideas accentuated the alien nature of the new migrants and for some Britons fed a sense of being under siege from the former empire. This sense of otherness persists into the present despite the fact that at this point most of Britain's non-white population is native born, raising the question of at what point will the descendents of migrants be viewed as truly British or English.[9]

While popular culture and perceptions formed one part of the response to immigration, academic disciplines with their own connections to empire helped place the new arrivals in context. Fields like sociology, anthropology, and medicine responded to this new population in ways that drew on preexisting understandings of colonial peoples.[10] The growth of a multiethnic Britain contributed to the emergence of the new field of race relations.[11] Aided by the formulation of race relations policies by postwar governments, the discipline established itself as an interpreter of race and culture and a proponent of the ideas of multiculturalism and pluralism.[12] Despite its progressive claims, even this field can trace its roots back to the work of racial geographers like Huntington and East in the early twentieth century and can be seen as potentially essentializing race and racism.[13] In social work the provision of services to immigrants became a special branch of the field that traced its roots back to work of T.S. Simey and other social welfare experts who applied their expertise to the West Indies under British rule and then brought their work to Britain in the form of the British Caribbean Welfare Service.[14]

Colonial demography influenced how immigration came to be understood in postimperial Britain. In the interwar years it made the connection among race, population growth, and migration. Discussions of Asian populations emphasized that the only "true" solution for their problems lay in birth control and that migration would disrupt receiving societies while not significantly reducing population pressure. The proliferation of studies of "overpopulated" regions in the 1940s and 1950s reinforced these arguments, and early studies of Commonwealth migration linked population growth and migration.[15]

The representation of immigration as a by-product of overpopulation in the underdeveloped world ignored how global labor markets have shaped migration since the nineteenth century. The emphasis on movements from outside Europe to Britain overlooked the long history of labor migration within the empire and the role played by Britain in trying to shape the flow of migrants to serve imperial interests in the West Indies, Africa, Oceania, and Asia.[16] It also underplayed how war and decolonization, especially in South Asia, encouraged immigration by disrupting existing patterns of migration and displacing people.[17] Rather than a set of separate streams of migration, linked to previous movements within the global system in the twentieth century and motivated by particular social and economic forces, postwar immigration came to be seen as a tidal wave of people seeking to escape poverty in their overpopulated homelands.[18]

This construction of migration portrayed the immigration of the 1950s and 1960s as unprecedented and threatening to Britain. In demographic terms, non-white or New Commonwealth migration differed in two significant ways from so-called Old Commonwealth migration. Unlike Australians or the Irish, West Indians, Africans, and Asians came from countries perceived as overpopulated. This idea, reinforced by the population explosion literature of the 1960s, raised the specter of a limitless queue of people waiting to enter Britain. Concerns about immigrants also focused on differential fertility. New Commonwealth migrants came from areas with higher fertility than Britain, which led to fears of a dramatic shift in Britain's racial composition.[19] While these fears appeared throughout Western Europe, in Britain they continued a debate about fertility and population growth that dated back to the early twentieth century.[20] Concern about the impact of low fertility among white Europeans upon Europe for has led to calls for the creation of pronatalist policies.[21]

The construction of immigration as a demographic threat to Britain formed part of an emerging postimperial understanding of population in the 1960s. This discourse focused on the possibility that political unrest and ecological crises triggered by global population growth could imperil the planet. Within Britain, the environmental movement highlighted the problems created by an expanding domestic population, particularly the growth of urban areas. Immigration, by creating higher rates of growth, threatened the future of an overcrowded and polluted island. The connection between immigration and global population became a staple for the environmental movement, as embodied in publications like *Blueprint for Survival*. In this view, the best response to demands for entry from New Commonwealth immigrants would be restrictions on entry into Britain and support for population control abroad.[22]

The focus on non-white immigration as a potential cause of domestic overpopulation ignored several features about migration in postwar Britain. Despite the new waves of immigration, Britain remained a country of net emigration into the 1990s.[23] At the same time, while the race and culture of Caribbean and South Asian migrants made them more visible, an equivalent number of Old Commonwealth and Irish migrants came in the postwar era without provoking controversy. The belief that New Commonwealth migrants differed from other types of migrants obscured their similarities to other groups in postwar Britain. West Indian migrations came not simply as a result of population pressure at home but in response to demand for West Indian workers and their skills in a tight labor market.[24] This pattern repeated itself in the debate over South Asian migration in the 1960s and 1970s. Pakistani and Indian migrants often came as a result of labor recruitment and most immigrants came from a few regions within South Asia and East Africa rather than the subcontinent as a whole.[25] Their ranks contained a number of educated professionals who easily found employment in Britain. Even as the British debated the suitability of these new migrants, others raised fears of a brain-drain from the former colonies as highly skilled workers migrated to Britain.[26]

The role of postimperial population discourse in the emerging politics of race and immigration is complex, in part due to the variety of pressures that influenced politicians and officials. Historians disagree about the evolution of immigration policy in postwar Britain. Some argue that politicians responded to popular unrest by moving toward immigration controls to prevent being outflanked on the issue. Thus, Labour, despite its previous opposition to immigration controls, expanded the Immigration Act of 1962 during its time in office. Although Labour linked these actions to new initiatives in race relations, it faced renewed pressure from within its working-class base in the wake of Enoch Powell's "Rivers of Blood" speech.[27] Despite its efforts, Labour struggled with the issue in the late 1970s and 1980s in the face of willingness of Conservatives to increase restrictions on immigration.[28] Some observers believe that debates about race and immigration helped restructure the political landscape in favor of the Conservatives, who became the principal beneficiaries of racial politics.[29]

Other historians discount the role of popular anti-immigrant and racist sentiment in determining policy.[30] They point to deeply rooted antiracist ideals within the trade union movement and the limited appeal of racist politics within the political system as a whole.[31] Public support for anti-immigrant politicians like Powell reflected not only fear of strangers but a larger discontent with elites over housing, wages, and the direction of Britain and its economy in the 1960s and 1970s.[32] Instead of public outrage, these scholars focus on the attitudes and behavior of officials and politicians. They see the increasing restriction on New Commonwealth migrants compared to the relative ease of entry enjoyed by Irish and Old Commonwealth migrants as indicative of a racially based immigration regime in the postwar era, starting with the Nationality Act of 1948. The unwillingness of British elites to accept non-white migrants reflected deeply held views about race and national identity that led first to informal limits on immigration to legislative controls in 1962.[33] The survival of imperial attitudes into the postcolonial age led to a hardening of racial lines in Britain and increasing tension with the Commonwealth.

However, the imperial factor in immigration politics operated in other ways. As Randall Hansen argues, although the British eventually imposed controls, their inability to do so until 1962, despite political pressure and personal attitudes toward non-whites, needs to be explained. For Hansen, the imperial factor—the desire to preserve the Commonwealth and fear about the impact of racially sensitive changes in immigration— limited the actions of the government.[34] A similar perspective affected Irish immigration; British politicians hesitated to control southern Irish migration for fear of reaction in Northern Ireland.[35] The declining importance of the Commonwealth in the late 1950s opened the door to controls over immigration.³⁶ This willingness to abandon the non-white Commonwealth and the desire to avoid openly expressing racial views of immigration highlights the contradictions of Britain's postimperial role.

Ideas about population played a part in the realignment of British attitudes and policies. Fears about the potential threat of migration from overpopulated areas of the empire predated the onset of colonial and New Commonwealth migration, and many of the racial concerns of the 1950s first appeared in the 1920s. While attention focused primarily on controlling movements into colonies and the Dominions, by the late 1940s, Colonial Office officials feared that West Indian overpopulation would lead to migration to Britain. Once colonial and Commonwealth migration accelerated in the 1950s, these same officials abandoned their reluctance to restrict immigration while calling for the British government to openly support population control. As part of this effort, officials experimented with ways to administratively restrict immigration using techniques pioneered in the empire and Commonwealth. Despite the decline of scientific racism, race played a role in the construction of postimperial polices. While the racial attitudes of individual officials and politicians varied, most of them shared a racialized view of immigration and population. They continued to make fundamental distinctions between the behavior and values of races that led them to view Asian, African, and Caribbean peoples as unsuitable migrants.³⁷

The reluctance of officials and politicians to accept non-white migration structured the possible solutions to the perceived problems of overpopulation and migration in the postcolonial era. Unlike many European countries, the British rejected the idea of controlled migration to relieve labor shortages through either guest worker or sponsored migrant programs. The pursuit of restriction as the only policy often produced unintended consequences. The Immigration Act of 1962 actually encouraged the permanent settlement of immigrants in two ways. Anticipation of restrictions led to a wave of last-minute migration to beat the restrictions that dramatically expanded the migrant community. Although the act reduced male migration, by allowing family reunification it encouraged the creation of permanent communities as men, fearing an inability to travel back and forth to their home countries, chose to stay and bring their families. The fumbling efforts to find a way to restrict immigration without provoking protest from abroad finally led to the passage of the Nationality Act of 1981, which inaugurated a much stricter regime of immigration control.³⁸

The debate over immigration starkly displayed the contradictions of

Conclusion: Population and the Legacies of Empire / 199

postimperial Britain. The British desire to retain influence and a unique role in the world collided with the desire to limit the impact of decolonization upon Britain. These contradictions appeared with a vengeance during the Labour government of Harold Wilson. Labour spoke of racial harmony and planned new development initiatives aimed at former colonies while restructuring immigration policy on racial lines. Committed to fostering better relations with former colonies and reviving the Commonwealth, Labour faced a series of problems including Rhodesian independence, a foreign exchange crisis and the expulsion of South Asians from East Africa that undercut the usefulness and reputation of the Commonwealth.[39] It was at this juncture that the British government announced its support for a new regime of international population control and greatly expanded British support for population programs in the former empire even as it reduced overseas aid and further restricted immigration.

For Labour under Wilson, as for other postwar governments, the desire to reconcile the needs of Britain with its perceived mission abroad could not be accomplished without highlighting the fundamental differences between the British and their former subjects. In the postimperial age, the immigration of former colonial subjects eroded the boundaries erected during four hundred years of empire building that separated groups at the center of empire from those at its periphery. In demographic terms, Britain sought to seal itself off from threats from abroad that could not be contained in the short run. The desire for insularity contrasts sharply with the continued pursuit of a new role in Europe and the broader world. After the terrorist attacks in the United States on September 11, 2001, and bombings in London on July 7, 2005, this desire became intertwined with questions of security, especially for the Muslim population of Britain.[40] Despite evidence of slowing global population growth, the influence of postimperial demographic discourse remains strong; as debates over asylum and repatriation continue to stir British politics and some observers call for a reduction in British population. The abandonment of "Greater Britain" and the return to "little England" marks another dividing line between the imperial and postimperial. The impact of immigration, combined with the resurgence of local identities within the British Isles, makes it unclear whether a uniquely British understanding of population will survive in the twenty-first century. However, the demise of Britishness may allow the emergence of a new demographic discourse based on a renewed interest in Englishness or an emphasis on concerns about race and culture shared across Europe.

Notes

INTRODUCTION

1. Robert Kuczynski, "Demography: Science and Administration," *Eugenics Review* 37, no. 1 (1945): 22.
2. Obituary, "R.R. Kuczynski, 1876–1947," *Population Studies* 1, no. 4 (1948): 471–72.
3. Karl Ittmann, "Demography as Policy Science in the British Empire, 1919–1969," *Journal of Policy History* 15, no. 4 (2003): 417–48.
4. Howard Johnson, 'The West Indies and the Conversion of the British Official Classes to the Development Idea," *Journal of Commonwealth and Comparative Politics* 15, no. 1 (1977): 55–83; R.D. Pearce, *The Turning Point in Africa: British Colonial Policy 1938–48* (London: Frank Cass, 1982); Penelope Hetherington, *British Paternalism and Africa 1920–1940* (London: Frank Cass, 1978); Stephen Constantine, *The Making of British Colonial Development Policy 1914–1940* (London: Frank Cass, 1984); J.M. Lee and Martin Petter, *The Colonial Office, War and Development Policy* (London: M.T. Smith, 1982).
5. D.A. Low and A. Smith, "The New Order," in Low and Smith, eds., *History of East Africa*, vol. III (Oxford: Clarendon Press, 1976), 12. For counterinsurgency and security see David Mockaitis, *British Counter Insurgency 1919–1960* (Manchester: Manchester University Press, 1995); David Percox, *Britain, Kenya and the Cold War: Imperial Defense, Colonial Security and Decolonization* (London: I.B. Tauris, 2004); David Anderson and David Killingray, eds., *Policing the Empire: Government, Authority and Control, 1830–1940* (Manchester: Manchester University Press, 1991); David Anderson, *Histories of the Hanged: The Dirty War in Kenya and the End of Empire* (New York: Norton, 2005).
6. While acknowledging the special circumstances the British faced after 1945, historians see these efforts as a continuation of a policy of imperial modernization that stretched to Joseph Chamberlain's push for greater integration of the empire in the 1890s. Joseph Hodge, *Triumph of the Expert:*

Agrarian Doctrines of Development and the Legacies of British Colonialism (Athens: Ohio University Press, 2007); Michael Cowen and Robert Shenton, "The Origins and Course of Fabian Colonialism in Africa," *Journal of Historical Sociology* 4, no. 2 (1991): 143–74; Michael Havinden and David Meredith, *Colonialism and Development: Britain and its Tropical Colonies, 1850–1960* (London: Routledge, 1993).

7. Ritchie Ovendale, *The English Speaking Alliance: Britain, the United States, the Dominions and the Cold War 1945–1951* (London: Allen & Unwin, 1985); John Darwin, *Britain and Decolonization* (New York: St. Martins, 1988); John Kent, *British Imperial Strategy and the Origins of the Cold War 1944–49* (Leicester: University of Leicester Press, 1993); Partha Sarathi Gupta, *Imperialism and the British Labour Movement, 1914–1964* (New York: Holmes and Meier, 1975), 303–48; P. J. Cain and A. G. Hopkins, *British Imperialism: Crisis and Deconstruction 1914–1990* (London: Longman, 1993), 263–81.

8. Bruce Berman, "The Perils of Bula Matari: Constraint and Power in the Colonial State," *Canadian Journal of African Studies* 31, no. 3 (1997): 556–70, and John Darwin, "What Was the Late Colonial State?" *Itinerario* 23, nos. 3–4 (1999): 73–82. For studies that demonstrate these limits see Frederick Cooper, *Decolonization and African Society: The Labor Question in French and British Africa* (Cambridge: Cambridge University Press, 1996) and Monica van Beusekom, *Negotiating Development: African Farmers and Colonial Experts at the Office du Niger 1920–1960* (Portsmouth, NH: Heinemann, 2002).

9. Hodge, *Triumph of the Expert*, 225–53; William Beinart, Karen Brown, and Daniel Gilfoyle, "Experts and Expertise in Colonial Africa Reconsidered: Science and the Interpenetration of Knowledge," *African Affairs* 108, no. 432 (2009): 413–33; Helen Tilley, *African as a Living Laboratory: Empire, Development and the Problem of Scientific Knowledge, 1870–1950* (Chicago: University of Chicago Press, 2011).

10. Donald Mackenzie, *Statistics in Britain, 1865–1930* (Edinburgh: Edinburgh University Press, 1981); Chris Renwick, "From Political Economy to Sociology: Francis Galton and the Social Scientific Origins of Eugenics," *British Journal for the History of Science* 44, no. 3 (2011): 343–69; Francisco Louca, "Emancipation through Interaction: How Eugenics and Statistics Converged and Diverged," *Journal of the History of Biology* 42, no. 4 (2009): 649–84. For economics see Sandra Pert and David Levy, "Denying Human Homogeneity: Eugenics and the Making of Post-Classical Economics," *Journal of the History of Economic Thought* 25, no. 3 (2003): 261–88.

11. The work of Edmund Ramsden has focused on this question and the significance of eugenics in demography and genetics. See his "Eugenics from the New Deal to the Great Society: Genetics, Demography and Population Quality," *Studies in the History and Philosophy of Biological and Biomedical Sciences* 39 (2008): 391–496, and ———, "Confronting the Stigma of Eugenics: Genetics, Demography and the Problems of Population," *Social Studies of Science* 39, no. 6 (2009): 853–84; Dennis Hodgson, "The Ideological Origins of

the Population Association of America," *Population and Development Review* 17, no. 1 (1991): 1–34.

12. For example, see David Coleman and Roger Schofield, *The State of Population Theory: Forward from Malthus* (Oxford: Blackwell, 1984).

13. Dorothy Ross, *The Origins of American Social Science* (Cambridge: Cambridge University Press, 1991); Mark Bevir, "Political Studies as Narrative and Science, 1880–2000," *Political Studies* 54, no.3 (2006): 583–606.

14. In addition to his *Discipline and Punish* and *the History of Sexuality* see Michel Foucault, "Governmentality," in Graham Burchell et al., eds., *The Foucault Effect: Studies in Governmentality* (Chicago: University of Chicago Press, 1991), 87–104. For a discussion of Foucault's concept of population see Bruce Curtis, "Foucault on Governmentality and Population: The Impossible Discovery," *Canadian Journal of Sociology* 27, no. 4 (2002): 505–33.

15. Edward Higgs uses the term "information truncation" to describe this process. Edward Higgs, "The General Register Office and the Tabulation of Data, 1837–1939," in M. Campbell Kelly et al., *The History of Mathematical Tables* (Oxford: Oxford University Press, 2003): 209–32.

16. Alain Desrosieres, *The Politics of Large Numbers: A History of Statistical Reasoning* (Cambridge, MA: Harvard University Press, 1998); Theodore Porter, *The Rise of Statistical Thinking, 1820–1900* (Princeton: Princeton University Press, 1986); Ian Hacking, *The Taming of Chance* (Cambridge: Cambridge University Press, 1990).

17. Bruce Curtis, *The Politics of Population: State Formation, Statistics and the Census of Canada, 1840–1875* (Toronto: University of Toronto Press, 2010); David Kertzer and Dominique Arel, *Census and Identity: The Politics of Race, Ethnicity, and Language in National Censuses* (Cambridge: Cambridge University Press, 2002); Simon Szreter, *Fertility, Class and Gender in Britain, 1860–1940* (Cambridge: Cambridge University Press, 1995), 254–82.

18. Benedict Anderson, *Imagined Communities* (London: Verso, 1991), 163–70. Much of this work focuses on India. Bernard Cohen, "The Census, Social Structure and Objectification in South Asia," in Bernard Cohn, *An Anthropologist among the Historians and Other Essays* (Oxford: Oxford University Press, 1987), 224–54; David Ludden, "Orientalist Empiricism: Transformations of Colonial Knowledge," in Carol Breckenridge and Peter van der Veer, eds., *Orientalism and the Postcolonial Predicament: Perspectives on South Asia* (Philadelphia: University of Pennsylvania Press, 1993), 250–78; Gyan Prakash, *Another Reason: Science and the Imagination of Modern India* (Princeton: Princeton University Press, 1999).

19. Richard Baxstrom, "Governmentality, Bio-Power and the Emergence of the Malayan-Tamil Subject on the Plantations of Colonial Malaya," *Crossroads: An Interdisciplinary Journal of Southeast Asian Studies* 14, no. 2 (2000): 49–78; Nicholas Thomas, *Colonialism's Culture* (Princeton: Princeton University Press, 1994), 112–23; Myron Echenberg, "'Faire du negre': Military Aspects of Population Planning in French West Africa, 1920–1940," in Dennis Cordell and Joel Gregory, eds., *African Population and Capitalism* (Madi-

son: University of Wisconsin Press, 1994), 95–108; John Caldwell, "The Social Repercussions of Colonial Rule: Demographic Aspects," in A. Adu Boahen, ed., *UNESCO General History of Africa*, vol. VII: *Africa under Colonial Domination 1880–1935* (London: Heinemann, 1985), 458–86.

20. This was the method employed by the best-known British book on demography prior to the late 1930s: Alexander Carr-Saunders's *The Population Problem: A Study in Human Evolution* (Oxford: Clarendon Press, 1922). See Norman Etherington, "A False Emptiness: How Historians May Have Been Misled by Early Nineteenth Century Maps of South-Eastern Africa," *Imago Mundi* 56, no. 1 (2004): 67–86.

21. See John Caldwell and Thomas Schindlmayr, "Historical Population Estimates: Unraveling the Consensus," *Population and Development Review* 28, no. 2 (2002): 183–204.

22. Raymond Gervais and Issiaka Mande, "How to Count the Subjects of Empire? Steps toward an Imperial Demography in French West Africa before 1946," in Karl Ittmann, Dennis Cordell, and Gregory Maddox, eds., *The Demographics of Empire: The Colonial Order and the Creation of Knowledge* (Athens: Ohio University Press, 2010): 89–129.

23. For an analysis of the census process in one region see Dmitri van den Bersselaar, "Establishing the Facts: P. A. Talbot and the 1921 Census in Nigeria," *History in Africa* 31 (2004): 69–102.

24. Philip Kreager, "Objectifying Demographic Identities," in Simon Szreter, Hania Sholkamy, and A. Dharmalingam, eds., *Categories and Contexts: Anthropological and Historical Studies in Critical Demography* (Oxford: Oxford University Press, 2004), 33–56.

25. Ann Stoler, *Carnal Knowledge and Imperial Power: Race and the Intimate in Colonial Rule* (Berkeley: University of California Press, 2002).

26. Anthony Christopher, "Race and the Census in the Commonwealth," *Population, Space and Place* 11, no. 2 (2005): 103–18: Tom Moultrie and Rob Dorrington, "Used for Ill; Used for Good: A Century of Collecting Data on Race in South Africa," *Ethnic and Racial Studies* 35, no. 8 (2012): 1447–65; Melissa Nobles, "Racial Categorization and Censuses," in Kertzer and Arel, *Census and Identity*, 43–70.

27. Tim Alborn, "Age and Empire in the Indian Census, 1871–1931," *Journal of Interdisciplinary History* 30, no. 1 (1999): 61–89; Norbert Peabody, "Cents, Sense, Census: Human Inventories in Late Precolonial and Early Colonial India," *Comparative Studies in Society and History* 43, no. 4 (2001): 819–50; Sumit Guha, "The Politics of Identity and Enumeration in India c. 1600–1990," *Comparative Studies in Society and History* 45, no. 1 (2003): 148–67; A. B. Shamsul, "A History of Identity, an Identity of a History: The Idea and Practice of 'Malayness' in Malaysia Reconsidered," *Journal of Southeast Asian Studies* 32, no. 3 (2001): 355–66; Charles Hirshman, "The Meaning and Measurement of Ethnicity in Malaysia: An Analysis of Census Classifications," *Journal of Asian Studies* 46, no. 3 (1987): 555–82.

28. Simon Szreter, "The Right of Registration: Development, Identity

Registration, and Social Security—A Historical Perspective," *World Development* 20, no. 10 (2006): 1–20.

29. Bruce Fetter, "Decoding and Interpreting African Census Data: Vital Evidence from an Unsavory Witness," *Cahiers D'Etudes Africaines* 27, no. 105/106 (1987): 83–105.

30. Much of this work occurred under the UN Population Division, which also sought to produce new estimates for previous colonial populations. For Africa see Frank Lorimer, *Demographic Information on Tropical Africa* (Boston: Boston University Press, 1961; K. M. Barbour and R. M. Prothero, eds., *Essays on African Population* (New York: Praeger, 1962); William Brass et al., *The Demography of Tropical Africa* (Princeton: Princeton University Press, 1968).

31. Ted McCormick, "Transmutation, Inclusion and Exclusion: Political Arithmetic from Charles II to William III," *Journal of Historical Sociology* 20, no. 3 (2007): 259–78.

32. Julian Hoppit, "Political Arithmetic in Eighteenth-Century England," *Economic History Review* 49, no. 3 (1996): 516–40; Porter, *Rise of Statistical Thinking, 1820–1900*, 4–5, 17–39; Peter Buck, "People Who Counted: Political Arithmetic in the Eighteenth Century," *Isis* 73, no. 1 (1982): 28–45; David Glass, "The Population Controversy in Eighteenth-Century England, Part I: The Background," *Population Studies* 6, no. 1 (1952): 69–91; Paul Langford, *A Polite and Commercial People: England 1727–1783* (Oxford: Oxford University Press, 1989), 145–49.

33. For the eighteenth-century context see Frederick Whelan, "Population and Ideology in the Enlightenment," *History of Political Thought* 12, no. 1 (1991): 35–72; Ann Firth, "From Oeconomy to the 'Economy': Population and Self-Interest in Discourses on Government," *History of Human Sciences* 11, no. 3 (1998): 19–35; Jacqueline Hecht, "From 'Be Fruitful and Multiply' to Family Planning: The Enlightenment Transition," *Eighteenth-Century Studies* 32, no. 4 (1999): 536–51; Sylvana Tomaselli, "Moral Philosophy and Population Questions in Eighteenth-Century Europe," *Population and Development Review* 14, Supplement: Population and Resources in Western Intellectual Tradition (1988): 7–29; Carol Blum, *Strength in Numbers: Population, Reproduction, and Power in Eighteenth-Century France* (Baltimore: John Hopkins University Press, 2002).

34. Lisa Cody, *Birthing the Nation: Sex, Science and the Conception of Eighteenth-Century Britons* (Oxford: Oxford University Press, 2005).

35. David McNally, *Against the Market: Political Economy, Market Socialism and the Marxist Critique* (London: Verso, 1993), 78–91.

36. Edward Higgs, *Life, Death and Statistics: Civil Registration, Census and the work of the General Register Office, 1837–1952* (Hatfield, UK: Local Population Studies, 2004), 64–98; Desrosieres, *The Politics of Large Numbers*, 166–72.

37. Higgs, *Life, Death and Statistics*, 156–85; Libby Schweber, *Disciplining Statistics: Demography and Vital Statistics in France and England, 1830–1885* (Durham, NC: Duke University Press, 2006), 91–131.

38. For the divergence of the two see Tim Alborn, "A Calculating Profession: Victorian Actuaries among the Statisticians," *Science in Context* 7, no. 3 (1994): 433–68.

39. Szreter, *Fertility, Class and Gender*, 76–128, 182–262; Schweber, *Disciplining Statistics*, 177–211.

40. For the importance of empire to Pearson, see Theodore Porter, *Karl Pearson* (Princeton: Princeton University Press, 2004), 282–84.

41. Francis Galton, "Address to the Anniversary Meeting of the Anthropological Institute," *Journal of the Royal Anthropological Institute of Great Britain and Ireland* 16 (1887): 386–402. See Raymond Fancher, "Francis Galton's African Ethnography and Its Role in the Development of his Psychology," *British Journal for the History of Science* 16, no. 1 (1983): 67–79.

42. Karl Pearson, *National Life from the Standpoint of Science* (Cambridge: Cambridge University Press, 1919).

43. Thomas Malthus, *An Essay on the Principle of Population*, vol. 1 (London: J.M. Dent, 1914), 75–138. Malthus worked for the East India Company in his later years, and his ideas resonated with company officials. See Simon Commander, "Malthus and the Theory of 'Unequal Powers': Population and Food Production in India, 1800–1947," *Modern Asian Studies* 20, no. 4 (1986): 661–701.

44. Charles Darwin, *The Descent of Man*, reprint of 1879 edition (London: Penguin, 2004), 190–240. For the intellectual background see Gregory Claeys, "The 'Survival of the Fittest' and the Origins of Social Darwinism," *Journal of the History of Ideas* 61, no. 2 (2000): 223–40. For Darwin's views on race see Adrian Desmond and James Moore, *Darwin's Sacred Cause: How a Hatred of Slavery Shaped Darwin's Views on Human Evolution* (Boston: Houghton Mifflin Harcourt, 2009).

45. Charles Dilke, *Greater Britain* (London: Macmillan, 1869) and J.R. Seeley, *The Expansion of England*, reprint of 1881 edition (Chicago: University of Chicago Press, 1971).

46. Christina Bolt, *Victoria Attitudes to Race* (London: Routledge and Kegan Paul, 1971); Douglas Lorimer, *Colour, Class and the Victorian* (Leicester: University of Leicester Press, 1978); Henrika Kuklick, *The Savage Within: The Social History of British Anthropology* (Cambridge: Cambridge University Press, 1991); Douglas Lorimer, "Theoretical Racism in Late Victorian Anthropology," *Victorian Studies* 31, no. 3 (1988): 405–30.

47. See Daniel Pick, *Face of Degeneration: A European Disorder, c. 1848-c. 1918* (Cambridge: Cambridge University Press, 1989) and William Greenslade, *Degeneration, Culture and the Novel, 1880–1940* (Cambridge: Cambridge University Press, 1994).

48. The best overviews of the eugenics movement are Richard Soloway, *Demography and Degeneration* (Chapel Hill: University of North Carolina Press, 1990) and Daniel Kevles, *In the Name of Eugenics* (New York: Knopf, 1985).

49. Dorothy Porter, "'Enemies of the Race': Biologism, Environmental-

ism, and Public Health in Edwardian England," *Victorian Studies* 34, no. 2 (1991): 159–78; Gareth Steadman Jones, *Outcast London* (Oxford: Clarendon Press, 1971); Anna Davin, "Imperialism and Motherhood," *History Workshop Journal* 5 (1978): 9–65; Roger Davidson, *Whitehall and the Labour Problem in Late-Victorian and Edwardian Britain* (London: Croom Helm, 1985).

50. Richard Soloway, "Counting the Degenerates: The Statistics of Race Deterioration in Edwardian England," *Journal of Contemporary History* 17, no. 1 (1982): 137–64.

51. Porter, *Karl Pearson*, 249–86, and MacKenzie, *Statistics in Britain*, 101–19.

52. Szreter, *Fertility, Class and Gender*, 67–282.

53. Higgs, *Life, Death and Statistics*, 156–85.

54. Ibid., 134–39.

55. H. J. Mackinder, "Manpower as a Measure of National and Imperial Strength," *National Review* 45, no. 1 (1905): 136–43. C. V. Drysdale, *The Empire and the Birth Rate* (London: Royal Colonial Institute, 1914), 2.

56. D. P. Crook, *Darwinism, War, and History* (Cambridge: Cambridge University Press, 1994) and Nancy Leys Stepan, "'Nature's Pruning Hook': War, Race and Evolution, 1914–1918," in J. Bean, ed., *The Political Culture of Modern Britain* (London: Hamilton, 1987), 129–48; Franz Coetzee, *For Party or Country: Nationalism and the Dilemmas of Popular Conservatism in Edwardian England* (Oxford: Oxford University Press, 1990).

57. Seth Koven and Sonya Michael, eds., *Mothers of a New World: Maternalist Politics and the Origins of Welfare States* (New York: Routledge, 1993); Keith Laybourn, "'The Defence of the Bottom Dog': The Independent Labour Party in Local Politics," in Tony Jowitt and D. G. Wright, eds., *Victorian Bradford* (Bradford, UK: City of Bradford Metropolitan Council, 1981), 223–44; E. H. Green, *The Crisis of Conservatism* (London: Routledge, 1995).

58. Bernard Semmel, *Imperialism and Social Reform* (Cambridge, MA: Harvard University Press, 1960), G. R. Searle, *The Quest for National Efficiency* (Berkeley: University of California Press, 1971).

59. Enid Charles, *Twilight of Parenthood* (London: Norton, 1934). For a discussion of the panic see Michael Teitelbaum and Jay Winter, *The Fear of Population Decline* (Orlando, FL: Academic Press, 1985), 45–62, and Soloway, *Demography and Degeneration*, 226–58.

60. J. W. Gregory, *The Menace of Colour* (London: Seeley, Service, 1925); Basil Mathews, *The Clash of Colour* (London: Edinburgh House, 1925); L. C. Money, *The Peril of the White Race* (London: W. Collins Sons, 1925); J. Swinburne, *Population and the Social Problem* (London: Allen & Unwin, 1924).

61. The most significant work was that of Warren Thompson, whose books *Population Problems* (New York: McGraw Hill, 1930) and *Danger Spots in World Population* (New York: Knopf, 1929) were widely read during the interwar era. See also W. R. Crocker, *The Japanese Population Problem: The Coming Crisis* (New York: Macmillan, 1931) and John Megaw, "Pressure of Population in India," *Journal of the Royal Society of Arts* 87, no. 4491 (1938): 134–57.

62. Muriel Nissel, *People Count: A History of the General Register Office* (London: HMSO, 1987), 44–45, 133–35, and Higgs, *Life, Death and Statistics*, 188–202.

63. Soloway, *Demography and Degeneration*, 233–34, 247–52.

64. A. J. Christopher, "The Quest for an Imperial Census, 1840–1940," *Journal of Historical Geography* 34 (2008): 268–85, and Jean-Pierre Beaud and Jean-Guy Prevost, "Statistics as the Science of Government: The Stillborn British Empire Statistical Bureau, 1918–1920," *Journal of Imperial and Commonwealth History* 33, no. 3 (2005): 369–91.

65. Martin Bulmer, "Mobilizing Social Knowledge for Social Welfare: Intermediary Institutions in the Political Systems of the United States and Great Britain between the First and Second World Wars," in Paul Weindling, ed., *International Health Organizations and Movements, 1918–1939* (Cambridge: Cambridge University Press, 1995), 305–25, and ———, *The Use of Social Research* (London: Allen & Unwin, 1982), 19–29.

66. Eugene Grebenik, "Demographic Research in Britain 1936–1986," *Population Studies* 45, Suppl. (1991): 4–11.

67. Ibid., 18–23; Higgs, *Information State*, 133–67; Jay Winter, "Population, Economists and the State: The Royal Commission on Population, 1944–49," in Mary Furner and Barry Supple, eds., *The State and Economic Knowledge: The American and British Experience* (Cambridge: Cambridge University Press, 1990), 436–60. For this expansion as part of a larger process see David Edgerton, *Warfare State, Britain, 1920–1970* (Cambridge: Cambridge University Press, 2006), 145–90.

68. Desmond King, "The Politics of Social Research: Institutionalizing Public Funding Regimes in the United States and Great Britain," *British Journal of Political Science* 28, no. 3 (1998): 415–44; Cyril Smith, "Networks of Influence: The Social Sciences in the United Kingdom since the War," in Peter Wagner et al., eds., *Social Sciences and Modern States* (Cambridge: Cambridge University Press, 1991), 131–47; Michael Savage, *Identities and Social Change in Britain since 1940: The Politics of Method* (Oxford: Oxford University Press, 2010), 51–134.

69. John Caldwell and Pat Caldwell, *Limiting Population Growth and the Ford Foundation Contribution* (London and Dover, NH: F. Pinter, 1986); John Sharpless, "Population Science, Private Foundations and Development Aid," in Frederick Cooper and Randall Packard, eds., *International Development and the Social Sciences* (Berkeley: University of California Press, 1997), 176–200; John Harr and Peter Johnson, *The Rockefeller Century* (New York: Scribner, 1988), 368–69, 452–67.

70. For an assessment by the chief statistician of the Colonial Office see W. F. Searle, E. J. Phillips, and C. J. Martin, "Colonial Statistics," *Journal of the Royal Statistical Society* 113, no. 3 (1950): 271–98.

71. David Anderson, *Histories of the Hanged: The Dirty War in Kenya and the End of Empire* (New York: Norton, 2005), 122–25, 235–38, 293–97; Wade

Markel, "Draining the Swamp: The British Strategy of Population Control," *Parameters* 36, no. 1 (2006): 35–48.

72. Ian Spencer, *British Immigration Policy since 1939: The Making of Multi-racial Britain* (London: Routledge, 1997); Zig Layton-Henry, *The Politics of Immigration: Immigration, "Race" and "Race" Relations in Post-War Britain* (Oxford: Blackwell, 1992); Kathleen Paul, *Whitewashing Britain: Race and Citizenship in Post-War Britain* (Ithaca, NY: Cornell University Press, 1997); Randall Hansen, *Citizenship and Immigration in Post-War Britain* (Oxford: Oxford University Press, 2000).

73. See Alison Bashford, "Nation, Empire, Globe: The Spaces of Population Debate in the Interwar Years," *Comparative Studies in Society and History* 49, no. 1 (2007): 170–201, and Mathew Connelly, *Fatal Misconceptions: The Struggle to Control World Population* (Cambridge, MA: Harvard University Press, 2008).

74. See Kevin Grant, Philippa Levine, and Frank Trentmann, eds., *Beyond Sovereignty: Britain, Empire and Transnationalism, c. 1880–1950* (London: Palgrave Macmillan, 2007), 1–15; Simon Potter, "Webs, Networks, and Systems: Globalization and the Mass Media in the Nineteenth- and Twentieth-Century British Empire," *Journal of British Studies* 46, no. 3 (2007): 621–46; Gary Magee and Andrew Thompson, *Empire and Globalization: Networks of People, Goods and Capital in the British World. C. 1850–1914* (Cambridge: Cambridge University Press, 2010).

75. Sanjam Ahluwalia, *Reproductive Restrains: Birth Control in India, 1877–1947* (Urbana: University of Illinois Press, 2008), 115–42; Sarah Hodges, *Contraception Colonialism and Commerce: Birth Control in South India, 1920–1940* (Aldershot: Ashgate, 2008), 21–46; David Arnold, "Official Attitudes to Population, Birth Control and Reproductive Health in India, 1921–1946," in Sarah Hodges, ed., *Reproductive Health in India: History, Politics, Controversies* (New Delhi: Orient Longman, 2006), 22–50; Rahul Nair, "The Construction of a 'Population Problem' in Colonial India, 1919–1947," *Journal of Imperial and Commonwealth History* 39, no. 2 (2011): 227–47.

76. Stephen Constantine, ed., *Emigrants and Empire* (Manchester: University of Manchester Press, 1990); Kent Fedorowich, *Unfit for Heroes: Reconstruction and Soldier Settlement in the Empire between the Wars* (Manchester: University of Manchester Press, 1995); Paul, *Whitewashing Britain*, 25–63.

CHAPTER 1

1. C.P. Blacker, "Obituary Alexander Carr-Saunders," *Population Studies* 20, no. 3 (1967): 367.

2. See Matthew Connelly, *Fatal Misconception: The Struggle to Control World Population* (Cambridge, MA: Harvard University Press, 2008), 46–76, and Alison Bashford, "Nation, Empire, Globe: The Spaces of Population Debate in the Interwar Years," *Comparative Studies in Society and History* 49, no. 1 (2007): 170–201.

3. Chris Langford, *The IUSSP* (London: Population Investigation Committee, 1984). The BPS appears to have been primarily a project of the Eugenics Society, which dominated its membership in the early years.

4. Glenda Sluga, "UNESCO and the (One) World of Julian Huxley," *Journal of World History* 21, no. 3 (2010): 393–418.

5. Harold Cox, "A League of Low Birth-Rate Nations," in Margaret Sanger, ed., *The Sixth International Neo-Malthusian and Birth Control Conference* (New York: American Birth Control League, 1926), 145–52.

6. Harold Wright, *Population* (New York: Harcourt Brace 1923), 157–69; George Knibbs, *The Shadow of the World's Future* (London: E. Benn, 1928), 72–95.

7. For more on British internationalism see Daniel Gorman, "Liberal Internationalism, the League of Nations Union and the Mandates System," *Canadian Journal of History* 40, no. 4 (2005): 449–77; Jo Vellacott, "A Place for Pacifism and Transnationalism in Feminist Theory: The Early Work of the Women's International League for Peace and Freedom," *Women's History Review* 2, no. 1 (1993): 23–56; Christine Bolt, *Sisterhood Questioned? Race, Class and Internationalism in American and British Women's Movements, c. 1880s-1970s* (London: Routledge, 2004), 76–105.

8. Richard Symonds and Michael Carder, *The United Nations and the Population Question 1945–1970* (New York: McGraw Hill, 1973), 20–29; Alison Bashford, "Global Biopolitics and the History of World Health," *History of the Human Sciences* 19, no. 1 (2006): 67–88.

9. Sluga, "UNESCO and the (One) World of Julian Huxley," 405–14; Gorman, "Liberal Internationalism," 451–55; Bolt, *Sisterhood Questioned*, 84–86.

10. See, for example, G. F. McCleary, *Population: Today's Question* (London: Allen & Unwin, 1938).

11. Enid Charles and Pearl Moshinsky, "Differential Fertility in England and Wales during the Past Two Decades," in Lancelot Hogben, ed., *Political Arithmetic* (London: Allen & Unwin, 1938), 106–60.

12. Harold Cox, *The Population Problem* (London: G. P. Putnam's Sons, 1922); John Toye, *Keynes on Population* (Oxford: Oxford University Press, 2000), 161–80; A. L. Bowley, "Births and Population in Great Britain," *Economic Journal* 34, no. 134 (1924): 188–92; Robert Kuczynski, *The Balance of Births and Deaths*, vol. 1 (New York: Brookings Institution, 1928); E. W. Shanahan, "Over-Population, Emigration and Empire Development," *Economica* 9 (1923): 215–23.

13. Michael Teitelbaum and Jay Winter, *The Fear of Population Decline* (Orlando, FL: Academic Press, 1985), 45–62, and Richard Soloway, *Demography and Degeneration* (Chapel Hill: University of North Carolina Press, 1990), 226–58.

14. Enid Charles, *Twilight of Parenthood* (London: Norton, 1934).

15. A. M. Carr-Saunders, *World Population*, reprint of 1936 edition (New York: Barnes and Noble, 1964), 129–32; Grace Leybourne, "An Estimate of

the Future Population of Great Britain," *Sociological Review* 26, no. 2 (1934): 130–38.

16. Lionel Robbins, "Notes on Some Probable Consequences of the Advent of a Stationary Population in Great Britain," *Economica* 25 (1929): 71–82. See Pat Thane, "The Debate on the Declining Birth Rate in Britain, 1920s-1950s," *Continuity and Change* 5, no. 2 (1990): 283–305.

17. For the attitude of the Church of England in the 1920s, see Richard Soloway, *Birth Control and the Population Question in England, 1877–1930* (Chapel Hill: University of North Carolina Press, 1982), 233–55.

18. Charles, *Twilight*, 191–223.

19. Richard Titmuss, *Poverty and Population* (London: Macmillan, 1938).

20. British demographers questioned the efficacy of such policies and the legitimacy of territorial demands. David Glass, *Population Policies and Movements in Europe* (Oxford: Clarendon Press, 1940), 219–313, and Robert Kuczynski, *'Living Space' and Population Problems* (Oxford: Oxford University Press, 1939).

21. While considerable uncertainty existed about demographic trends in the USSR, many demographers saw its population growing. Warren Thompson, *Danger Spots in World Population* (New York: Knopf, 1929), 292–93, and Carr-Saunders, *World Population*, 135–36. Enid Charles, like many observers, linked presumed Soviet population growth to new state policies.

22. Harold Cox, "The Peopling of the British Empire," *Foreign Affairs*, 2, no. 1 (1923): 117–29; George McCleary, *The Menace of Depopulation* (London: Allen & Unwin, 1937); Robert Kuczynski, "The White Population of the Empire," *Sociological Review* 29, no. 3 (1937): 221–31; J.A. Thomas, *Our Invincible Empire: An Appeal to Patriotism* (London: n.p., 1939).

23. Charles Pearson, *National Life and Character: A Forecast* (London: Macmillan, 1893), 31–90. For a reading of Pearson that emphasizes his concerns about Asian population growth see Marilyn Lake, "The White Man under Siege: New Histories of Race in the Nineteenth Century and the Advent of White Australia," *History Workshop Journal* 58 (2004): 41–62.

24. Lothop Stoddard, *The Rising Tide of Color* (New York: Scribner, 1920); Edward Reuter, *Population Problems* (Philadelphia: J.B. Lippincott, 1923); Edward Ross, *Standing Room Only* (New York: Century, 1927).

25. J.W. Gregory, *The Menace of Colour* (London: Seeley, Service, 1925); Basil Matthews, *The Clash of Colour* (London: Edinburgh House, 1925); L.C. Money, *The Peril of the White Race* (London: W. Collins Sons, 1925); J. Swinburne, *Population and the Social Problem* (London: Allen & Unwin, 1924).

26. Ross, *Standing Room*, 93–101; Stoddard, *Rising Tide*, 8–11.

27. Gregory, *Menace*, 24.

28. Edward East, *Mankind at the Crossroads* (New York: Scribner, 1923) and Alexander Carr-Saunders, *The Population Problem* (Oxford: Clarendon Press, 1922).

29. Wright, *Population*, 63–122; Knibbs, *Shadow of the World's Future*, 29–71.

30. John and Pat Caldwell, *Limiting Population Growth: The Ford Foundation Contribution*, (London and Dover, NH: F. Pinter, 1986), 10.

31. Warren Thompson, *Population Problems* (New York: McGraw Hill, 1930), 41–67, and *Danger Spots*, 3–17.

32. Thompson, *Danger Spots*, 19–48, 71–209.

33. While demographers saw the Dutch East Indies (present-day Indonesia) growing rapidly, they believed that the stability of Dutch rule combined with abundant land and resources made them less likely to threaten Western interests in the region. East, *Mankind*, 92; Ross, *Standing Room*, 300–301; Reuter, *Population*, 104–6, Carr-Saunders, *World Population*, 279–83; Thompson, *Danger Spots*, 95–104.

34. C. Allen, "The Population Problem in Japan," *Economica* 17 (1926): 170–86; John Orchard, "The Pressure of Population in Japan," *Geographical Review* 18, no. 3 (1928): 374–401; J. B. Condliffe, ed., *Problems of the Pacific: Proceedings of the Second Conference of the Institute of Pacific Relations, 1927* (Chicago: University of Chicago Press, 1928); E. F. Penrose, *Population Problems and their Application with Special Reference to Japan* (Stanford, CA: Food Institute, 1934); W. R. Crocker, *The Japanese Population Problem: The Coming Crisis* (New York: Macmillan, 1931).

35. J. B. Condliffe, "The Pressure of Population in the Far East," *Economic Journal* 42, no. 166 (1932): 196–210; Etienne Dennery, *Asia's Teeming Millions: And Its Problems for the West*, reprint of 1931 edition (Port Washington, NY: Kennikat, 1970).

36. Estimates varied from about 300 million to 440 million. Percy Roxby, "The Distribution of Population in China: Economic and Political Significance," *Geographical Review* 15, no. 1 (1925): 1–3; Walter Mallory, *China: Land of Famine* (New York: American Geographic Society, 1928); Thompson, *Danger Spots*, 49–70; Glass, *World Population*, 286–90; East, *Mankind*, 94–96; Ross, *Standing Room*, 120–35.

37. East, *Mankind*, 88–92; Ross, *Standing Room*, 287–97; Thompson, *Danger Spots*, 140–58, Carr-Saunders, *World Population*, 269–77; G. Findlay Shirras, "The Population Problem in India," *Economic Journal* 43, no. 169 (1933): 56–73; Taraknath Das, "The Population Problem in India," in Sanger, *Neo-Malthusian and Birth Control Conference*, 224–27. For changing views in India see David Arnold, "Official Attitudes to Population, Birth Control and Reproductive Health in India, 1921–1946," in Sarah Hodges, ed., *Reproductive Health in India: History, Politics, Controversies* (New Delhi: Orient Longamn, 2006), 22–50, and Rahul Nair, "The Construction of a 'Population Problem' in Colonial India, 1919–1947," *Journal of Imperial and Commonwealth History* 39, no. 2 (2011): 227–47.

38. Denney, *Teeming*, 103–80; Thompson, *Danger Spots*, 66–70, 159–81; Das, "Population Problem," 216–24.

39. Charles Darwin, *The Descent of Man*, reprint of 1879 edition (London: Penguin 2004), 213–22. For a discussion of the "biologizing of colonial extinction" by Darwin see Adrian Desmond and James Moore, *Darwin's Sacred*

Cause: How a Hatred of Slavery Shaped Darwin's Views on Human Evolution (Boston: Houghton Mifflin Harcourt), 146–51, and Tony Barta, "Mr. Darwin's Shooters: On Natural Selection and the Naturalizing of Genocide," *Patterns of Prejudice* 32, no. 2 (2005): 116–37.

40. Donald Denoon, "New Economic Orders: Land, Labour and Dependency," in Denoon et al., eds., *The Cambridge History of the Pacific Islanders* (Cambridge: Cambridge University Press, 1997), 243–49.

41. Stephen Roberts, *Population Problems of the Pacific*, reprint of 1927 edition (New York: AMS, 1969), 58–101. See also G. H. Pitt-Rivers, *The Clash of Culture and the Contact of Races*, reprint of 1927 edition (New York: Negro Universities Press, 1969).

42. Roberts, *Population Problems*, 229–76. For a discussion of British work in the southwest Pacific see Nicholas Thomas, "Sanitation and Seeing: The Creation of State Power in Early Colonial Fiji," *Comparative Studies in Society and History* 32, no.1 (1990): 149–70.

43. Ross, *Standing Room*, 342; Thompson, *Population Problems*, 253–54; East, *Mankind*, 98–102; Stoddard, *Clash*, 87–91.

44. Carr-Saunders, *Population Problem*, 174–83. Carr-Saunders asserted that Africans possessed a diminished sex drive and smaller sex organs, which exacerbated the difficulties they faced in maintaining their numbers.

45. Julian Huxley, *Africa View* (London: Chatto & Windus, 1931), 418.

46. William Macmillan, *Africa Emergent* (London: Faber & Faber, 1938), 40.

47. Ibid., 9–49.

48. See John Caldwell and Thomas Schindlmayr, "Historical Population Estimates: Unraveling the Consensus," *Population and Development Review* 28, no. 2 (2002): 183–204. For Africa see Patrick Manning, "African Population Projections, 1850–1960," in Karl Ittmann, Dennis Cordell, and Gregory Maddox, eds., *The Demographics of Empire: The Colonial Order and the Creation of Knowledge* (Athens: Ohio University Press, 2010), 245–75.

49. For debates prior to 1914 see Theodore Porter, *Karl Pearson* (Princeton: Princeton University Press, 2004), 249–86; Donald Mackenzie, *Statistics in Britain, 1865–1930* (Edinburgh: University of Edinburgh Press, 1981), 101–19; Simon Szreter, *Fertility, Class and Gender in Britain, 1860–1940* (Cambridge: Cambridge University Press, 1995), 67–282; Edward Higgs, *Life, Death and Statistics: Civil Registration, Census and the Work of the General Register Office, 1837–1952* (Hatfield, UK: Local Population Studies, 2004), 156–85.

50. Edward Higgs, "The Statistical Big Bang of 1911: Ideology, Technological Innovation and the Production of Medical Statistics," *Social History of Medicine* 9, no. 3 (1996): 409–26.

51. The brief revival of biological explanations of British fertility decline in the 1920s represented one variant of this trend. J. Brownlee, "The History of the Birth and Death Rates in England and Wales," *Public Health* 29 (1915–16), 211–22, 228–38.

52. Raymond Pearl, *The Biology of Death* (Philadelphia: J. B. Lippincott,

1922) and "The Population Problem," *Geographical Review* 12, no. 4 (1922): 636–45.

53. For a discussion of Pearl and his work see Garland Allen, "Old Wine in New Bottles: From Eugenics to Population Control in the Work of Raymond Pearl," in Keith Benson, Jane Maienschein, and Ronald Rainger, eds., *The Expansion of American Biology* (New Brunswick, NJ: Rutgers University Press, 1991), 231–61, and Michael Mezzano, "The Progressive Origins of Eugenics Critics: Raymond Pearl, Herbert S. Jennings, and the Defense of Scientific Inquiry," *Journal of the Gilded Age and Progressive Era* 4, no. 1 (2005): 83–97.

54. A. B. Wolfe, "Is There a Biological Law of Human Population Growth?" *Quarterly Journal of Economics* 41, no. 4 (1927): 557–94.

55. Raymond Pearl, *The Natural History of Population* (New York: Oxford University Press, 1939).

56. Ellsworth Huntington, *Civilization and Climate* (New Haven: Yale University Press, 1916).

57. M. Aurousseau, "The Geographical Study of Population Groups," *Geographical Review* 13, no. 2 (1923): 266–82; T. Griffith Taylor, *Environment and Race* (Oxford: Oxford University Press, 1927).

58. Taylor produced estimates of future white populations of 100 million each for Argentina, Canada, and Siberia and more than 60 million for South Africa and Australia.

59. Porter, *Karl Pearson*, 261–78; Mackenzie, *Statistics in Britain*, 182–213. For efforts to distance demography and eugenics see Edmund Ramsden, "Eugenics from the New Deal to the Great Society: Genetics, Demography and Population Quality," *Studies in the History and Philosophy of Biological and Biomedical Sciences* 39 (2008): 391–496, and "Confronting the Stigma of Eugenics: Genetics, Demography and the Problems of Population," *Social Studies of Science* 39, no. 6 (2009): 853–84.

60. Nathan Keyfitz, "Pascal K. Whelpton," in Paul Demeny and Geoffrey McNicoll, eds., *The Encyclopedia of Population*, vol. 2 (New York: Macmillan Reference, 2003): 972–73.

61. Dennis Hodgson, "The Ideological Origins of the Population Association of America," *Population and Development Review* 17, no. 1 (1991), 16–20, and Ramsden, "Eugenics from the New Deal to the Great Society," 393; Simon Szreter, "History of Demography," *International Encyclopedia of the Social and Behavioral Sciences* (Oxford: Elsevier, 2002), 3491.

62. Major Greenwood, "On the Value of Royal Commissions in Sociological Research, with Special Reference to the Birth Rate," *Journal of the Royal Statistical Society* 100, no. 3 (1937): 396–414.

63. John Hajnal, "Aspects of Recent Trends in Marriage in England and Wales," *Population Studies* 1, no. 1 (1947): 72–98. See John Hobcraft, "Fertility in England and Wales: A Fifty Year Perspective," *Population Studies* 50, no. 3 (1996): 485–524.

64. See Szreter's discussion of the implications of T.H. Stevenson's diffusion model of fertility decline. Szreter, *Fertility, Class and Gender*, 238–71.

65. Susan Greenhalgh, "The Social Construction of Population Science," *Comparative Studies in Society and History* 38, no. 1 (1996): 26–65; Simon Szreter, "The Idea of the Demographic Transition and the Study of Fertility Change: A Critical Intellectual History," *Population and Development Review* 19, no. 4 (1993): 659–70; Dennis Hodgson, "Demography as Social Science and Policy Science," *Population and Development Review* 9, no. 1 (1983): 1–33.

66. Edmund Ramsden, "Frank W. Notestein, Frederick H. Osborn, and the Development of Demography in the United States," *Princeton Library Review* 65, no. 2 (2004), 282–316; Jennifer Gunn, "A Few Good Men: The Rockefeller Approach to Population, 1911–1936," in Theresa Richardson and Donald Fisher, eds., *The Development of the Social Sciences in the United States and Canada: The Role of Philanthropy* (Ann Arbor: University of Michigan Press, 1999), 97–114.

67. Soloway, *Demography and Degeneration*, 233–34, 247–52.

68. Muriel Nissel, *People Count: A History of the General Register Office* (London: HMSO, 1987), 44–45, 133–35; Eugene Grebenik, "Demographic Research in Britain 1936–1986," *Population Studies* 45, Suppl. (1991), 10–11; Higgs, *Life, Death and Statistics*, 188–202.

69. For the private sources of "gentlemanly" social science see Mike Savage, *Identities and Social Change in Britain Since 1940* (Oxford: Oxford University Press, 2010), 93–105. More generally see Martin Bulmer, *The Uses of Social Research: Social Investigation in Policy Making* (London: Allen & Unwin, 1982), 1–29, and "Mobilizing Social Knowledge for Social Welfare: Intermediary Institutions in the Political Systems of the United States and Great Britain between the First and Second World Wars," in Paul Weindling, ed., *International Health Organizations and Movements, 1918–1939* (Cambridge: Cambridge University Press, 1995), 305–25.

70. Porter, *Karl Pearson*, 261–78; Mackenzie, *Statistics in Britain*, 101–19.

71. G. Udny Yule, "The Growth of Population and the Factors Which Control It," *Journal of Royal Statistical Society* 88, no. 1, (1925): 1–58.

72. Donald Fisher, "The Rockefeller Foundation and the Development of Scientific Medicine in Great Britain," *Minerva* 16 (1978): 20–41; Edward Higgs, "Medical Statistics, Patronage and the State: The Development of the MRC Statistical Unit, 1911–1948," *Medical History* 44 (2000): 323–40; Grebenik, "Demographic Research," 4.

73. Rosaleen Love, "Alice in Eugenics Land: Feminism and Eugenics in the Careers of Alice Lee and Ethel Elderton," *Annals of Science* 36 (1979): 145–58.

74. The Royal Statistical Society hosted a public discussion of these issues in 1937. Major Greenwood, "Discussion on the Quantity and Quality of Official Statistics," *Journal of the Royal Statistical Society* 95, no.2 (1937): 279–302.

75. Soloway, *Demography and Degeneration*, 246–52; C.M. Langford, *The Population Investigation Committee* (London: Population Investigation Committee, 1988). For the role of American foundations see Donald Fisher,

"American Philanthropy and the Social Sciences in Britain, 1919–1939: The Reproduction of a Conservative Ideology," *Sociological Review* 28, no. 2 (1980): 277–315. Martin Bulmer and Joan Bulmer, "Philanthropy and Social Science in the 1920s: Beardsley Ruml and the Laura Spelman Rockefeller Memorial 1922–1929," *Minerva* 19 (1981): 347–407. More generally see Ellen Lagemann, *The Politics of Knowledge: The Carnegie Corporation, Philanthropy, and Public Policy* (Middletown, CT: Wesleyan University Press, 1989).

76. For LSE's role see Bulmer, *Uses of Social Research*, 21–23.

77. Ralf Dahrendorf, *LSE: A History of the London School of Economics and Political Science 1895–1995* (Oxford: Oxford University Press, 1995), 249–66; Jose Harris, *William Beveridge: A Biography* (Oxford: Oxford University Press, 1997), 277–83. The interest of T. H. Marshall, who was a leading figure in the social sciences at LSE, also played a role.

78. Dahrendorf, *LSE*, 260, and Grebenik, "Demographic Research," 7–10.

79. Grebenik, "Demographic Research," 4–6.

80. Kuczynski's work garnered enough respect to that he was invited to be a founding member of the Population Association of American in 1931.

81. The net reproduction rate measures changes in women's fertility by representing it as the sum of period birth rates during their fertile years. It is expressed as the ratio of female children to women of child-bearing age. "Memoir: R. R. Kuczynski," *Population Studies* 1, no. 4 (1948): 471–72; David Glass, "Robert Rene Kuczynski," *Journal of the Royal Statistical Society* 110, no. 4 (1947): 383–84; F. M.M. Lewes, "A Note on the Origin of the Net Reproduction Ratio," *Population Studies* 38, no. 2 (1984): 321–24.

82. In addition to his earlier work see his contribution to the Hogben volume. Robert Kuczynski, "The International Decline of Fertility," in Hogben, *Political Arithmetic*, 47–72.

83. Hogben described him as the leading European demographer. Adrian and Anne Hogben, eds., *Lancelot Hogben Scientific Humanist: An Unauthorized Autobiography* (Woodbridge, UK: Merlin, 1998), 131–32.

84. These included two book length studies, *The Struggle for Population* (Oxford: Clarendon Press, 1936) and *Population Policies and Movements in Europe*.

85. For more on Glass's career see W. D. Borrie, "David Victor Glass 1911–1978," *Proceedings of the British Academy* 68 (1982): 537–60.

86. Eva Durbin, *New Jerusalems: The Labour Party and the Economics of Democratic Socialism* (London: Routledge & Kegan Paul, 1986).

87. Ann Oakley, "Eugenics, Social Medicine and the Career of Richard Titmuss in Britain 1935–1950," *British Journal of Sociology* 42, no. 2 (1991): 165–94.

88. William McGucken, *Scientists, Society, and State: The Social Relations of Science Movement in Great Britain 1931–1947* (Columbus: Ohio State University Press, 1984).

89. Solly Zuckerman, *From Apes to Warlords* (London: Hamilton, 1978), 393–404; Gary Werskey, *The Visible College* (London: Allen Lane, 1978),

264–64; Ralph Demaris, "Tots and Quots," in H.G.C. Matthew and Brian Harrison, eds., *Oxford Dictionary of National Biography* (Oxford: Oxford University Press, 2004). http://www.oxforddnb.com/view/theme/95704.

90. Robert Kuczynski, *The Cameroons and Togoland* (London: Oxford University Press, 1939), preface.

91. For the background to the survey see A.D. Roberts, "The Early Historiography of Colonial Africa," *History in Africa* 5 (1978), 156–60; Helen Tilley, *African as a Living Laboratory: Empire, Development and the Problem of Scientific Knowledge, 1870–1950* (Chicago: University of Chicago Press, 2011), 69–113; John Cell, "Lord Hailey and the Making of the African Survey," *African Affairs* 88, no. 353 (1989): 481–505.

92. Robert Kuczynski, *Colonial Population* (London: Oxford University Press, 1937).

93. Colonial Office (CO) 323/1523/1 Population Problems in the Colonies, 1937, National Archives; Minutes 9–11-37 and 9–6-38, Minutes of the PIC, 1935–43, SA-PIC A/1/1, Papers of the PIC, CMAC. The original amount was £1,150.

94. For Africa see F. Dixey, "The Distribution of Population in Nyasaland," *Geographical Review* 18, no. 2 (1928): 274–90; J.K. Baker, "The Distribution of Native Population over East Africa," *Africa: Journal of the International African Institute* 10, no. 1 (1937): 37–54; C.R. Niven, "Some Nigerian Population Problems," *Geographical Journal* 85, no. 1 (1936): 54–58; A.T. Culwick and G.M. Culwick, "A Study of Population in Ulanga, Tanganyika Territory," *Sociological Review* 30, no. 4 (1938): 365–79, and *Sociological Review* 31, no. 1 (1939): 25–43.

95. Kuczynski, *Colonial Population*, xiii–xiv.

96. For example, his discussion of declining fertility invoked the idea of the "small family system." Carr-Saunders, *World Population*, 106–16, 243–59.

97. P. Granville Edge, *Vital Records in the Tropics* (London: Routledge, 1932) and "The Demography of British Colonial Possessions," *Journal of the Royal Statistical Society* 100, no. 2 (1937): 181–231.

98. P.G.E., "Review of *Cameroons and Togoland: A Demographic Study*," *Journal of the Royal Statistical Society* 103, no. 3 (1940): 406–7.

99. Stephen Howe, *Anti-colonialism in British Politics: The Left and the End of Empire 1918–1964* (Oxford: Oxford University Press, 1993), 27–52, 134–39; Michael Cowen and Robert Shenton, "The Origins and Course of Fabian Colonialism in Africa," *Journal of Historical Sociology* 4, no. 2 (1991): 143–74.

100. The political and racial views of demographers ran the gamut. Many on the left, including Enid Charles and Richard Titmuss, took a keen interest in the political implications of demographic analysis. Kuczynski, who was forced into exile from Germany after 1933 for his political views, appears to have been a man of the left. Some scholars, like Harold Wright, opposed eugenics as misguided, while others, like David Glass, maintained a neutral

stance. Still others, like Alexander Carr-Saunders and George Knibbs, continued to express hereditarian ideas throughout their careers.

101. Dennis Hodgson, "Ideological Currents and the Interpretation of Demographic Trends: The Case of Francis Amasa Walker," *Journal of the History of the Biological Sciences* 28, no. 1 (1992): 28–44; Matthew Guterl, *The Color of Race in America 1900–1940* (Cambridge, MA: Harvard University Press, 2001), 27–67; Paul Kramer, *The Blood of Government: Race, Empire, the United States and the Philippines* (Chapel Hill: University of North Carolina Press, 2006).

102. Myron Echenberg, "Paying the Blood Tax: Military Conscription in French West Africa, 1914–1929," *Canadian Journal of African Studies* 9, no. 2 (1975): 171–92.

103. The Colonial Social Science Research Council predated its domestic counterpart by twenty years. For the greater freedom of colonial research and policy see Jane Lewis, *Empire and State-Building: War and Welfare in Kenya 1925–52* (Athens: Ohio University Press, 2000) and Alice Conklin, *A Mission to Civilize: The Republican Idea of Empire in France and West Africa, 1895–1930* (Stanford, CA: Stanford University Press, 1997).

104. Historians have studied this in India in particular. See Bernard Cohn, "The Census, Social Structure and Objectification in South Asia," in Bernard Cohn, *An Anthropologist Among the Historians and Other Essays* (Oxford: Oxford University Press, 1987), 224–54, and David Ludden, "Orientalist Empiricism: Transformations of Colonial Knowledge," in Carol Breckenridge and Peter van der Veer, eds., *Orientalism and the Postcolonial Predicament: Perspectives on South Asia* (Philadelphia: University of Pennsylvania Press, 1993), 250–78.

105. G. Broberg and N. Rolle-Hansen, eds., *Eugenics and the Welfare State: Sterilization Policy in Denmark, Sweden, Norway and Finland* (East Lansing: Michigan State University Press, 1996) and Angus McLaren, *Our Own Master Race: Eugenics in Canada, 1885–1945* (Toronto: McClelland and Steward, 1990), 89–106; P.R. Reilly, *The Surgical Solution: A History of Involuntary Sterilization in the U.S.* (Baltimore: John Hopkins University Press, 1991).

106. Carl Ipsen, *Dictating Demography: The Problem of Population in Fascist Italy* (Cambridge: Cambridge University Press, 1996); Paul Weindling, *Health Race and German Politics Between National Unification and Nazism, 1870–1945* (Cambridge: Cambridge University Press, 1989); David Horn, *Social Bodies: Science, Reproduction, and Italian Modernity* (Princeton: Princeton University Press, 1994); Mark Adams, "Eugenics in Russia, 1900–1940," in Mark Adams, ed., *The Wellborn Science* (Oxford: Oxford University Press, 1990), 153–216; Andres Reggiani, "Alexis Carrel, the Unknown: Eugenics and Population Research under Vichy," *French Historical Studies* 25, no. 2 (2002): 331–56.

107. William Seltzer, "Population Statistics, the Holocaust, and the Nuremberg Trials," *Population and Development Review* 24, no. 3 (1998): 511–52.

108. For the history of eugenics in Britain see Soloway, *Demography and*

Degeneration, and Daniel Kevles, *In the Name of Eugenics: Genetics and the Uses of Human Heredity* (New York: Knopf, 1985).

109. Soloway, *Demography and Degeneration,* 163–225; Kevles, *Eugenics,* 164–75.

110. Diane Paul, "Eugenics and the Left," *Journal of the History of Ideas* 45, no. 4 (1984): 567–90.

111. John MacNicol, "The Voluntary Sterilization Campaign in Britain, 1918–1939," *Journal of the History of Sexuality* 2, no. 3 (1992): 422–38, and Matthew Thompson, *The Problem of Mental Deficiency: Eugenics, Democracy and Social Policy in Britain c. 1870–1959* (Oxford: Oxford University Press, 1998), 180–205.

112. The continued focus on class can be seen the discussion of the social problem group, a supposed concentration of lesser endowed families in poorer areas. See C. P. Blacker, "Social Problem Families in the Limelight," *Eugenics Review* 38, no. 3 (1946): 117–27.

113. Dan Stone, "Race in British Eugenics," *European History Quarterly* 31, no. 3, (2001): 397–425.

114. Elazar Barkan, *The Retreat of Scientific Racism* (Cambridge: Cambridge University Press, 1992).

115. For Huxley's rather complicated views see Barkan, *Scientific Racism,* 178–89, 235–48, 296–310; Garland Allen, "Julian Huxley and the Eugenical View of Human Evolution," in C. Kenneth Water and Albert Van Helden, eds., *Julian Huxley: Biologist and Statesman of Science* (Houston: Rice University Press, 1992), 193–222; Tilley, *Africa as a Living Laboratory,* 238–22.

116. Julian Huxley to Oliver Stanley, 17–7–43, CO/859/62/17, Birth Control-West Africa, 1943.

117. Soloway, *Demography and Degeneration,* 195–202.

118. Ibid., 203–15.

119. A.S. Parkes to C.P. Blacker 29–10–34 (?), Memo, 26-12-34, Rockefeller archives material on Eugenics Society Funding, SA/EUG/GC/88/1, Eugenics Society Papers, (hereafter ES), Contemporary Medical Archives Centre (hereafter CMAC). See Richard Soloway, "The 'Perfect Contraceptive': Eugenics and Birth Control Research in Britain and America in the Inter-war Years," *Journal of Contemporary History* 30, no. 4 (1995): 637–64.

120. For Blacker's correspondence with Sanger see Correspondence with Margaret Sanger 1922–60, SA/EUG C.304, ES Papers, CMAC.

121. Rockefeller Archives Eugenics Society Material 1934–40 SA/EUG/GC/88/1, ES Papers, CMAC.

122. Blacker in particular found the work of George Knibbs important. Blacker called his book, *The Shadow of the World's Future,* "an excellent introduction to problem of world population." *Eugenics Review* 20, no. 4 (1929): 269–70.

123. C.P. Blacker, *Birth Control and the State: A Plea and a Forecast* (London: Taylor & Francis, 1926), 22–27, 70–78.

124. Ibid., 59–70, 85–89.

125. Letter to the Empire Settlement Committee, n.d., and Letter to Prominent People in the Dominions, n.d. The letters were not dated, but surrounding papers are from the mid-1920s. File on Immigration and Emigration of the Eugenics Society 1925-58 SA/EUG/D.103, ES Papers, CMAC.

126. Eric Richards, *Britannia's Children: Emigration from England, Scotland, Wales and Ireland since 1600* (London: Hambledon and London, 2004), 117-231. For Greater Britain see Andrew Thompson, *Imperial Britain: The Empire in British Politics c. 1880-1932* (Harlow: Longman, 1999) and Duncan Bell, *The Idea of Greater Britain: Empire and the Future of the World Order, 1860-1900* (Princeton: Princeton University Press, 2007).

127. Robert Huttenback, *Racism and Empire: White Settlers and Colored Immigrants in the British Self-Governing Colonies 1830-1910* (Ithaca, NY: Cornell University Press, 1976).

128. Angus McLaren and Arlene McLaren, *The Bedroom and the State: The Changing Practices and Politics of Contraception and Abortion in Canada, 1880-1997* (Toronto: Oxford University Press, 1997). Stefania Siedlecky and Dianna Wyndam, *Populate or Perish: Australian Women's Fight for Birth Control* (Sydney: Allen & Unwin, 1990), 16-23.

129. Victor Wallace, *Women and Children First* (Melbourne: Oxford University Press, 1946), 2.

130. David Walker, *Anxious Nation: Australia and the Rise of Asia 1850-1939* (St. Lucia: University of Queenlands Press, 1999); Roger Thompson, *Australian Imperialism in the Pacific: The Expansionist Era, 1820-1920* (Carlton: Melbourne University Press, 1980). For contemporary accounts see Hector Bywater, *Sea Power in the Pacific* (New York: Houghton Mifflin, 1921); E.I. Piesse, "Australia and Imperial Defence," *Austral-Asiatic Bulletin* 1, no. 1 (1937): 8-9; H.L. Wilkinson, *The World's Population* (London: P.S. King, 1930); W.D. Forsyth, *The Myth of Open Spaces* (Melbourne: Oxford University Press, 1942); F.W. Eggleston and G. Packer, *The Growth of Australian Population* (Sydney: Eggleston & Packer, 1937).

131. Stephen Constantine, ed., *Emigrants and Empire* (Manchester: University of Manchester Press, 1990) and Kent Fedorowich, *Unfit for Heroes: Reconstruction and Soldier Settlement in the Empire between the Wars* (Manchester: University of Manchester Press, 1995).

132. C.S. Stock, "Emigration," *Eugenics Review* 9, no. 4 (1918): 277-95; ———, "Eugenics and Imperial Development," *Eugenics Review* 11, no. 3 (1919): 124-35; Vaughn Cornish, "The Geographical Aspect of Eugenics," *Eugenics Review* 16, no. 4 (1925): 267-69; G.P. Mudge, "The Menace to the English Race and Its Traditions of Present-Day Immigration and Emigration," *Eugenics Review* 11, no. 4 (1920): 202-12.

133. Alexander Carr-Saunders, "Migration in Relation to Racial Problems, *Eugenics Review* 18, no. 4 (1927): 302-311.

134. Richards, *Britannia's Children*, 233-51. The depression of the 1930s put plans for settling the interior and northern coasts of Australia on hold.

Michael Roe, "'We Can Die Just as Easy Out Here'": Australia and British Migration, 1916–1939," in Constantine, *Emigrants*, 96–120.

135. For Australia see Stuart Macintyre, *Oxford History of Australia*, vol. 4: *The Succeeding Age 1901–42* (Melbourne: Oxford University Press, 1986), 198–296.

136. The foremost exponent of this view was the American geographer Ellsworth Huntington. See his *Civilization and Climate* (New Haven: Yale University Press, 1922), 11–29, 306–9. Warren Thompson cited the unsuitability of the tropical regions of Australian for whites as a justification for their settlement by Asian people. Thompson, *Danger Spots*, 71–73, 88–89. For a discussion of this debate and its resolution in the 1930s see Warwick Anderson, *The Cultivation of Whiteness: Science, Health and Racial Destiny in Australia* (Durham, NC: Duke University Press, 2006).

137. J.E. Duerden, "Genesis and Reclamation of the poor White in South Africa," *Eugenics Review* 14, no. 4 (1923): 270–75.

138. Tony Taylor, "Thomas Hunter and the Campaign Against Eugenics," *New Zealand Journal of History* 39, no. 2 (2005): 195–210, and Angela Wanhalla, "To 'Better the Breed of Men': Women and Eugenics in New Zealand, 1900–1935," *Women's History Review* 16, no. 2 (2007): 163–82.

139. McLaren, *Our Own Master Race*, 89–106.

140. Carol Bacchi, "The Nature-Nurture Debate in Australia, 1900–1914," *Historical Studies* 19, no. 75 (1980): 199–212; Stephen Garton, "Sound Minds and Healthy Bodies: Reconsidering Eugenics in Australia, 1914–1940," *Historical Studies* 33, no. 103 (1994): 163–81; Rob Watts, "Beyond Nature and Nurture: Eugenics in Twentieth Century Australian History," *Australian Journal of Politics and History* 40, no. 3 (1994): 318–34; Ross Jones, "The Master Potter and the Rejected Pots: Eugenic Legislation in Victoria, 1918–1939," *Australian Historical Studies* 11, no. 3 (1999): 319–42; Alison Bashford, "'Is White Australia Possible'?: Race, Colonialism and Tropical Medicine," *Ethnic and Racial Studies* 23, no. 2 (2000): 248–71.

141. Letter from C.P. Blacker to Arthur Packard. 26–11–34, Rockefeller archives material on Eugenics Society Funding, SA/EUG/GC/88/1, 2, ES Papers, CMAC. See Soloway, "Perfect Contraceptive," 645–47, and Susanne Klausen, "'Poor Whiteism,' White Maternal Mortality, and the Promotion of Public Health in South Africa: The Department of Public Health's Endorsement of Contraceptive Services, 1930–1938," *Southern African Historical Journal* 45, no. 1 (2001): 53–78.

142. For eugenics in Kenya see Chloe Campbell, *Race and Empire: Eugenics in Colonial Kenya* (Manchester: University of Manchester Press, 2007).

143. One South African labeled the threat of poor white reproduction as greater than the threat from a growing African population. N. Romeyn to Eugenics Society 15–12–30, Correspondence with other Eugenics Organizations SA/EUG E.22 South Africa 1930–1, ES papers, CMAC.

144. Susanne Klausen, "For the Sake of the Race: Eugenic Discourses of Feeblemindedness and Motherhood in the South African Medical Record,"

Journal of Southern African Studies 23, no. 1 (1997): 27–50, and "Women's Resistance to Eugenic Birth Control in Johannesburg, 1930–39," *South African Historical Journal* 50, no. 1 (2004): 152–69.

145. John Oldham, "Population and Health in Africa," *International Review of Missions* 15, no. 3 (1926): 414–17.

146. Alexander Carr-Saunders, "Eugenics in the Light of Population Trends," *Eugenics Review* 27, no. 1 (1935): 11–20.

147. Soloway, *Demography and Degeneration*, 226–82.

148. Memo on Formation of the Institute of Family Relations, SA EUG/C.57 Letters 1933–37, ES Papers, CMAC.

149. Soloway, *Demography and Degeneration*, 245–52; Grebenik, "Demographic Research," 9–10.

150. Carr-Saunders published a pamphlet, "Standing Room Only," based on five radio talks in 1930. In 1937, the radio program *One Generation to Another* broadcast a series of discussions entitled "The Population Problem: the Experts and the Public" that included Carr-Saunders and Kuczynski as panelists. The talks were published as a book edited by the LSE sociologist T. H. Marshall, *The Population Problem* (London: Allen & Unwin, 1938).

151. Richard Soloway, *Birth Control and the Population Question*, 159–318; June Rose, *Marie Stopes and the Sexual Revolution* (London: Faber & Faber, 1992); Audrey Leathard, *The Fight for Family Planning: The Development of Family Planning Services in Britain 1921–74* (London: Macmillan, 1980), 1–50, Rosanna Ledbetter, *The Malthusian League, 1877-1927*, (Columbus: Ohio State University Press, 1982).

152. American birth control advocates faced a more difficult task, complicated by the Comstock Act and the need to address differing state and local laws about contraception. James Reed, *From Private Vice to Public Virtue: The Birth Control Movement and American Society since 1830* (New York: Basic, 1978), 97–128, and Ellen Chesler, *Woman of Valor: Margaret Sanger and the Birth Control Movement in America* (New York: Simon & Schuster, 1992), 200–42, 269–354.

153. Patricia Thane, "What Difference Did the Vote Make? Women in Public and Private Life since 1918," *Historical Research* 76, no. 192 (2003): 268–85; Barbara Caine, *English Feminism 1780–1980* (New York: Oxford University Press 1987), 173–221.

154. Jane Lewis, "The Ideology and Politics of Birth Control in Inter-War Britain," *Women's Studies International Quarterly* 2, no. 1 (1979): 33–48.

155. For a discussion of the role of feminism in the earlier eugenics movement see Soloway, *Demography and Degeneration*, 122–37.

156. Linda Gordon, *The Moral Property of Women: A History of Birth Control Politics in America* (Urbana: University of Illinois Press, 2002), 190–203; Richard Soloway," Marie Stopes, Eugenics and the Birth Control Movement," in Robert Peel, ed., *Marie Stopes, Eugenics and the Birth Control Movement* (London: Galton Institute, 1997); Chesler, *Woman of Valor*, 215–17.

157. Ann Taylor, "Feminism and Eugenics in Germany and Britain 1900–

1940: A Comparative Perspective," *German Studies Review* 23, no. 3 (2000): 477–505; Claire Makepeace, "To What Extent was the Relationship between the Feminists and Eugenics Movement a 'Marriage of Convenience' in the Inter-war Years?" *Journal of International Women's Studies* 11, no. 3 (2009): 66–80; Lesley Hall, "Women, Feminism and Eugenics," in Robert Peel, ed., *Essays in the History of Eugenics: Proceedings of a Conference Organized by the Galton Institute* (London: Galton Institute, 1997), 36–51.

158. Edith How-Martyn to Margaret Sanger, 15-3-29, Box 21, Reel 14, Sanger papers, Library of Congress Collection.

159. Edith How-Martyn to Anonymous, 18-10-37, Papers on India 1934–38, Eileen Palmer Papers, Coll Misc 0639, LSE Archives. Palmer was Edith How-Martyn's assistant.

160. Clare Midgley, *Women against Slavery* (London: Routledge, 1992).

161. Margaret Strobel, *European Women and the Second British Empire* (Bloomington: Indiana University Press, 1991); Antoinette Burton, *The Burdens of Empire: British Feminists, Indian Women and Imperial Culture, 1865–1915* (Chapel Hill: University of North Carolina Press, 1994); Catherine Hall, Keith McClelland, and Jane Rendell, *Defining the Victorian Nation: Class, Race, Gender and the Reform Act of 1867* (Cambridge: Cambridge University Press, 2000); Clare Midgley, *Feminism and Empire: Women Activists in Imperial Britain 1790–1865* (London: Routledge, 2007).

162. Susan Pedersen, "The Maternalist Moment in British Colonial Policy: The Controversy over 'Child Slavery' in Hong Kong, 1917–1941," *Past and Present* 171, no. 1(2001): 161–202.

163. Barbara Bush, "'Britain's Conscience on Africa': White Women, Race and Imperial Politics in Inter-war Britain," in Clare Midgley, ed., *Gender and Imperialism* (Manchester: Manchester University Press, 1998), 200–223.

164. Draft of broadcast speech by Edith How-Martyn, February 1937, Materials on India, 1/25, Palmer Papers, Coll Misc 0639, LSE Archives.

165. Helen Beck to Malcolm MacDonald 24-9-38, CO 273/633/9 Birth Control Straits Settlement, 1937.

166. Bolt, *Sisterhood Questioned*, 83, 87–88.

167. Sanjam Ahluwalia, *Productive Restraints* (Urbana: University of Illinois Press, 2008), 54–84; Genevieve Burnett, "Fertile Fields: A History of the Ideological Origins and Institutionalization of the International Birth Control Movement 1870–1940," PhD diss., University of New South Wales, 1998.

168. Edith How-Martyn to Margaret Sanger, 5-2-35, S09:0616, Sanger Papers, Smith Collection, cited in Sanjam Ahluwalia, "Rethinking Boundaries: Feminism and (Inter)Nationalism in Early Twentieth Century India," *Journal of Women's History* 14, no. 4 (2003): 190.

169. Lisa Cody, "The Politics of Illegitimacy in the Age of Reform: Women, Reproduction and Political Economy in England's New Poor of 1834," *Journal of Women's History* 11, no. 4 (2000): 131–56.

170. Meredeth Turshen, "Reproducing Labor: Colonial Government Reg-

ulation of African Women's Reproductive Lives," in Ittmann, Cordell, and Maddox, *The Demographics of Empire*, 217–44.

171. Thomas Malthus, *An Essay on the Principle of Population*, vol. 1 (London: J.M. Dent, 1914), 75–138.

172. See Anne Stoler, *Carnal Knowledge and Imperial Power: Race and the Intimate in Colonial Rule* (Berkeley: University of California Press, 2002).

173. Susan Pedersen, *Eleanor Rathbone and the Politics of Conscience* (New Haven: Yale University Press, 2004).

174. Margaret Sanger and Edith How-Martyn, *Round the World for Birth Control* (London: BCIIC, 1936); Beryl Suitters, *Be Brave and Angry: Chronicles of the International Planned Parenthood Federation* (London: International Planned Parenthood Federation, 1973), 12–16; Connelly, *Fatal Misconception*, 77–114.

175. Correspondence about Australia 1919–43, PP/MCS A 307; Letters about India CC/MCS A.313, Marie Stopes Papers, CMAC.

176. Rose, *Marie Stopes*, 208–9; Peter Neushul, "Marie Stopes and the Popularization of Birth Control Technology," *Technology and Culture* 39, no. 2 (1998): 245–72; Susanne Klausen, "The Imperial Mother of Birth Control: Marie Stopes and the South African Birth Control Movement, 1930–1950," in Gregory Blue, Martin Bunton, and Ralph Crozier, eds., *Colonialism and the Modern World* (Armonk, NY: M.E. Sharpe, 2002), 182–99.

177. Chesler, *Woman of Valor*, 235–36, 258–59, 358–59.

178. Margaret Sanger to C. Blacker 14–11–35, Birth Control International Information Centre 1933–37 SA/EUG/D.14, ES Papers, CMAC.

179. Sanger has been the subject of a number of biographies. In addition to Chesler, see David Kennedy, *Birth Control in America; the Career of Margaret Sanger* (New Haven: Yale University Press, 1976).

180. Soloway, *Birth Control*, 154; Chesler, *Woman of Valor*, 258–59; Helen Rappaport, *Encyclopedia of Women Social Reformers*, vol. 1 (Santa Barbara: ABC-CLIO, 2001), 312–13; Olive Banks, *The Biographical Dictionary of British Feminists*, vol. 1 (New York: Harvester Wheatsheaf, 1985–90), 105–6.

181. Edith How-Martyn to Margaret Sanger, 2–7-29, Box 21, Reel 14, Sanger Papers, Library of Congress Collection.

182. She also wrote an account of her 1935–36 tour with Sanger, *Round the World for Birth Control*, with a foreword by Julian Huxley.

183. Travel Books, 1/7 Ceylon 1931–35, 1/8 China 1935–36, 1/13 press cuttings India 1929–36, 1/16 Indian tour 1934–35, 1/22 India correspondence, 1935–39, Palmer Papers, Misc 0639, LSE Archives.

184. Travel Book, 2/5 Egypt 1934, Palmer Papers, Coll Misc 0639, LSE Archives. The American social scientist Walter Cleland was among the first to raise the issue of overpopulation. Walter Cleland, *The Population Problem in Egypt* (Lancaster, PA: Science Press, 1936).

185. Chesler, *Woman of Valor*, 235–37, 355–70; Sanger and How-Martyn, *Round the World for Birth Control*.

186. She had previously visited in 1935. Birth Control World Wide, Report

October 1938–39, 7, 1/33 Miscellaneous Papers, Palmer Papers, Coll Misc 0639, LSE Archives.

187. For more on Jamaica see Jill Briggs, "'As Fool-Proof as Possible': Overpopulation, Colonial Demography and the Jamaican Birth Control League," *The Global South* 4, no. 2 (2010): 57–77, and Nicole Bourbonnais, "'Dangerously Large': The 1938 Labor Rebellion and the Debate over Birth Control in Jamaica," *New West Indian Guide* 83, nos. 1 and 2 (2009): 39–69.

188. Minutes of Meeting of the International Subcommittee of the National Birth Control Association, 3-2-39, Minutes of the International Subcommittee of the FPA, 1938-1942, SA/FPA A5/43, FPA Papers, CMAC.

189. Michael Fielding, ed., *Birth Control in Asia* (London: BCIIC, 1935).

190. Edith How-Martyn to Margaret Sanger 10-5-37, C 06:0484, Sanger Papers, Collected Document Series.

191. Edith How-Martyn to Margaret Sanger, 19-7-37, Sanger Papers, Smith Collection, S11:0408; Margaret Sanger to Edith How-Martyn, 29-10-37, C06:0637, Sanger Papers, Collected Document Series.

192. Edith How-Martyn to Margaret Sanger 28-1--36, S10:0952, Sanger Papers, Smith Collection.

193. *Eugenics Review* 28, 1 (1936): 60–61. Connelly, *Fatal Misconception*, 110.

194. Klaussen, "Imperial Mother," 192–93; Minutes, 10–5-38, Minutes, 3–4-39, Minutes of International Sub-Committee of the Family Planning Association, 1938–42, SA/FPA A5/43, FPA Papers, CMAC; CO 129/565/5 Hong Kong Eugenics League, 1938.

195. Sir John Megaw, "Pressure of Population in India," *Journal of the Royal Society of Arts* 87, no. 4491 (1938): 134–57. For more on his work see Arnold, "Official Attitudes to Population," 30–34.

196. CO/859/62/16/ Birth Control in the West Indies 1941–42. Blacker discussed Brander in a 1963 letter to George Cadbury. PP/CPB/B.18/5 Correspondence 1963, C. P Blacker Papers, CMAC.

197. Hong Kong Eugenics League, 1937, CO 129/565/5; Hong Kong Eugenics League, 1938, CO/129/571/17; Birth Control-Straits Settlements, 1938, CO 273/645/8.

198. Edith How-Martyn to Margaret Sanger 9–6-37, S13:0170, Margaret Sanger Papers, Smith Collection.

199. CO 37/282/9, Birth Control-Bermuda, 1934 and CO 37/208/8 Birth Control-Bermuda, 1935. Governor Hillyard invited Margaret Sanger to tour Bermuda at government expense in 1937. Margaret Sanger to Havelock Ellis 25-5-37, S13:0117, Sanger Papers, Smith Collection.

200. Barbara Evans, *Freedom to Choose: The Life and Work of Dr. Helena Wright, Pioneer of Contraception* (London: Bodley Head, 1984).

201. For India see Ahluwalia, *Reproductive Restraints*, 115–42; Sarah Hodges, *Contraception Colonialism and Commerce: Birth Control in South India, 1920-1940* (Aldershot: Ashgate, 2008), 21–46; Arnold, "Official Atti-

tudes to Population," 22–50; Nair, "The Construction of a 'Population Problem'", 227–47.

202. Omnia El Shakry, "Barren Land and Fecund Bodies: The Emergence of Population Discourse in Interwar Egypt," *International Journal of Middle East Studies* 37, no. 3 (2005): 351–72.

203. Barbara Ramusack, "Embattled Advocates: The Debate over Birth Control in India, 1920–1940," *Journal of Women's History* 1, no. 2 (1989): 34–64, and Ahluwalia, *Reproductive Restraints*, 23–53.

204. Travel book of Edith How-Martyn, Jamaica, 2/9, Palmer Papers, Coll Misc 0639. LSE Archives.

205. Briggs, "'As Fool-Proof as Possible,'"166–74, and Bourbonnais, "'Dangerously Large,'" 47–64.

206. This idea is somewhat at odds with David Cannadine's argument about ties between elites within the empire. David Cannadine, *Ornamentalism: How the British Saw their Empire* (Oxford: Oxford University Press, 2001).

207. For more on the publicity about depopulation see Soloway, *Demography and Degeneration*, 241–46.

208. General publicity about global population growth did not appear until after 1945, and this material found a mass audience only in the 1960s. For an analysis of American coverage, see John Wilmoth and Patrick Ball, "The Population Debate in American Popular Magazines, 1946–90," *Population and Development Review* 18, no. 1 (1992): 631–68.

CHAPTER 2

1. In 1900, the Colonial Service employed about 1,500 British or expatriate officials and in 1938, the number had reached 7,000–9,000. Anthony Kirk-Greene, *A Biographical Dictionary of the British Colonial Service 1939–1966* (London: H. Zell, 1991), vii.

2. Maria Missra, "Colonial Officers and Gentleman: The British Empire and the Globalization of Tradition," *Journal of Global History* 3, no. 2 (2008): 149–59.

3. Charles Jeffries, *Whitehall and the Colonial Service: An Administrative Memoir, 1939–1956* (London: Athlone, 1972), 9–17; Charles Jeffries, *The Colonial Office* (London: Allen & Unwin, 1956), 24–115; Anthony Kirk-Greene, *On Crown Service: A History of HM Colonial and Overseas Services, 1837–1997* (London: I. B. Taurus, 1999), 15–37.

4. Stephen Constantine, *The Making of British Colonial Development Policy 1914–1940* (London: Frank Cass, 1984), 9–29.

5. For an overview see Robert Holland, "The British Empire and the Great War, 1914–1918," in Judith Brown and Wm. Roger Louis, eds., *The Oxford History of the British Empire*, vol. 4: *The Twentieth Century* (Oxford: Oxford University Press, 1999), 114–37.

6. Howard Johnson, 'The West Indies and the Conversion of the British

Official Classes to the Development Idea," *Journal of Commonwealth and Comparative Politics* 15, no. 1 (1977): 55–83; R. D. Pearce, *The Turning Point in Africa: British Colonial Policy 1938-48* (London: Frank Cass, 1982); Penelope Hetherington, *British Paternalism and Africa 1920-1940* (London: Frank Cass, 1978); Stephen Constantine, *The Making of British Colonial Development Policy 1914-1940* (London: Frank Cass, 1984); J. E. Lewis, "'Tropical East Ends' and the Second World War: Some Contradictions in Colonial Office Welfare Initiatives," *Journal of Imperial and Commonwealth History* 28, no. 2 (2000): 42–66.

7. George Knibbs, "The Organization of Imperial Statistics," *Journal of the Royal Statistical Society* 83, no. 2 (1920): 201–24.

8. A. J. Christopher, "The Quest for an Imperial Census, 1840–1940," *Journal of Historical Geography* 34, no. 2 (2008): 268–85, and Jean-Pierre Beaud and Jean-Guy Prevost, "Statistics as the Science of Government: The Stillborn British Empire Statistical Bureau, 1918–1920," *Journal of Imperial and Commonwealth History* 33, no. 3 (2005): 369–91.

9. For the census process in one region see Dmitri van den Bersselaar, "Establishing the Facts: P. A. Talbot and the 1921 Census in Nigeria," *History in Africa* 31 (2004): 69–102.

10. Hugh Tinker, *A New System of Slavery: The Export of Indian Labour Overseas 1830-1920* (London: Oxford University Press, 1974); Colin Newberry, "Labour Migration in the Imperial Phase," *Journal of Imperial and Commonwealth History* 3, no. 2 (1975): 234–56; David Northrup, *Indentured Labor in the Age of Imperialism 1834-1922* (Cambridge: Cambridge University Press, 1995).

11. Stephen Constantine, ed., *Emigrants and Empire* (Manchester: Manchester University Press, 1990); Kent Fedorowich, *Unfit for Heroes: Reconstruction and Soldier Settlement in the Empire between the Wars* (Manchester: Manchester University Press, 1995).

12. For an overview of global migration before 1940 see Adam McKeown, "Global Migration, 1846–1940," *Journal of World History* 15, no. 2 (2004): 155–89.

13. Michael Roe, "'We Can Die Just as Easy Out Here': Australia and British Migration, 1916–1939," in Constantine, ed., *Emigrants and Empire*, 96–120.

14. Laura Tabili, *"We Ask for British Justice": Black Workers and the Construction of Racial Difference in Late Imperial Britain* (Ithaca, NY: Cornell University Press, 1994). See also Ian Spencer, *British Immigration Policy since 1939: The Making of Multi-racial Britain* (London: Routledge 1997), 8–13.

15. Franklin W. Knight, "Jamaican Migrants and the Cuban Sugar Cane Industry," in Manuel Fraginlas, Frank Pons, and Stanley Engerman, eds., *Between Slavery and Free Labor: The Spanish-Speaking Caribbean in the Nineteenth Century* (Baltimore: John Hopkins University Press, 1985), 94–114; Barry Carr, "Identity, Class, and Nation: Black Immigrant Workers, Cuban

Communism, and the Sugar Insurgency," *Hispanic American Historical Review* 78, no. 1 (1998): 83–116.

16. Minute by Poynton 20-4-38, CO 318/432/10 Emigration-West Indies, 1938.

17. Minute by Sidebottom 8-3-38, CO 28 322/4 Emigration Barbados, 1938.

18. CO 28/325/12 Surplus Population Problem-Barbados, 1939.

19. R. Graham to Sir W. G. Tyrrell, 2-2-26, CO 111/66/41 Surplus population of Italy Suggested absorption by British Guiana.

20. Another scheme was proposed in 1939, CO 111/757/13 Miscellaneous Resettlement Project of George Lloyd 1939. Despite these problems, the idea would be renewed in the 1940s and would be the subject of a Royal Commission, the Evans Commission, in 1948.

21. Minute on Immigration of Refugees to the West Indies, CO 318/440/5 Immigration-General Policy, West Indies, 1939.

22. Note of a discussion 31-3-38, CO 318/432/10 Emigration-West Indies, 1938.

23. Amarjit Kaur, "Tappers and Weeders: South Indian Plantation Workers in Peninsular Malaysia," *South Asia* 21, Special Issue (1998): 73–102.

24. A. B. Shamsul, "A History of Identity, an Identity of a History: The Idea and Practice of 'Malayness' in Malaysia Reconsidered," *Journal of Southeast Asian Studies* 32, no. 3 (2001): 355–66; Charles Hirshman, "The Meaning and Measurement of Ethnicity in Malaysia: An Analysis of Census Classifications," *Journal of Asian Studies* 46, no. 3 (1987): 555–82.

25. Christopher Baker, "Economic Reorganization and the Slump in South and Southeast Asia," *Comparative Studies in Society and History* 23, no. 3 (1981): 325–49; W. G. Huff, "Entitlements, Destitution, and Emigration in the 1930s Singapore Great Depression," *Economic History Review* 14, no. 2 (2001): 290–323.

26. CO 273/566/2 Unemployment in Malaya, 1930; CO 273/654/1; Emigration from India to Malaya, 1939.

27. CO 129/587/15 Excess Population Reduction Committee Report Chinese Immigration Bill, 1940.

28. CO 822/99/17 Indians in East Africa; CO 37 294/17 Bermuda Overpopulation and Emigration, 1943.

29. Naomi Shepard, *Ploughing Sand: British Rule in Palestine 1917–1948* (New Brunswick, NJ: Rutgers University Press, 2000), 76–99.

30. Optimal population theory represented an attempt to refine Malthusian concepts of overpopulation. Proponents argued that population size and growth rates were relative to resources and the level of economic development. Hugh Dalton, "The Theory of Population," *Economica* 22 (1928): 28–50; Lionel Robbins, "The Optimum Theory of Population," in *London Essays in Economics* (Freeport, NY: Books for Libraries, 1967), 103–34; Alexander Carr-Saunders, *The Population Problem* (Oxford: Clarendon Press, 1922), 197–202.

31. Roza I. M. El-Eini, "The Implementation of British Agricultural Policy in Palestine in the 1930s," *Middle Eastern Studies* 32, no. 4 (1996): 211–50.

32. Shalom Reichman, Yossi Katz, and Yair Paz, "The Absorptive Capacity of Palestine, 1882–1948," *Middle Eastern Studies* 33, no. 2 (1997): 338–61.

33. Memo from High Commissioner for Palestine Sir Arthur Wauchope On Immigration Policy in Palestine, CO 733/254/7 Immigration Policy-Palestine, 1934.

34. CO 733/387 Policy Settled Population Proportion of Jews to Arabs, 1938.

35. For a discussion of the 1931 Census as well as the broader demographic background, see Justin McCarthy, *The Population of Palestine: Population History and Statistics of the Late Ottoman Period and the Mandate* (New York: Columbia University Press, 1990).

36. W.D. Battershill to H. F. Downie 12-30-38, CO 733/387 Settled Population Proportion of Jews to Arabs, 1938.

37. CO 733/309/9 Palestine Census, 1936.

38. CO 733/415/1 Palestine Fertility of Marriage 1939. For a discussion of the issue of Arab migration see McCarthy, *Population of Palestine*, 33–34.

39. Minute by J. S. Bennett 1-10-39, CO 733/387 Settled Population Proportion of Jews to Arabs, 1938.

40. CO 733/409/6 Settled Population: Proportion of Jews to Arabs, 1939.

41. Bernard Wasserstein, *Britain and the Jews of Europe 1939–1945* (London: Leicester University Press, 1999), 16–32.

42. Minute by C. Eastwood, CO 323/1626/3 Immigration Regulations Entry of Foreigners into British Colonies, 1938–39.

43. Spencer, *British Immigration Policy*, 8–20.

44. CO 859/9/7 Migration of Workers-Labour ILO, 1939.

45. Robin Oakley, "The Control of Cypriot Migration to Britain between the Wars," *Immigrants and Minorities* 6, no. 1 (1987): 30–43.

46. Despite the widespread incidence of forced labor, there is no comprehensive study of forced labor during this era. For Africa, a number of regional and local studies exist, but the most comprehensive study remains A. T. Nzula, I. I. Potekhin, and A. Z. Zusmanovich, *Forced Labour in Colonial Africa* (London: Zed, 1979).

47. For one study of North Borneo see CO 874/1080 Health of Native Races and Depopulation Problem, 1933–36.

48. For the complexity of the situation in East Africa see Shane Doyle, "Population Decline and Delayed Recovery in Bunyoro, 1860–1960," *Journal of African History* 41, no. 3 (2000): 429–58. For more on the biomedical analysis of Africa see Megan Vaughan, *Curing Their Ills* (Stanford, CA: Stanford University Press, 1991) and Sheldon Watts, *Epidemics and History: Disease, Power and Imperialism* (New Haven: Yale University Press, 1997), 213–68.

49. Kwabena Opare Akurang-Parry, "Colonial Forced Labor Policies for Road-Building in Southern Ghana and International Forced Labor Pressures, 1900–1940," *African Economic History* 28 (2000): 1–25.

50. Frederick Cooper, "Conditions Analogous to Slavery: Imperialism and Free Labor Ideology in Africa," in Frederick Cooper, Thomas Holt, and Rebecca Scott, eds., *Beyond Slavery: Explorations of Race, Labor, and Citizenship in Postemancipation Societies* (Chapel Hill: University of North Carolina Press, 2000), 107–49.

51. Raymond Dumett, "Disease and Mortality among Gold Miners of Ghana: Colonial Government and Mining Company Attitudes and Polices, 1900–1938," *Social Science and Medicine* 37, no. 2 (1993): 212–32. For an overview see John Caldwell, "The Social Repercussions of Colonial Rule: Demographic Aspects," in A. Adu Boahen, ed., *UNESCO General History of Africa*, vol. VII: *Africa under Colonial Domination 1880–1935* (London: Heinemann, 1985), 458–86.

52. G. H. Pitt-Rivers, *The Clash of Culture and the Contact of Races*, reprint of 1927 edition (New York: Negro Universities Press, 1969); Stephen Roberts, *Population Problems of the Pacific*, reprint of 1927 edition (New York: AMS, 1969).

53. Kevin Grant, *A Civilized Savagery: Britain and the New Slaveries in Africa, 1894–1926* (New York: Routledge, 2005), 135–66.

54. Nancy Rose Hunt, "'Le Bebe En Brousse': European Women, African Birth Spacing and Colonial Intervention in Breast-Feeding in the Belgian Congo," *International Journal of Historical Studies* 21, no. 3 (1988): 401–32; Myron Echenberg, "'Faire du negre': Military Aspects of Population Planning in French West Africa, 1920–1940," in Dennis Cordell and Joel Gregory, eds., *African Population and Capitalism* (Madison: University of Wisconsin Press, 1994), 95–108; Nicholas Thomas, "Sanitation and Seeing: The Creation of State Power in Early Colonial Fiji," *Comparative Studies in Society and History* 32, no. 1 (1990): 149–70.

55. Frederick Cooper, *Decolonization and African Society: The Labor Question in French and British Africa* (Cambridge: Cambridge University Press, 1996), 1–170 and Alice Conklin, *A Mission to Civilize: The Republican Idea of Empire in France and West Africa, 1895–1930* (Stanford, CA: Stanford University Press, 1997), 38–72, 212–45.

56. Orde-Brown's report on unrest in that colony in 1937 played a role in the creation of his position and the establishment of labor departments throughout the empire. Cooper, *African Society and Decolonization*, 58–73; L. J. Butler, *Copper Empire: Mining and the Colonial State in Northern Rhodesia, c. 1930–1964* (Basingstoke: Palgrave Macmillan, 2007), 53–59.

57. Oldham, as head of the Church Missionary Society, was an influential contributor to colonial policy. His critique of British policy in East Africa stirred controversy in the 1920s. He helped found the Institute for African Languages and Culture and became an advisor to Malcolm MacDonald. For his work see John Cell, "Lord Hailey and the Making of the African Survey," *African Affairs* 88, no. 353 (1989): 483–85, and Helen Tilley, *Africa as a Living Laboratory* (Chicago: University of Chicago Press, 2010), 77–91.

58. John Oldham, "Population and Health in Africa," *International Review*

of Missions 15, no. 3 (1926): 402–17. For a somewhat different version see "The Population Question in Africa," 1926, typescript in School of Oriental and African Studies, Council of British Missionary Societies Archive, Box 206, African-General.

59. Oldham, "Population Question in Africa," 34.

60. For a semi-official view of the issue of underpopulation see Study Group of the Royal Institute of International Affairs, "The Population Problem," in *The Colonial Problem* (London: Oxford University Press, 1937), 127–39.

61. *Proceedings of the Imperial Social Hygiene Congress, 1925* (London: British Social Hygiene Council, 1925), 1–2.

62. W. Ormsby-Gore, "The Economic Development of Tropical Africa and Its Effect on the Native Population," *Geographical Journal* 68, no. 3 (1926): 240–53.

63. Hetherington, *British Paternalism and Africa*.

64. David Arnold, "Introduction: Disease, Medicine and Empire," in David Arnold, ed., *Imperial Medicine and Indigenous Societies* (Manchester: Manchester University Press, 1988), 1–26. For a discussion of the influenza pandemic see David Killingray, "A New 'Imperial Disease': The Influenza Pandemic of 1918–19 and Its Impact on the British Empire," *Caribbean Quarterly* 49, no. 4 (2003): 30–49; Terrence Ranger, "The Influenza Pandemic in Southern Rhodesia: A Crisis of Comprehension," in Arnold, *Imperial Medicine*, 172–88; K. David Patterson, "The Influenza Epidemic of 1918–1919 in the Gold Coast," *Journal of African History* 24, no. 4 (1983): 485–502.

65. Tilley, *Africa as a Living Laboratory*, 169–208.

66. Kirk Arden Hoppe, *Lords of the Fly: Sleeping Sickness Control in British East Africa, 1900–1960* (Westport, CT: Greenwood, 2003), 105–42. In one case in Nigeria, officials hoped to create a forest reserve in the evacuated area. CO 583/296/3 Anchua Rural Development and Resettlement Scheme Report by Dr. T.A.M. Nash, 1946–47.

67. Donald Fisher, "Rockefeller Philanthropy and the British Empire: The Creation of the London School of Hygiene and Tropical Medicine," *History of Education* 7, no. 2 (1978): 129–43; ———, "The Rockefeller Foundation and the Development of Scientific Medicine in Great Britain," *Minerva* 16 (1978): 20–41; Edward Higgs, "Medical Statistics, Patronage and the State: The Development of the MRC Statistical Unit, 1911–1948," *Medical History* 44 (2000): 323–40; Eugene Grebenik, "Demographic Research in Britain 1936–1986," *Population Studies* 45, Suppl. (1991): 4.

68. Tilley, *Africa as a Living Laboratory*, 208–11.

69. Joseph Hodge, *Triumph of the Expert: Agrarian Doctrines of Development and the Legacies of British Colonialism* (Athens: Ohio University Press, 2007), 119–25; Lenore Manderson, "Health Services and the Legitimation of the Colonial State: British Malaya 1786–1941," *International Journal of the Health Services* 17, no. 1 (1987): 91–112.

70. Sierra Leone in the late 1920s employed five European doctors and

four African medical officers to service a population estimated at 1.5 million. In order to improve infant welfare, the British government agreed to subsidize the work of four missionary hospitals. The grant totaled £2,400 per year. Dispatch, 12-4-28 CO 267/625/10 Sierra Leone Infant Welfare Work, 1928.

71. Kerrie MacPherson, "Health and Empire: Britain's National Campaign to Combat Venereal Diseases in Shanghai, Hong Kong and Singapore," in Roger Davidson and Lesley Hall, eds., *Sex, Sin and Suffering: Venereal Disease and European Society since 1870* (London: Routledge, 2001), 173–90. For a discussion of colonial medicine and venereal disease in Africa see Vaughan, *Curing Their Ills*, 39–76, 129–54.

72. Rita Pemberton, "A Different Intervention: the International Health Commission/Board, Health, Sanitation in the British Caribbean, 1914–1930," *Caribbean Quarterly* 49, no. 4 (2003): 87–103; John Farley, *To Cast Out Disease: A History of the International Health Division of the Rockefeller Foundation, 1913–1951* (Oxford: Oxford University Press, 2003), 61–79.

73. Lenore Manderson, *Sickness and the State: Health and Illness in Colonial Malaya, 1870–1940* (Cambridge: Cambridge University Press, 1996) and Margaret Jones, *Health Policy in Britain's Model Colony: Ceylon, 1900–1948* (New Delhi: Orient Longman, 2004).

74. Jones, *Health Policy*, 173–208.

75. Ibid., 209–58; Manderson, *Sickness and the State*, 201–29; Carol Summers, "Intimate Colonialism: The Imperial Production of Reproduction in Uganda, 1907–1925," *Signs* 16, no. 41 (1991): 387–407; Jean Allman, "Making Mothers: Missionaries, Medical Officers and Women's Work in Colonial Assante, 1924–1945," *History Workshop* 38, no. 1 (1994): 23–47; Walter Bruchhausen, "Public Health and Child Health in German East Africa and Tanganyika Territory, 1900–1960," *Dynamis* 23 (2003): 85–113; Juanita de Barros, "'Improving the Standard of Motherhood': Infant Welfare in Post-Slavery British Guiana," in Juanita de Borros, Steven Palmer, and David Wright, eds., *Health and Medicine in the circum-Caribbean, 1800–1968* (London: Routledge, 2009), 165–94; Margaret Jolly, "Other Mothers: Maternal 'Insouciance' and the Depopulation Debate in Fiji and Vanuatu, 1890–1930," in Kalpana Ram and Margaret Jolly, eds., *Maternities and Modernities: Colonial and Postcolonial Experiences in Asia and the Pacific* (Cambridge: Cambridge University Press, 1998), 177–212.

76. Jolly, "Other Mothers," 199–202, De Borros, "Improving the Standard of Motherhood," 179–82; Meredeth Turshen, "Reproducing Labor: Colonial Government Regulation of African Women's Reproductive Lives," in Karl Ittmann, Dennis Cordell, and Gregory Maddox, eds., *The Demographics of Empire: The Colonial Order and the Creation of Knowledge* (Athens: Ohio University Press, 2010), 217–44.

77. De Borros, "Improving the Standard of Motherhood," 176–78.

78. Jones, *Health Policy*, 228–31; Lenore Manderson, "Bottle Feeding and

Ideology in Colonial Malaya: The Production of Change," *International Journal of Health Services* 12, no. 4 (1982): 611–12.

79. Deborah Neill, *Networks in Tropical Medicine: Internationalism, Colonialism and the Rise of a Medical Specialty, 1890–1930* (Stanford, CA: Stanford University Press, 2012). For a discussion of scientific networks in the British Empire see Brett Bennett and Joseph Hodge, eds., *Science and Empire: knowledge and networks of science across the British Empire, 1800–1970* (Basingstoke: Palgrave Macmillan, 2011).

80. Alison Bashford, "Global Biopolitics and the History of World Health," *History of the Human Sciences* 19, no. 1 (2006): 67–88; Iris Borowy, "The League of Nations Health Organization: From European to Global Health Concerns," in Astri Andresen, William Hubbard, and Teemu Rymin, eds., *International and Local Approaches to Health and Health Care* (Bergen: University of Bergen Press, 2010), 11–30; Lenore Manderson, " Wireless Wars in the Eastern Arena: Epidemiological Surveillance, Disease Prevention and the Work of the Eastern Bureau of the League of Nations Health Organization," in Paul Weindling, ed., *International Health Organizations and Movements, 1918–1939* (Cambridge: Cambridge University Press, 1995), 109–53, Tilley, *Africa as a Living Laboratory*, 172–81.

81. Michael Worboys, "The Discovery of Colonial Malnutrition between the Wars," in Arnold, *Imperial Medicine*, 208–25.

82. Steven Palmer, *Launching Global Health: The Caribbean Odyssey of the Rockefeller Foundation* (Ann Arbor: University of Michigan Press, 2010), 69–76, 80–83, 205–7.

83. CO 323/1067/1 Native Women and Children, 1930.

84. CO 323/1067/2–6 Health of Native Women and Children, 1930.

85. CO 323/1067/1 Native Women and Children, 1930.

86. Summary of Lord Passfield's reply, CO 323/1177/21 Health and Progress of Native Populations, 1932.

87. CO 323/1177/21 Health and Progress of Native Populations, 1932.

88. Joanna Lewis, *Empire State Building War and Welfare in Kenya 1925–52* (Athens: Ohio University Press, 2001), 61–62.

89. Barbara Bush, "'Britain's Conscience on Africa': White Women, Race and Imperial Politics in Inter-war Britain," in Clare Midgley, ed., *Gender and Imperialism* (Manchester: Manchester University Press, 1998), 200–23; Susan Pedersen, "National Bodies, Unspeakable Acts: The Sexual Politics of Colonial Policy Making," *Journal of Modern History* 63, no. 4 (1991): 647–80; ———, "The Maternalist Moment in British Colonial Policy: The Controversy over 'Child Slavery' in Hong Kong, 1917–1941," *Past and Present* 171, no. 1 (2001): 161–202; Lynn Thomas, "Imperial Concerns and Women's Affairs: State Efforts to Regulate Clitoridectomy and Eradicate Abortion in Meru Kenya, c. 1910–1950," *Journal of African History* 39, no. 1 (1998): 121–45.

90. Minute by J. Flood, CO 323/1331/11 Medical Welfare Work amongst Native Women and Children, 1935; CO 323/1465/7, Maternity and Child Welfare Conference, London, June 1937.

91. Nicole Bourbonnais, "One Woman to Another: Birth Control in the Caribbean 1936–1958," Conference Paper, 2012 Congress of the Latin American Studies Association, San Francisco, 10–11.

92. Mary Blacklock, "Certain Aspects of the Welfare of Women and Children in the Colonies," *Annals of Tropical Medicine* 30, no. 2 (1936): 221–64.

93. For more on her work see Hodge, *Triumph of the Expert*, 189–91; Manderson, *Sickness and the State*, 225–27. For a more critical view of her work see Denise Allen, *Managing Motherhood, Managing Risk: Fertility and Danger in West Central Tanzania* (Ann Arbor: University of Michigan Press, 2004), 22–25.

94. Lewis, *Empire State Building*, 62–63. For women and the colonial service see Helen Callaway, *Gender, Culture and Empire: European Women in Colonial Nigeria* (Urbana: University of Illinois Press, 1987), 139–43.

95. Note by J.J. Paskins, 11-7-42, CO/859/77/11, 1942–3 Social Service, Maternity and Child Welfare, Women's Services in the Colonies and Training of Personnel for, Report by Dr Mary Blacklock.

96. Joseph Hodge has explored this effort at some length. Hodge, *Triumph of the Expert*, 144–206.

97. John Perkins, *Geopolitics and the Green Revolution: Wheat, Genes and the Cold War* (New York: Oxford University Press, 1997).

98. James Long, "Can the Empire Feed its People?" *Nineteenth Century* 34 (1896): 16–27.

99. C.B. Fawcett, *A Political Geography of the British Empire* (London: University of London Press, 1933). See James Vernon, *Hunger: A Modern History* (London and Cambridge, MA: Belknap Press of Harvard University Press, 2007), 91–117.

100. Fawcett, *A Political Geography of the British Empire*, 299–330. Harold Cox, "The Peopling of the British Empire," *Foreign Affairs* 2, no. 1 (1923): 117–29; E.W. Shanahan, "Over-Population, Emigration and Empire Development," *Economica* 9 (1923): 215–33.

101. R. Mukerjee, *Food Planning for Four Hundred Millions* (London: Macmillan, 1938); Carr-Saunders, *World Population*, 269–76.

102. Joseph Hodge, "Science, Development and Empire: The Colonial Advisory Council on Agriculture and Animal Health, 1929–43," *Journal of Imperial and Commonwealth History* 30, no. 1 (2002): 1–26.

103. G.B. Masefield, *A History of the Colonial Agricultural Service* (Oxford: Clarendon Press, 1972).

104. David Anderson, "Depression, Dust Bowl, Demography and Drought: The Colonial State and Soil Conservation in East Africa during the 1930s," *African Affairs* 83, no.332 (1984): 321–41.

105. Edward East, *Mankind at the Crossroads* (New York: C. Scribner's Sons, 1928), 64–109; O.D. Von Engeln, "The World's Food Resources," *Geographical Review* 9, no. 3 (1920): 170–90; O.E. Baker, "Population, Food Supply, and American Agriculture," *Geographical Review* 18, no.3 (1928): 353–73;

Sir Daniel Hall, "The Relation between Cultivated Area and Population," *Scientific Monthly* 23, no. 4 (1926): 356–65.

106. Minute by Frank Stockdale 10–8-36, CO 318/422/9, File on *Warning from the West Indies* by W.M. Macmillan, 1936. Both Johnson and Constantine see Stockdale as an advocate for smallholdings, but his comments about the inability of peasants to cultivate their plots without constant supervision seems to contradict such assertions. Constantine, *Colonial Development*, 235–36, and Johnson, "Conversion," 65–66.

107. Royal Commission on the West Indies (Moyne Commission), *Report* (London: HMSO, 1945), 244–45, 287–93.

108. For concerns elsewhere in Africa see F. Dixey, "The Distribution of Population in Nyasaland," *Geographical Review* 18, no. 2 (1928): 274–90; C.R. Niven, "Some Nigerian Population Problems," *Geographical Journal* 85, no. 1 (1936): 54–58.

109. In addition to Anderson, "Depression," 321–41, see Hodge, *Triumph*, 146–66.

110. A. Walter, a government statistician, estimated African population growth at 1 to 1.5 percent per year in his testimony to the Kenyan Land Commission in 1933. S.J.K. Baker, "The Distribution of Native Population over East Africa," *Africa: Journal of the International African Institute* 10, no. 1 (1937): 37–54; Lord Hailey, *An African Survey* (London: Macmillan, 1938), 811–13.

111. E.B. Worthington, *Science in Africa* (London: Oxford University Press, 1938), 376–99, 566–67.

112. Sir A. Daniel Hall, *The Improvement of Native Agriculture in relation to Population and Public Health* (Oxford: Oxford University Press, 1936), 27.

113. Cynthia Brantley, "Kikuyu-Maasai Nutrition and Colonial Science: The Orr and Gilks Study in Late 1920s Kenya Revisited," *International Journal of African Historical Studies* 30, no. 1 (1997): 49–86.

114. Hall, *Improvement*, 65–82, Worthington, *Science*, 167–68, 571–86.

115. Worboys, "The Discovery of Colonial Malnutrition," 217–25.

116. Committee on Nutrition in the Colonial Empire, *First Report, Part I* (London: HMSO, 1939), 43–44.

117. Ibid., 130–31.

118. John Flint, "Macmillan as Critic of Empire: The Impact of an Historian on Colonial Policy," in Hugh Macmillan and Shula Marks, eds., *Africa and Empire: W.H. Macmillan, Historian and Social Critic* (London: Temple Smith, 1989), 212–31, and John Cell, *Hailey: A Study in Imperial Administration* (Cambridge: Cambridge University Press, 1992).

119. This agreement grew in part from the influence of Macmillan on Hailey, who read Macmillan's *Africa Emergent* in draft form before embarking on his project. Flint, "Macmillan," 224.

120. Johnson, "Conversion," 67–76; Constantine, *Colonial Development*, 195–266.

121. Jeffries, *Whitehall and the Colonial Service*, 11–17; Jeffries, *The Colonial Office*, 157–66; Kirk-Greene, *On Crown Service*, 19–37.

122. Barbara Ingram, "Shaping Opinion on Development Policy: Economists at the Colonial Office during World War II," *History of Political Economy* 24, no. 3 (1992): 689–710; J. M. Lee and Martin Petter, *The Colonial Office, War and Development Policy* (London: M. T. Smith for the Institute for Commonwealth Studies, 1982), 13–46.

123. David Mills, "How Not to be a 'Government House Pet': Audrey Richards and the East African Institute for Social Research," in Mwenda Ntarangwi, David Mills, and Mustafa Babiker, eds., *African Anthropologies: History, Critique and Practice* (London: Zed, 2006), 76–98.

124. The literature on anthropology and colonial administration is quite extensive. In this context see Henrika Kuklick, *The Savage Within* (Cambridge: Cambridge University Press, 1991), 27–74, 184–242, John Burton, "Representing Africa: Colonial Anthropology Revisited," *Journal of African and Asian Studies* 27, no. 3–4 (1992): 181–201; Adam Kuper, "Alternative Histories of British Social Anthropology," *Social Anthropology* 13, no. 1 (2005): 47–64; Nicholas Thomas, *Colonialism's Culture: Anthropology, Travel and Government* (Princeton: Princeton University Press, 1994); Tilley, *Africa as a Living Laboratory*, 261–311.

125. For the Treasury role see Peter Clark, "The Treasury's Analytical Model of the British Economy between the Wars," in Mary Furner and Barry Supple, eds., *The State and Economic Knowledge: The American and British Experiences* (Cambridge: Cambridge University Press, 1990), 171–207. For a view that emphasizes the impact of war on the deployment of expertise see David Edgerton, *Warfare State, Britain, 1920–1970* (Cambridge: Cambridge University Press, 2006).

126. Eric Butterworth and Robert Holma, eds., *Social Welfare in Modern Britain* (London: Fontana, 1975) and Wolfgang Mommsen and W. Mock, *The Emergence of the Welfare State in Britain and Germany* (London: Croom Helm, 1981); Keith Laybourn, *The Evolution of British Social Policy and the Welfare State* (Keele, UK: Keele University Press, 1995); Kathleen Jones, *The Making of Social Policy in Britain 1830–1990* (Atlantic Highlands, NJ: Humanities Press, 1994); Pat Thane, *The Foundations of the Welfare State* (New York: Longman, 1982).

127. For a discussion of the pre-1914 state and experts see Roy MacLeod, ed., *Government and Expertise: Specialists, Administrators and Professionals, 1860–1914* (Cambridge: Cambridge University Press, 1988).

128. Cyril Smith, "Networks of Influence: The Social Sciences in the United Kingdom since the War," in Peter Wagner et al., eds., *Social Sciences and Modern States* (Cambridge: Cambridge University Press, 1991), 131–47; Martin Bulmer, *The Use of Social Research* (London: Allen & Unwin, 1982), 19–29.

129. Barry Supple, "The State and Social Investigation in Britain between the World Wars," in Michael Lacey and Mary Furner, eds., *The State and*

Social Investigation in Britain and the United States (Cambridge: Cambridge University Press, 1993), 365–87.

130. Martin Bulmer, "Mobilizing Social Knowledge for Social Welfare: Intermediary Institutions in the Political Systems of the United States and Great Britain between the First and Second World Wars," in Weindling, *International health organizations*, 305–25.

131. Richard Glotzer, "A Long Shadow: Frederick P. Keppel, the Carnegie Corporation and the Dominions and Colonies Fund Area Experts 1923–1945," *History of Education* 38, no. 5 (2009): 621–48.

132. This would be particularly the case in the Colonial Office, which experienced rapid turnover of senior ministers during the late 1930s and 1940s.

133. Gail Savage, *The Social Construction of Expertise: The English Civil Service and Its Influence, 1919–1939* (Pittsburgh: University of Pittsburg Press, 1996).

134. Martin Bulmer, "The Governmental Context: Interaction between Structure and Influence," in Martin Bulmer, ed., *Social Science Research and Government: Comparative Essays on Britain and the United States* (Cambridge: Cambridge University Press, 1987), 27–39.

135. Elizabeth Durbin, *New Jerusalems: The Labour Party and the Economics of Democratic Socialism* (London: Routledge & Kegan Paul, 1985).

136. See Janet Manson, "Margery Perham, the Fabians, and Colonial Policy," in Wayne Chapman and Janet Manson, eds., *Women in the Milieu of Leonard and Virginia Woolf: Peace, Politics and Education* (New York: Pace University Press, 1998), 171–90.

137. For more on Cohen's career see Ronald Robinson, "Andrew Cohen and the Transfer of Power in Tropical Africa, 1941–1951," in W. H. Morris-Jones and G. Fischer, eds., *Decolonization and After* (London: Frank Cass, 1980), 50–72.

138. Grant, *Civilized Savagery*, 11–78.

139. Stephen Howe, *Anticolonialism in British Politics: The Left and the End of Empire 1918–1964* (Oxford: Oxford University Press, 1993), 82–142.

140. CO 323/1023/5, IUSIPP, 1928.

141. CO 129/571/17/ Hong Kong Eugenics League, 1938. The officials included H. Cowell, the head of the Eastern Department and Arthur O'Brien, the chief medical officer. Minutes of Meeting of the International Subcommittee of the National Birth Control Association, 7–7–38, Minutes of the International Sub-Committee of the Family Planning Association, 1938–1942, SA/FPA A5/43, FPA Papers, CMAC. Pyke would later contact the colonial secretary to weigh in about the controversy over a proposed birth control clinic in Singapore. CO 273/633/9 Birth Control Straits Settlement 1937 and Letter of 10-2-37, 1/17 Papers on India, Eileen Palmer Papers, LSE Archives.

142. Alexander King spoke of the "free, easy, but often unplanned contacts" between senior civil servants and members of research councils and

the Royal Society at the Athenaeum in the interwar years. Alexander King, *Science and Politics: The International Stimulus* (London: Oxford University Press, 1974), 11

143. Daniel Kelves, "Huxley and the Popularization of Science," in C. Kenneth Walters and Albert Van Helden, eds., *Julian Huxley: Biologist and Statesman of Science* (Houston: Rice University Press, 1992), 238–51.

144. Clyde Dander, *Malcolm MacDonald: Bringing an End to Empire* (Montreal: McGill-Queens University Press, 1995), 148–49.

145. For more his career see Thomas Osborne and Nicholas Rose, "Populating Sociology: Carr-Saunders and the Problem of Population," *Sociological Review* 56, no. 4 (2008): 552–78.

146. Michael Roe, *Australia, Britain, and Migration, 1915–1940: A Study of Desperate Hopes* (Cambridge: Cambridge University Press, 1995), 146–47. Minutes of twenty-fifth meeting of OSB 23-2-37, Overseas Settlement Board, M 554/6; Dominions Office (DO) 35/709/5 Trend of Population in Relation to Migration, 1937, National Archives.

147. A. S. Carr-Saunders, to Ormsby-Gore 27-3-37, CO 323/1523/2 Population Problems in the Colonies, 1937.

148. Minute by R. V. Vernon 5-5-37, CO 323/1523/2 Population Problems in the Colonies, 1937.

149. Carr-Saunders to J. A. Calder, 6–10–38, CO 323/1613/10 Population Problems in the Colonies, 1938.

150. Ibid.

151. Carr-Saunders to J. A. Calder, 6–10–38, CO 323/1613/10 Population Problems in the Colonies, 1938.

152. Minute by S. Caine 29/6/40, CO 859/39/8 Proposed Census 1941 Social Service.

153. Memo of Miss Robertson 6–8–43, CO /859/62/17 Birth Control West Africa. He was given a further £500 in October 1942. Minutes of meeting 30–11–42, Minutes of the PIC, 1935–43, SA-PIC A/1/1, Papers of the PIC, CMAC.

154. Granville Edge to CO 18–12–34, CO 874/1080 Health of Native Races and Depopulation Problem 1933–36. Edge was an expert in colonial medical statistics at the LSHTM who published a number of works on the subject. P. Granville Edge, *Vital Records in the Tropics* (London: G. Routledge, 1932) and "The Demography of British Colonial Possessions," *Journal of the Royal Statistical Society* 100, no. 2 (1937): 181–231.

155. Minute by S. Caine 29–6–40, CO 859/39/8 Proposed Census 1941, 1940.

156. Edge had been asked by Dr. Arthur O'Brien, the medical advisor, for assistance in preparing estimates of future West Indian population. Edge found his work hampered by the limitations of the data made available to him. Granville Edge to O'Brien 9–27–38 CO 950/48 Population Estimates of West Indies population by London School of Hygiene and Tropical Medicine, 1938.

157. Royal Commission on the West Indies, *Report*, 9.
158. For Kuczynski's view of African statistics see Hailey, *African Survey*, 124–29.
159. Suke Wolton, *Lord Hailey, the Colonial Office and the Politics of Race and Empire in the Second World War* (New York: St. Martins, 2000); Tilley, *Africa as a Living Laboratory*, 217–59.
160. Minute by R. W. 2–38, DO 37/710/1 Trends of Population in Relation to Migration 1938–43.
161. Susan Klausen, "'Poor Whiteism': White Maternal Mortality, and the Promotion of Public Health in South Africa: The Department of Public Health's Endorsement of Contraceptive Services, 1930–1938," *South African Historical Journal* 45, no. 1 (2001): 53–78.
162. CO 950/906 Memo on Emigration of Poor Whites to Dominions.
163. Minute by F. Stockdale 10/4/40, ibid. For a discussion of this community see Karl Watson, "'Walk and Nyam Buckras'": Poor-White Emigration from Barbados, 1834–1900," *Journal of Caribbean History* 34, no. 1/2, (2000): 130–56.
164. Malcolm MacDonald to E. J. Waddington 24-4-40, CO 318/444/35 Royal Commission Report Population Barbados, 1940.
165. For a discussion of how class and gender were implicated in the construction of race see Anne Stoler, *Carnal Knowledge and Imperial Power: Race and the Intimate in Colonial Rule* (Berkeley: University of California Press, 2002).
166. Lynn Thomas, *The Politics of the Womb: Women, Reproduction and the State in Kenya* (Berkeley: University of California Press, 2003), 21–51.
167. E. A. Waddington to Sir Cosmo Parkinson 12–9–35, CO 37/282/9 Birth Control-Bermuda, 1935.
168. Dora Ibberson, "A Note on the Relationship between Illegitimacy and the Birthrate," *Social and Economic Studies* 5, no. 1 (1956): 93–99, and G. W. Roberts, "Some Aspects of Mating and Fertility in the West Indies," *Population Studies* 8, no. 3 (1955): 199–227. Ibberson served as social welfare advisor, and Roberts was the vital statistics officer for the Comptroller for Social Welfare and Development in the West Indies.
169. CO 323/1067/1–6 Health of Native Women and Children, 1930.
170. CO 323/1067/6 Native Women and Children-Customs Affecting Fiji and Western Pacific Region, 1930.
171. CO 323/1067/5 Native Women and Children Customs Affecting their Health-West Africa, 1930.
172. E. J. Waddington to H. Beckett 2–2–34, CO 37/280/8 Bermuda, 1934.
173. Minute by Sidney Caine 1–5–36, CO 318 /422/9 File on Warning from the West Indies by W. M. Macmillan, 1936.
174. Major Orde-Brown, *Labour Conditions in the West Indies* (London: HMSO, 1939), 35–36.
175. Minute by Frank Stockdale 10–8–36, CO 318 /422/9 File on Warning from the West Indies by W. M. Macmillan, 1936; W. H. Flinn to H. Beckett 23–10–39, CO 28 325/12 Surplus Population Problem-Barbados, 1939.

176. Carr-Saunders spoke at one of the meetings and outlined the problem of non-European population growth. M 554/6 Minutes of twenty-fifth meeting of OSB 23-2-37, DO 37/710/1 Trends of Population in Relation to Migration, 1938–43.

177. Minutes of Meeting of the International Subcommittee of the National Birth Control Association, 3-2-39, Minutes of the International Subcommittee of the FPA, 1938–42, SA/FPA A5/43, CMAC.

178. Moyne Commission, *Report*, 245.

179. Ibid., 245–46.

180. Minute by Dr. O'Brien 27-2-34, CO 37/280/8 Bermuda.

181. The legislature voted to provide a grant of £150–£200 per year for the provision of birth control in health clinics. Note from (illegible) 30-5-39, CO 23 684 Birth Control: Provision for Clinics in Bermuda, 1939; Wilkinson to Margaret Sanger, 19-6-37, Box 17, Reel 11, Margaret Sanger Papers, Library of Congress Collection. For more on Wilkinson see Bourbonais, "One Woman to Another," 10–12.

182. Nancy Astor to Malcolm MacDonald, 1-8-35, CO 37/282/9 Birth Control Bermuda, 1935. Waddington assured the Colonial Office that the proposals would probably not pass. E. A. Waddington to Sir Cosmo Parkinson 12-9-35.

183. Lord Fitzalan to William Ormsby-Gore 24-1-37, CO 37/285/5 Birth Control-Bermuda, 1937.

184. Copy of *The Negro Worker*, February 1937, ibid.

185. C. H. Talbott, secretary to governor of Bermuda, to Margaret Sanger, 2-3-37, Box 17, Reel 11, Margaret Sanger Papers, Library of Congress Collection.

186. Nancy Astor to Malcolm MacDonald, 1-8-35, CO 37/282/9 Birth Control-Bermuda, 1935.

187. Ormsby Gore to Lord Fitzalan 1-2-37, CO 37/285/5 Birth Control-Bermuda, 1937.

188. Lord Fitzalan to William Ormsby Gore 27-6-37, CO 129/565/5, Hong Kong Eugenics League, 1938; CO 37/285/5 Birth Control-Bermuda, 1937.

189. Minute by Sir John Shuckburgh 2-7-37, CO 129/565/5 Hong Kong Eugenics League, 1937.

190. Minute by J. Vernon 1-7-37, ibid.

191. Letter of 7-7-38, 1/17 Papers on India, 1934–38, LSE and 1/38 Material on Malaya, Straits Settlement, Singapore, Eileen Palmer Papers, LSE Archives. Beck's request followed visits by Edith How-Martyn and Margaret Sanger to Malaya in 1936. Beck apparently met during Picton-Tuberville's visit to Malaya as part of her work on the issue of child marriage for the Colonial Office. For more on Picton-Tuberville see Pedersen, "The Maternalist Moment," 191–94.

192. Helen Beck to Malcolm MacDonald 24-9-38, CO 273/633/9 Birth Control Straits Settlement, 1937.

193. Helen Beck to BCIC, 7-7-38, 1/17 Papers on India, 1934-38, Palmer Papers, Coll Misc 0639, LSE Archives.
194. Minute by H. Cowell, 21-5-37, CO 273/633/9 Birth Control Straits Settlement, 1937.
195. Minute by P. Rogers 26-4-38, CO 129 571/17 Hong Kong Eugenics League, 1938.
196. Draft letter for Sir S. Thomas from H. Cowell, 17-10-38, CO 273/645/8 Birth Control Straits Settlement, 1938; Minute by (illegible), 3-5-37 CO 273/633/9 Birth Control Straits Settlement, 1937.
197. W. Ormsby Gore to S. Thomas, 31-5-37, CO 273/633/9 Birth Control Straits Settlement, 1937.

CHAPTER 3

1. Warren Thompson, *Danger Spots in World Population* (New York: Knopf, 1929), 212-54, 292-93; David Glass, *Population Policies and Movements* (Oxford: Clarendon Press, 1940), 219-313; A.M. Carr-Saunders, *World Population* (London: Clarendon Press, 1936), 135-36; Robert Kuczynski, *'Living Space' and Population Problems* (Oxford: Oxford University Press, 1939).
2. Thompson, *Danger Spots*, 113-34. See also W.R Crocker, *The Japanese Population Problem: The Coming Crisis* (New York: Macmillan, 1932) and E.F. Penrose, *Population Problems and Their Application with Special Reference to Japan* (Stanford, CA: Food Institute, 1934).
3. R. Graham, British Embassy at Rome 26-2-26 to Sir W.G. Tyrell, CO 111/664/1 Surplus population of Italy: Suggested absorption by British Guiana 10-3-26.
4. W.G. Tyrrell to Brigadier-General Sir S.H. Wilson 10-3-26, ibid.
5. Report from Rome Embassy on population figures for 1938, Minute by Sargent, Foreign Office (FO), 371/23824 file 1145 1939 Italian Population Statistics for 1938, National Archives.
6. FO 262/1952 Population Japan 1936; FO 371/22193 File 8991 August 1938; FO 371/23563 File 533/69 1939; FO/371/ 23563 File 4575/73/1939.
7. Barbara Ingram, "Shaping Opinion on Development Policy: Economists at the Colonial Office during World War II," *History of Political Economy* 24, no. 3 (1992): 689-710.
8. Alan Milward, *War, Economy and Society 1939-1945* (Berkeley: University of California Press, 1977), 111-12, 119-21.
9. Martin Wilmington, *The Middle East Supply Centre* (Albany: State University of New York Press, 1971); FO 922/172 Middle East Supply Centre, Populations 1942.
10. Wilmington, *Middle East Supply*, 140-62.
11. MESC, *Proceedings of the Conference on Middle East Agricultural Development*, Cairo, 1944 (Cairo: Middle East Supply Centre, 1944).
12. This scheme resembled the one used by Worthington in his work with

the Hailey Survey that was published separately as *Science in Africa* (Oxford: Oxford University Press, 1938).

13. E.B. Worthington, *Middle East Science: A Survey of Subjects Other Than Agriculture* (London: HMSO, 1946), 181–89.

14. FO 921/347 Middle East Office Scientific Advisory Mission MESC, 1945.

15. Toynbee was a member of the Foreign Office's Political Intelligence Department during the First World War. R.A. Longmire, *Herald of a Noisy World: Interpreting the News of All Nations: The Research and Analysis Department of the Foreign and Commonwealth Office* (London: Foreign and Commonwealth Office, 1995).

16. The result was a series of volume on European population. Frank Notestein et al., *The Future Population of Europe and the Soviet Union* (Geneva: League of Nations, 1944); Wilbert Moore, *Economic Demography of Eastern and Southern Europe* (Geneva: League of Nations, 1945); Frank Lorimer, *The Population of the Soviet Union: History and Prospects* (Geneva: League of Nations, 1946); Dudley Kirk, *Europe's Population in the Interwar Years* (Geneva: League of Nations, 1946).

17. FO 371/41102 File 2663 1944 Estimates of European population at end of 1943.

18. Minute by N. O'Neil, 15–10–43, Comments on paper by Notestein on European population, FO 371 34463 1943 File 14891/279/18. O'Neil was the assistant to the foreign office advisor on Germany.

19. FO 371/34461, Paper to be prepared regarding future population of Germany, 1943; FO 371 34462 Foreign Office Research Department forecast of the future population of Germany; FO 371 34463 1943 Comments on Paper by Notestein on European Population; FO 371/40764 Future Population of Europe U 5005 June 1944; FO 371/40567 Post War Relief Population Reproduction, 1944.

20. FO 371/38648 1944 World Trends in Population.

21. FO 371/45621 Population of Syria and Lebanon 1945.

22. J.M. Lee, "Forward Thinking and War: The Colonial Office during the 1940s," *Journal of Imperial and Commonwealth History* 6, no. 1 (1977): 65–79.

23. For an overview see John Darwin, *Britain and Decolonization* (New York: St. Martins, 1988), 32–68, and J.M. Lee and Martin Petter, *The Colonial Office, War and Development Policy* (London: M.T. Smith for the Institute for Commonwealth Studies, 1982), 115–43. For imperial propaganda see Rosaleen Smyth, "Britain's African Colonies and British Propaganda during the Second World War," *Journal of Imperial and Commonwealth History* 23, no. 1 (1985): 65–82, and "War Propaganda during the Second World War in Northern Rhodesia," *African Affairs* 83, no. 332 (1984): 345–58; S. Shattacharya and B. Zachariah, "A Great Destiny: The British Colonial State and the Advertisement of Post-War Reconstruction in India, 1942–45," *South Asia Research* 19, no. 1 (1999): 71–100.

24. Paul Addison, *The Road to 1945: British Politics and the Second World War* (London: Random House, 1994).

25. Kevin Jefferys, "British Politics and Social Policy during the Second World War," *Historical Journal* 30, no. 1 (1987): 123–44; Jose Harris, *William Beveridge: A Biography* (Oxford: Clarendon Press, 1997), 412–50; Rodney Lowe, "The Second World War, Consensus and the Foundation of the Welfare State," *Twentieth Century British History* 1, no. 2 (1990): 152–82.

26. Maria Missra, "Colonial Officers and Gentleman: The British Empire and the Globalization of Tradition," *Journal of Global History* 3, no. 2 (2008): 135–61.

27. Joanna Lewis, *Empire State Building: War and Welfare in Kenya 1925–52* (Athens: Ohio University Press, 2000), 1–81.

28. The exam system was suspended from 1918 to 1925, and by the late 1930s this older generation dominated the upper levels of the Colonial Office. Lee and Petter, *Colonial Office*, 37.

29. John Cell, *Hailey: A Study in British Imperialism 1872–1969* (Cambridge: Cambridge University Press, 1992), 266–74.

30. Lee and Petter, *Colonial Office*, 206–19. For the conflicts within the council see Robert Tignor, *W. Arthur Lewis and the Birth of Development Economics* (Princeton: Princeton University Press, 2006), 56–67.

31. For an overview see Keith Jeffries, "The Second World War," in William Roger Louis and Judith Brown, eds., *Oxford History of the British Empire*, vol. IV: *The Twentieth Century* (Oxford: Oxford University Press, 1998), 306–38.

32. Anthony Kirk Greene, *On Crown Service: A History of HM Colonial and Overseas Services 1837–1997* (London: I. B. Tauris, 1999), 39–41.

33. Lee and Petter, *Colonial Office*, 59–65. The domestic nonindustrial civil service reached a peak of 686,000 in 1943, and the Colonial Office establishment grew from 471 in 1939 to 817 by 1945.

34. CO 129/587/15 Excess Population Reduction Committee Report Chinese Immigration Bill 1940; CO 537/3701 Immigration Control Threatened Influx of Refugees 1948; CO 927/67/4 Demography and Census-Hong Kong, 1947–48.

35. Bernard Wasserstein, *Britain and the Jews of Europe 1939–1945* (London: Leicester University Press, 1999), 36–72; Arieh Kochavi, *Post-Holocaust Politics: Britain, the United States, and Jewish Refugees, 1945–1948* (Chapel Hill: University of North Carolina Press, 2001), 7–10, 60–61; Louise London, *Whitehall and the Jews, 1933–1948: British Immigration Policy, Jewish Refugees and the Holocaust*(Cambridge: Cambridge University Press, 2000), 173–74.

36. CO 733/409/14 Immigration Palestine, 1939; Minute by R. Kuczynski 3–12–46, CO 733/471/7 Area and population of Palestine, 1946.

37. Minute by W. Mathieson 12–5-46, CO 733/471/7 Area and population of Palestine, 1946.

38. London, *Whitehall and the Jews*, 42–45.

39. Memo by Sir H. Emerson, CO 323/1668/1 Jews and Refugees General, 1939.

40. Max Nicholson, An Approach to the Refugee Problem, ibid.
41. CO 323/1750/12 Settlement of Jews and Refugees, 1940.
42. London, *Whitehall and the Jews*, 100–102.
43. CO 318/440/5 Immigration General Policy, West Indies, 1939.
44. CO 28 325/12 Surplus Population Problem Barbados, 1939.
45. Minute by J.G. Hibbert 25–8–42, CO 323/1845/7 Jews and Refugees Post-War Settlement of Refugees, 1942.
46. This colony contained only about thirty people. Comment on Sir Alan Pim's Memo by Arthur Hailey, CO 323/1845/7, 1942.
47. CO 822/118/1 Immigration (Non-native) Control of East Africa, 1944.
48. Note by Sir Charles Dundas, CO 822/118/2 Immigration(Non-Native) Control of, 1945–46.
49. CO 323/1863/5 Manpower: West Indies Recruitment of Unskilled Men for Training for Munitions Work, 1942; CO 323/1863/6 Manpower: West Indies General Matters Recruitment of Unskilled Men for Training for Munitions Work, 1943.
50. J.L. Keith, Colour Discrimination in the UK, CO 859/80/13 Colour Discrimination in the Colonies General Policy of the CO Social Service, 1941.
51. Marika Sherwood, *Many Struggles: West Indian Workers and Service Personnel in Britain, 1939–45* (London: Karia, 1985).
52. Oliver Stanley to W. Murray 15–11–43, CO 37 294/17 Bermuda Overpopulation and Emigration, 1943.
53. The quote is from Sir John Campbell, economic and financial advisor to the Colonial Office, cited in Steven Constantine, *The Making of British Colonial Development Policy 1914–1940* (London: Frank Cass, 1984), 235.
54. From 1940 to 1946, about 38 percent of all funds went to the West Indies. Michael Havinden and David Meredith, *Colonialism and Development: Britain and Its Tropical Colonies, 1850–1960* (London: Routledge, 1993), 218–27. D.J. Morgan, *The Official History of Colonial Development*, vol. 1: *The Origins of British Aid Policy 1924–1945* (Atlantic Highlands, NJ: Humanities Press 1980), 137–56.
55. Howard Johnson, "The Anglo-American Commission and the Extension of American Influence in the British Caribbean, 1942–45," *Journal of Commonwealth and Comparative Politics* 22, no. 2 (1984): 180–203; Charley Whitham, *Bitter Rehearsal: British and American Planning for a Post-War West Indies* (Westport, CT: Greenwood, 2002), 77–82.
56. DO 35/684/6 Australian Population Statistics 1935–41; DO 35/1141 Series of files on Dominion issues, including migration.
57. See Kathleen Paul, *Whitewashing Britain: Race and Citizenship in the Postwar Era* (Ithaca, NY: Cornell University Press, 1997), 88–90.
58. Brian Murphy, *The Other Australia: Experiences of Migration* (Cambridge: Cambridge University Press, 1993), 88.
59. Ibid., 65–94.
60. Constantine, *Colonial Development*, 198.
61. Alan Pim, *The Financial and Economic History of the African Tropical*

Territories (Oxford: Clarendon Press, 1940) and *Colonial Agricultural Production* (Oxford: Oxford University Press, 1946).

62. CO 323/1845/7, Comment on Sir Alan Pim's Memo by Arthur Hailey, 1942.

63. Lee and Petter, *Colonial Office*, 73–114, and Michael Cowen and Nicholas Westcott, "British Imperial Economic Policy during the War," in David Killingray and Richard Rathbone, eds., *Africa and the Second World War* (New York: St. Martins, 1986), 20–67.

64. David Killingray, "Labour Mobilization in British Colonial Africa for the War Effort, 1939–46," in Killingray and Rathbone, *Africa and the Second World War*, 89–90.

65. Frederick Cooper, *Decolonization and African Society: The Labor Question in French and British Africa* (Cambridge: Cambridge University Press, 1996), 110–41.

66. Reginald A. Cline Cole, "Wartime Forest Energy Policy and Practice in British West Africa: Social and Economic Impact on the Labouring Classes 1939–1945," *Africa* 63, no. 1 (1993): 56–79.

67. Killingray, "Labour Mobilization," 68–96.

68. Hamilton Sipho Simelane, "Labor Mobilization for the War Effort in Swaziland, 1940–42," *International Journal of African Historical Studies* 26, no. 3 (1993): 541–74.

69. Kenneth Vickery, "The Second World War Revival of Forced Labor in the Rhodesias," *International Journal of African Studies* 22, no. 3 (1989): 423–37.

70. David Killingray, "Labour Exploitation for Military Campaigns in British Colonial Africa 1870–1945," *Journal of Contemporary History* 24, no. 3 (1989): 483–501.

71. M. Perham to Warden of Nuffield College 23–10–39, CO 847/17/12 Nuffield College Proposed Labour Investigation-Africa-1939. For more on her career see Janet Manson, "Margery Perham, the Fabians, and Colonial Policy," in Wayne Chapman and Janet Manson, eds., *Women in the Milieu of Leonard and Virginia Woolf: Peace, Politics and Education* (New York: Pace University Press, 1998), 170–90.

72. Meshack Owino, "Panyako: The Discourse of Over-Population in Western Kenya, and the Creation of Panyako-the Pioneer Corps," in Karl Ittmann, Dennis Cordell, and Greg Maddox, eds., *The Demographics of Empire: The Colonial Order and the Creation of Knowledge* (Athens: Ohio University Press, 2010), 157–73.

73. Major Orde-Brown, *Labour Conditions in East Africa* (London: HMSO, 1946); *Labour Conditions in Ceylon, Mauritius, and Malaya* (London: HMSO, 1943); *Labour Conditions in West Africa* (London: HMSO, 1941).

74. CO 927/10/1 Demography, 1943–44. In addition to the CDW grant of £500, he received a salary of £900 per year, a raise over his salary at LSE. To prevent Kuczynski, a German émigré, from being interned as an enemy

alien, the Colonial Office certified his work as being of national importance in July 1940. CO 859/39/8 Proposed Census, 1941.

75. Lee and Petter, *Colonial Office*, 56.

76. A.J. Christopher, "The Quest for an Imperial Census, 1840–1940," *Journal of Historical Geography* 34, no. 2 (2008): 268–85.

77. Memo by R. Kuczynski, Proposal for the Modernization of Colonial Population and Vital Statistics, CO 927/10/1 Demography, 1944.

78. Memo from Robert Kuczynski, Personnel for Reorganization of Colonial Population and Vital Statistics, 7–12–44, CO 927/10/1 Demography, 1943–44.

79. Kuczynski worked with L.G. Hopkins, the chief statistician of the Colonial Development Welfare Fund, who had previously worked as an assistant to Eric Mills in Palestine in the 1930s. Hopkins would eventually oversee the 1946 Census of the West Indies as part of his duties. Twelfth meeting of the CSSRC, 25–9–45, CO 901/2 CSSRC Minutes and Papers 1945.

80. Lee and Petter, *Colonial Office*, 188–89.

81. Joseph Hodge, *Triumph of the Expert: Agrarian Doctrines of Development and the Legacies of British Colonialism* (Athens: Ohio University Press, 2002), 90–116; Helen Tilley, *Africa as a Living Laboratory* (Chicago: University of Chicago Press, 2010).

82. Comment by Orde-Brown, CO 847/17/12 Nuffield College Proposed Labour Investigation-Africa-1939.

83. Minute by F.J. Pedler 9–2–39, CO 847/13/18 Labour Migration need for study of demographic and social effects. Lord Hailey's recommendation, 1938.

84. Manson, "Margery Perham," 174–75. Nuffield College and Oxford gave £7,000 to support Perham's work, CO 859/79/17 Colonial Research Nuffield College Schemes, 1942–43.

85. Minute by OGRW 24–4–42, CO 859/79/17 Colonial Research Nuffield College Schemes; Minute by (illegible), 11–5–42, CO 852/509/13 Nuffield College Colonial Research, 1942.

86. Minute by (illegible), 17–10–42, CO 859/79/17 Colonial Research Nuffield College Schemes, 1942. CO 852/509/13 Nuffield College Colonial Research, 1942.

87. Minute by Eastwood, CO 859/79/17 Colonial Research Nuffield College Schemes. 1942–43.

88. Minute by (illegible) 1/4/42, CO 859/79 Colonial Research Advisory Council, 1942–43.

89. David Mills, "How Not to Be a 'Government House Pet': Audrey Richards and the East African Institute for Social Research," in Mwenda Ntarangwi, David Mills, and Mustafa Babiker, eds., *African Anthropologies: History, Critique and Practice* (London: Zed, 2006), 76–98.

90. CO 859/79/16 Organization of Social Studies, 1942.

91. Lee and Petter, *Colonial Office*, 188–89; S.R. Ashton and S.E. Stockwell, *Imperial Policy and Colonial Practice 1925-45, Pt 1* (London: HMSO,

1996), lxxxii–lxxxiv; David Mills, "British Anthropology at the End of Empire: The Rise and Fall of the Colonial Social Science Research Council, 1944–1962," *Revue d'histoire des Sciences Humaines* 1, no. 6 (2001): 166–75.

92. CO 927/10/1 Demography, 1943–44.

93. CO 859/126/1 Census East Africa, 1944.

94. Memo by Robert Kuczynski, Personnel for Reorganization of Colonial Population and Vital Statistics, 7-12-44, CO 927/10/1 Demography, 1943–44.

95. Minute by John Patterson 26-7-45, CO 859/126/3 Census Nigeria.

96. CO 927/10/3 Research Social Services Demography and Census, 1946.

97. Note by Colonial Office on Proposed Sociological and Economic Survey and Population Census in Zanziba, CSSRC 44(8), CO 901/1, Minutes and Papers of the CSSRC, 1944. Dutton, a former major in the British army, served throughout Africa in the 1920s and '30s. An advocate of the new development ethos within the colonial service, he became responsible for postwar development planning in Zanzibar, where he served during the 1940s and '50s. He became associated with a several important projects, notably efforts to create new urban environments in northern Rhodesia (Zambia) and Zanzibar. For more in Dutton's career see Garth Andrew Myers, "Intellectual of Empire: Eric Dutton and Hegemony in British Africa," *Annals of the Association of American Geographers* 66, no. 1 (1998): 1–27.

98. Sir George Gater to Lord Hailey, 10–12–45, CO 927/10/3 Demography and Census, 1946.

99. Ibid.

100. Minute by (illegible), 26–6–44, ibid.

101. CO 859/62/17 Birth Control-West Africa, 1943.

102. Andrew Cohen to J. B. Williams 16–2–45, CO 927/10 Demography, 1945.

103. Native Land Tenure (CSSRC (44) 33 Memo by Colonial Office, CO 901/1, CSSRC Minutes and Papers, 1944.

104. Paper by A. R. Peterson, "Some Figures and Opinions Bearing on Population Growth," Notes for an Address at the Nairobi Rotary Club, 6–12–46; in the papers of Edgar Baron Worthington, MSS Africa 1425 5/3 Rhodes House, Oxford. Also see David Anderson, "Depression, Dust Bowl, Demography and Drought: The Colonial State and Soil Conservation in East Africa during the 1930s," *African Affairs* 83, no. 332 (1984): 328–31.

105. H. L. Gordon, "The Population Problem in a Crown Colony," CO 537/13 Population in East Africa, 1945.

106. Minute by Sidney Caine, 30–3–40, CO 859/40/12901/Part II, originally cited in Cooper, *Decolonization*, 114.

107. Memo, 6/41, CO 859/62/16, Social Services Birth Control West Indies, 1941–42.

108. Hill visited India to report on scientific research as part of a effort to accelerate development planning for India. Deepak Kumar, "Reconstructing

India: Disunity in the Science and Technology for Development Discourse, 1900–1947," *Osiris* 15, no. 1 (2001): 241–57.

109. Kumar, "Disunity," 252–54.

110. Minute by Andrew Cohen, 13–6–44, CO 927/10/1 Demography, 1944.

111. Frank Stockdale to Eileen Palmer 26–8–40, CO 1042/46 Population Birth Control Papers, 1942. This meeting was most likely the last one with officials for How-Martyn, who left shortly afterward on a tour that ended with her decision to immigrate to Australia, where she lived until her death in 1954.

112. J. Brander to Lord Lloyd 18–10–40, CO/859/62/16/ Birth Control in the West Indies, 1941–42. Brander previously worked under Lloyd as collector of Bombay.

113. Extract of letter from J. Huxley to Oliver Stanley 17–7–43, CO 859/62/17 Birth Control-West Africa, 1943.

114. Sir Alan Burns to Cosmo Parkinson 29–12–39, CO 318/445/5, Royal Commission on the West Indies-Report and Recommendations-Population, 1940.

115. Ibid.

116. Ibid.

117. Memo by A. Smart, CO 859/62/17 Birth Control West Africa, 1943.

118. This statement, referring to suspicions about birth control in the West Indies, appeared in a discussion of population issues in Africa. Memo of Miss Robertson 6–8–43, CO 859/62/17, Birth Control West Africa, 1943.

119. F. Stockdale note 3–7–40, CO 318/445/5 Royal Commission on the West Indies-Report and Recommendations-Population, 1940.

120. Minute by S. Caine 10–6–40, ibid.

121. Extract from secret dispatch from Sir Arthur Richards 19–2–40 and Report by F.A. Norman, "Population," April 1940, CO 318/445/5 Royal Commission on the West Indies Report and Recommendations Population, 1940.

122. Minute by E. 15-6-44 CO 927/10/1 Demography, 1944.

123. Memo by P. Rogers, 12–5–42, CO/859/62/16/ Birth Control in the West Indies 1941–42.

124. Arthur Green, "Rogers, Sir Philip (1914–1990)," in H. C. G. Matthew and Brian Harrison, eds., *Oxford Dictionary of National Biography* (Oxford: Oxford University Press, 2004). http://www.oxforddnb.com/view/article/76262.

125. Memo by P. Rogers 12–5–42, CO/859/62/16/ Birth control in the West Indies, 1941.

126. E.A. Waddington to Sir Cosmo Parkinson 12–9–35, CO 37/282/9 Birth Control-Bermuda, 1935.

127. Report by F.A. Norman, "Population," April 1940, CO 318/445/5 Royal Commission on the West Indies Report and Recommendations Population.

128. Orde-Brown, *Labour Conditions in the West Indies*, 35–36.

129. Memo by J. J. Paskin 16–1–42, CO/859/62/16/ Birth Control in the

West Indies, 1941–42. To facilitate discussion, Paskin produced a memo summarizing existing birth control work within the empire as well as the guidelines established by Ormsby-Gore and MacDonald in the late 1930s.

130. F.J. Pedlar, "Post War Labor Issues," CO 852/503/4 Lord Hailey's Committee on Colonial Post-War Problems Part 1, 1941. Pedlar served as Lord Hailey's private secretary and the editor of the *African Survey*.

131. Extract from Minutes of thirty-fourth meeting of CO Committee on Post-War Problems, 19–3–42, CO/859/62/16/ Birth Control in the West Indies, 1941–42.

132. Minute by Cranborne, 5–6–42, CO/859/62/16/ Birth Control in the West Indies, 1941–42.

133. Minute by R. Hancock 13–4–46, FO 371 56627 File N5428/2615/55 Polish Settlement in the Colonies, 1946.

CHAPTER 4

1. Robert Kuczynski, Comments on Memo for Proposed General Census for East Africa, CO 859/126/1 Census East Africa, 1944.

2. D.A. Low and A. Smith, "The New Order," in Low and Smith, eds., *History of East Africa*, vol. III (Oxford: Clarendon Press, 1976), 12.

3. Joseph Hodge makes this argument about colonial agricultural policies. Joseph Hodge, *Triumph of the Expert: Agrarian Doctrines of Development and the Legacies of British Colonialism* (Athens: Ohio University Press, 2007), 254–76.

4. For a general account of this period see Kenneth Morgan, *Labour in Power, 1945–1951* (Oxford: Oxford University Press, 1986), 94–187, and Peter Hennesey, *Never Again Britain, 1945–1951* (London: J. Cape, 1992), 119–215.

5. Ritchie Ovendale, *The English-Speaking Alliance: Britain, the United States, the Dominions and the Cold War 1945–1951* (London: Allen & Unwin, 1985).

6. William Louis, *Imperialism at Bay: The United States and the Decolonization of the British Empire 1941–1945* (New York: Oxford University Press, 1978).

7. William Roger Louis and Ronald Robinson, "The Imperialism of Decolonization," *Journal of Imperial and Commonwealth History* 22, no. 3 (1994): 462–511; John Kent, "United States Reactions to Empire, Colonialism, and Cold War in Black Africa, 1949–1957," *Journal of Imperial and Commonwealth History* 33, no. 2 (2005): 195–220.

8. The question of intention and planning for decolonization sparked an exchange on how and why political change occurred in the empire after 1945. See Ronald Robinson, "Andrew Cohen and the Transfer of Power in Tropical Africa, 1941–1951," in W.H. Morris-Jones and G. Fischer, eds., *Decolonization and After: The British and French Experience* (London: Frank Cass, 1980), 50–72, as well as John Flint, "Planned Decolonization and Its Failure in British Africa," *African Affairs* 82, no. 328 (1983): 389–411, and Robert Pearce, "The

Colonial Office and Planned Decolonization in Africa," *African Affairs* 83, no. 330 (1984): 77–93.

9. For the war see J. M. Lee and Martin Petter, *The Colonial Office, War and Development Policy* (London: M. T. Smith for the Institute for Commonwealth Studies, 1982). For the postwar era see John Darwin, *Britain and Decolonization* (New York: St. Martins, 1988); John Kent, *British Imperial Strategy and the Origins of the Cold War 1944-49* (Leicester: Leicester University Press, 1993); Partha Sarathi Gupta, *Imperialism and the British Labour Movement, 1914-1964* (New York: Holmes & Meier, 1975), 303–48; P. J. Cain and A. G. Hopkins, *British Imperialism: Crisis and Deconstruction 1914-1990* (London: Longman, 1993), 263–81.

10. Frederick Cooper, "Modernizing Bureaucrats, Backward Africans, and the Development Concept," in Frederick Cooper and Randall Packard, eds., *International Development and the Social Sciences* (Berkeley: University of California Press, 1997), 64–92; A. J. Stockwell, "British Imperial Policy and Decolonization in Malaya, 1942-52," *Journal of Commonwealth and Imperial History* 13, no. 1 (1984): 68–87; Michael Cowen and Robert Shenton, "The Origin and Course of Fabian Colonialism in Africa," *Journal of Historical Sociology* 4, no. 2 (1991): 143–74.

11. For the politics and limitations of the Labour government's planning see Jim Tomlinson, "Planning: Debate and Policy in the 1940s," *Twentieth Century British History* 3, no. 2 (1992): 154–74, and Richard Toye, "Gosplanners versus Thermostatters: Whitehall Planning Debates and their Political Consequences, 1945–1949," *Contemporary British History* 14, no. 4 (2000): 81–104.

12. A. J. Stockwell, "Colonial Planning during World War II: The Case of Malaya," *Journal of Imperial and Commonwealth History* 2, no. 3 (1974): 331–51; Nicholas Tarling, "A New and Better Cunning: British Wartime Planning for Postwar Burma 1942-43," *Journal of Southeast Asian Studies* 13, no. 1 (1982): 33–59.

13. D. J. Morgan, *The Official History of Colonial Development*, vol. 1: *The Origins of British Aid Policy, 1924-1945* (Atlantic Highlands, NJ: Humanities Press, 1980), 137–56.

14. S. Shattacharya and B. Zachariah, "A Great Destiny: The British Colonial State and the Advertisement of Post-War Reconstruction in India, 1942-45," *South Asia Research* 19, no. 1 (1999): 71–100.

15. Ronald Hyam, "Africa and the Labour Government, 1945-1951," *Journal of Imperial and Commonwealth History* 16, no. 3 (1988): 148–72; R. D. Pearce, *The Turning Point in Africa: British Colonial Policy 1938-48* (London: Frank Cass, 1982), 90–161; Gupta, *Imperialism and the British Labour Movement*, 309–35; Frederick Cooper, *Decolonization and African Society: The Labor Question in French and British Africa* (Cambridge: Cambridge University Press, 1996), 111–24.

16. For a study of the vagaries of development in the West Indies see Richard Harris, "Making in the Leewards, 1929–51: The Negotiation of Colo-

nial Development," *Journal of Imperial and Commonwealth History* 33, no. 3 (2005): 393–418. For Africa, see Jane Lewis, *Empire State Building: War And Welfare in Kenya 1925-1952* (Athens: Ohio University Press, 2000); Roderick Neumann, "The Post-War Conservation Boom in British Colonial Africa," *Environmental History* 7, no. 1 (2002): 22–47; Dorothy Hodgson, "Taking Stock: Ethnic Identity and Pastoralist Development in Tanganyika, 1948–1958," *Journal of African History* 41, no. 1 (2000): 55–78; Andres Eckert, "Regulating the Social: Social Security, Social Welfare and the State in Late Colonial Tanzania," *Journal of African History* 45, no. 3 (2004): 467–89; Eric Worby, "Discipline without Oppression: Sequence, Timing and Marginality in Southern Rhodesia's Post-War Development Regime," *Journal of African History* 41, no. 1 (2000): 101–25.

17. Christopher Bonneuil, "Development as Experiment: Science and State Building in Late Colonial and Postcolonial Africa, 1930–1970," *Osiris* 15, no. 1 (2000): 258–81, and James Scott, *Seeing Like a State* (New Haven: Yale University Press, 1998), 223–63. For the limits of colonial state building see Bruce Berman, "The Perils of Bula Matari: Constraint and Power in the Colonial State," *Canadian Journal of African Studies* 31, no. 3 (1997): 556–70, and John Darwin, "What Was the Late Colonial State?" *Itinerario* 23, nos. 3–4 (1999): 73–82. For French programs see Monica van Beusekom, *Negotiating Development: African Farmers and Colonial Experts at the Office du Niger, 1920–1960* (Portsmouth, NH: Heinemann, 2002).

18. Nicholas Tarling, "An Empire Gem: British Wartime Planning for Post-War Burma, 1943–44," *Journal of Southeast Asian Studies* 13, no. 2 (1982): 310–48.

19. A.V. M. Horton, "'So Rich as to Be Almost Indecent': Some Aspects of Post-War Rehabilitation in Brunei, 1946–1953," *Bulletin of the School of Oriental and African Studies* 58, no. 1 (1995): 91–103.

20. For a discussion of the role of the sterling area in the postwar empire see Allister Hinds, *Britain's Sterling Colonial Policy and Decolonization, 1939–1958* (Westport, CT: Greenwood, 2001) and Gerald Krozewski, *Money and the End of Empire: British International Economic Policy and the Colonies, 1947-58* (Basingstoke: Palgrave, 2001).

21. R.J. Butler, "The Ambiguities of British Colonial Development Policy, 1938–1948," in Anthony Gorst, Lewis Johnson, and W. Scott Lucas, eds., *Contemporary British History, 1939–1961: Politics and the Limits of Policy* (London: Pinter, 1991), 119–40, and ———,"Reconstruction, Development and the Entrepreneurial State: The British Colonial Model, 1939–1951," *Contemporary British History* 13, no. 4 (1999): 29–55.

22. Michael Hogan, *The Marshall Plan: America, Britain, and the Reconstruction of Western Europe, 1947–1952* (Cambridge, Cambridge University Press, 1987), 227–56.

23. J.M. Lee, *Colonial Development and Good Government: A Study of the Ideas Expressed by the British Official Classes in Planning Decolonization 1939-1964* (Oxford: Oxford University Press, 1967), 112–14; D.J. Morgan,

Developing British Colonial Resources, 1945-1951 (Atlantic Highlands, NJ: Humanities Press, 1980), 63–83; Michael Havinden and David Meredith, *Colonialism and Development: Britain and Its Tropical Colonies, 1850-1960* (London: Routledge, 1993), 252–55.

24. Cited in Lee, *Colonial Development*, 112.

25. Robert Tignor, *W. Arthur Lewis and the Birth of Development Economics* (Princeton: Princeton University Press, 2006), 56–71.

26. Morgan, *Colonial Resources*, 17–20.

27. In 1949 and 1950 an additional £20 million was allocated.

28. Havinden and Meredith, *Colonialism and Development*, 235–75.

29. Lee, *Colonial Development*, 100–104.

30. The Colonial Service began the campaign in June 1945 and made some 4,000 appointments from 1946 to 1948. The Colonial Service reached 11,000 in 1947 and peaked at 18,000 in 1954. Anthony Kirk-Greene, *On Crown Service: A History of HM Colonial and Overseas Civil Services 1837-1997* (London: I. B. Tauris, 1999), 49–53.

31. David Goldsworthy, *Colonial Issues in British Politics 1945-1961* (Oxford: Oxford University Press, 1971), 43–48.

32. For a discussion of this transition see Melvyn Leffler, *A Preponderance of Power: National Security, the Truman Administration and the Cold War* (Stanford, CA: Stanford University Press, 1992).

33. For the origins of Marshall Aid see Hogan, *Marshall Plan*, 1–134.

34. Kent, "Colonialism, and Cold War in Black Africa," 197–200.

35. Vernon Rutton, *United States Development Assistance Policy: The Domestic Politics of Foreign Economic Aid* (Baltimore: John Hopkins University Press, 1996), 38–93.

36. For a discussion of the link of population programs and U.S. aid and security planning see John Sharpless, "World Population Growth, Family Planning and American Foreign Policy," *Journal of Policy History* 7, no. 1 (1995): 72–102.

37. Ademola Adeleke, "Playing Fairy Godfather to the Commonwealth: The United States and the Colombo Plan," *Commonwealth and Comparative Politics* 42, no. 3 (2004): 393–411.

38. Rutton, *Development Assistance*, 45–47, 387–97.

39. CO 733/471/7 Area and population of Palestine, 1946.

40. CO 927/10/4 Demography and Census-Malaya, 1946.

41. CO 927/160/1 Demography and Census, 1948–50 Publication of Dr. Kuczynski's Survey.

42. CO 927/154 Demography and Census, 1948–50.

43. CSSRC meeting 9-1-45, CO 927/10/2, Demography, 1945. For the Devonshire scheme see Kirk Greene, *Crown Service*, 46–48.

44. He consulted with the Oxford Institute of Statistics and in February 1950 made a trip to Oxford to recruit statistics students. Annual salaries were about £1,000 per year. CO 877/39/2 Appointment of Statisticians General, 1948–50.

45. Minute by W. F. Searle 19–1–50, CO 852/1076/1 Staff Training of Colonial Government Statisticians, 1950.
46. CO 877/39/2 Appointment of Statisticians General, 1948–50.
47. CO 1034/10 Extract from Report of African Statistical Conference, Second Conference of Colonial Government Statisticians, 1953.
48. CO 1042/146 Conference of Colonial Government Statisticians, 1951–53.
49. W. F. Searle, E. T. Phillips, and C. J. Martin, "Colonial Statistics," *Journal of the Royal Statistical Society* 113, no. 3 (1950): 271–98.
50. CO 852/1076/1 Staff Training of Colonial Government Statisticians, 1950; Minutes of Conference, CO 852/1127/4 Conference of Colonial Government Statisticians, 1950; Progress Report March 1950 to March 1953, CO 1034/1 Conference of Colonial Government Statisticians, 1953.
51. CO 901/3 CSSRC Minutes and Papers, 1946. In addition Kuczynski's salary and expenses came to about £2,400.
52. David Mills, "How Not to Be a 'Government House Pet': Audrey Richards and the East African Institute for Social Research," in Mwenda Ntarangwi, David Mills, and Mustafa Babiker, eds., *African Anthropologies: History, Critique and Practice* (London: Zed, 2006), 76–98.
53. CO 1023/85 South Pacific Commission Research Council Demographic Survey of the South Pacific, 1953.
54. CO 822/999 Future Arrangements for Development Finance Demographic Research, 1954–56; CO 927/374 Scheme for the Study of Demographic Data in East Africa, 1954–56. Frank Lorimer, already well known for his work at Princeton on Eastern European demography, began to focus on African demography in the 1950s. He presented his work to the East African Social Research Institute and attracted the interest of Searle. CO 901/11 CSSRC Minutes and Papers, 1952; CO 1034/16 Second Conference of Colonial Government Statisticians, 1953–54.
55. J. K. Thompson to Searle, 9–6–50, CO 852/1076/1 Staff Training of Colonial Government Statisticians, 1950.
56. Note by Kenneth Robinson, Meeting (59)5, CO 901/18 CSSRC Minutes and Papers, 1959.
57. Eugene Grebenik, "Demographic Research in Britain," *Population Studies* 45, Suppl. (1991), 22.
58. Roberts, whose first book was published by the Conservation Foundation, continued a close association with Kurt Black and Stycos, whom he met while working on the Jamaican Family Life project. See Lloyd Braithwaite, "Sociology and Demographic Research in the West Indies," *Social and Economic Studies* 6, no. 4 (1957): 531–40.
59. T. S. Simey, *Welfare and Planning in the West Indies* (Oxford: Clarendon Press, 1946).
60. CO 1042/244 West Indies Social Welfare Family Planning 1951, 1952, 1955.
61. Clarke, a birth control activist since the 1930s, facilitated Edith How-

Martyn's visit to Jamaica in 1939 and corresponded with the Colonial Office about the birth control movement on the island. CO 950/279 Pamphlet on birth control by Dr. W. E. McCulloch.

62. W. D. Huggins, an economist at the University of the West Indies, made a similar suggestion to the Colonial Office in 1949. CO 318/495/5 Population Problems West Indies, 1949.

63. Minute by P. Rogers 21-3-56, CO 1031/1967 Population Problems in Jamaica, 1954-56.

64. Minute by A. S. Gann 31-10-55; Note of meeting between Norman Manley and Nuffield Foundation at Nuffield Lodge 18-2-56, ibid.

65. The committee soon disbanded and the first and only trainee appears to have been Douglas Manley, son of Norman Manley. Robert Snider to Solly Zuckerman, 6-12-56, SZ/CF/4/1 Correspondence with Robert Snider, Zuckerman Archives, University of East Anglia.

66. J. Mayone Stycos and Kurt Black, *Prospects for Fertility Reduction: The Jamaican Family Life Project of the Conservation Foundation—A Preliminary Report* (New York: Conservation Foundation, 1957), 86-87.

67. Population Trends in British Colonial Territories and Policy in Regard to Population Control, Cabinet (CAB) 124/2843 World Food Supplies and Population Trends, Papers by Professor Zuckerman, 1948-58, National Archives.

68. FO 371/88830 UN Population and Vital Statistics Working Party 1950; CO 927/374 Scheme for the Study of Demographic Data in East Africa, 1954-56.

69. Richard Glotzer, "A Long Shadow: Frederick P. Keppel, the Carnegie Corporation and the Dominions and Colonies Fund Area Experts 1923-1945," *History of Education* 38, no. 5 (2009): 621-48. The Carnegie Corporation provided the funding for the *African Survey*. The Rockefeller Foundation supported a number of medical and public health projects. Donald Fisher, "Rockefeller Philanthropy and the British Empire: The Creation of the London School of Hygiene and Tropical Medicine," *History of Education* 7, no. 2 (1978): 129-43, and John Farley, *To Cast Out Disease: A History of the International Health Division of the Rockefeller Foundation, 1913-1951* (New York and Oxford: Oxford University Press, 2003), 61-79.

70. CO 323/1885/1 General Carnegie Corporation Grants, 1946; CO 859/339 Ford Foundation, 1952.

71. Minutes of ACSP meeting 2-1-56; CO 859/666, ACSP: Colonial Population Problems, 1954-56.

72. Nuffield, the founder of Morris Motors, had already provided supported for African studies through Nuffield College, Oxford.

73. Minute by R. S. Furse 17-2-44, CO 852/217/11 Nuffield Scholarships, 1944-45.

74. CO 876/255 Proposed Survey of Colonial Population of the UK, 1950.

75. Minutes of the fifty-first meeting 20-10-53, Nuffield Foundation, Minutes held by the foundation.

76. For the history of FORD see R. A. Longmire, *Herald of a Noisy World: Interpreting the News of All Nations: The Research and Analysis Department of the Foreign and Commonwealth Office* (London: Foreign and Commonwealth Office, 1995).

77. FO 943/304 File E.1/13/2 Part I Control Office for Germany and Austria Central Registry Population of Germany, 1946–47; FO 371/64529 File 2193 Germany Population, 1947; FO 371/69025 File 3530 Population Trends in Europe, 1948.

78. FO 371/54087 Control of Japan, 1946; FO 371/69836 Population Problems in Japan, 1948; FO 371/84042 Latest U.S. information on the population trend in Japan, 1950.

79. FO 371/99401 Japanese Expansion Attitude toward Japanese Population Problem, 1952; FO 371/110520 Japanese Population, 1954.

80. FO 381/79534 File 1823 Italian Emigration and Population Issues, 1949.

81. Z 7436/1823/22 Conversation between Labour Minister Fanfani and Labour attaché, 3–11–49, ibid.

82. FO 371/73151, 1948, Italian Labour in Africa, FO 381/79534 File 1823 1949 Italian Emigration, FO 371/69153 File J 5392 Association of Italy with African Development, 1948. For a discussion of the policy of labor recruitment in Italy see Joseph Behar, "Diplomacy and Essential Workers: Official British Recruitment of Foreign Labor in Italy, 1945–1951," *Journal of Policy History* 15, no. 3 (2003): 324–44.

83. Saul Kelly, *Cold War in the Desert: Britain, the United States and the Italian Colonies, 1945–52* (New York: Palgrave Macmillan, 2000).

84. FO 371 34463 File 14891/279/18 Comments on paper by Notestein on European population, published in *American Philosophical Society* 87, no. 2 (August 1943), 1943; FO 371 56627 File N5428/2615/55 Polish Settlement in the Colonies, 1946; FO 371 77940 File 7564 European Recovery Department Memo on European Population Problems by Douglas Jay, 1949; FO 371 8253 Further Comments on Jay's Memo; FO 371/88834 UN Relief of Over-Population of Europe, 1950.

85. Richard Bosworth, "Australia and Assisted Immigration from Britain, 1945–1954," *Australian Journal of Politics and History* 34, no. 2 (1988): 187–200.

86. The Foreign Office showed particular interest in population trends in the Middle East. FO 921/347 Middle East Office Scientific Advisory Mission, Middle East Supply Centre, 1945; Eric Pridie, The Effect of Raising the Standard of Living on the Birth Rate and Increase in Population in the Middle East and Tropical Africa, CO 927/73, Demography and census; FO 371/75085 Economic Development in the Middle East, 1949.

87. A Foreign Office official relying on such estimates argued that Eastern Europe's population would exceed that of Western Europe by 25 percent in 1970, which would give the communist bloc a larger pool of military manpower. FO 371/135138 High Population Increases in Poland, 1958; FO

371/116840 Estimates of Soviet Population, 1955 N S1822/1; FO 371/135404 N S 1823/1 Discussion of Soviet Population Prospects during the Next Few Decades.

88. Memo on the Problem of Chinese Immigration, CO 537/4871, 1948. This memo in turn drew on another one created by the Far East Defence Secretariat, which detailed changes in Chinese population in Southeast Asia from 1920 to 1947. Only the title of the latter file is available; the file itself has been retained in department.

89. FO 371/121008 China Population, 1956.

90. Ian Spencer, *British Immigration Policy since 1939: The Making of Multi-racial Britain* (London: Routledge, 1997), 82–128; Zig Layton-Henry, *The Politics of Immigration: Immigration, "Race" and "Race Relations" in Post-War Britain* (Oxford: Blackwell, 1992).

91. Brian Murphy, *The Other Australia: Experiences of Migration* (Cambridge: Cambridge University Press, 1993), 88.

92. CO 323/1845/7 Comment on Sir Alan Pim's Memo by Arthur Hailey, 1942.

93. Kathleen Paul, *Whitewashing Britain: Race and Citizenship in Post-War Britain* (Ithaca, NY: Cornell University Press, 1997), 25–63.

94. Memo on Shipping Migrants to Australia, Overseas Settlement in the Dominions, 1945–47, Papers, Ministry of Labour (LAB) 199/13, National Archives. See also CO 537/2667, Implication of Dispersal of Population and Industry throughout the Commonwealth, 1948.

95. Memo by H. T. Tizard, 25–11–1947, CAB 124/1033 Dispersal of Population and Industry throughout the Commonwealth, 1947–48.

96. CO 537/2667 Implications of Dispersal of Population into the Commonwealth, 1948.

97. CAB 124/1033 Dispersal of Population and Industry throughout the Commonwealth, 1947–48. Despite this setback, supporters of dispersal continued to call for new plans to ensure Britain's long-run security. See Wayne Reynolds, "Atomic War, Empire Strategic Dispersal and the Origins of the Snowy Mountain Scheme," *War and Society* 14, no. 1 (1996): 121–44.

98. G. Myrddin Evans to John Stephenson at Dominions Office. 15–11–44, CO 968/152/5 Empire Settlement Post-War Migration Interdepartmental Committee, 1944–45.

99. Diana Kay and Robert Miles, *Refugees or Migrant Workers? European Volunteer Workers in Britain 1946–1951* (London: Routledge, 1992).

100. CO 1032/123 Use of Quota Systems to Control Immigration, 1954–56. Spencer, *British Immigration*, 21–48; David Walker, "General Cariappa Encounters 'White Australia': Australia, India and the Commonwealth in the 1950s," *Journal of Imperial and Commonwealth History* 34, no. 3 (2006): 389–406.

101. This concern was voiced by the CSSRC as well. CSSRC (46) 9 Census and Labour Problems Major Orde-Brown 27–2–46, CO 901/3 CSSRC Minutes and Papers, 1946.

102. Arieh Kochavi, *Post-Holocaust Politics: Britain, the United States and Jewish Refugees, 1945–1948* (Chapel Hill: University of North Carolina Press, 2001), 60–86.

103. CO 537/4871, Memo on the Problem of Chinese Immigration, 1948.

104. CO 537/1653 Future Policy Immigration Control Policy, 1946; CO 927/67/4 Demography and Census Hong Kong 1947–8; CO 537/3701 Immigration Control Threatened Influx of Refugees, 1948.

105. CO 129/604/4, Hong Kong Immigration Control, 1947.

106. Chi Kwan Mark, "The 'Problem of People': British Colonials, Cold War Powers, and the Chinese Refugees in Hong Kong, 1949–1962," *Modern Asian Studies* 41, no. 6 (2007): 1145–81.

107. Despite their efforts, recruitment proved disappointing, with only 500 white settlers entering in the last official effort after 1945. Levi Izakor, "Kenya: Demographic Constraints on the Growth of European Settlement, 1900–1956," *Africa; rivista trimestrale di studi e documentazione* 42, no. 3 (1987): 400–416. For Kenya's settler population see Alison Smith, "The Immigrant Communities (1): The Europeans," in Low and Smith, *History of East Africa*, 457–66.

108. Minute by R. Hancock 13-4-46, FO 371 56627 File N5428/2615/55 Polish Settlement in the Colonies, 1946. Several thousand POWs and refugees were temporarily housed in camps in Tanganyika before being repatriated. Smith, "Immigrant Communities," 458–59.

109. A. Cohen, 19-7-1948, FO 371/73151. File Z 5964/65/22, Italian population and the possible use of Italian labor in Africa.

110. Marginal note by Hall Patch, File Z3784/65/22, FO 371/73151 Italian population and the possible use of Italian labor in Africa, 1948.

111. Minute by D. W. Lascelles 18-2-48, File Z 4060/65/22, ibid..

112. Minute by Mr. Sargent 3-8-48, FO 371/69153 File J 5392 Association of Italy with Development, 1948.

113. P. M. Crossthwaite to A. Cohen 18-6-48, File Z3784/65/22 1948 FO 371/73151 Italian population and the possible use of Italian labor in Africa, 1948.

114. File Z6995/65/22, ibid.

115. Minute by F. D. W. Brown 5-2-49, File Z1411/1823/22, FO 371 79534, Italian Emigration and Population Issues, 1949.

116. CO 822/115/13 Indians in East Africa, 1946.

117. CO 822/143/7 Indians in East Africa Political, Social and Economic Position, 1951.

118. CO 822/581 Asian Immigration into East Africa, 1951–54.

119. CO 822/143/7 Indians in East Africa Political, Social and Economic Position, 1951.

120. Secret Memo Necessity for Immigration Control 9-6-51, CO 822/581 Asian Immigration into East Africa, 1951–54.

121. Note by Sir Charles Dundas, CO 822/118/2 Immigration(Non-Native) Control of, 1945–46; CO 537/5910 Immigration Legislation East Africa, 1950.

122. Minute by P. Rogers, 6–11–51, CO 822/581, Asian Immigration into East Africa, 1951–54.

123. Memo Necessity for Immigration Control 4659 9–6–51, CO 822/581 Asian Immigration into East Africa, 1951–54.

124. Minute by A. Cohen 6–11–50, CO 537/5910 Immigration Legislation East Africa, 1950.

125. Minute of J.S. Ward 6–6–55, CO 822/861 Asian Immigration into East Africa, 1954–56.

126. Minute by I. Wallace 16–11–51, CO 822/581 Asian Immigration into East Africa, 1951–54.

127. CO 822/118/2 Control of Non-Native Immigration, 1945–46; CO 537/5910, Immigration Legislation East Africa, 1950; CO 822/581, Asian Migration into East Africa, 1951–54.

128. J.S. Mangat, "The Immigrant Communities (2): The Asians," in Low and Smith, *History of East Africa*, 483–84.

129. Report of Joint Meeting 14–1–48, Colonial Advisory on Council of Agriculture, Animal Health and Forestry, CO 996/7 Papers Colonial Advisory Council on Agriculture, 1948.

130. Minute by (illegible) 21–3–49, CO 537/4472 World Food Supplies-Strategic Aspects of World Food Production, Working Party on Food Supplies and Communism, 1949.

131. Pridie, who previously served as medical director of the Sudan Service and the Health Advisor to the Middle East Office in Cairo, became an important figure in postwar population debates. His report on population trends in the Middle East and Africa, produced for the Foreign Office, painted a picture of increasing population pressure in both regions. Eric Pridie, The Effect of Raising the Standard of Living on the Birth Rate and Increase in Population in the Middle East and Tropical Africa, CO 927/73, Demography and census.

132. Memo by J.H. Seddon, CO 859/154/6 Medical Population, 1949.

133. In 1945 Andrew Cohen had warned of predictions that the introduction of DDT would dramatically lower death rates from malaria, leading to increased population growth. CO 927/10, Demography-Social Service Research, 1945.

134. Extracts from CAMC's 443rd meeting 23–3—48 CO 859/154/6 Medical-Population.

135. Minute by Poynter, 3–3—48, CO 859/154/6 Growth of Tropical Population, 1949.

136. Minute by P. Deane 22–6—48, ibid.

137. Minute by C. Eastwood, 14–6—48, ibid.

138. From 1940 to 1946, about 38 percent of all funds went to the West Indies. Morgan, *Colonial Development*, 137–56; Havinden and Meredith, *Colonialism and Development*, 218–27.

139. Howard Johnson, "The Anglo-American Commission and the Exten-

sion of American Influence in the British Caribbean, 1942–45," *Journal of Commonwealth and Comparative Politics* 22, no. 2 (1984): 180–203.

140. For a discussion of the Labour government's policy on colonial migration see D. W. Dean, "Coping with Colonial Immigration, the Cold War and Colonial Policy: The Labour Government and Black Communities in Great Britain 1945–1951," *Immigrants and Minorities* 6, no. 3 (1987): 304–34.

141. James Vining, "Grandiose Schemes for Foreign Colonization in Guyana: A Survey of their Origin, Provisions and Abandonment," *Caribbean Quarterly* 24, nos. 1–2 (1978): 86–87. C. W. W. Greenidge, director of the Anti-Slavery Society and an advocate of West Indian interests, authored the Fabian report. C. W. Greenidge, "Overpopulation in the West Indies," 25-9—44, Greenridge Papers, MSS British Empire since 1877, Fabian Colonial Bureau Papers, Box 142/2, Rhodes House Archives, Oxford University.

142. Minute for Sir Thomas Lloyd by N. L. Mayle 23–2—51, CO 318 511/9 Population Problems-West Indies, 1951.

143. CO 859/151/1 Labour Conference West Indies, 1947–49.

144. LAB 13/42 Use of Surplus Colonial Manpower, 1948–50.

145. Spencer, *British Immigration*, 39–42.

146. CO 859/151/4 Minutes of the Working Party on Employment of Surplus Colonial Population in the United Kingdom, 1949.

147. Minute by A. J. Fairclough 3/1/50, CO 859/151/3 Surplus Labour in the Colonies Social Service, 1949.

148. Spencer in particular emphasizes the importance of the increasing size of the West Indian community as a factor shaping policy, Spencer, *British Immigration*, 87–98.

149. CO 318/495/4 Population Problems West Indies, 1948–49.

150. Lord Listowel to Hubert Rance from 31-1—49, CO 1042/244, Social Welfare Family Planning, 1949. Rance called attention to population problems in his report, *Development and Welfare in the West Indies, 1947-49* (London: HMSO, 1949), 13.

151. CO 318/495/4, Population Problems West Indies, 1948; CO 318/495/5, Population Problems West Indies, 1949.

152. Governor of British Honduras to Creech Jones 30-6—49, CO 1042/244 West Indies Social Welfare Family Planning, 1945–55.

153. J. Shaw to Creech Jones 30-6—49, ibid.

154. Note by Mr. Vernon, CO 318/511/9, Population Problems-West Indies, 1951.

155. Dora Ibberson, "A Note on the Relationship between Illegitimacy and the Birthrate," *Social and Economic Studies* 5, no. 1 (1956): 93–99, and G. W. Roberts, "Some Aspects of Mating and Fertility in the West Indies," *Population Studies* 8, no. 3 (1955): 199–227. Ibberson served as social welfare advisor and Roberts was the vital statistics officer for the Comptroller for Social Welfare and Development in the West Indies.

156. Minute by W. Sweaney 20–12–50, CO 318/511/8 Population Problems West Indies, 1950.

157. W. F. Searle and his statisticians became involved, as did the Colonial Office's education advisor, who envisioned a broad-based campaign, using a variety of media, targeted to different audiences. Minute by J. L. Nicol, education advisor 4–4–51, CO 318/511/9, Population Problems West Indies, 1951.

158. Minute by Hewitt-Myring 2–22–51, CO 1042/48 West Indies Population Pamphlet on the Population Problem of West Indies, 1951.

159. Minute by M. Maccoll, 18–1–51, CO 318/511/8 Population Problems-West Indies, 1950.

160. For Conservative colonial policy see Goldsworthy, *Colonial Issues*, 113–253; Philip Murphy, *Party Politics and Decolonization: The Conservative Party and British Colonial Policy in Tropical Africa, 1951-1964* (Oxford: Oxford University Press, 1995), 13–57; Nicholas Owens, "Decolonization and Postwar Consensus," in Harriet Jones and Michael Kandiah, eds., *The Myth of Consensus: New Views of British History* (New York: St. Martins, 1996), 157–81; Martin Lynn, ed., *The British Empire in the 1950s: Retreat or Revival* (New York: Palgrave Macmillan, 2005); L. J Butler, *Britain and Empire: Adjusting to a Post-Imperial World* (London: I. B. Tauris, 2002), 97–170.

161. CO 1032/120 Employment of Coloured Peoples in the UK and Bill to Restrict Immigration of British Subjects from Overseas, 1954–55.

162. Spencer, *British Immigration*, 58–81; See also D. W. Dean, "Conservative Governments and the Restriction of Commonwealth Immigration in the 1950s: The Problems of Constraint," *Historical Journal* 35, no. 1 (1992): 171–94.

163. CO 1032/123, Use of Quota Systems to Control Immigration, 1954–56.

164. Minute of K. Woolverton 6–10–55, CO 822/861 Asian Immigration into East Africa, 1954–56.

165. For an overview see Spencer, *British Immigration*, 21–48, 82–108. Also see Paul, *Whitewashing Britain*, 131–69.

166. P. Rogers to governor of Jamaica. 1–5–54, CO 1032/119 Employment of Coloured People in the UK and Bill to Restrict Immigration of British Subjects from Overseas, 1954.

167. Minute by T. Lloyd, 26–3—56, CO 1032/121 Employment of Coloured People in the UK and Bill to Restrict Immigration of British Subjects from Overseas, 1955–56.

168. R. A. Butler 24–2—58, DO 35/9103 Problem of Over-Population in Certain Commonwealth Countries Proposed Colonial Development and Welfare grant to the FPA, 1958–59.

169. P. Rogers, 2–3–55, CO 1031/1969, Family Planning in the West Indies, 1954–55.

170. In addition to Barbados, medical officers provided birth control advice in St. Vincent and Antigua, though without public notice. Kenneth Blackburne to P. Rogers, 18–9—56, CO 1031/1970 Family Planning in the West Indies, 1954–56; Sir Colville Deverell to P. Rogers 13–3–58, CO 1031/2787 Population Problems, 1957–59. For the work of the IPPF see Jean Gearing,

"Family Planning in St. Vincent, West Indies: A Population History Perspective," *Social Science and Medicine* 35, no. 10 (1992): 1273–82.

171. Minutes of ACSP July 1953 and October 1953, CAB 132/07, Minutes and Papers of the ACSP, 1953.

172. CAB 132/08 Minutes and Papers of the ACSP, 1954–56.

173. In addition to the Statistical Department and the West Indian Department, R. Terrell, W. H. Chinn, E. M. Chilver, and Sir Hilton Poynton participated in the drafting of the report. Phillip Rogers, J. K. Thompson, and M. Monson served as an editorial committee to put together the final draft of the paper. Minute by M. Monson, 16–1—56, CO 859/666 ACSP: Colonial Population Problems, 1954–56.

174. Minute by R. Terrell, 12–1–56, CO 859/666 ACSP: Colonial Population Problems, 1954–56.

175. Population Trends in British Colonial Territories and Policy in Regard to Population Control, ibid.

176. Minutes of ASCP second meeting, 1957, CAB 132/155 Minutes and Papers, 1957.

177. Solly Zuckerman to Robert Snider, 25–11–55 SZ/CF/4/1 Correspondence with Robert Snider, Zuckerman Archives, University of East Anglia.

178. Minute by Sir J. MacPherson, 17–9—56, CO 1031/1970 Family Planning in the West Indies, 1954–56.

179. The list included David Glass, Richard Titmuss, and Audrey Richards. Minute by E. M. Chilver, 28–9—56; Minute by J. Thompson, 1–57, CO 927/699 ACSP: Review and Coordination of Research in Human Fertility, 1957–59.

180. Minute by Monson, 3–1—57, ibid.

181. Alan Lennox Boyd to Solly Zuckerman 2–58, CAB 124/2843 World Food Supplies and Population Trends, Papers by Professor Zuckerman, 1948–58.

182. Brief for secretary of state's meeting with Sir Solly Zuckerman 28–1–59, CO 859/1028, Population Control Policy, 1957–59.

183. Note by J. Thompson, 9–12–57, CO 859/1026 Population-General Information and Enquiries, 1957–59.

184. CO 859/1026, Population General Information and Enquiries, 1957–59.

185. CO 859/666 ACSP: Colonial Population Problems, 1954–56.

186. Draft Brief for Lord Hailsham 6–62, CO 859/1444 Population Control Policy, 1960–62.

187. Hyam, "Africa and the Labour Government," 148–72, and John Kent, "Bevin's Imperialism and the Idea of Euro-Africa," in M. Dockrill and John Young, eds., *British Foreign Policy, 1945-56* (London: Macmillan, 1989), 47–76.

188. In the postwar funding allocation, the share of the West Indies fell to 18 percent, while those of the East and Central African colonies rose to 25 percent. Havinden and Meredith, *Colonialism and Development*, 252–53.

189. R. Kuczynski, *Demographic Survey of the Colonial Empire*, vol. 1:

West Africa (London: Oxford University Press, 1948), 13–15. Both E.D. Pridie and T.H. Davey argued that populations in some parts of Africa were growing. E.D. Pridie, The Effect of Raising the Standard of Living on Population, CO/927/73/1,1948; CO 537/4472, Working Party on Food Supplies and Communism, 1949; J.H. Davey, The Growth of Tropical Populations, CO/859/152/4, Growth of Tropical Population, 1949.

190. C.J. Martin, "The East African Population Census, 1948. Planning and Enumeration," *Population Studies* 3, no. 3 (1949): 303–20; R. Mansell Prothero, "The Population Census of Northern Nigeria 1952: Problems and Results," *Population Studies* 10, no. 2 (1952): 166–83, Estimates produced by government statisticians in the early 1950s put Nigeria's population growth at 1.3 percent to 1.7 percent per year, the Gold Coast at 2.0 percent and the Central African Federation at 2.8 percent. R.A. Cooper of CO Statistical Office to the secretary of the East Africa Royal Commission 7-7–53, CO 1034/16, second conference of Colonial Government Statisticians, 1953–54. The governor of southern Rhodesia claimed that his territory had one of the highest growth rates in world, which led to pressure on the land. Governor of southern Rhodesia to secretary of state, 9–11–50, CO 936/62/3 Affairs in Southern Rhodesia, 1950. For outside views see L.T. Badenhurst, "Population Distribution and Growth in African," *Population Studies* 5, no. 1 (1951): 23–34; A.T. Grove, "Soil Erosion and Population Problems in South-East Nigeria," *Geographical Journal* 117, no. 3 (1951): 291–304; J.F.M. Middleton and D.J. Greenland, "Land and Population in West Nile District, Uganda," *Geographical Journal* 120, no. 4 (1954): 446–55; Glenn Trewartha and Wilber Zelinsky, "Population Patterns in Tropical Africa," *Annals of the Association of American Geographers* 44, no .2 (1954): 135–62; W.B. Morgan, "Farming Practices, Settlement Patterns and Population Density in South-Eastern Nigeria," *Geographical Journal* 121, no.3 (1955): 320–33; Glenn Trewartha, "New Population Maps of Uganda, Kenya, Nyasaland and Gold Coast," *Annals of the Association of American Geographers* 47, no. 1 (1957): 1–58.

191. Fiona Mackenzie," Contested Ground: Colonial Narratives and the Kenyan Environment, 1920–1945," *Journal of African Studies* 26, no. 4 (2000): 698–718.

192. David Throup, *Economic and Social Origins of Mau-Mau* (Athens: Ohio University Press, 1988). John McCracken, "Conservation and Resistance in Colonial Malawi: The 'Dead North' Revisited," in William Beinart and Joann McGregor, eds., *Social History and African Environments* (Athens: Ohio University Press 2003), 155–74; L. Cliffe, "Nationalism and the Reaction to Enforced Agricultural Change in Tanganyika during the Colonial Period," in L. Cliffe and J. Saul, eds., *Socialism in Tanganyika: An Interdisciplinary Reader* (Nairobi: East African Publishing House, 1972), 17–24.

193. Note on Land Distribution in the African Territories, CO 936/46/1 Special Committee on Information Submitted by NSGT Land Distribution, 1951.

194. European representatives from East Africa raised the issue at the

East African Medical Conference in 1945. In August 1946, another representative met with Robert Kuczynski and Andrew Cohen, then undersecretary of state for the colonies, to press for a census in East Africa. In August 1947 the Fabian Colonial Bureau wrote to Creech Jones to raise the question of overpopulation in the region, CO 859/155/1, Memo on Colonial Medical Policy, 1945–48; Notes of a Meeting 14–8–46, Worthington Papers, Rhodes House, MSS Africa 1425 5/3; Letter from the Fabian Colonial Bureau to A. Creech Jones, 24-4-47, Greenridge Papers, MSS British Empire since 1877, 285 Box 14, File 2, Rhodes House, Oxford.

195. *Land and Population in East Africa: An Exchange between the Secretary of State of State and the Governor of Kenya on the Appointment of a Royal Commission* (London: HMSO, 1952).

196. East Africa Royal Commission, 1953–55, *Report* (London: HMSO, 1955), 30–40.

197. Kirk Arden Hoppe, *Lords of the Fly: Sleeping Sickness Control in British East Africa, 1900-1960* (Westport, CT: Praeger, 2003), 105–42. In one case in Nigeria, officials hoped to create a forest reserve in the evacuated area. CO 583/296/3 Anchua Rural Development and Resettlement Scheme Report by Dr. T.A.M. Nash, 1946–47.

198. CO 691/215 East Africa Agricultural Policy, 1951. For a discussion of such schemes see Scott, *Seeing Like a State*, 225–29, and Bonneuil, "Development," 261–69.

199. CO 583/311/4 Resettlement of Africans from Overpopulated Areas, 1951; CO 525/196/2 Congested Areas in Cholo District, 1944–45 Nyasaland; CO 583/296/3 Anchua Rural Development and Resettlement Scheme Report by Dr. T.A.M. Nash, 1946–47; CO 583/296/4 Resettlement of Africans from Overpopulated Area, 1947–48; CO 892/15/8 Uganda Protectorate Agricultural Development and Resettlement Schemes, 1953.

200. The Nyasaland project affected 28,000 people; a Ugandan plan to resettle former soldiers in the Kigezi district involved 15,000 people. The Kigezi scheme cost £18,000, and one in Nigeria from 1946 to 1951 ran to £240 per settler. For more on the Kigezi plan see Grace Carswell, *Cultivating Success in Uganda: Kigezi Farmers and Colonial Policies* (Athens: Ohio University Press, 2007), 59–62.

201. Throup, *Roots of Mau-Mau*, 120–38.

202. In Rhodesia alone 450,000 squatters were moved. Chris Youe, "Rebellion and Quiescence: Kenyan and Rhodesian Responses to Forced Removals in the 1950s," in Chris Youe and Tim Stapleton, eds., *Agency and Action in Colonial Africa: Essays for John Flint* (New York: Palgrave, 2001), 172–94.

203. A.T. Lennox-Boyd to Reverend R.W. Sorenson 22–11–51, CO 554/370 The Resettlement of Africans from Birom in the Jos Division of Nigeria, 1951.

204. Grace Carswell, "Multiple Historical Geographies: Responses and

Resistance to Colonial Conservation Schemes in East Africa," *Journal of Historical Geography* 32, no. 2 (2006): 398–421.

205. The refusal of a local authority court to enforce the ban on settlement led to its dismissal by colonial officials.

206. See Throup for the role played by Norman Humphreys in this process. Throup, *Roots of Mau-Mau*, 69–72.

207. UN Report on *Non-Self-Governing Territories Settlement* Policies, 1951 A/AC.35.L.61 17–10–51, CO 936/46/1 Special Committee on Information Submitted by NSGT, Land Distribution, 1951.

208. By one estimate, officials devoted £3 million to resettlement and agricultural schemes in Kenya from 1945 to 1950. Ibid. For more on land and insurgency see David Anderson, *Histories of the Hanged: The Dirty War in Kenya and the End of Empire* (New York: Norton, 2005), 119–51, Throup, *Roots of Mau-Mau*, 91–119.

209. Hodge, *Triumph of the Expert*, 146–66, 180–96, 231–51; Hodgson, "Taking Stock," 56–57; Worby, "Discipline," 104–5; McCracken, "Conservation and Resistance," 163–73. The British extended this critique to Africa's relationship to forests and wild game. See Neuman, "Postwar Conservation," 31–35; James Fairhead and Melissa Leach, "Rethinking the Forest Savanna Mosaic: Colonial Science and Its Relics in West Africa," in Melissa Leach and Robin Mearns, *The Lie of the Land: Challenging Received Wisdom on the African Environment* (Oxford: International African Institute in association with James Currey, 1996), 105–23.

210. E. B. Worthington, *Science in Africa* (London: Oxford University Press, 1938) and Sir A. Daniel Hall, *The Improvement of Native Agriculture in Relation to Population and Public Health* (Oxford: Oxford University Press, 1936). For a discussion of this discourse on a broader African scale see the essays in Leach and Mearns, *The Lie of the Land*, and David Anderson, "Depression, Dust Bowl, Demography and Drought: The Colonial State and Soil Conservation in East Africa During the 1930s," *African Affairs* 83, no. 332 (1984): 321–41.

211. The geographer Robert Steel, whose work was supported by Colonial Welfare and Development funds, warned of erosion and soil exhaustion as a consequence of population pressure in the Gold Coast and Sierra Leone. R.W. Steel, "Some Geographical Problems of Land Use in West Africa," *Transactions and Papers (Institute of British Geographers)* no. 14 (1948): 27–42, and ———, "The Population of Ashanti: A Geographical Analysis," *Geographical Journal* 112, no. 1/3 (1948): 64–77.

212. Hodge, *Triumph*, 206–51.

213. Throup, *Roots of Mau-Mau*, 6–8, 77; Anderson, "Dust Bowl," 325–26.

214. Cooper, *Decolonization*, 43–56, 208–6; Throup, *Roots of Mau-Mau*, 72–77.

215. Native Land Tenure (CSSRC (44) 33 Memo by Colonial Office, CO 901/1, CSSRC Minutes and Papers, 1944.

216. CO 583/296/3 Anchua Rural Development and Resettlement Scheme

Report by Dr. T.A.M. Nash 1946. Helen Tilley, "African Environments and Environmental Sciences: The African Research Survey, Ecological Paradigms and British Colonial Development 1920–1940," in Beinart and McGregor, *African Environments*, 109–30.

217. Memo by J.K. Greer 11–3–48, CO 859/154/6, 180–196, 231–51.

218. Worby, "Discipline," 109–11.

219. Minute by Francis, 18–3–48, CO 859/154/6, Growth of Tropical Population, 1949.

220. Cooper, "Modernizing Bureaucrats," 78–81; Lewis, *State Building*, 363–73.

221. Richard Symonds, *The British and their Successors: A Study of the Development of Government Services in the New States* (Evanston, IL: Northwestern University Press, 1966), 119–208.

222. Kirk-Greene, *On Crown Service*, 64–91; Hodge, *Triumph*, 251–53.

223. Minute by J. Thompson 13–1–58, CO 1031/2783 Population Problems in Jamaica, 1957–59.

224. The Seychelles was also targeted in these efforts, although in that case it was primarily a Catholic, Afro-European population. CO 1036/433 Population Problems Seychelles, 1957–59.

225. For ethnic tensions see Terrence Carroll, "Owners, Immigrants and Ethnic Conflict in Fiji and Mauritius," *Ethnic and Racial Studies* 17, no. 2 (1994): 301–24. For the complexities of classification of ethnicity see A.J. Christopher, "Ethnicity, Community and the Census in Mauritius, 1830–1990," *Geographical Journal* 158, no. 1 (1992): 57–64.

226. CO 1036/155 Overpopulation Problems Mauritius, 1954–56.

227. H.C. Brookfield, "Mauritius: Demographic Upsurge and Prospect," *Population Studies* 11, no. 2 (1957): 102–22.

228. Minute by S.J. Moore 7–9–54, CO 1036/155 Overpopulation Problems Mauritius, 1954–56. See Klaus Neumann, "Anxieties in Colonial Mauritius and the Erosion of the White Australia Policy," *Journal of Imperial and Commonwealth History* 32, no. 3 (2004): 1–24.

229. W.J. Coe, High Commissioners Office in Canberra, 16–7–58 to R.J. Johnson at Commonwealth Relations Office, DO 35/10239 Migration from Mauritius to Commonwealth Countries, 1956.

230. Minute by J.H. Robertson 9–3–59, CO 118/13/01 Overpopulation Problems Family Planning in Mauritius, 1957–59.

231. Minute by R. Terrell 14–6–60 CO 859/1444 Population Control Policy, 1960–62.

232. For Britain's entanglement in the politics of ethnicity see Robert Norton, "Accommodating Indigenous Privilege: Britain's Dilemma in Decolonizing Fiji," *Journal of Pacific History* 37, no. 2 (2000): 133–56.

233. Eila Campbell, "Land and Population Problems in Fiji," *Geographical Journal* 118, no. (1952): 477–82.

234. Sir R. Garvey to J.L. Sidebottom 2–26–53, CO 1023/12 Commission of Inquiry to Investigate Population Problems-Fiji, 1952–53.

235. Extract from Fiji Supplementary Report for April 1953, CO 1023/12 Commission of Inquiry to Investigate Population Problems-Fiji, 1952–53.

236. Telegram from governor of Fiji to secretary of state for colonies 7–27-1960, CO 118/1/01 Population Problems Fiji, 1960–62.

237. In addition to Philip Rogers, W.H. Chinn, Richard Terrell, and J.K. Thompson became advocates for a more forward policy. Terrell had served as the secretary of PEP before the war. Richard Terrell, *Civilians in Uniform: A Memoir, 1937–1945* (London: Radcliffe Press, 1998), 1–7.

238. Minute by R. Terrell 14–11–58, CO 1031/2783 Population Problems in Jamaica, 1957–59; Minute by W.H. Chinn 24–6–59, CO 859/1028 Population Control Policy, 1957–59; Minute by R. Terrell 14–6–60, CO 859/1444 Population Control Policy, 1960–62.

239. David Goldsworthy, "Britain and the International Critics of British Colonialism, 1951–56," *Journal of Commonwealth and Comparative Politics* 19, no. 1 (1991): 1–24.

240. John Profumo to Robert Scott 28–7–58, CO 118/13/01 Overpopulation Problems Family Planning in Mauritius, 1957–59.

241. Minute by W. Wallace 24–8–56, CO 1031/1965 Measures to Alleviate the Over-Population Problem in Barbados, 1954–56 Part B.

242. Letter from Lord Privy Seal 7–12–59, CO 859/1028 Population Control Policy, 1957–59.

243. Minute by Hailsham, 5–10–59, CAB 124/2844, World Food Supplies and Population Trends Papers by Professor Sir Solly Zuckerman.

244. Letter from Lord Holme 1–12–59, CO 859/1028 Population Control Policy, 1957–59.

245. Confidential Note of Meeting of ACSP on Population Control 25–1–56, CO 859/666 ACSP: Colonial Population Problems, 1954–56.

246. Zuckerman and the ACSP followed American efforts to develop a birth control pill closely. Minutes of meeting, 1–2–56, CO 859/666: ACSP: Colonial Population Problems, 1954–56.

247. Ibid.

248. Minute by J. Chadwick 8–10–59, DO 35/10175 Australian Immigration with Regard to Asians and Coloured Peoples, 1954–60.

249. CO 1031/3951 Emigration from the West Indies to New Zealand, 1960–62.

250. Jill Briggs, "'As Fool-Proof as Possible': Overpopulation, Colonial Demography and the Jamaican Birth Control League," *The Global South* 4, no. 2 (2010): 57–77, and Nicole Bourbonnais, "'Dangerously Large': The 1938 Labor Rebellion and the Debate over Birth Control in Jamaica," *New West Indian Guide* 83, nos. 1 and 2 (2009): 39–69.

251. Eddie Burke, 6–56, CO 1031/1967 Population Problems in Jamaica, 1954–56.

252. Christopher Tietze and Charles Alleyne, "A Family Planning Service in the West Indies," *Fertility and Sterility* 10, no. 3 (1959): 259–71.

253. This was the argument advanced by D. Smith at the second IPPF conference in 1958, CO 859/1028 Population Control Policy, 1957–59.

254. Copy of letter from Alexander Bustamante, 29–5–59 CO 1031/2783 Population Problems in Jamaica, 1957–59.

255. Extract from the *Barbados Advocate* 15–1–59 CO 1031/2782 Population Problems in British Guiana, 1957–59.

256. Secretary of state's private secretary to W. Sweaney, 29–10–48, CO 318/495/4 Population Problems-West Indies, 1948.

257. Steve Garner, Trevor Munroe, and Arnold Bertram, *Adult Suffrage and Political Administrations in Jamaica, 1944-2002: A Compendium and Commentary* (Kingston, Jamaica: Ian Randle, 2006), 177–78.

258. Minute by N. L. Mayle 31–12–51, CO 1031/953 Report on the Growth of Population and Illegitimacy in Bermuda, 1951–53.

259. P. Rogers to Solly Zuckerman, 23–11–55, SZ/ACSP/24/2, Zuckerman Archives, University of East Anglia; Nancy Astor to Malcolm MacDonald, 1–8–35, CO 37/282/9 Birth Control-Bermuda, 1935.

260. Minute by Mr. Luke 1–1–52, CO 1031/953 Report on the Growth of Population and Illegitimacy in Bermuda, 1951–53.

261. Minute by W. Sweaney 15–3–49, CO 318/495/5 Population Problems-West Indies, 1949.

262. H. L. Gordon, "The Population Problem in a Crown Colony," CO 537/13 Population in East Africa, 1945. For more on Gordon see Chloe Campbell, *Race and Empire: Eugenics in Colonial Kenya* (Manchester: University of Manchester Press, 2007), 39–61.

263. Huxley cited in Lewis, *State Building*, 183; A. R. Patterson, "The Human Situation in East Africa: Part I on the Increase of the People," *East African Medical Journal* 24, no. 2 (1947): 81–97.

264. General Correspondence, Africa, 1952–60, SP/FPA A21/1, FPA Papers, CMAC; CO/859/1026, Population-General Information and Enquiries, 1957–59.

265. Frank Furedi, *Colonial Wars and the Politics of Third World Nationalism* (London: I. B. Tauris, 1994), 91, 111.

266. Unemployment in Malaya, 1930, CO 273/566/2; Emigration from India to Malaya, 1939, CO 273/654/1.

267. For the role of the census and survey see T. N. Harper, *The End of Empire and the Making of Malaya* (Cambridge: Cambridge University Press, 1998), 195–96. Also see Karl Hack, "Screwing Down the People: The Malayan Emergency, Decolonization and Ethnicity," in Hans Antlov and Stein Tonnensson, eds., *Imperial Policy and Southeast Asian Nationalism, 1930–1957* (Richmond, UK: Curzon, 1995), 83–109.

268. Wade Markel, "Draining the Swamp: The British Strategy of Population Control," *Parameters* 36, no. 1 (2006): 35–48. For a contemporary view see E. Dobby, "Resettlement Transforms Malaya: A Case-History of Relocating the Population of an Asian Plural Society," *Economic Development and*

Cultural Change 1, no. 3 (1952): 163–89. As in Africa, authorities used the term *squatter* to mark populations for removal or control.

269. Harper, *End of Empire*, 275–382.

270. Anderson, *Histories of the Hanged*, 122–25, 235–38, 293–97; David Percox, *Britain, Kenya, and the Cold War: Imperial Defense, Colonial Security, and Decolonization* (London: I. B. Tauris, 2004), 60–63, Caroline Elkins, *Imperial Reckoning: The Untold Story of Britain's Gulag in Kenya* (New York: Macmillan, 2005), 103–6, 116–17, 125–30, 265–68.

271. These projects included several long-planned irrigation schemes. The Hola camp, the site of a massacre of detainees, provided labor to one of these projects. William Adams and David Anderson, "Irrigation before Development: Indigenous and Induced Change in Agricultural Water Management in East Africa," *African Affairs* 87, no. 349 (1988): 520; Elkins, *Imperial Reckoning*, 345–46.

272. Anderson, *Histories of the Hanged*, 328–44.

CHAPTER 5

1. David Glass, "The Interpretation of Population Statistics," *Political Quarterly* 15, no.1 (1944): 50–56; R. R. Kuczynski, "World Population Problems," *International Affairs* 20, no. 4 (1944): 449–57.

2. William Beveridge, *Social Insurance and Allied Services* (New York: Macmillan, 1942), 8.

3. For example see George McCleary, *Race Suicide?* (London: Allen & Unwin, 1945).

4. Enid Charles, "Post-War Demographic Problems in Britain," *American Sociological Review* 11, no. 5 (1946): 578–90.

5. The phrase was used by Richard Titmuss, *The Parents Revolt* (London: Secker and Warburg, 1942), 170.

6. R. F. Harrod, *Britain's Future Population* (London: Oxford University Press, 1943), 25–29.

7. Eva Hubback, *The Population of Britain* (London: Penguin, 1947), 227–38.

8. For a discussion of the Royal Commission see Richard Soloway, *Demography and Degeneration* (Chapel Hill: University of North Carolina Press, 1990), 337–50, and Jay Winter, "Population, Economists and the State: The Royal Commission on Population, 1944–49," in Mary Furner and Barry Supple, eds., *The State and Economic Knowledge: The American and British Experiences* (Cambridge: Cambridge University Press, 1990), 436–60.

9. The Fabian Society, *Population and the People: A National Policy* (London: Allen & Unwin, 1945), 42.

10. PEP, *Population Policy in Great Britain: A Report* (London: PEP, 1948), 39–60.

11. Ibid., 119–58.

12. Charles Arden-Close, "Our Crowded Island," *Eugenics Review* 40, no. 1

(1948): 23–31. The article cited a speech by Hugh Dalton on February 27, 1948, that called Britain overpopulated. For public comments on this idea, see the correspondence in *The New Statesman* in March and April 1948 over C. M. Joad's review of Eva Hubback's *The Population of Britain*.

13. *Times*, December 6, 1950.

14. *Population and the People*, 40–41. Harrod agreed with that assessment, *Future Population*, 20–23.

15. CAB 124/1033 Dispersal of Population and Industry throughout the Commonwealth 1947–48. For a discussion of postwar migration policy, see Kathleen Paul, *Whitewashing Britain: Race and Citizenship in the Postwar Era* (Ithaca, NY: Cornell University Press, 1997), 25–63.

16. George McCleary, "Peopling the Dominions," *Contemporary Review* 170 (1946): 280–85.

17. "Population and Empire: Imperial Aspects of Empire," *Round Table* 143 (1946): 254–59. For a more pessimistic assessment see Donald Cowie, "Empires without Men," *Quarterly Review* 555 (1943): 50–73.

18. Brinley Thomas, "Does Our Migration Policy Make Sense," *Political Quarterly* 18, no. 3 (1947): 189–99.

19. Richard Bosworth, "Australia and Assisted Immigration from Britain, 1945–1954," *Australian Journal of Politics and History* 34, no. 2 (1988): 186–200.

20. Draft of Pamphlet by Dudley Barker, 25-4-51, Correspondence, Migration Council Materials 1950–54 SA/EUG D.125, ES Papers, CMAC.

21. Ibid.

22. Reprint from *Sunday Chronicle*, March 25, 1951, Migration Council Materials 1950–54, Correspondence SA/EUG/D127 1953, ES Papers, CMAC.

23. Memo on Government Policy 6-53, Migration Council Materials 1950–54, SA/EUG/D.123 Minutes of Migration Council 1952, ES Papers, CMAC.

24. Paul, *Whitewashing Britain*, 60.

25. For a discussion of these issues see Pat Thane, "Population Politics in the Post-War British Culture," in Becky Conekin, Frank Mort, and Chris Waters, eds., *Moments of Modernity: Reconstructing Britain 1945–1964* (New York: Rivers Oram, 1999), 114–33.

26. The report generated debate during the war. Some demographers, like David Glass, remained agnostic about the implications of these trends during the war, while others, like Robert Kuczynski attacked the White Paper's conclusions and continued to insist on the threat of population decline. Glass, "Population Statistics," 52–55; Kuczynski, "World Population," 452–53; E. Grebenik, "The Quantitative Aspect of the British Population Movement-A Survey," *Review of Economic Studies* 10, no. 1 (1942–43): 43–52.

27. John Hajnal, "Aspects of Recent Trends in Marriage in England and Wales," *Population Studies* 1, no. 1 (1947): 72–98.

28. Royal Commission on Population, *Report* (London: HMSO, 1949), 56–59, 220–21.

29. Frank Notestein, "The Royal Commission on Population: A Review," *Population Studies* 3, no. 3 (1949): 232–40.

30. Glen O'Hara, "'We Are Faced Everywhere with a Growing Population': Demographic Change and the British State, 1955–64," *Twentieth Century British History* 15, no. 3 (2004): 243–66.

31. Memo by C.P. Blacker on Age Distribution of GB in 1972, 12-3-51, Correspondence of C.P. Blacker, Ia 1948–51 SA/EUG C21, ES Papers, CMAC.

32. Royal Commission on Population, *Report*, 226.

33. Mary Stocks, "The Malthusian Devil in Chains," *Political Quarterly* 21, no. 1 (1950): 18.

34. For many, it seemed unclear whether the United States would continue to grow, and estimates varied at the end of the war. See A.J.B., "Population Trends and Power," *International Affairs* 21, no. 1 (1945): 79–86, and Philip Hauser and Conrad Taeuber, "The Changing Population of the United States," *Annals of the American Academy of Political and Social Science* 237 (1945): 12–21. By the late 1940s, however, demographers predicted continuing growth. See Henry Shyrock, "Forecasts of Population in the United States," *Population Studies* 3, no. 4 (1950): 406–12, and Joseph Davis, "Fifty Million More Americans," *Foreign Affairs* 28, no. 7 (1949–50): 412–26.

35. PEP, *Population Policy*, 34–36.

36. PEP, *World Population and Resources* (London: Allen & Unwin, 1955), 311.

37. Ibid., 309.

38. Ibid., 325.

39. The journal *Nature* devoted attention to population, agricultural science, and colonial development in the 1940s and 1950s, See Sir Frank Stockdale's article on "Some Biological Elements of Colonial Development," *Nature* 162, no. 4117 (1948): 476–78.

40. G.C. Bertram, "Population Trends and the World's Resources," *Geographical Journal* 107, no. 5/6 (1946): 191–205; A.V. Hill, "Health, Food and Population in India: The Emergency of the Next Twenty-Five Years," *International Affairs* 21, no. 1 (1945): 40–52.

41. For more on Hill's work in India see G.C. Deepak Kumar, "Reconstructing India: Disunity in the Science and Technology for Development Discourse, 1900–1947," *Osiris* 15, no. 1 (2001): 252–54.

42. Hill, "Health," 45.

43. Karl Sax, *Standing Room Only: The World's Exploding Population*, 2nd ed. (Boston: Beacon, 1960).

44. Garrett Hardin, "The Tragedy of the Commons," *Science* 162, no. 3559 (1968): 1243–48.

45. Garrett Hardin, *Biology: Its Human Implications*, 2nd ed. (San Francisco: W.H. Freeman, 1966), 682–93.

46. *Lancet*, June 14, 1952.

47. His speeches to various Indian organizations are included in his papers in Belfast. See also Sir John Megaw, "Pressure of Population in India,"

Journal of the Royal Society of Arts 87, no. 4491 (1938): 134–57. In addition, he wrote an editorial about the subject for the *Indian Medical Gazette.*

48. Sir John Megaw, *Overpopulation as a World Problem* (London: British Social Hygiene Council, 1947).

49. See John Perkins, *Geopolitics and the Green Revolution: Wheat, Genes and the Cold War* (New York: Oxford University Press 1997) for a discussion of these issues.

50. Joseph Hodge, *Triumph of the Expert: Agrarian Doctrines of Development and the Legacies of British Colonialism* (Athens: Ohio University Press, 2007).

51. For more on British agricultural science in this era, see Perkins, *Green Revolution*, 186–209.

52. Cynthia Brantley, "Kikuyu-Maasai Nutrition and Colonial Science: The Orr and Gilks Study in Late 1920s Kenya Revisited," *International Journal of African Historical Studies* 30, no. 1 (1997): 49–86.

53. John McCormick, *Reclaiming Paradise: The Global Environmental Movement*, (Bloomington: Indiana University Press, 1989), 27–29.

54. John Boyd-Orr, *The White Man's Dilemma: Food and the Future* (London: Allen & Unwin, 1953).

55. John Russell, *World Population and Food Supplies* (London: Allen & Unwin, 1954), 182.

56. Ibid., 245.

57. Ibid., 495–98.

58. For more on the context of their work on agriculture, see Perkins, *Green Revolution*, 131–39.

59. For more on Vogt's and Osborne's relationship to environmentalism see McCormick, *Reclaiming Paradise*, 29–32.

60. William Vogt, *The Road to Survival* (New York: W. Sloane, 1948), 70–71.

61. Ibid., 228, 186.

62. Ibid., 77.

63. See John Wilmoth and Patrick Ball, "The Population Debate in American Popular Magazines, 1946–1990," *Population and Development Review* 18, no. 1 (1992): 631–38.

64. These talks were published as a pamphlet *Man and the Soil* (London: British Council, 1953), edited by Ritchie Calder, an important figure in internationalist and environmental circles and a close friend of Huxley.

65. Julian Huxley, "Population Planning and Quality of Life," *Eugenics Review* 51, no.3 (1959), 149.

66. Solly Zuckerman, *Monkeys, Men and Missiles (1946–1988)* (New York: Norton, 1988), 403–17, and ———, "Environmental Planning for an Increased Population," in Fairfield Osborn, ed., *Our Crowded Planet* (New York: Doubleday, 1962), 109–14. For Nicholson and Huxley's work in establishing the Nature Conservancy see Stephen Bocking, *Ecologists and Environmental*

Politics: A History of Contemporary Politics (New Haven: Yale University Press, 1997), 13–60.

67. Julian Huxley to Myer Cohen Director, Bureau of Operations, UN Special Fund, 4-2-64, Box 36 January–June 1964, Huxley Papers, Woodson Collection, Rice University Library.

68. Horace Herring, "The Conservation Society: Harbinger of the 1970s Environmental Movement in the UK," *Environment and History* 7, no. 4 (2001): 381–401.

69. Edward Goldsmith, Robert Allen, Michael Allaby, John Davoll, and Sam Lawrence, *Blueprint for Survival* (Boston: Houghton Mifflin, 1972).

70. Ian Spencer, *British Immigration Policy since 1939: The Making of Multi-racial Britain* (London: Routledge, 1997), 129–46.

71. William Vogt, *The Road to Survival* (London: Gollancz, 1949), preface.

72. Blacker and Glass entered national service, while Max Nicholson helped direct the Middle East Supply Center. Both LSE and the Eugenics Society moved their operations outside of London.

73. Soloway, *Demography*, 336–62.

74. Bradley Hart, "Watching the 'Eugenic Experiment' Unfold: The Mixed Views of British Eugenicists toward Nazi Germany in the Early 1930s," *Journal of the History of Biology* 45, no. 1 (2012): 33–63.

75. In 1939, C. P. Blacker spoke of the "substantial and indeed remarkable" results of German policy in a letter to Alexander Carr-Saunders. C. Blacker to A. Carr-Saunders, 8-2-39, Alexander Carr Saunders Correspondence, Letters 1933–37, SA/EUG/C. 57 II ES Papers, CMAC.

76. William Beveridge. "The Population Problem," *Political Quarterly* 17, no. 2 (1946): 133–36.

77. See John Thompson, *The Problem of Mental Deficiency: Eugenics, Democracy and Social Policy in Britain c. 1870–1959* (Oxford: Oxford University Press, 1990), 278–84, and Edmund Ramsden, "A Differential Paradox: The Controversy Surrounding the Scottish Mental Surveys of Intelligence and Family Size," *Journal of the History of the Behavioral Sciences* 43, no. 2 (2007): 109–34.

78. For example see Vera Houghton, "The Bombay Conference and Its Aftermath: The Reactions of the Press," *Eugenics Review* 45, no. 1 (1953): 41–43.

79. The Eugenics Society initially suggested this idea in its submission to the Royal Commission on Population in 1945. Memo January 1945, SA/EUG D.185 Evidence for Royal Commission on Population 1943–45, ES Papers, CMAC.

80. Correspondence, Migration Council Materials 1950–1954, SA/EUG D.125, ES Papers, CMAC.

81. Minute by T. C. Jerrom 29-7-57, CO 118/13/01 Overpopulation Problems Family Planning in Mauritius 1957–59.

82. Lord Simon Correspondence, 1952–60, SA/EUG/C 356, ES Papers, CMAC.

83. After his death, he endowed the trust with £15,000, followed by £179,000 after Lady Simon's death in 1972. C. Blacker to Max Nicholson, 14-12-69, Max Nicholson Papers, Correspondence with C. P. Blacker GC/142/2, ES Papers, CMAC.

84. Penny Kane, "The Simon Population Trust: A Brief History," *Journal of Family Planning and Reproductive Health Care* 28, no. 2 (2002) Suppl.

85. C. P. Blacker, "Stages in Population Growth," *Eugenics Review* 39, no. 3 (1947): 88–102. Also see chapter 8, "Stages in Population Growth," in his book *Eugenics: Galton and After* (Cambridge, MA: Harvard University Press, 1952).

86. R. Shattock to C. Blacker, 9–7–53, Correspondence of C. P. Blacker Ia 1948–51 SA/EUG C21, ES Papers, CMAC.

87. Memo by C. Blacker on Birth Control Work and Methods, CAB 124/2843 World Food Supplies and Population Trends, Papers by Professor Zuckerman, 1948–58.

88. Memo from A. Lennox Boyd to R. A. Butler 14-2-58, DO 35/9103 Problem of Over-Population in Certain Commonwealth Countries, 1958–59.

89. Memo by C. Blacker on Age Distribution of Great Britain in 1972, 12-3-51, Correspondence of C. P. Blacker, Ia 1948–51 SA/EUG C21, ES Papers, CAMC.

90. C. Blacker to Frederick Osborn 30–8–56, Correspondence 1956, PP/CPB B 18.1 1956, Blacker Papers, CMAC.

91. C. Blacker to James, 18–1–58, Correspondence of C. P. Blacker, II, 1953–60, SA/EUG C21, ES Papers, CMAC.

92. C. Blacker to E. F. G. Haig, 6–2–57, Correspondence, 1957, PP/CPB/B.18/2, 1957, Blacker Papers, CMAC.

93. For a discussion of Gamble's work see Philip Reilly, *The Surgical Solution: A History of Involuntary Sterilization in the United States* (Baltimore: John Hopkins University Press, 1991), 133–35, and Edward Larson, *Sex, Race and Science: Eugenics in the Deep South* (Baltimore: John Hopkins University Press, 1995), 147–60.

94. C. Blacker to Margaret Sanger, 13–1–54, Correspondence with Margaret Sanger 1922–60, SA/EUG C.304, ES Papers, CMAC.

95. Margaret Sanger to C. Blacker, 1–18–54; C. Blacker to Margaret Sanger, 29–1–54, Correspondence of C. P. Blacker II 1953–60, SA/EUG C21, ES Papers, CMAC.

96. For Carr-Saunders's career at LSE see Ralf Dahrendorf, *LSE: A History of the London School of Economics and Political Science, 1895–1995* (Oxford: Oxford University Press, 1995), 337–97.

97. For example, officials consulted him about Singapore in 1951, fifty-sixth meeting of the CSSRC, 13–2–51, CO 901/10 CSSRC Minutes and Papers 1951 Meetings 56–59.

98. See Michael Carder and Richard Symonds, *The United Nations and the Population Question, 1945-1970* (New York: McGraw Hill, 1973), 33–66.

99. Clipping of December 16, 1961, Julian Huxley on the radio show, *I Remember*, Correspondence with Julian Huxley, 1950–65, SA/FPA/A14/47.2,

FPA Papers, CMAC. For a discussion of Huxley's views on race and population control, see Garland Allen, "Julian Huxley and the Eugenical View of Human Evolution," in C. Kenneth Water and Albert Van Helden, eds., *Julian Huxley: Biologist and Statesman of Science* (Houston: Rice University Press, 1992), 193–222.

100. Unpublished letter by Julian Huxley to the *Times*, dated December, 19, 1959, ibid.

101. Nicholas Deakin, "Besieging Jericho: Episodes from the Early Career of Francois Lafitte, 1931–1945," *Cercles, Occasion Papers* (2004): 1–28.

102. Ann Oakley, "Eugenics, Social Medicine and the Career of Richard Titmuss in Britain 1935–1950," *British Journal of Sociology* 42, no. 2 (1991): 165–94.

103. Richard Titmuss and Brian Abel-Smith, *Social Policies and Population Growth in Mauritius* (London: Methuen, 1961).

104. Proposal by Eugenics Society to Form Population Policies Committee with PEP, 1368/38/Pop 23/3/38, PEP February–June 1938 PWS 1/1 PEP Papers, LSE Archives.

105. Obituary, Sir Geoffrey Wilson, *The Independent*, March 4, 2004. http://www.independent.co.uk/news/obituaries/sir-geoffrey-wilson-550114.html.

106. For Zuckerman's life and career see Bernard Donovan, *Zuckerman: Scientist Extraordinary* (Bristol, UK: Bradley Stoke, 2005) as well as his own two-volume autobiography, *From Apes to Warlords (1904–1946)* (London: Hamilton, 1978) and *Monkeys, Men and Missiles (1946–1988)* (New York: Norton, 1988).

107. Solly Zuckerman to Julian Huxley, 12-12-55, SZ/Gen/50 Julian Huxley, Zuckerman Archives, University of East Anglia.

108. Despite government support for the conference, the Colonial Office declined to pay for Zuckerman's attendance because of his well-known advocacy of birth control. Zuckerman, who attended as an observer, suffered from the heat and spent most of the conference drinking and swimming with Robert Snider at the American naval base in Trinidad. Zuckerman, *Monkeys, Men and Missiles*, 141–44.

109. Solly Zuckerman to Robert Snider, 29-3-57, SZ/CF/4/1 Correspondence with Robert Snider, Zuckerman Archives, University of East Anglia.

110. Zuckerman, *Monkeys, Men and Missiles*, 135–41.

111. Solly Zuckerman to Lord Simon 5-12-53 SZ/ACSP/24/10, Zuckerman Archives, University of East Anglia. See also his paper for the ACSP "The Scale of Research into Ideal Methods of Birth Control," May 1954, SZ PEP/2/3 Documents, Zuckerman Archives, University of East Anglia.

112. Minutes of Meeting of Advisory Council on Scientific Policy 1-2-56, CO 859/666 ACSP: Colonial Population Problems, 1954–56.

113. For the international context of the IPPF's work see Matthew Connelly, *Fatal Misconception: The Struggle to Control World Population* (Cambridge, MA: Harvard University Press 2008), 177–90.

114. Firoze Manju and Carl O'Coil, "The Missionary Position: NGOs and Development in Africa," *International Affairs* 78, no. 3 (2003): 567–83.

115. John Hailey, "Ladybirds, Missionaries and NGOs: Voluntary Organizations and Co-operatives in 50 Years of Development: A Historical Perspective on Future Challenges," *Public Administration and Development* 19, no. 5 (1999): 467–86; John Stuart, "Overseas Mission, Voluntary Service and Aid to Africa: Max Warren, the Church Missionary Society and Kenya, 1945–1963," *Journal of Imperial and Commonwealth History* 36, no. 3 (2008): 527–43.

116. Audrey Leathard, *The Fight for Family Planning* (London: Macmillan, 1980), 78–234.

117. The only comprehensive history of the IPPF is Beryl Suitters, *Be Brave and Angry: Chronicles of the International Planned Parenthood Federation* (London: International Planned Parenthood Federation, 1973).

118. Ibid., 38–40. In addition, the society gave £250 a year.

119. Lord Simon gave £1,000; George Cadbury gave £300, as well as £2,400 for work in Jamaica. Report by Vera Houghton 15–6–56, International Planned Parenthood Federation, General Correspondence Files, 1954-57, SA/FPA A10/2A, FPA Papers, CMAC.

120. Chair of FPA to Captain Oliver Bird, 17–9–56, ibid.

121. Fundraising Appeal 14–6–56, ibid.

122. Suitters, *Be Brave*, 60–63, 80–84, 115–16, 135–41, 151–54.

123. General Correspondence-Africa, 1952–60 SA/FPA A21/1, FPA Papers, CMAC. Also Suitters, *Be Brave*, 136–41.

124. Barbara Brown, "Facing the 'Black Peril': The Politics of Population Control in South Africa," *Journal of Southern African Studies* 13, no. 2 (1987): 256–73; Michael White, "Nationalism, Race and Gender: The Politics of Family Planning in Zimbabwe, 1957–1990," *Social History of Medicine* 7, no. 3 (1994): 447–71; Amy Kaler, *Running after Pills: Politics, Gender, and Contraception in Colonial Zimbabwe* (Portsmouth, NH: Heinemann, 2003), 43–56.

125. Report of Conversation of Mrs. Pyke with Mrs. Medawar and Brooks 15–7–57; N. L. Wintersgill to Dr. Beric Wright Trinidad. 22–1–58; Correspondence with West Indian Welfare Service, 1950–63, SA/FPA A21/26, FPA Papers, CMAC.

126. De Souza attended the Caribbean Commission Conference on the Demographic Problems of the West Indies in 1957 along with Solly Zuckerman. Minute by J. Thompson 6–6–57, CO 1031/2096 The Caribbean Commission Conference on Demographic Problems in the Caribbean Area, 1957–59.

127. J. E. Fraser of West Indies High Commission Office of Migrant Welfare Service to FPA, 26–5–59, Correspondence with West Indian Welfare Service 1950–63, SA/FPA A21/26, FPA Papers, CMAC.

128. Edith How-Martyn to Margaret Sanger, 10–10–30, Box 21, Reel 14, Sanger Papers, Library of Congress Collection.

129. From January 1 to August 31, 1954, the FPA trained fourteen overseas doctors and ten overseas nurses. In 1955, thirty-one doctors and six

nurses gained FPA certificates. Up to the end of November 1956, thirty-three doctors and ten nurses had taken courses. Memo 28-6-58, International Planned Parenthood Federation, General Correspondence Files,1954-57, SA/FPA, A10/2/A; Memo 12-3-58, International Planned Parenthood Federation, General Correspondence Files, 1954–57, SA/FPA A10/2 B, FPA Papers, CMAC.

130. H.A. Sandiford to secretary of FPA 14-9-51, Correspondence with Empire Medical Advisory Bureau, 1951–52, SA/FPA A/13/18, FPA Papers, CMAC.

131. Eleanor Mears to J. Thompson 19-6-58, Correspondence with the Colonial Office, 1957–64, SA/FPA 293/A8/9, FPA Papers, CMAC.

132. Notes on 28/29 November conference in Edinburgh, ibid.

133. See Richard Soloway, "The 'Perfect Contraceptive': Eugenics and Birth Control Research in Britain and America in the Inter-war Years," *Journal of Contemporary History* 30, no. 4 (1995): 637–64.

134. These questions were first raised in the 1930s and continued into the 1950s. Meeting of BCIC 4–5–38, BCIC Committee Papers and Minutes 1937–39, SA/FPA A13/5M, FPA Papers, CMAC; Mrs. Clifford Smith to Solly Zuckerman 11-9-56, SZ/FPA/1 Correspondence 1956–92, Zuckerman Archives, University of East Anglia. For its use in Africa see Report of the Bulawayo FPA in Southern Rhodesia, January 1960, General Correspondence-Africa 1952–60, SA/FPA A21/1, FPA Papers, CMAC.

135. Mary Calderone to Vera Houghton 12-5-58, CO 1031/2785 Population Problems in the Leeward Islands, 1957–59.

136. Connelly, *Fatal Misconception*, 175–76, 200–205.

137. Suitters, *Be Brave*, 105–9.

138. FPA to Lord Simon 23-10-56, SA/FPA A14/82 Correspondence with Lord Simon, FPA Papers, CMAC; Eleanor Mears to J. Thompson 19-6-58, Correspondence with the Colonial Office 1957–64. SA/FPA 293/A8/9, FPA Papers, CMAC.

139. Laura Marks, *Sexual Chemistry: A History of the Contraceptive Pill* (New Haven: Yale University Press, 2001).

140. Eleanor Mears to J. Buchanan 4-11-59 Correspondence with the Colonial Office 1957–64, SA/FPA 293/A8/9, SA/FPA 293/A8/9, FPA Papers, CMAC.

141. Marks, *Sexual Chemistry*, 183–215.

142. Stephen Brooke, *Sexual Politics: Sexuality, Family Planning, and the British Left from the 1880s to the Present Day* (Oxford: Oxford University Press, 2011), 135, 164–67.

143. Note from J. Thompson, 9-12-57, CO 859/1026 Population-General Information and Enquiries, 1957–59.

144. Jean Gearing, "Family Planning in St. Vincent, West Indies: A Population History Perspective," *Social Science and Medicine* 35, no. 10 (1992), 1273–82. For Barbados see Christopher Tietze and Charles Alleyne, "A Family

Planning Service in the West Indies," *Fertility and Sterility* 10, no. 3 (1959): 259–71.

145. Confidential letter from Sir John Macpherson to Wolfson Trust 21-5-59, Correspondence with the Colonial Office 1957–64, SA/FPA 293/A8/9, FPA Papers, CMAC.

146. The Colonial Office turned down this request despite support from senior officials. Colonial Office to Mrs. Clifford 3–1–60, CO 859/1028 Population Control Policy 1957–59; Note of Interview at Colonial Office 4–8–60, Correspondence with the Colonial Office 1957–64, SA/FPA 293/A8/9, FPA Papers, CMAC.

147. Eugene Grebenik, "Demographic Research in Britain," *Population Studies* 45, Suppl. (1991), 18–23; Edward Higgs, *The Information State in England* (London: Macmillan Palgrave, 2004), 133–67; Jay Winter, "Population, Economists and the State: The Royal Commission on Population, 1944–49," in Mary Furner and Barry Supple, eds., *The State and Economic Knowledge: The American and British Experiences* (Cambridge: Cambridge University Press, 1990), 436–60. For this expansion as part of a larger process see David Edgerton, *Warfare State, Britain, 1920–1970* (Cambridge: Cambridge University Press, 2006), 145–90.

148. Muriel Nissel, *People Count: A History of the General Register Office* (London: HMSO, 1987), 136–38.

149. CAB 139/394 Estimates of future population Pt. 1, 1947–60.

150. Desmond King, "The Politics of Social Research: Institutionalizing Public Funding Regimes in the United States and Great Britain," *British Journal of Political Science* 28, no. 3 (1998): 415–44; Cyril Smith, "Networks of Influence: The Social Sciences in the United Kingdom since the War," in Peter Wagner et al., eds., *Social Sciences and Modern States* (Cambridge: Cambridge University Press, 1991), 131–47; Michael Savage, *Identities and Social Change in Britain since 1940: The Politics of Method* (Oxford: Oxford University Press, 2010), 51–134.

151. Grebenik, "Demographic Research," 18–20.

152. Glass called him the worst student he had ever had. Minute by A. E. Robertson, Overseas Development (OD) 27/128 Possible British Assistance to Family Planning Programme in India, 1967–69, National Archives.

153. Chris Langford, *The Population Investigation Committee* (London: Population Investigation Committee, 1988).

154. Kingsley Davis, "The World Demographic Transition," *Annals of the American Academy of Political and Social Science* 237 (1945): 1–11; Frank Notestein, "Population: The Long View," in Theodore Schultz, ed., *Food for the World* (Chicago: University of Chicago Press, 1945), 36–57.

155. Dennis Hodgson, "Orthodoxy and Revisionism in American Demography," *Population and Development Review* 14, no. 4 (1988): 541–69; Simon Szreter, "The Idea of the Demographic Transition and the Study of Fertility Change: A Critical Intellectual History," *Population and Development Review* 19, no. 4 (1993): 659–701; Susan Greenhalgh, "The Social Construction of

Population Science," *Comparative Studies in Society and History* 38, no. 1 (1996): 26–65.

156. Michael Latham, *The Right Kind of Revolution: Modernization and U.S. Foreign Policy from the Cold War to the Present* (Ithaca, NY: Cornell University Press, 2010), 36–64, 95–109, and Mark Berger, "Decolonization, Modernization and Nation Building: Political Development Theory and the Appeal of Communism in Southeast Asia, 1945–1975," *Journal of Southeast Asian Studies* 34, no. 3 (2003): 421–48.

157. Ibid., 431–34.

158. Frank Notestein, "Problems of Policy in Relations to Areas of Heavy Population Pressure," *Milbank Memorial Fund Quarterly* 22, no. 4 (1944): 424–44. This was one of a series by Notestein, Kingsley Davis, Warren Thompson, Irene Tauber, and Frank Lorimer published in the July 1944 and October 1944 volumes of the *Milbank Memorial Fund Quarterly* and in *The Annals of the Academy of Political and Social Science* 237 (1945).

159. Dennis Hodgson, "Demography as Social Science and Policy Science," *Population and Development Review* 9, no. 1 (1983): 1–33; Szreter, "The Idea of the Demographic Transition," 675–82; Frank Furedi, *Population and Development: A Critical Introduction* (New York: St. Martins, 1997).

160. See James Reed, *From Private Vice to Public Virtue: The Birth Control Movement and American Society since 1830* (New York: Basic Books, 1979), 97–128.

161. Jennifer Gunn, "A Few Good Men: The Rockefeller Approach to Population, 1911–1936," in Theresa Richardson and Donald Fisher, eds., *The Development of the Social Sciences in the United States and Canada: The Role of Philanthropy* (Stamford, CT: Ablex, 1999), 97–114.

162. John Sharpless, "Population Science, Private Foundations and Development Aid," in Frederick Cooper and Randall Packard, eds., *International Development and the Social Sciences* (Berkeley: University of California Press, 1997), 176–200.

163. John Harr and Peter Johnson, *The Rockefeller Century* (New York: Scribner, 1988), 368–69, 452–67.

164. See John Caldwell and Pat Caldwell, *Limiting Population Growth and the Ford Foundation Contribution* (London and Dover, NH: F. Pinter, 1986).

165. It also generated the occasional spasm of envy, as reflected in David Glass's description of Kingsley Davis as a crude empire builder. Minute by W. F. Searle 27–9–54, CO 1031/1971 Conference on the Problems of Population and Public Health in the Caribbean, 1954–56.

166. Dennis Hodgson, "The Ideological Origins of the Population Association of America," *Population and Development Review* 17, no. 1 (1991): 1–34; Szreter, "The Idea of the Demographic Transition," 663–67.

167. Edmund Ramsden, "Frank W. Notestein, Frederick H. Osborn, and the Development of Demography in the United States," *Princeton Library Review* 65, no. 2 (2004), 293.

168. Gamble's work both inside and outside the United States proved

awkward, and his insistence of going his own way without consulting local organizations created tensions in the population movement. For Gamble's relationship to the larger movement see Reed, *From Private Vice*, 225–77.

169. Ibid., 294–306.

170. Ibid., 308–12. For U.S. work in Puerto Rico see Annette Ramierez de Arellano and Conrad Seipp, *Colonialism, Catholicism, and Contraception: A History of Birth Control in Puerto Rico* (Chapel Hill: University of North Carolina Press, 1983) and Laura Briggs, *Reproducing Empire: Race, Sex, Science, and U.S. Imperialism in Puerto Rico* (Berkeley: University of California Press, 2002). For the perceived racial threat posed by Filipino migration to the United States see Paul Kramer, *The Blood of Government: Race, Empire, the United States and the Philippines* (Chapel Hill: University of North Carolina Pres, 2006), 397–418.

171. Demographers also offered briefings to officials and military leaders, such as Frank Lorimer's talk to the Industrial College of the Armed Forces in March 1947. "Changing Patterns of Economic Potential for War –Population," The Industrial College of the Armed Forces, Publication Number L-47-98.

172. Harr and Johnson, *The Rockefeller Century*, 462–63. The group published its report under the title *Public Health and Demography in the Far East* in 1950. For MacArthur's attitude see Ellen Chesler, *Woman of Valor: Margaret Sanger and the Birth Control Movement in America* (New York: Simon & Schuster, 1992), 421–22.

173. Michael Hogan, *The Marshall Plan: America, Britain, and the Reconstruction of Western Europe, 1947-1952* (Cambridge: Cambridge University Press, 1987) and Vernon Rutton, *United States Development Assistance Policy: The Domestic Politics of Foreign Economic Aid* (Baltimore: John Hopkins University Press, 1996).

174. For example, see Eugene Staley, *The Future of Underdeveloped Countries: The Political Implications of Economic Development* (New York: Harper, 1954), 273–85. The Council on Foreign Relations published the book.

175. John Sharpless, "World Population Growth, Family Planning, and American Foreign Policy," *Journal of Policy History* 7, no. 1 (1995): 72–102.

176. Caldwell and Caldwell, *Ford Foundation*, 48–49; Peter Donaldson, *Nature against Us: The United States and the World Population Crisis, 1965-1980* (Chapel Hill: University of North Carolina Press, 1990), 22–25; Oscar Harkavy, *Curbing Population Growth: An Insider's Perspective on the Population Movement* (New York: Plenum, 1995), 33–37.

177. For J.D. Rockefeller's role see John Harr and Peter Johnson, *The Rockefeller Conscience: An American Family in Public and Private Life* (New York: Scribner, 1991), 31–45, 159–63.

178. The Ford Foundation alone contributed $88.9 million to population programs from 1952 to 1967. Harkavy, *Curbing Population Growth*, 37. See also Caldwell and Caldwell, *Ford Foundation*, 52–76.

179. Minutes of ACSP meeting 2-1-56, CO 859/666, ACSP: Colonial Population Problems 1954-56.

180. Minutes, fifty-third meeting, 16-3-54, Nuffield Foundation, held by the Nuffield Foundation.

181. Confidential Note of Meeting of ACSP on Population Control 25-1-56, CO/859/666 ACSP: Colonial Population Problems, 1954-56.

182. Solly Zuckerman to Alan Lennox-Boyd, 2-17-58, CAB 124/2843 World Food Supplies and Population Trends, Papers by Professor Zuckerman, 1948-58.

183. Linda Gordon, *The Moral Property of Women* (Chicago: University of Illinois Press, 2002); Ruth Dixon-Mueller, *Population Policy and Women's Rights: Transforming Reproductive Choice* (Westport, CT: Praeger, 1993); Betsy Hartmann, *Reproductive Rights and Wrongs: The Global Politics of Population Control* (Boston: South End Press, 1995); Dennis Hodgson and Susan Watkins, "Feminists and Neo-Malthusians: Past and Present Alliances," *Population and Development Review* 23, no. 3 (1997): 469-523; Helen Simons, "Cairo: Repackaging Population Control," *International Journal of Health Services* 25, no. 3 (1995): 559-66.

184. Richard Soloway, "Perfecting the Imperfect: The Eugenic Origins of Genetic Engineering," the 2005 E.M. Adams Lecture on the Humanities and Human Values, October 2005, Programs in the Humanities and Human Values; Diane Paul, "Eugenic Origins of Medical Genetics," in *The Politics of Heredity: Essays on Eugenics, Biomedicine, and the Nature-Nurture Debate* (Albany: State University of New York Press, 1998), 133-56; Edmund Ramsden, "Eugenics from the New Deal to the Great Society: Genetics, Demography and Population Quality," *Studies in the History and Philosophy of the Biological and Biomedical Sciences* 39 (2008): 391-406. For the use of eugenics as a means of attacking the goals of the family planning movement see Angela Franks, *Margaret Sanger's Eugenic Legacy: The Control of Female Fertility* (Jefferson, NC: McFarland, 2011) and Ann Farmer, *By Their Fruits: Eugenics, Population Control and the Abortion Campaign* (Washington, DC: Catholic University Press, 2008).

CHAPTER 6

1. Jim Tomlinson, "The Commonwealth, the Balance of Payments and the Politics of International Poverty: British Aid Policy, 1958-1971," *Contemporary European History* 12, no. 4 (2003): 413-29.

2. D.J. Morgan, *The Official History of Colonial Development*, vol.3: *A Reassessment of British Aid Policy* (Atlantic Highlands, NJ: Humanities Press, 1980), 236-70; vol. 4: *Changes in British Aid Policy* (Atlantic Highlands, NJ: Humanities Press, 1980), 13-32.

3. He produced a book on the subject for the left-wing publisher Victor Gollancz. Harold Wilson, *The War on World Poverty: An Appeal to the Conscience of Mankind* (London: Gollancz, 1953); Paul Streeten, "Balogh, Thomas, Baron Balogh (1905-1985)," in H.C.G. Matthew and Brian Harrison, eds.,

Oxford Dictionary of National Biography rev ed. (Oxford: Oxford University Press, 2004). http://www.oxforddnb.com/view/article/30788.

4. Anthony Kirk-Greene, "Decolonization: The Ultimate Diaspora," *Journal of Contemporary History* 36, no. 1 (2001): 133–51.

5. John Toye, "Herbert Frankel: From Colonial Economics to Development Economics," *Oxford Development Studies* 37, no. 2 (2009): 175–79. The South African industrialist Ernest Oppenheimer contributed £100,000.

6. D.K. Fieldhouse, "The Cambridge Development Conferences, 1963–1970," *Journal of Imperial and Commonwealth History* 16, no. 2 (1988): 173–99.

7. Lord Balogh, "Bilateral Aid," in Ronald Robinson, ed., *Developing the Third World: The Experiences of the Nineteen Sixties* (Cambridge: Cambridge University Press, 1971), 242–45.

8. A.H. Kirk-Greene. "Public Administration and the Colonial Administrator," *Public Administration and Development* 19, no. 5 (1999): 507–19.

9. Kirk-Greene, "Decolonization," 133–51.

10. Uma Kothari, "From Colonialism to Development: Reflections of Former Colonial Officers," *Commonwealth and Comparative Politics* 44, no. 1 (2006): 118–36.

11. Joseph Hodge, *Triumph of the Expert: Agrarian Doctrines of Development and the Legacies of British Colonialism* (Athens: Ohio University Press, 2007), 254–62; Catherine Watson, "Working at the World Bank," in Teresa Hayter and Catherine Watson, eds., *Aid: Rhetoric and Reality* (London: Pluto, 1985), 271–74.

12. Balogh, "Bilateral Aid," 232.

13. Minute by A. Cohen 16-4-63, OD 10/32, DTC, Population Control Policy, 1961–63, Part A.

14. Minute by T.B. Williamson 11-1-61, ibid.

15. Minute by A. Cohen 13-1-67, OD 25/233 Population Control Cooperation with IPPF Part A, 1967–69.

16. OD29/46, Population Control Advisory Panel on Family Planning, 1964–66.

17. Draft Memo on Population Policy and UK Aid by R.H. Cassen, OD 25/222 Population Control General Policy Part A, 1967–69.

18. OD 25/233 Population Control Cooperation with IPPF Part A, 1967–69; OD 62/59 Cooperation with IPPF, 1973–75.

19. OD 29/46 Population Control Advisory Panel on Family Planning, 1964–66.

20. By 1972, the British gave £350,000 to the IPPF. British Official Aid for Family Planning and Population Activities, 26-1-71, CAB 134/3705 Official Committee on Future World Trends Sub Committee on Population, 1973.

21. Note of meeting held 11-5-63, DTC, OD 10/33 Population Control Policy DT, Social Development Department, 1961–63.

22. P. Hewlett to W.J. Smith 26-3-64, OD 10 146 Population Control: India Part A, 1964–66.

23. Tomlinson, "British Aid Policy," 425–26.

24. J.T. Thompson to K.C. Christofas at Aid Department of Commonwealth Office 28-2-67, FCO 49/25 Planning Committee The Population Crisis second meeting 18-1-67.

25. Minute by A. Cohen 29-6-67, OD 25/223 Population Control General Policy, 1967-69 Part B.

26. Minute by E.M. West 23-8-67, OD 25/223 Population Control General Policy, 1967-69 Part B.

27. A. Cohen to Sir Paul Gore-Booth 22-5-67, FCO 49/25 Planning Committee The Population Crisis second meeting 18-1-67.

28. K.C. Christofas to J.A. Thompson 17-4-67, ibid.

29. F.E. Bland to J.E. Powell Jones at FO 13-12-65, OD 29/45 Population Control International Policy, 1964-66.

30. Confidential memo by Burke Trend 14-2-68, OD 32/48 Committee on World Population, 1967-69.

31. First Report of World Population Committee, ibid.

32. Minute by G.M. Wilson, 5-16-69, OD 25/225 Committee on World Population Correspondence and Draft Papers, 1967-69.

33. The United States had similar concerns. See Peter Donaldson, *Nature against Us: The United States and the World Population Crisis, 1965-1980* (Chapel Hill: University of North Carolina Press, 1990), 43.

34. Minute by G.M. Wilson 26-7-67, OD 25/237 Population Control UN Fund for Population Activities, 1967-69.

35. Minute by N. Leach 7-7-69, OD 43/3 British Government Aid on Family Planning, 1968-71.

36. The IPPF would receive £350,000 and the UNFPA £450,000. Aid for Family Planning, OD 43/3 British Government Aid on Family Planning, 1965-70; British Official Aid for Family Planning and Population Activities, 26-1-71, CAB 134/3705 Official Committee on Future World Trends Sub Committee on Population, 1973.

37. ODM 25/241 Population Control Proposed Population Bureau Part A, 1967-69.

38. Minute by J.D. Anderson 3-7-68, OD 25/242 Population Control Proposed Population Bureau Part B, 1967-69.

39. Eugene Grebenik, "Demographic Research in Britain 1936-1986," *Population Studies* 45, Suppl. (1991), 22.

40. Memo by D. Wolfers 24-1-69, OD 43/1 Population Bureau General Policy, 1968-71.

41. Lena Jeger, "The Politics of Family Planning, "*Political Quarterly* 33, no. 1 (1962): 48-58.

42. Minute by D. Wolfers, 23-3-71, OD 43/2 Population Bureau, 1968-71.

43. CAB 134/3669 Population Panel, 1973.

44. K. George to D. Wolfers 15-9-69, FCO 44/146 West Indies: Committee on World Population, 1969.

45. Philip Rogers to Sir Burke Trend at Cabinet Office, 10-12-70, CAB 168/241 Population Control, 1969-71.

46. Draft Brief for Lord Hailsham, CO 859/1444 Population Control Policy, 1960–62.
47. Minute by W. Wallace 3–1–61, CO 1030/1347 Family Planning Hong Kong, 1960–62.
48. Sir Robert Black to W. Wallace 22–2–61, ibid.
49. F. E. Bland to R. Jones, 22–11–65, OD 29/46 Population Control Advisory Panel on Family Planning, 1964–66.
50. Summary of Requests for U.K. Technical Assistance in the Field of Family Planning as of 1–2–67, OD 25/222 Population Control General Policy Part A, 1967–69.
51. British Aid for Population Activities and Family Planning, OD 62/59 Cooperation with IPPF, 1973–75.
52. Letter from Geoffrey Wilson, director of Bureau for Technical Cooperation, in South and South East Asia, Colombo, Ceylon, 3–9–51, PEP PWS 8/5 1951–54, PEP papers, LSE Archives.
53. Solly Zuckerman to Malcolm MacDonald, high commissioner in New Delhi 2–4–57, DO 35/5770 Colombo Plan Assistance for Research into Birth Control Question in India, 1957.
54. V. C. Martin to H. Rumbold 12–7–57; Thompson to B. R. Curson at Commonwealth Relations Office 25–7–57, ibid.
55. Internal Memo on Family Planning by E. A. Midgley, OD 10 146, Population Control: India Part A, 1964–66.
56. B. K. Sheorey, medical advisor to High Commission of India to FPA, 25–3–60, correspondence with High Commission of India 1954–62, SA/FPA A21/11, FPA Papers, CMAC; Summary of Requests for U.K. Technical Assistance in the Field of Family Planning as of 1–2–67, OD 25/222 Population Control General Policy Part A, 1967–69.
57. Donald Lublin of IPPF to Energy Ministry, 4–2–74, OD 62/59 Cooperation with IPPF, 1973–75.
58. Internal Memo on Family Planning by E. A. Midgley, OD 10/146 Population Control: India Part A, 1964–66.
59. Solly Zuckerman suggested £2 million for India alone. Minutes of meeting held 25–9–69, OD 27/221 Population Control General Family Planning Programme for South Asia, 1967–69.
60. Eric William 5–18–67 to IPPF, OD 24/230 Population Control Trinidad and Tobago A, 1967–69.
61. Draft memo on population policy and UK aid by R. H. Cassen, OD 25/222 Population Control General Policy Part A, 1967–69.
62. Brief for Economic Commission for Africa Eighth Session Lagos February 1967, OD 25/222 Population Control General Policy Part A, 1967–69.
63. In addition to Kenya, Malawi, Gambia, and Ghana received aid. OD 30/312 Family Planning the Gambia, 1970–72.
64. Howard White, "British Aid and the White Paper on International Development: Dressing a Wolf in Sheep's Clothing in the Emperor's New Clothes?" *Journal of International Development* 10, no. (1998), 152–55; Owen

Barder, "Reforming Development Assistance: Lessons from the U.K. Experience," in Lael Brainard, ed., *Security by Other Means: Foreign Assistance, Global Poverty and American Leadership* (Washington, DC: Brookings Institute, 2007), 278–85.

65. OD 25/225 Ministry of Overseas Development Natural Resources, FAO and Voluntary Organizations Department, Population Control Committee on World Population Correspondence and Draft Papers, 1967–69.

66. John C. Caldwell and Pat Caldwell, *Limiting Population Growth and the Ford Foundation Contribution* (London: F. Pinter, 1986), 98–107; Oscar Harkavy, *Curbing Population Growth: An Insider's Perspective on the Population Movement* (New York: Plenum, 1995), 46–50; Donaldson, *Nature*, 31–52.

67. For a discussion of British attitudes to the United Nations see David Goldsworthy, "'Britain and the International Critics of British Colonialism, 1951–56,'" *Journal of Commonwealth and Comparative Politics* 19, no. 1 (1991), 6–7.

68. Memo from Colonial Office, undated, CO 927/72/1, Demography and Census-UNESCO-Population Commission, 1946–48.

69. Minute by A. N. Galsworthy 27–11–47, CO 927/72/2 Demography and Census UN Economic and Social Council Population Commission, 1946–47.

70. Note on Land Distribution in the African Territories, CO 936/46/1 Special Committee on Information Submitted by NSGT Land Distribution, 1951.

71. Minute by P. Rogers 19–5–51, ibid.

72. Michael Carder and Richard Symonds, *The United Nations and the Population Question, 1945-1970* (New York: McGraw Hill, 1973), 69–88.

73. FO 371/153387 Roman Church Attitudes to BC, 1960.

74. Minute by W. J. Smith 11–1–61, OD 10/32 DT C, Social Development, Population Control Policy, 1961–63.

75. Minute by D. M. Kitching 25–3–64, File UN S 1824/2, FO 371/178333 UN Department Population Increase.

76. P. W. Dill-Russell to P. Lee 20–4–64, OD 10/143 Population Control Policy, 1964–66.

77. W. Whyte to Powell Jones 5–8–64, File UNS 1824/3, FO 371/178333 UN Department Population Increase.

78. Stanley Johnson, *World Population and the United Nations: Challenge and Response* (Cambridge: Cambridge University Press, 1987), 14–33.

79. Minute by A. Cohen 28–7–67, OD 25/237 Population Control UN Fund for Population Activities, 1967–69.

80. Minute by Joan Chapman, OD 62/68 Review of Population Aid Policy, 1973–75.

81. Joseph Hodges, "Colonial Expertise, Post-Colonial Careering and the Early History of International Development," *Journal of Modern European History* 8, no. 1 (2010): 24–46.

82. Brian Urquhart, "Owen, Sir (Arthur) David Kemp (1904–1970)," in H. C. G. Matthew and Brian Harrison, eds., *Oxford Dictionary of National*

Biography, rev. ed. (Oxford: Oxford University Press, 2004). http://www.oxforddnb.com/view/article/35346.

83. Johnson, *World Population*, 48–49.

84. Obituary, Sir Geoffrey Wilson, *The Independent*, March 4, 2004. http://www.independent.co.uk/news/obituaries/sir-geoffrey-wilson-550114.html.

CONCLUSION

1. For a perspective from the left see Tom Nairn, *The Breakup of Britain* (London: New Left Books, 1977).

2. See Ian Spencer, *British Immigration Policy since 1939: The Making of Multi-racial Britain* (London: Routledge, 1997); Zig Layton-Henry, *The Politics of Immigration: Immigration, "Race" and "Race" Relations in Post-War Britain* (Oxford: Blackwell, 1992); Kathleen Paul, *Whitewashing Britain: Race and Citizenship in Post-War Britain* (Ithaca, NY: Cornell University Press, 1997); Randall Hansen, *Citizenship and immigration in Post-War Britain* (Oxford: Oxford University Press, 2000); James Hampshire, *Citizenship and Belonging: Immigration and the Politics of Demographic Governance in Post-War Britain* (London: Palgrave Macmillan, 2005).

3. See Chris Waters, "'Dark Strangers' in Our Midst: Discourses of Race and Nation in Britain, 1947–1963," *Journal of British Studies* 36, no. 2 (1997): 207–38.

4. Mary Hickman, "Reconstructing Deconstructing 'Race': British Political Discourses about the Irish in Britain," *Ethnic and Racial Studies* 21, no. 2 (1998): 289–307, and David Feldman, "The Importance of Being English: Jewish Immigration and the Decay of Liberal England," in David Feldman and Gareth Stedman Jones, eds., *Metropolis-London: Histories and Representations since 1800* (London: Routledge, 1989), 56–84. For an overview on ethnicity in Britain see Paul Ward, *Britishness since 1870* (London: Routledge, 2004), 113–23.

5. Bill Schwarz, "'The Only White Man in There': The Re-racialization of England, 1956–1968," *Race and Class* 38, no.1 (1996): 65–78, and ——,"Reveries of Race: The Closing of the Imperial Moment," in Becky Conekin, Frank Mort, and Chris Waters, eds., *Moments of Modernity: Reconstructing Britain 1945-1964* (New York: Rivers Oram, 1999), 189–207.

6. The term "New Commonwealth" referred to the former colonies in Asia, Africa, and the Caribbean that joined the Commonwealth after 1945. Elspeth Huxley, *Back Streets, New Worlds: A Look at Immigrants in Britain* (London: Chatto & Windus, 1964); Elspeth Huxley to Edith How-Martyn, 8–9-48, 9/02/259, Autograph Collection: General Women's Movement, The Women's Library, London Metropolitan University.

7. Wendy Webster, *Imagining Home: Gender, Race and National identity, 1945-64* (London: UCL Press, 1999) and *Englishness and Empire 1935–1965* (Oxford: Oxford University Press, 2005).

8. In addition to Webster, *Imagining Home*, 46–61, see Hampshire, *Citizenship and Belonging*, 111–49, and Waters, "Dark Strangers," 228–30.

9. As reflected in the continuing debate over the need for integration or assimilation of ethnic, religious, and racial minorities.

10. Roberta Bivins, "'The English Disease' of 'Asian Rickets'? Medical Responses to Postcolonial Immigration," *Bulletin of the History of Medicine* 81, no. 3 (2007): 533–68. For a contemporary account see Michael Banton, *The Coloured Quarter: Negro Immigrants in an English City* (London: Cape, 1955).

11. Waters, "Dark Strangers," 218–21.

12. Michael Banton, "The Race Relations Problematic," *British Journal of Sociology* 42, no. 1 (1991): 115–30.

13. Alison Bonnett, "Constructions of 'Race,' Place and Discipline: Geographies of 'Racial' Identity and Racism," *Ethnic and Racial Studies* 19, no. 4 (1996): 864–83.

14. For the uses and ideology of colonial social work see Joan French, "Women and Colonial Policy in Jamaica after the 1938 Uprising," in Saskia Wieringa, ed., *Subversive Women: Women's Movements in Africa, Asia, Latin America and the Caribbean* (Atlantic Highlands, NJ: Humanities Press 1995), 121–46.

15. Michael Banton, "Recent Migration from West Africa and the West Indies to the United Kingdom," *Population Studies* 7, no. 1, (1953): 2–13.

16. Adam McKeown, "Global Migration 1846–1940," *Journal of World History* 15, no. 2 (2004): 155–89.

17. Shompa Lahiri, "South Asians in Post-imperial Britain: Decolonization and the Imperial Legacy," in Stuart Ward, ed., *British Culture and the End of Empire* (Manchester: Manchester University Press, 2001), 200–216.

18. Adam McKeown, "Regionalizing World Migration," *International Review of Social History* 52, no. 1 (2007): 134–42.

19. This is one of the factors that motivated Enoch Powell to attack immigration. See Nicholas Hillman, "A 'Chorus of Execration'? Enoch Powell's Rivers of Blood Forty Years On," *Patterns of Prejudice* 42, no. 1 (2008), 100–103.

20. Michael Teitelbaum and Jay Winter, *A Question of Numbers: High Migration, Low Fertility, and the Politics of National Identity* (New York: Hill & Wang, 1998); David Coleman, "Immigration and Ethnic Change in Low-Fertility Countries: A Third Demographic Transition," *Population and Development Review* 32, no. 3 (2006): 401–46.

21. Peter McDonald, "Low Fertility and the State: The Efficacy of Policy," *Population and Development Review* 32, no. 3 (2006): 485–510, and Jacques Vallin, "The End of the Demographic Transition: Relief or Concern," *Population and Development Review* 28, no. 1 (2002): 105–20.

22. Edward Goldsmith, Robert Allen, Michael Allaby, John Davoll, and Sam Lawrence, *Blueprint for Survival* (Boston: Houghton Mifflin, 1972).

23. Timothy Hatton, "Emigration from the UK, 1870–1913 and 1950–1998," *European Review of Economic History* 8, no.2 (2004): 149–71.

24. Ceri Peach, "West Indian Migrants to Britain," *International Migration Review* 1, no. 2 (1967): 34–45.

25. Ceri Peach, "South Asian Migration and Settlement in Great Britain, 1951–2000," *Contemporary South Asia* 15, no. 2 (2006): 133–46.

26. For the characteristics of New Commonwealth immigration see Spencer, *British Immigration*, 156–61.

27. Dennis Dean, "The Race Relations Policy of the First Wilson Government," *Twentieth Century British History* 11, no. 3 (2000): 259–83; Shamit Saggar, "Re-examining the 1964–70 Labour's Government's Race Relations Strategy," *Contemporary Record* 7, no. 2 (1993): 253–81.

28. Layton-Henry, *Politics of Immigration*, 154–214.

29. Anthony Messina, "The Impact of Post-WWII Migration to Britain: Policy Constraints, Political Opportunism and the Alteration of Representational Politics," *Review of Politics* 63, no. 2 (2001): 260–85.

30. For a discussion of this point for a later period see Paul Statham and Andrew Geddes, "Elites and the 'Organized Public': Who Drives British Immigration Politics and in Which Direction," *West European Politics* 29, no. 2 (2006): 248–69.

31. Fred Londop, "Racism and the Working Class: Strikes in Support of Enoch Powell," *Labour History Review* 66, no. 1 (2001): 79–100; Neville Kirk, "Traditionalists and Progressives: Labor, Race and Immigration in Post-World War II Australia and Britain," *Australian Historical Studies* 39, no.1 (2008): 53–71.

32. Landon, "Racism and the Working Class," 83–85, and Amy Whipple, "Revisiting the 'Rivers of Blood' Controversy: Letters to Enoch Powell," *Journal of British Studies* 48, no. 3 (2009): 717–35.

33. Paul, *Whitewashing Britain*; Spencer, *British Immigration*; and Hampshire, *Citizenship and Belonging* make this argument.

34. Hansen, *Citizenship and Immigration*, 62–99. Also see David Welsh, "The Principal of the Thing: The Conservative Government and the Control of Commonwealth Immigration, 1957–1959," *Contemporary British History* 12, no. 2, (1998): 51–79, and D. W. Dean, "Conservative Governments and the Restriction of Commonwealth Immigration in the 1950s: The Problems of Constraint," *Historical Journal* 35, no. 1 (1992): 171–94.

35. Edna Delaney, "'Almost a Class of Helots in an Alien Land': The British State and Irish Immigration, 1931–1945," *Immigrants and Minorities* 18, no. 2 (1999): 240–65; Hickman, "Reconstructing Deconstructing 'Race,'" 291–301.

36. Krishnan Spinivasan, "Nobody's Commonwealth? The Commonwealth in Britain's Post-Imperial Adjustment," *Commonwealth and Comparative Politics* 44, no 2 (2006): 257–69.

37. Frederick Cooper, "Modernizing Bureaucrats, Backward Africans, and the Development Concept," in Frederick Cooper and Randall Packard, eds., *International Development and the Social Sciences* (Berkeley: University of California Press, 1997), 64–92.

38. Spencer, *British Immigration*, 147–51.

39. Philip Alexander, "A Tale of Two Smiths: the Transformation of Commonwealth Policy, 1964–70," *Contemporary British History* 20, no. 3 (2006): 303–21.

40. Jef Huysmans and Alessandra Buonfino, "Politics of Exception and Unease: Immigration, Asylum and Terrorism in Parliamentary Debates in the UK," *Political Studies* 56, no. 4 (2008): 766–88. For British Muslims see Scott Poynting and Victoria Mason, "The Resistible Rise of Islamophobia: Anti-Muslim Racism in the UK and Australia before 11 September 2001," *Journal of Sociology* 43, no. 1 (2007): 61–86.

Index

Aboriginal Protection Society, 70
Adams, Grantley, 142–43
Advisory Council on Scientific Policy (ACSP), 131, 133
Africa: IPPF and, 166; population and development in postwar, 135–38; population concerns about, 21. *See also specific country*
Africa Emergent (Macmillan), 22
An African Survey (Hailey), 67
The African Survey, 48
Africa View (Huxley), 21–22, 72
Agency for International Development (AID), 112
agricultural reforms, 64
AID (Agency for International Development), 112
Allen, H. B., 86
American demography, development of, 25
Amery, Leo, 59
Anderson, Benedict, 5
anthropology, imperial administration and, 68, 236n124
Anti-Slavery Society, 70
ASCP. *See* Advisory Council on Scientific Policy (ACSP)
Asia. *See specific country*
Astor, Lady Nancy, 79
Atlee, Clement, 93, 119

Bagehot, Walter, 9
Bailey, Amy, 43
Baker, John, 34
Balogh, Thomas, 178
Barker, Dudley, 150–51
BCIC. *See* Birth Control Investigation Committee (BCIC)
BCIIC. *See* Birth Control International Information Centre (BCIIC)
Beck, Helen, 39, 45, 80
Bermuda, population issues of, 78–79. *See also* West Indies
Bertram, G. C., 153
Beveridge, William, 26, 33, 70, 159
Beveridge Report, 88, 149
Biology: Its Human Implications (Hardin), 154
Bird, Oliver, 166
birth control: Colonial Office and, during Second World War, 99–105; Hong Kong and, 79–81; as international movement, 17; opposition of religious groups, 140–41; politics of, 140–41; politics of, in Kenya, 143–44; politics of, in West Indies, 142–43. *See also* family planning; population control
birth control advocates, 16; American, 222n152
Birth Control and the State (Blacker), 34

289

Birth Control International Information Centre (BCIIC), 34, 41, 42, 71
Birth Control Investigation Committee (BCIC), 33–34
birth control movement, 38–45; in the empire, 39; feminism and, 39; improving lives of women and, 40; organizations for, 41
Birth Control World Wide, 44, 101
Birth International Information Centre, 167
Black, Kurt, 116
Blacker, C. P., 15, 26, 42; as activist, 157, 158; as demographic expert, 159–61; eugenics movement and, 161; joint population policy committee of PEP and PIC and, 165; as leading activist, 72; as public intellectuals, 72–73; questions of imperial and global population and, 159, 163; racial differences and immigration and, 161; racist members of population movement and, 161–62; strategy of, for involvement of Eugenic Society in population movement, 33–35, 37; work with American demographers and population activists and, 174
Blacklock, Mary, 63–64
Boyd-Orr, Sir John, 66, 155, 188
Brander, J. P., 37, 101
Brass, William, 115, 182
Britain: colonial policy of, and population science, 1–2; contradictions over population programs and, 199; debate over population of, 9–10; emergence of field of race relations in, 194–95; evolution of immigration policy in postwar, 197–98; immigration as demographic threat to, 196; influence of colonial demography on understanding immigration in postimperial, 195–96; international population programs and, 185–90; population in interwar, 18–22; position of, in postcolonial era, 193–94; postimperial demographic discourse in, 199; race and immigration in postimperial, 194

Britain's Future Population (Harrod), 148–49
British Empire, interwar: labor and development in, 57–59; migration and population in, 52–57
British Empire, population and race in, 7–13
British Empire, postwar: development and, 108–12; Labour Government and, 124–26
British Empire, wartime, colonial governance and, 83
British population movement, 16–17
British population science, influences of, 7
British Population Society (BPS), 17, 71
British Social Hygiene Council, 61
Brush, Dorothy, 172
Bulmer, Martin, 69
Burke, Eddie, 142
Burns, Sir Alan, 101–2, 128, 140
Bustamante, Adam, 142–43
Butler, R. A., 130

CACA. *See* Colonial Advisory Council on Agriculture (CACA)
Cadbury, George, 166, 188
Caine, Sir Sidney, 71, 77, 89, 102, 111
Campbell, Eila, 139
capitalism, declining fertility and, 149
Carnegie Foundation, 171, 172, 173
Carr-Saunders, Alexander, 23, 218n100; demographic estimates and, 87; demographic transition and, 170; Eugenics Society and, 33, 37–38; as head of Sociology Group of CRAC, 98; influence of, 162; joint population policy committee of PEP and PIC and, 163; as leading activist, 72; as leading figure in British demography, 26, 27, 28, 29–30; 1933 conference on birth

Index / 291

control in Asia and, 43; origins of colonial demography and, 15; population movement and, 158, 159; as public intellectuals, 72–73; threat of non-white population growth and, 20
CAS (Colonial Agricultural Service), 65
Castle, Barbara, 178
CDW (Colonial Development and Welfare) Acts, 111
CEDC (Colonial Economic and Development Council), 111
censuses: in England, 8, 10; invention of modern, 5
Centre for Overseas Population Studies, 115, 182
Chandrasekhar, Sripati, 169
Charles, Enid, 10, 18–19, 27, 149, 217n100
China, population concerns about, 21
Chinn, W. H., 179
Churchill, Winston S., 90, 150
Civilization and Climate (Huntington), 23
civil servants, colonial policy formation and, 69
Clarke, Edith, 116
The Class of Colour (Matthew), 19
Clubs, as networking centers for activists, 71–72
CMAC (Colonial Medical Advisory Council), 124–25
Coale, Ansley, 87, 170
Cohen, Andrew, 70, 72, 100, 123, 180, 188, 192
Cohen, Sir Robert Whaley, 91
Cold War, non-Western population growth and, 171
Colombo Plan, 112; population programs and, 184–85
Colonial Advisory Council on Agriculture (CACA), 65, 124
Colonial Agricultural Service (CAS), 65
colonial demography: birth of, 22–32; decline of, 170–71; development of,
2; emergence of, 191–92; failure of, 192–93; failure to secure stability of Births imperial state, 3; in France, 31; Kuczynski's vision of, 2–3; political environment and, 7; race and, 2; role of Eugenics Society in launching, 32; transformation of the imperial state and, 48–49; understanding of immigration and, 195–96; weaknesses of, 6. *See also* demography
Colonial Development and Welfare (CDW) Acts, 111
Colonial Economic and Development Council (CEDC), 111
Colonial Medical Advisory Council (CMAC), 124–25
Colonial Office, 12; challenges of twentieth-century empire and, 50–52; clubs as centers for activists and officials of, 71–72; demographic information in, during Second World War, 95–99; experts and, 67–70; health policies, 63; influence of population movement on, 71; International Planned Parenthood Federation (IPPF), 168; Jewish immigration issues during Second World War, 90–91; labor and resource issues during Second World War, 93–95; lobbying groups and, 70–71; merging with Commonwealth Relations Office, 177–78; migration issues during Second World War, 91–92; overpopulation issues during Second World War, 99–105; planning development for postwar empire, 108–12; population issues during Second World War and, 88–93; population politics in, 79; postwar expansion of statistical services by, 115–17; postwar pro-settler policy and, 121–22; race and overpopulation issues in West Indies and, 79–80; race and population issues in interwar empire and, 74–81

colonial policy, British, population science and, 1–2
colonial population growth, 2
colonial populations, efforts to control, 3
Colonial Research Advisory Committee (CRAC), 96–98
Colonial Service, 67, 226n1
Colonial Social Science Research Council (CSSRC), 12, 98, 115, 218n103
Colonial Welfare and Development Act (1940), 88
Committee on World Population, 181–82
Congo Reform Association, 70
Conservation Foundation, 174
Conservation Society, 157
Conservative government, population policy of, in 1950s, 130–35
Coupland, Reginald, 97
Cowell, H. R., 80
Cox, Harold, 17, 37, 43
CRAC (Colonial Research Advisory Committee), 96–98
Cranborne, Lord, 104–5
Creech Jones, Arthur, 71, 127, 128, 129
CSSRC. See Colonial Social Science Research Council (CSSRC)
Culwick, G. M., 98
Culwick, Theodore, 98

Danger Spots in World Population (Thompson), 20
Darwin, Charles, 9
Davey, T. H., 125
Davis, Kingsley, 11, 170, 172
demographers, 1; in authoritarian states, 31; political and racial views of, 217–18n217; role of, 31; sterilization policies and, 31
Demographic Advisory Council, 11–12
A Demographic Survey of the British Colonial Empire (Kuczynski), 1, 29
demographic techniques, 5–6
demographic transition theory, 2, 24–25, 137, 147–48, 170–71
demography, British: as academic discipline, 2, 169; development of, 25–26; institutional development of, in postwar era, 170; in interwar wars, 11; Kuczynski's comments on, 1; as policy science, in postwar era, 69–176; in postwar years, 11–12; scientific community and postwar debates over, 153–54. *See also* colonial demography
Demography Group (CSSRC), 98. *See also* Colonial Social Science Research Council (CSSRC)
Department of Technical Cooperation (DTC), 178; assessment of British population policy and, 179–81; development studies and, 178; endorsement of family planning, 184–85; shift in population policy by, 184
depopulation, fears of, 151–52
The Descent of Man (Darwin), 9
De Souza, Ivo, 166–67
development: in interwar empire, 57–59; in postwar Africa, 135–38; in postwar empire, 108–12
development institutes, 178–79
Deverell, Sir Colville, 180
Devonshire schemes, 114
diffusion model, 24
Dilke, Charles, 191
Dilke, William, 9
Dorothy Brush Foundation, 166, 172
Draper Committee, 173
Drysdale, C. V., 10, 37
DTC. *See* Department of Technical Cooperation (DTC)
Dublin, Louis, 24
Dundas, Sir Charles, 91–92
Dunlop, Binnie, 37
Durex condoms, 184
Dutton, Eric, 99

East, Edward, 20, 23, 194

East African Institute of Social Research, 115
East African Statistical Department (EASD), 114
Eastwood, C., 97
Edge, P. Granville, 30
Ehrlich, Paul, 157
Eisenhower, Dwight, 173
Elderton, Ethel, 26
Ellis, Havelock, 162
Emerson, Sir Hugh, 90
emigration, British, debate over, 150–51
Empire Medical Advisory Bureau, 167
enumeration forms, 6
ethnicity, efforts to map, 6
eugenicists, 16
eugenics: population movement and, 32–38; population movement and, in postwar era, 158
eugenics movement: Blacker and, 161; colonies and, 36
Eugenics Review (journal), 34, 159
Eugenics Society, 26, 28, 149; IPPF and, 165–66; PEP and, 163–64; population movement and, 33–34; in postwar era, 158–59; postwar influence of, 162–63; role of, in launching colonial demography, 32
European Recovery Plan (ERP), 112
Evans Commission, 127
experts, Colonial Office and, 67–70

Fabian Colonial Bureau, 70–71
Fabian Society, 149, 150
Fairclough, A. J., 128
The Family and the State (Blacker), 73
family-based assistance, 149
family planning, 103; DTC's endorsement of, 184–85; emergence of, in postwar era, 165–69; need to change attitudes about, 133–34; opposition of religious groups, 140. *See also* birth control; population control
Family Planning Association (FPA), 41, 44, 141, 165, 275n129; in West Indies, 166–67
FAO (Food and Agriculture Organization), 188
Farr, William, 8
feminism, birth control movement and, 39
fertility, racial, 152
Fiji, applying lessons of population control in, 139–40
Fisher, R. A., 33
Fitzalan, Lord, 79–80
Food and Agriculture Organization (FAO), 188
food production: in East Africa, 65–66; population growth and, 155
Foot, Sir Hugh, 116
FORD. *See* Foreign Office Research Department (FORD)
Ford Foundation, 171, 172, 173–74
Foreign Office: tracking demographic trends and, 84–87
Foreign Office Research Department (FORD), 86; postwar expansion of demographic services, 117–19
Forrest, Robert, 45
Foucault, Michel, 5
FPA. *See* Family Planning Association (FPA)
France, colonial demography in, 31
Friends of Africa, 70

Galton, 8, 9
Galton, Francis, 24
Gamble, Clarence, 161–62, 172, 278n168
Garvey, Sir Reginald, 139
Gater, Sir George, 99
Gates, Edith, 166
Gates, R. Ruggles, 161–62
General Register Office (GRO), 8, 11, 25–26, 169
geopolitics, of population, 84–87
Gilks, John, 66
Glass, David, 11, 29, 73, 217n100; background of, 27; Blacker and, 174; Eugenics Society and, 162,

Glass, David *(continued)*
163; Jewish immigration discussions and, 90; London School of Economics and, 169; as member of Royal Commission on Population, 158; postwar British population debate and, 148; as UK representative to United Nations Population Commission, 113, 186–87
Gordon, H. L., 143
Government Actuaries, 26
Great Britain. *See* Britain
Grebenik, Eugene, 169
Green Revolution, 155
Greenwood, Major, 24, 26, 30
Greer, J. K., 138
Gregg, Alfred, 9
Gregory, J. W., 19, 20, 37
GRO. *See* General Register Office (GRO)

Hacking, Iian, 5
Hailey, Lord, 97
Hailsham, Lord, 141
Hajnal, John, 151
Hall, Sir A. Daniel, 66
Hansen, Randall, 197
Hardin, Garrett, 154
Harrod, Sir Roy, 148–49
Hibbert, J. G., 91
Hildyard, Reginald, 79
Hill, A. V., 100–101, 153–54
Hill, Ruben, 116
Hodgson, Cora, 39
Hogben, Lancelot, 26–27, 28
Hong Kong: birth control efforts issues and, 79–81; family planning program of, 183–84; refugee crisis during Sino-Japanese War, 89–90
Horder, Lord, 33, 43, 71
Horton, Gertrude, 63
Houghton, Douglas, 168
Houghton, Vera, 165, 168
How-Martyn, Edith, 37, 39, 40, 42–44, 77, 101, 167
Hubback, Eva, 39, 63, 149
Huntington, Ellsworth, 23, 194

Hutton, J. H., 98
Huxley, Elspeth, 143, 194
Huxley, Julian, 15, 100, 101, 141; on Africa's population, 21–22; Demography Group of CSSRC and, 98; eugenics and, 33; Eugenics Society and, 37–38; as head of UNESCO, 188; Kuczynski and, 28, 29; as leading activist, 72; as lobbyist, 72; as population activist, 17; population growth and, 153, 157; population movement and, 158, 159, 163, 164, 165; postwar population movement and, 162

Ibberson, Dora, 130
IDS (Institute for Development Studies), 178–79
immigration: as demographic threat to Britain, 196; focus on non-white, 196; influence of colonial demography on understanding, in postimperial Britain, 195–96
Immigration Act (1962), 198
immigration policy, evolution of, in postwar Britain, 197–98
immigration politics, British: ideas about population and, 198; imperial factor in, 197–98
Ince, Sir Godfrey, 127
India: population concerns about, 21; postwar migration and, 122–23
Institute for African Studies, 97
Institute for Development Studies (IDS), 178–79
International Planned Parenthood Committee, 165
International Planned Parenthood Federation (IPPF), 44, 132, 134–35, 147, 168; in Africa, 166; American support of, 174; Colonial Office and, 168; Council for Investigation of Fertility Control, 167; Eugenics Society and, 165–66; funding of research on new contraceptive methods and, 167; Medical Committee, 167; in postwar era, 165–69;

training courses of, 167; in West Indies, 166–67
international population programs, emergence of, 185–90
International Union for the Scientific Investigation of Population Problems (IUSSP), 17
IPPF. *See* International Planned Parenthood Federation (IPPF)
Italian immigration, postwar, 122

Jamaican Birth Control League, 44
Jamaican Family Life Project, 134, 174, 175
Jamaican Family Life Survey, 116
Japan, population concerns about, 21

Keen, B. A., 86
Kenya: ethnic tensions in, 144–45; politics of birth control in, 143–44; population growth concerns in, 135–36; resettlement as means of population control in, 136–37
Keynes, John Maynard, 18, 33, 70
Kigezi plan, 263n200
Kirkwood, Robert, 143
Knibbs, George, 17, 20, 34, 218n100
Kuczynski, Robert, 11–12, 34, 43, 217n100; British postwar population debate and, 148; call for imperial census after Second World War, 107; Colonial Office and, 73–74; Demography Group and, 98–99; detractors of, 30; influence of, 29–30; Jewish migration to Palestine and, 90; origins of interest in non-European populations, 28–29; reputation as quantitative demographer, 27; review of British demography by, 1; Royal Commission on Population and, 158; vision of colonial demography, 2–3; work at Colonial Office, during Second World War, 95–97

labor, in interwar empire, 57–59
Labour government: postwar British Empire and, 124–26; postwar population policy and, 126–30
Lafitte, Francois, 162–63
The Lancet (journal), 154
Laski, Frida, 43
League of Coloured Peoples, 70
League of Nations, 17
League of Nations Health Agency (LNHA), 62
Lennox Boyd, Alan, 134, 141, 175
Lewis, Arthur, 111
Lewis, Joanna, 88
Lewis, W. A., 88–89
Lister, Samuel Cunliffe, 63
Listowel, Lord, 129
Lloyd, Sir Thomas, 127, 130
LNHA (League of Nations Health Agency), 62
lobbying groups, Colonial Office and, 70–71
London Rubber Company, 184
London School of Economics (LSE), 11, 26, 27–28; Rockefeller Foundation support of, 174
London School of Hygiene and Tropical Medicine (LSHTM), 61, 115, 182
Lorimer, Frank, 172
Lotka, Alfred, 24
LSE. *See* London School of Economics (LSE)
LSHTM. *See* London School of Hygiene and Tropical Medicine (LSHTM)
Lugard, Sir Frederick, 54

MacArthur, N. R., 115
MacDonald, Malcom, 57, 71, 72, 76, 79
Mackinder, H. J., 10
Macmillan, W. M., 67
Macmillan, William, 22, 77
Macpherson, Sir John, 134, 168
Malaya: ethnic tensions in, 144
Malinowski, Bronislav, 68
Mallet, Sir Bernard, 33, 71
Malthus, 8, 9
Manley, Norman, 43, 116, 142

296 / Index

Marshall, T. H., 86–87
Marshall Plan, 112
Martin, C. J., 114
Maternal and child health care, 63
Matthew, Basil, 19
Mau-Mau insurgency, 144
Mauritius: applying lessons of population control in, 138–39; politics of birth control in, 143
McCleary, George, 150
McDougall, Frank, 188
Mears, Eleanor, 168
medical care, colonial, 59–64
medical research, British, in interwar years, 60–61
Medical Research Council, 26
Megaw, Sir John, 44, 154, 157
The Menance of Colour (Gregory), 19
MESC (Middle East Supply Centre), 85–86
Middle East Supply Centre (MESC), 85–86
migration: British, after Second World War, 119–24; in interwar British Empire, 52–57; Jewish, during interwar years, 55–56; in postwar British Empire, 120–24; race-based, in postwar empire, 120–24; West Indies and, during interwar years, 54
Migration Council, 150–51, 160
Milbank Memorial Fund, 172
Mills, Eric, 56
Ministry of Health, 26
Ministry of Overseas Development (ODM), 177, 178; as agency in Foreign Office, 181; aid programs and, 180–81; creation of Population Bureau, 182; development studies and, 178; support of family planning and, 185
Mitchell, Sir Phillip, 136
Money, Lionel, 19
Moyne, Lord, 72
Moyne Commission, 74, 77, 88, 126
My Mother Who Fathered Me (Clarke), 116

National Birth Control Association (NBCA), 33–34, 41, 44, 71
National Health Service (NHS), 165
Nationality Act (1948), 197
NBCA. *See* National Birth Control Association (NBCA)
Neo-Malthusian League, 38
net reproduction rate (NRR), 1, 27, 216n81
NHS (National Health Service), 165
Nicholson, Max, 72, 90, 156, 157, 160, 163
Nicolson, Max, 28
1911 Census, 10
1911 Fertility Census, 24
Notestein, Frank, 11, 25, 87, 151, 170, 172, 173, 174
NRR (net reproduction rate), 1, 27
Nuffield Foundation, 174
nutrition: scientific agriculture and, 66–67
Nyasaland project, 263n200

Oceania: population concerns about, 21; sexual behavior and population problems of, 76
ODA (Overseas Development Administration), 181. *See also* Ministry of Overseas Development (ODM)
ODM. *See* Ministry of Overseas Development (ODM)
Office of Population Research (Princeton University), 173
Oldham, J. H., 59, 230n57
Oldham, John, 37, 68
Oliver Bird Trust, 166, 167, 174
optimal population theory, 228n30
Orde-Brown, Granville, 58–59, 77, 95, 97, 104
Ormsby-Gore, William, 60, 72, 81
Osborne, Frederick, 161, 172, 174
Osborne, Henry Fairchild, 25, 134, 156, 173, 175
overpopulation: focus on, in postwar era, 154–57; immigration to Britain and debates over, 157–58

Overseas Development Administration (ODA), 181. *See also* Ministry of Overseas Development (ODM)
Overseas Settlement Board, 92
Owen, Sir David, 72, 188–89
Oxfam, 165

Palestine, 121
Palmer, Eileen, 101
Parents Revolt (Titmuss), 148–49
Parkinson, Sir Cosmo, 101–2
Paskin, J. J., 104
Passfield, Lord (Sydney Webb), 63
Pathfinder Fund, 172
Patterson, A. R., 143
Pearl, Raymond, 23
Pearson, Karl, 8–9, 23, 24, 26
Pederson, Susan, 39
Pedlar, F. J., 104
Pedler, F. J., 97
PEP. *See* Political and Economic Planning (PEP)
Perham, Margery, 97
The Peril of the White (Money), 19
Petty, William, 7
Picton-Tuberville, Edith, 80
Pim, Sir Alan, 93, 119
Pinkus, Gregory, 168
Planned Parenthood, 171–72
The Plundered Planet (Osborne), 156
Point Four Program, 112
Political and Economic Planning (PEP), 27–28, 149, 152–53, 157–58, 160; Eugenics Society and, 163–64
population: Britain's postwar debate on, 148–58; environmental determinants of, 23; geopolitics of, 84–87; in interwar British Empire, 52–57; in postwar Africa, 135–38
The Population and Resources of Barbados (Simon), 160
Population and the Future (Blacker), 73
Population and the People (Fabian Society), 149
Population and the Social Problem (Swinburne), 19–20

Population and World Food Supplies (Russell), 155
Population Association of America, 25
The Population Bomb (Ehrlich), 157
Population Bureau, 182
population control: applying lessons of, in Mauritius, 138–39; *The Lancet* as advocate, 154; politics of, 140–45; race as factor in, 141; U.S. government and, 173. *See also* birth control; family planning
Population Council, 173
population growth: food production and, 155; non-Western, Cold War and, 171
Population Investigation Committee (PIC), 26, 28, 71, 73; in postwar era, 169–70; Rockefeller Foundation support of, 174
population movement: eugenics and, 32–38; eugenics and, in postwar era, 158–65; evolution of, in postcolonial Britain, 147; influence of, on Colonial Office, 71; in postcolonial era, 193–94; racist members of, 161–62
The Population of Britain (Hubback), 149
population policy: assessment of British, by DTC, 179–81; British reassessment of, in postcolonial era, 181–85; Conservative government in 1950s and, 130–35; Labour Government's postwar, 126–30; race as factor in, 141
Population Policy in Great Britain (PEP), 149
The Population Problem (Carr-Saunders), 29, 72
Population Problems (Reuter), 19
Population Problems (Thompson), 20
population programs: contradictions over, in postcolonial Britain, 199; international, emergence of, 175–76
population quality, 159

population science, 5; British colonial policy and, 1–2; eugenicists and birth controllers as consumers of, 16
Porter, Theodore, 5
Powell, Enoch, 191, 197
Pridie, Sir Eric, 72, 124–25, 258n131
Profumo, John, 140
public health, colonial, 59–64
Pyke, Margaret, 71

race: colonial demography and, 2; efforts to map, 6; as factor in population policy, 141; migration and, in postwar empire, 120–24; and overpopulation issues in West Indies, 79–80
racial fertility, 152
Rance, Sir Hubert, 129
Rathbone, Eleanor, 39, 43, 63, 149
reproduction, colonial, 59–64
research, British medical, in interwar years, 60–61
resettlement, as means of population control in Africa, 136–37
Reuter, Edward, 19
Richards, Audrey, 68, 98
The Rising Tide of Color (Stoddard), 19
The Road to Survival (Vogt), 156
Roberts, G. W., 115, 130
Robinson, Ronald, 178
Rockefeller Foundation, 171, 172, 174
Rogers, Philip, 70, 80; as advocate for birth control in Colonial Office, 103; as advocate of birth control, 128, 132; immigration restrictions and, 123; postwar population control in colonies and, 139, 141, 143, 144, 160, 179, 183, 192; review of global population trends and, 133, 134
Ross, Edward, 19
Royal Commission on Population, 149, 151–52, 169; population movement and, 158–59
Russell, Sir John, 155–56, 157

Sanger, Margaret, 17, 25, 39, 42, 157, 174
Save the Children, 165
Sax, Karl, 154
scientific agriculture, 64; nutrition and, 66–67
Scripps Foundation for Research in Population Problems, 25
Searle, W. F., 113–14
Second World War: demand for labor and resources during, 93–95; Jewish immigration issues during, 90–91; population issues and Colonial Office during, 88–93
Seddon, J. H., 125
Seely, J. R., 9
sexual behavior, population problems and, 76
Simey, T. S., 115–16, 195
Simon, Lord, 160, 166, 273n83
Simon Population Trust, 160, 174
Smart, Archibald, 100
Smith, T. E., 115
Snider, Robert, 134, 164, 175
Social Hygiene Council, 70
Society for Progressive Birth Control, 41
South Asian immigration, postwar, 122–23
South Pacific Commission Research, 115
Spencer, Herbert, 9
Standing Room Only (Ross), 19
Standing Room Only (Sax), 154
Stanley, Oliver, 33, 72
state intervention, expansion of, 3
statistics: development of, 8–9; use of, 5
sterilization, as birth control method, 184–85
Stevenson, T. C., 10
Stevenson, T. H., 24
Stockdale, Sir Frank, 65, 76, 92, 101, 102
Stoddard, Lothrop, 19
Stopes, Marie, 38, 39, 41
Stycos, J. Mayone, 116

Sweaney, W. D., 128, 130, 143
Swinburne, J., 19–20
Swynnerton Plan, 145
Sykes, G. G., 80
Symonds, Richard, 163, 189

Tauber, Irene, 173
Terrell, Richard, 163
Thomas, Brinley, 150
Thompson, J. K., 179
Thompson, Warren, 20–21, 25, 34, 170
Titmuss, Richard, 19, 28, 148–49, 162, 163, 217n100
Tizard, H. T., 120, 164
Todd, Sir Alexander, 134
Tots and Quots (dining club), 28
Toynbee, Arnold, 86
Truman, Harry S., 12
The Twilight of Parenthood (Charles), 18–19

United Kingdom. *See* Britain
United Nation Relief and Recovery Administration, 112
United Nations, development aid and, 112
United Nations Development Programme, 112
United Nations Educational, Scientific and Cultural Organization (UNESCO), 88
United Nations Population Commission, 186–87
United Nations Population Fund (UNFPA), 189
United Nations Technical Assistance Administration (UNTAA), 188
United Nations Technical Assistance Board (UNTAB), 189

Vivian, Sylvanus, 25–26, 72
Vogt, William, 156, 157, 158, 172, 174

Waddington, E. J., 76–77, 78, 104
Ward, J. S., 123
Warnings from the West Indies (Macmillan), 67

Wauchope, Sir Arthur, 55–56
Webb, Sydney (Lord Passfield), 63
Welfare and Planning in the West Indies (Simey), 116
West Indies: Colonial Office and race and overpopulation issues and, 79–80; FPA and, 166–67; IPPF and, 166–67; Labour's postwar population policy and, 126–30; late 1940s mass migration from, 127–28; migration issues, 92; politics of birth control in, 142–43; race and population issues of, 76–77
Whelpton, P. K., 24, 25
The White Man's Dilemma (Boyd-Orr), 155
Wilkinson, Henry, 63
Wilson, Harold, 178, 181, 199
Wilson, Sir Geoffrey, 163, 189
Wolfers, David, 182
World Population (Carr-Saunders), 29
World Population Committee, 160
World Population Conference of 1927 (Geneva), 17
World War Two. *See* Second World War
Worthington, E. B., 66, 86
Wright, Harold, 17, 20, 217n100
Wright, Helena, 43
Wright, Norman, 124

Yule, C. Udney, 26

Zuckerman, Solly, 274n106; ASCP's review of global population trends and, 133–34; Committee on World Population and, 181; Eugenics Society and, 33, 34; as exponent of population control, 192; as facilitator of relationships between American and British governments, 174–75; global overpopulation and environment movement, 157, 183; as leading figure in population movement, 163–65; on race and population control, 141–42; Tots and Quots club and, 28

www.ingramcontent.com/pod-product-compliance
Lightning Source LLC
Chambersburg PA
CBHW031707230426
43668CB00006B/133